IFIP Advances in Information and Communication Technology

586

Editor-in-Chief

Kai Rannenberg, Goethe University Frankfurt, Germany

Editorial Board Members

IFIP – The International Federation for Information Processing

IFIP was founded in 1960 under the auspices of UNESCO, following the first World Computer Congress held in Paris the previous year. A federation for societies working in information processing, IFIP's aim is two-fold: to support information processing in the countries of its members and to encourage technology transfer to developing nations. As its mission statement clearly states:

IFIP is the global non-profit federation of societies of ICT professionals that aims at achieving a worldwide professional and socially responsible development and application of information and communication technologies.

IFIP is a non-profit-making organization, run almost solely by 2500 volunteers. It operates through a number of technical committees and working groups, which organize events and publications. IFIP's events range from large international open conferences to working conferences and local seminars.

The flagship event is the IFIP World Computer Congress, at which both invited and contributed papers are presented. Contributed papers are rigorously refereed and the rejection rate is high.

As with the Congress, participation in the open conferences is open to all and papers may be invited or submitted. Again, submitted papers are stringently refereed.

The working conferences are structured differently. They are usually run by a working group and attendance is generally smaller and occasionally by invitation only. Their purpose is to create an atmosphere conducive to innovation and development. Refereeing is also rigorous and papers are subjected to extensive group discussion.

Publications arising from IFIP events vary. The papers presented at the IFIP World Computer Congress and at open conferences are published as conference proceedings, while the results of the working conferences are often published as collections of selected and edited papers.

IFIP distinguishes three types of institutional membership: Country Representative Members, Members at Large, and Associate Members. The type of organization that can apply for membership is a wide variety and includes national or international societies of individual computer scientists/ICT professionals, associations or federations of such societies, government institutions/government related organizations, national or international research institutes or consortia, universities, academies of sciences, companies, national or international associations or federations of companies.

More information about this series at http://www.springer.com/series/6102

Carolina Metzler · Pierre-Emmanuel Gaillardon ·
Giovanni De Micheli · Carlos Silva-Cardenas ·
Ricardo Reis (Eds.)

VLSI-SoC:
New Technology Enabler

27th IFIP WG 10.5/IEEE International Conference
on Very Large Scale Integration, VLSI-SoC 2019
Cusco, Peru, October 6–9, 2019
Revised and Extended Selected Papers

 Springer

Editors
Carolina Metzler (iD)
Universidade Federal do Rio Grande do Sul
Porto Alegre, Brazil

Pierre-Emmanuel Gaillardon (iD)
University of Utah
Salt Lake City, UT, USA

Giovanni De Micheli (iD)
EPFL
Lausanne, Switzerland

Carlos Silva-Cardenas (iD)
Pontificia Universidad Católica del Perú
Lima, Peru

Ricardo Reis (iD)
Universidade Federal do Rio Grande do Sul
Porto Alegre, Brazil

ISSN 1868-4238   ISSN 1868-422X   (electronic)
IFIP Advances in Information and Communication Technology
ISBN 978-3-030-53275-8   ISBN 978-3-030-53273-4   (eBook)
https://doi.org/10.1007/978-3-030-53273-4

This Springer imprint is published by the registered company Springer Nature Switzerland AG
The registered company address is: Gewerbestrasse 11, 6330 Cham, Switzerland

Preface

This book contains extended and revised versions of the highest quality papers, presented during the 27th edition of the IFIP/IEEE WG10.5 International Conference on Very Large Scale Integration (VLSI-SoC 2019), a global System-on-Chip Design and CAD conference. The 27th edition of the conference was held October 6–9, 2019, at the Cuzco Convention Center, Cuzco, Peru. Previous conferences have taken place in Edinburgh, Scotland (1981); Trondheim, Norway (1983); Tokyo, Japan (1985); Vancouver, Canada (1987); Munich, Germany (1989); Edinburgh, Scotland (1991); Grenoble, France (1993); Chiba, Japan (1995); Gramado, Brazil (1997); Lisbon, Portugal (1999); Montpellier, France (2001); Darmstadt, Germany (2003); Perth, Australia (2005); Nice, France (2006); Atlanta, USA (2007); Rhodes Island, Greece (2008); Florianopolis, Brazil (2009); Madrid, Spain (2010); Kowloon, Hong Kong (2011), Santa Cruz, USA (2012), Istanbul, Turkey (2013), Playa del Carmen, Mexico (2014), Daejeon, South Korea (2015), Tallin, Estonia (2016), Abu Dhabi, UAE (2017); and Verona, Italy (2018).

The purpose of this conference, which was sponsored by IFIP TC 10 Working Group 10.5, the IEEE Council on Electronic Design Automation (CEDA), and the IEEE Circuits and Systems Society, with the cooperation of ACM SIGDA, is to provide a forum for the presentation and discussion of the latest academic and industrial results and developments as well as the future trends in the field of System-on-Chip (SoC) design, considering the challenges of nano-scale, state-of-the-art, and emerging manufacturing technologies. In particular, VLSI-SoC 2019 addressed cutting-edge research fields like Heterogeneous Mobile Architectures, Reliability and Security of MPSoCs, Radiation Effects, Binary Neural Networks, Variability, Self-Test, and Test Generation. The chapters of this new book in the VLSI-SoC series continue its tradition of providing an internationally acknowledged platform for scientific contributions and industrial progress in this field.

For VLSI-SoC 2019, 28 papers out of 82 submissions were selected for oral presentation and 15 for poster presentation. Out of these 28 full papers presented at the conference as oral presentations, 15 papers were chosen by a Selection Committee to have an extended and revised version included in this book. The selection process of these papers considered the evaluation scores during the review process as well as the review forms provided by members of the Technical Program Committee and the session chairs as a result of the presentations.

The chapters of this book have authors from Brazil, Canada, Cyprus, England, Estonia, Germany, India, Israel, Italy, Portugal, Switzerland, Turkey, and England. The Technical Program Committee for the regular tracks comprised 89 members from 29 countries.

VLSI-SoC 2019 was the culmination of the work of many dedicated volunteers: paper authors, reviewers, session chairs, invited speakers, and various committee chairs. We thank them all for their contributions.

This book is intended for the VLSI community at large, and in particular the many colleagues who did not have the chance to attend the conference. We hope you will enjoy reading this book and that you will find it useful in your professional life and for the development of the VLSI community as a whole.

June 2020

Carolina Metzler
Pierre-Emmanuel Gaillardon
Giovanni De Micheli
Carlos Silva-Cárdenas
Ricardo Reis

Organization

The IFIP/IEEE International Conference on Very Large Scale Integration System-on-Chip (VLSI-SoC 2019) took place during October 6–9, 2019, at the Cuzco Convention Center, Cuzco, Peru. VLSI-SoC 2019 was the 27th in a series of international conferences, sponsored by IFIP TC 10 Working Group 10.5 (VLSI), IEEE CEDA, and ACM SIGDA. The Organization Committee of the conference consisted of the following colleagues:

General Chairs

Carlos Silva-Cárdenas	Pontifical Catholic University of Peru, Peru
Ricardo Reis	UFRGS, Brazil

Technical Program Chairs

Pierre-Emmanuel Gaillardon	The University of Utah, USA
Giovanni De Micheli	EPFL, Switzerland

Special Sessions Chair

Maciej Ogorzalek	Jagiellonian University, Poland

PhD Forum Chairs

Michael Huebner	Technical University Cottbus, Germany
Fatih Ugurdag	Ozyegin University, Turkey

Local Chairs

Vladimir Canal	UNSAAC, Peru
Jorge Arizaca	UNSAAC, Peru

Industry Chairs

Raul Camposano	SAGE, USA
Victor Grimblatt	Synopsys, Chile

Publicity Chairs

Salvador Mir	TIMA, France
Jose Ayala	UCM, Spain

Publication Chair

Carolina Metzler   Universidade Federal do Rio Grande do Sul, Brazil

Registration Chairs

Hugo Pratt   Pontifical Catholic University of Peru, Peru
Mario Raffo   Pontifical Catholic University of Peru, Peru

VLSI-SoC Steering Committee

Graziano Pravadelli   University of Verona, Italy
Ibrahim Elfadel   Masdar Institute of Science and Technology, UAE
Manfred Glesner   TU Darmstadt, Germany
Matthew Guthaus   UC Santa Cruz, USA
Luis Miguel Silveira   INESC ID, Portugal
Fatih Ugurdag   Ozyegin University, Turkey
Salvador Mir   TIMA, France
Ricardo Reis   UFRGS, Brazil
Chi-Ying Tsui   HKUST, Hong Kong, China
Ian O'Connor   INL, France
Masahiro Fujita   The University of Tokyo, Japan

As for the Technical Program Committee, it was composed as follows:

Technical Program Committee

1. Analog, mixed-signal, and sensor architectures

Track Chairs

Tetsuya Iizuka   University of Tokyo, Japan
Piero Malcovati   University of Pavia, Italy

2. Digital architectures: NoC, multi- and many-core, hybrid, and reconfigurable

Track Chairs

Haris Javaid   Xilinx, Singapore
Edith Beigne   Facebook, USA

3. CAD, Synthesis and Analysis

Track Chairs:

Srinivas Katkoori   University of South Florida, USA
Matthew Guthaus   UC Santa Cruz, USA

4. Prototyping, Verification, Modeling and Simulation

Track Chairs:

Graziano Pravadelli	University of Verona, Italy
Tiziana Margaria	Lero, Ireland

5. Circuits and systems for signal processing and communications

Track Chairs:

Carlos Silva Cardenas	Pontifical Catholic University of Peru, Peru
Fatih Ugurdag	Ozyegin University, Turkey

6. Embedded & Cyberph. Systems: Arch., design, and software

Track Chairs:

Michael Huebner	Brandenburg University of Technology Cottbus, Germany
Donatella Sciuto	Politecnico di Milano, Italy

7. Low-Power and Thermal-Aware IC Design

Track Chairs:

Alberto Macii	Politecnico di Torino, Italy
Dimitrios Soudris	National Technical University of Athens, Greece

8. Emerging technologies and computing paradigms

Track Chairs:

Ian O'Connor	Lyon Institute of Nanotechnology, France
Andrea Calimera	Politecnico di Torino, Italy

9. Variability, Reliability and Test

Track Chairs

Matteo Sonza Reorda	Politecnico di Torino, Italy
Salvador Mir	University of Grenoble Alpes, France

10. Hardware Security

Track Chairs

Odysseas Koufopavlou	University of Patras, Greece
Lilian Bossuet	University of Lyon, France

11. Machine learning for SoC design and for electronic design

Track Chairs:

Luc Claesen	University Hasselt, Belgium
Mike Niemier	University of Notre Dame, USA

Technical Program Committee Members

Abdulkadir Akin	ETHZ, Switzerland
Aida Todri-Sanial	LIRMM, France
Alberto Bosio	Lyon Institute of Nanotechnology, France
Bei Yu	The Chinese University of Hong Kong, Hong Kong, China
Brice Colombier	CEA, France
Cecile Braunstein	UPMC, LIP6, France
Chattopadhyay Anupam	Nanyang Technological University, Singapore
Chun-Jen Tsai	National Chiao Tung University, Taiwan
David Atienza	EPFL, Switzerland
Elena Ioana Vatajelu	TIMA Laboratory, France
Enrico Macii	Politecnico di Torino, Italy
Ettore Napoli	University of Napoli Federico II, Italy
Eugenio Villar	University of Cantabria, Spain
Federico Tramarin	CNR-IEIIT, Italy
Francesca Palumbo	Università degli Studi di Sassari, Italy
Franck Courbon	University of Cambridge, England
Fynn Schwiegelshohn	University of Toronto, Canada
Gildas Leger	Instituto de Microelectronica de Sevilla, Spain
Giorgio Di Natale	LIRMM, France
Hassan Mostafa	University of Waterloo, Canada
Henri Fraisse	Xilinx, USA
Ibrahim Elfadel	Masdar Institute of Science and Technology, UAE
Ioannis Savidis	Drexel University, USA
Jari Nurmi	Tempere University, Finland
Johanna Sepulveda	Technical University of Munich, Germany
Jose Monteiro	INESC-ID, University of Lisboa, Portugal

Ke-Horng Chen	National Sun Ya-sen University, Taiwan
Kostas Siozios	Aristotle University of Thessaloniki, Greece
Kun-Chih (Jimmy) Chen	National Sun Yat-sen University, Taiwan
Lars Bauer	Karlsruhe Institute of Technology, Germany
Lionel Torres	LIRMM, France
Luca Amaru	Synopsys, USA
Luciano Ost	Loughborough University, England
Massimo Poncino	Politecnico di Torino, Italy
Mathias Soeken	EPFL, Switzerland
Meng-Fan (Marvin) Chang	National Tsing Hua University, Taiwan
Michail Maniatakos	New York University Abu Dhabi, UAE
Mirko Loghi	Università di Udine, Italy
Mohamed Ibrahim	Intel, USA
Nadine Azemard	LIRMM, CNRS, France
Nele Mentens	Katholieke Universiteit Leuven, Belgium
Nektarios Georgios Tsoutsos	New York University, USA
Ozgur Tasdizen	ARM, England
Paolo Amato	Micron, Italy
Peng Liu	Zhejiang University, China
Per Larsson-Edefors	Chalmers University, Sweden
Philippe Coussy	Université de Bretagne Sud, France
Ricardo Reis	Universidade Federal do Rio Grande do Sul, Brazil
Robert Wille	Johannes Kepler University Linz, Austria
Ross Walter	The University of Utah, USA
Said Hamdioui	Delf Technical University, The Netherlands
Salvatore Pennisi	University of Catania, Italy
Selcuk Kose	University of Rochester, USA
Sezer Goren	Yeditepe University, Turkey
Shahar Kvatinsky	Technion - Israel Institute of Technology, Israel
Sicheng Li	HP, USA
Theocharis Theocharides	University of Cyprus, Cyprus
Tolga Yalcin	NXP, England
Tsung-Yi Ho	National Tsing Hua University, Taiwan
Valerio Tenace	Politecnico di Torino, Italy
Victor Champac	INAOE, Mexico
Victor Kravets	IBM, USA
Virendra Singh	Indian Institute of Technology Bombay, India
Volkan Kursun	The Hong Kong University of Science and Technology, Hong Kong, China
Wenjing Rao	University of Illinois at Chicago, USA
Xinfei Guo	NVidia, USA
Zebo Peng	Linkoping University, Sweden

Contents

Software-Based Self-Test for Delay Faults 1
  Michelangelo Grosso, Matteo Sonza Reorda, and Salvatore Rinaudo

On Test Generation for Microprocessors for Extended Class
of Functional Faults. 21
  Adeboye Stephen Oyeniran, Raimund Ubar, Maksim Jenihhin,
  and Jaan Raik

Robust FinFET Schmitt Trigger Designs for Low Power Applications 45
  Leonardo B. Moraes, Alexandra Lackmann Zimpeck,
  Cristina Meinhardt, and Ricardo Reis

An Improved Technique for Logic Gate Susceptibility Evaluation of Single
Event Transient Faults 69
  Rafael B. Schvittz, Denis T. Franco, Leomar S. da Rosa Jr.,
  and Paulo F. Butzen

Process Variability Impact on the SET Response of FinFET
Multi-level Design 89
  Leonardo H. Brendler, Alexandra L. Zimpeck, Cristina Meinhardt,
  and Ricardo Reis

Efficient Soft Error Vulnerability Analysis Using Non-intrusive Fault
Injection Techniques 115
  Vitor Bandeira, Felipe Rosa, Ricardo Reis, and Luciano Ost

A Statistical Wafer Scale Error and Redundancy Analysis Simulator 139
  Atishay, Ankit Gupta, Rashmi Sonawat, Helik Kanti Thacker,
  and B. Prasanth

Hardware-Enabled Secure Firmware Updates in Embedded Systems 165
  Solon Falas, Charalambos Konstantinou, and Maria K. Michael

Reliability Enhanced Digital Low-Dropout Regulator with Improved
Transient Performance 187
  Longfei Wang, Soner Seçkiner, and Selçuk Köse

Security Aspects of Real-Time MPSoCs: The Flaws and Opportunities
of Preemptive NoCs 209
  Bruno Forlin, Cezar Reinbrecht, and Johanna Sepúlveda

Offset-Compensation Systems for Multi-Gbit/s Optical Receivers 235
  László Szilágyi, Jan Pliva, and Ronny Henker

Accelerating Inference on Binary Neural Networks with Digital
RRAM Processing.   257
    João Vieira, Edouard Giacomin, Yasir Qureshi, Marina Zapater,
    Xifan Tang, Shahar Kvatinsky, David Atienza,
    and Pierre-Emmanuel Gaillardon

Semi- and Fully-Random Access LUTs for Smooth Functions   279
    Y. Serhan Gener, Furkan Aydin, Sezer Gören, and H. Fatih Ugurdag

A Predictive Process Design Kit for Three-Independent-Gate
Field-Effect Transistors   307
    Patsy Cadareanu, Ganesh Gore, Edouard Giacomin,
    and Pierre-Emmanuel Gaillardon

Exploiting Heterogeneous Mobile Architectures Through a Unified
Runtime Framework   323
    Chenying Hsieh, Ardalan Amiri Sani, and Nikil Dutt

Author Index   345

Contributors

David Atienza ESL, Swiss Federal Institute of Technology Lausanne (EPFL), Lausanne, Switzerland

Atishay ESL, DRAM Solutions, Samsung Semiconductor India Research and Development, Bengaluru, India

Furkan Aydin Department of Electrical and Computer Engineering, North Carolina State University, Raleigh, NC, USA

Vitor Bandeira PPGC/PGMicro, UFRGS, Porto Alegre, Brazil

Leonardo H. Brendler Institute of Informatics, PGMICRO, Universidade Federal do Rio Grande do Sul (UFRGS), Porto Alegre, RS, Brazil

Paulo F. Butzen Department of Electrical Engineering, Universidade Federal do Rio Grande do Sul, Porto Alegre, Brazil

Patsy Cadareanu Electrical and Computer Engineering Department, University of Utah, Salt Lake City, UT, USA

Leomar S. da Rosa Jr. Technologic Development Center, Universidade Federal de Pelotas, Pelotas, Brazil

Nikil Dutt Department of Computer Science, University of California, Irvine, CA, USA

Solon Falas Department of Electrical and Computer Engineering, KIOS Research and Innovation Centre of Excellence, University of Cyprus, Nicosia, Cyprus

Denis T. Franco Engineering Center, Universidade Federal de Pelotas, Pelotas, Brazil

Bruno Forlin Federal University of Rio Grande do Sul, Porto Alegre, RS, Brazil

Pierre-Emmanuel Gaillardon LNIS, Electrical and Computer Engineering Department, University of Utah, Salt Lake City, UT, USA

Y. Serhan Gener Department of Computer Science, University of California Riverside, Riverside, CA, USA

Edouard Giacomin LNIS, Electrical and Computer Engineering Department, University of Utah, Salt Lake City, UT, USA

Ganesh Gore Electrical and Computer Engineering Department, University of Utah, Salt Lake City, UT, USA

Sezer Gören Department of Computer Engineering, Yeditepe University, Istanbul, Turkey

Michelangelo Grosso STMicroelectronics s.r.l., AMS R&D, Turin, Italy

Ankit Gupta DRAM Solutions, Samsung Semiconductor India Research and Development, Bengaluru, India

Ronny Henker Circuit Design and Network Theory, Technische Universität Dresden, Dresden, Germany

Chenying Hsieh Department of Computer Science, University of California, Irvine, CA, USA

Maksim Jenihhin Centre for Dependable Computing Systems, Department of Computer Systems, Tallinn University of Technology, Tallinn, Estonia

Selçuk Köse Department of Electrical and Computer Engineering, University of Rochester, Rochester, NY, USA

Charalambos Konstantinou FAMU-FSU College of Engineering, Center for Advanced Power Systems, Florida State University, Tallahassee, FL, USA

Shahar Kvatinsky Andrew and Erna Viterbi Faculty of Electrical Engineering, Technion, Israel Institute of Technology, Haifa, Israel

Cristina Meinhardt Department of Informatics and Statistics, PPGCC, Universidade Federal de Santa Catarina (UFSC), Florianópolis, Brazil

Maria K. Michael Department of Electrical and Computer Engineering, KIOS Research and Innovation Centre of Excellence, University of Cyprus, Nicosia, Cyprus

Leonardo B. Moraes Instituto de Informática, PGMicro/PPGC, Universidade Federal do Rio Grande do Sul (UFRGS), Porto Alegre, Brazil

Luciano Ost Loughborough University, Loughborough, England

Adeboye Stephen Oyeniran Centre for Dependable Computing Systems, Department of Computer Systems, Tallinn University of Technology, Tallinn, Estonia

Jan Pliva Circuit Design and Network Theory, Technische Universität Dresden, Dresden, Germany

B. Prasanth Host Software, Samsung Semiconductor India Research and Development, Bengaluru, India

Yasir Qureshi ESL, Swiss Federal Institute of Technology Lausanne (EPFL), Lausanne, Switzerland

Jaan Raik Centre for Dependable Computing Systems, Department of Computer Systems, Tallinn University of Technology, Tallinn, Estonia

Cezar Reinbrecht Universidade Federal do Rio Grande do Sul, Porto Alegre, RS, Brazil

Ricardo Reis PGMICRO/PPGC, Instituto de Informática, Universidade Federal do Rio Grande do Sul (UFRGS), Porto Alegre, RS, Brazil

Salvatore Rinaudo STMicroelectronics s.r.l., AMS R&D, Catania, Italy

Felipe Rosa PPGC/PGMicro, UFRGS, Porto Alegre, Brazil

Ardalan Amiri Sani Department of Computer Science, University of California, Irvine, CA, USA

Rafael B. Schvittz Technologic Development Center, Universidade Federal de Pelotas, Pelotas, Brazil

Soner Seçkiner Department of Electrical and Computer Engineering, University of Rochester, Rochester, NY, USA

Johanna Sepúlveda Airbus Defence and Space GmbH, Taufkirchen, Germany

Rashmi Sonawat DRAM Solutions, Samsung Semiconductor India Research and Development, Bengaluru, India

Matteo Sonza Reorda Dipartimento di Automatica e Informatica, Politecnico di Torino, Turin, Italy

László Szilágyi Circuit Design and Network Theory, Technische Universität Dresden, Dresden, Germany

Xifan Tang LNIS, University of Utah, Salt Lake City, USA

Helik Kanti Thacker DRAM Solutions, Samsung Semiconductor India Research and Development, Bengaluru, India

Raimund Ubar Centre for Dependable Computing Systems, Department of Computer Systems, Tallinn University of Technology, Tallinn, Estonia

H. Fatih Ugurdag Department of Electrical and Electronics Engineering, Ozyegin University, Istanbul, Turkey

João Vieira INESC-ID, Instituto Superior Técnico, University of Lisboa, Lisbon, Portugal

Longfei Wang Department of Electrical and Computer Engineering, University of Rochester, Rochester, NY, USA

Marina Zapater ESL, Swiss Federal Institute of Technology Lausanne (EPFL), Lausanne, Switzerland

Alexandra Lackmann Zimpeck Instituto de Informática, PPGC, Universidade Federal do Rio Grande do Sul (UFRGS), Porto Alegre, Brazil

Software-Based Self-Test for Delay Faults

Michelangelo Grosso[1], Matteo Sonza Reorda[2(✉)],
and Salvatore Rinaudo[3]

[1] STMicroelectronics s.r.l., AMS R&D, Turin, Italy
`michelangelo.grosso@st.com`
[2] Dipartimento di Automatica e Informatica, Politecnico di Torino, Turin, Italy
`matteo.sonzareorda@polito.it`
[3] STMicroelectronics s.r.l., AMS R&D, Catania, Italy
`salvatore.rinaudo@st.com`

Abstract. Digital integrated circuits require thorough testing in order to guarantee product quality. This is usually achieved with the use of scan chains and automatically generated test patterns. However, functional approaches are often used to complement test suites. Software-Based Self-Test (SBST) can be used to increase defect coverage in microcontrollers, to replace part of the scan pattern set to reduce tester requirements, or to complement the defect coverage achieved by structural techniques when advanced semiconductor technologies introduce new defect types. Delay testing has become common practice with VLSI integration, and with the latest technologies, targeting small delay defects (SDDs) has become necessary. This chapter deals with SBST for delay faults and describes a case of study based on a peripheral module integrated in a System on Chip (SoC). A method to develop an effective functional test is first described. A comparative analysis of the delay faults detected by scan and SBST is then presented, with some discussion about the obtained results.

Keywords: Software-Based Self-Test · Transition delay faults · Small Delay Defects · VLSI · Microcontrollers · Peripherals

1 Introduction

Testing at the end of manufacturing is a mandatory requirement for digital integrated circuits, to guarantee product quality and minimize the number of field returns. Its cost constitutes a large part of the overall budget, and consequently designers and product engineers collaborate to find the best solutions in terms of test coverage and application costs for the products. The inclusion of additional Design-for-Testability (DfT) dedicated structures within the chip is considered a valid approach to simplify and accelerate test generation and application: the most common approach, in digital logic, is the use of scan chains, which provide direct controllability and observability to most flip-flops in the circuit. Today's scan chain-based methodologies overcome many limitations of the basic approach. Some examples include:

- Scan compression, to reduce the test pattern size and alleviate the memory requirement on the tester;

© IFIP International Federation for Information Processing 2020
Published by Springer Nature Switzerland AG 2020
C. Metzler et al. (Eds.): VLSI-SoC 2019, IFIP AICT 586, pp. 1–19, 2020.
https://doi.org/10.1007/978-3-030-53273-4_1

- On-chip clock controllers, to use available on-chip oscillator and phase-locked loop (PLL) for applying patterns at-speed, i.e., at the nominal circuit frequency;
- Power-aware pattern generation, to avoid the excessive energy dissipation during test due to a switching activity higher than normal.

Alternative and complementary approaches to scan chain-based testing have been developed and used in the past to provide a wider range of methods to designers and product engineers. Among those, Software-Based Self-Testing (SBST) methods [1] are based on the application of functional stimuli to an on-chip microprocessor, by forcing it to run a specific piece of code. With such a kind of stimulation, it is possible to guarantee the detection of structural faults within the logic, at the nominal circuit frequency (at speed) and without extra power consumption; however, test generation and coverage assessment processes are not as standardized, automated and widespread. The adoption of advanced semiconductor technologies even for safety-critical applications, requiring a high level of reliability, triggered the usage of SBST for in-field test, in the form of Self-Test Libraries (STLs) developed by the semiconductor company manufacturing the device and integrated by the system company in the application code [2].

While most of the papers describing techniques to generate SBST programs and assess their effectiveness focused on stuck-at faults, some of them also dealt with delay faults [3–8], whose importance is growing with shrinking semiconductor technologies. Several researchers (e.g., [9]) highlighted the fact that the percentage of functionally untestable delay faults (i.e., delay faults that cannot produce any failure when the circuit works in the operational mode) may be significant in many cases, thus reducing the achieved fault coverage. Clearly, the ideal approach would be to remove untestable faults from the fault list when computing the achieved fault coverage [10]. Unfortunately, given the complexity of modern processors, the task of identifying functionally untestable faults with a scalable effort still remains an open problem [9, 11].

Delay defects are usually modeled as path delay faults or transition delay faults. Transition delay faults are more easily handled by Electronic Design Automation (EDA) tools and test suites targeting stuck-at and transition delay faults in combination with scan are quite common in the industry. However, with the continuous shrinking of geometries and rising of frequencies, and as a direct consequence of process variations, the impact of more subtle delay defects has been rising, and the specific case of *Small Delay Defects* (SDDs) required in the last years the development of more advanced test generation techniques [12].

In this chapter, which extends a previously published paper [13], we propose a SBST methodology for testing a digital communication peripheral embedded in a mixed-signal ASIC device at the end of manufacturing focusing on both stuck-at and transition delay faults. The manually developed test stimuli include a specific code to be run by the embedded microcontroller, in parallel with the interaction from the outside handled by an Automatic Test Equipment (ATE). The effectiveness of the approach in detecting SDDs is also evaluated and discussed.

The goal of the chapter is first to demonstrate that SBST can be used to improve or replace part of traditional test procedures for digital logic, thus improving test coverage while containing test application cost. As a matter of fact, functional/embedded software-driven testing parts are commonly employed for analog components in mixed-signal circuits, disregarding the coverage that they may inherently obtain on the digital logic. Secondly, we compared the list of faults detected by the proposed SBST technique with the faults detected using scan. Results show that due to designer choices, some faults can only be detected resorting to a functional approach, while some of the faults which are only detected by the scan test proved to be functionally untestable, and hence their detection produces some overtesting. We also highlight the specific effort and computational time required for the process of fault grading the developed procedures, depending on the chosen fault model and observation strategy. Finally, for the first time, we compare the transition delay coverage and small delay defect coverage obtained with the use of the SBST approach.

In summary, the contribution of the chapter lies on the one side in proposing a technique to guide the test engineer in the generation of suitable SBST tests for a peripheral module, on the other on reporting detailed experimental results related to the stuck-at and delay (transitions and small delay) fault coverage figures achievable with SBST and scan on a real industrial case study.

This chapter is structured as follows: Sect. 2 provides an essential background to appreciate details and motivations of the work; Sect. 3 describes the flow used to develop the test set and to evaluate its test coverage. Experimental results on a case study are reported in Sect. 4, and conclusions are drawn in Sect. 5.

2 Related Works

This chapter focuses on the end-of-manufacturing test of a case study corresponding to a peripheral module managing communications with the outside of a System on Chip (SoC).

Test development for digital circuits relies on the definition of *fault models*, abstract models that represent the behavior of the circuit in the presence of a manufacturing defect. This kind of modeling provides a mathematical method to analyze and measure the effectiveness of a test in detecting the defect effects, and hence in discriminating good and faulty devices, using a logic netlist representation of the circuit. The fault coverage of a set of stimuli is represented by the ratio of faults that cause a difference between the real circuit outputs and the expected ones, and the total number of faults.

The most common and widely used fault model for digital blocks of logic is the stuck-at, corresponding to each single node in the circuit being fixed at the 0 (stuck-at-0) or 1 (stuck-at-1) logic level. The number of stuck-at faults is simply the number of nodes multiplied by two. To complement the effectiveness of a test targeting stuck-at faults, other fault models are used that consider other defect effects, such as bridging and delay faults.

Delay faults represent the behavior of a block of logic that is slower than expected, due, e.g., to the increased resistivity or capacitance of a circuit structure. Delay defects are usually modeled as path delay faults or transition delay faults. The former model is defined as the cumulative delay of a combinational path that exceeds some specified duration (e.g., the maximum propagation delay). The latter consists in a larger than normal delay in the toggling of the logic value of a node (slow-to-rise or slow-to-fall); such additional delay is considered to be large enough to cause an error on an output or on the next clock front, when data sampling occurs. The transition delay fault model is widely used due to its inherent simplicity, as it does not require timing models for pattern generation, and Automatic Test Pattern Generation (ATPG) algorithms are based on the ones for stuck-at faults.

Experimental data [14, 15] shows that the smaller delay defects are more likely to happen in the circuits. However, the transition delay fault coverage does not guarantee the detection of subtle defects that cause small delays within a combinational path. In fact, ATPG tools usually aim at covering the transition delay fault on a specific node with the lowest effort, i.e., not necessarily activating the worst path passing through that node. The detection of Small Delay Defects (SDDs) requires more specific patterns, and therefore more sophisticated ATPG and fault simulation flows [12, 16].

With respect to traditional transition delay fault ATPG flows, this kind of analysis requires timing analysis data – usually expressed in the Standard Delay Format (SDF). Figure 1.*a* (adapted from [16]) shows how a specific transition delay fault can be activated through different paths. Considering the endpoint flip flop always observable and the launch and capture clocks perfectly balanced, the delay fault on the combinational logic will be detected by the test activating the transition only if the additional delay is larger than the path slack (Fig. 1.*b*). Therefore, to detect a smaller delay defect, the transition has to be activated on a path with smaller slack, and thus this information has to be computed by the ATPG tool. This translates into additional algorithm complexity.

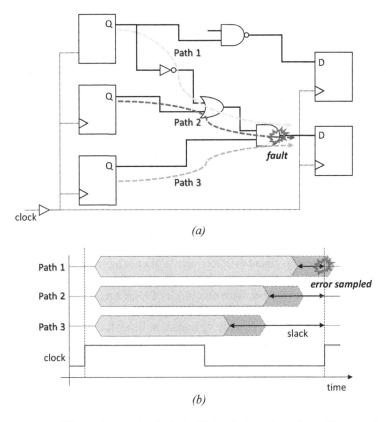

Fig. 1. In *a*) three different logic paths through which a fault can be activated in a sample circuit. In *b*) the timing diagram of the three paths showing the slack in each case: a small additional delay (highlighted in orange) causes an observable effect only along Path 1. (Color figure online)

The size of the delay to be considered is strictly correlated with the implementation technology and on slack distribution in the circuit. ATPGs usually address faults within a maximum timing margin (*max_tmgn*), representing the slack limit for targeting faults at their minimum slacks. To provide more expressive test quality measures with respect to fault coverage, different metrics are described in the literature, such as Delay Effectiveness (DE, [16, 17], which takes into account the size of the delay fault and the minimum slack of a path that can activate it, and probabilistic models considering slack and fault size distributions (e.g., [18, 19]). DE is defined as the ratio between the integral of the cumulative distribution of detected fault slacks F_D and the integral of the cumulative distribution of total fault slacks F_T within *max_tmgn*:

$$DE = \frac{\int F_D(t)dt}{\int F_T(t)dt} \tag{1}$$

Test of digital modules is typically performed resorting to DfT techniques, such as scan. While it guarantees an easy to apply and effective solution for stuck-at faults, scan is known to have some criticalities when delay faults are considered. In such a case, Launch on Capture (LoC) and Launch on Shift (LoS) can be used [20], which are widely supported by commercial tools. Both LoC and LoS are known to produce some overtesting, since they perform the test with full freedom in controlling and observing the flip-flop state. In normal operational conditions this is clearly not the case. When considering path delay faults, the overtesting issue can be tamed by identifying functionally untestable paths and removing them from the target fault list [21, 22]. While exact solutions are hardly scalable, approximate ones have also been proposed [10]. The role of temperature when facing delay faults has been explored in [23].

As an alternative to DfT solutions, functional ones (based on stimulating the circuit acting on the functional inputs and observing the functional outputs, only, without any DfT support) provide the advantage of not requiring any hardware overhead nor producing any overtesting. On the other side, test stimuli generation is not automated in this case, and its cost is clearly much higher. This solution may be particularly attractive for SoCs including at least one processor, where a functional test takes the form of a program suitably written to excite the target faults and make their possible presence visible on the circuit outputs (Software-based Self-Test, or SBST) [1]. Previous papers explored techniques to guide the test engineer in the development of suitable SBST programs targeting stuck-at and delay faults [4–6, 24]. Others focused on a comparison between the Fault Coverage achievable with scan with respect to the one of SBST, taking also into account the untestable delay faults [9]. Some works also tried to provide techniques allowing to automate the generation of such programs [3, 7], possibly resorting to a hybridization between DfT and SBST [25]. Finally, some recent works focused on new techniques to speed up the assessment of the quality of the developed test programs [26]. Once again, the issue of preliminarily identifying untestable delay faults to reduce the test generation effort and more precisely assess the achieved test effectiveness plays a key role [11]. Clearly, removing functionally untestable faults from the considered fault list allows to increase the achieved coverage, as it is routinely done when adopting standards (e.g., ISO 26262 in automotive) and performing Failure Modes, Effects and Diagnostic Analysis (FMEDA). On the other side, detecting them anyway may increase the overall quality of the product. The experimental results we report in this chapter allow to quantitatively assess the impact of functionally untestable faults and to better understand their origin.

In this chapter we do not focus on the usage of SBST for testing the faults in the CPU, but rather consider the test of a communication peripheral core, building over the techniques overviewed in [27]. We extend them to an interface based on the SPMI^{SM} standard, and analyze the results gathered on a test case where both the scan and SBST solutions were developed. For the first time, comparative results related to a peripheral component are reported with respect to both stuck-at and transition delay faults. An analysis of the results obtained with the two techniques provides the reader with some better understanding of their advantages and limitations. Furthermore, we present an evaluation of SDD coverage of the developed test set.

3   Proposed Approach

In order to test a peripheral module within a SoC with a functional approach, such as in SBST, a specific code for the embedded CPU needs to be written, accessing the peripheral registers by means of the system bus. In addition, in case of communication peripherals or modules interacting with the outside of the chip, further stimuli need to come from the external world, i.e., by the ATE. The operations of the embedded microcontroller and the external tester must be synchronized by means of precise timing control or handshake protocols.

For the validation of a SBST set and the assessment of test coverage, a hardware description language (hdl) testbench is used to activate the system and emulate external devices in simulation and fault simulation. The general flow is described in Fig. 2. After the code is written and the testbench is prepared, a functional simulation is performed to ascertain that the Unit Under Test (UUT) performs as planned. Then, fault simulation is required to assess the coverage on a list of faults on the peripheral logic structure.

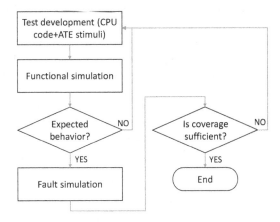

Fig. 2. Test generation flow.

3.1   Generation of the Test Program and External Stimuli

The development of a SBST set usually starts with a series of small program sections able to access each of the peripheral registers and activate all its functionalities (e.g., transmitting and receiving data in different configurations). Any available design validation code can be fruitfully employed in this step. Usually, each part is composed of a preliminary "setup" or configuration phase, and an operational step. It is possible to assume that the available code is already "short enough", i.e., avoids redundant parts, so as not to increase simulation time and also to limit test application duration/costs.

However, two important test-specific points have to be considered. First, the targeted fault model has an impact on the required stimuli: as an example, whereas a stuck-at test only requires that each register is written and then read first with '0' and then with '1' logic values, when dealing with delay-dependent fault models, such as the transition delay one, the sequence and the timing of operations is fundamental as well. In this case, a sequence of '0'-to-'1' and '1'-to-'0' operations are needed for each node. In this way, stuck-at faults are inherently covered.

Second, while validation usually requires the monitoring of a limited amount of functional results of an operation, in case of test, in order to guarantee high test coverage, the observation of fault effects requires more pervasive data sampling operations. The fault effects need to be propagated either to the outside of the device (to be read by the ATE) or to a bus or memory area readable by the embedded microprocessor.

After a preliminary all-encompassing functional stimulation, if additional coverage is required, it is possible to address the composing elements of the peripheral one at a time, with specific techniques for activating the logic of each part. The most common elements within a digital peripheral are controllers, combinational units such as comparators and algebraic units, sequential devices with a regular structure such as counters, and data buffers.

Controllers are the circuit sections used to handle the control signals regulating the datapath, and are typically implemented using Finite State Machines (FSMs), which are mathematical models of computation. An FSM is composed by a finite number of states; the current state evolves from one to another depending on the external inputs. A test procedure normally aims at activating all possible states and transitions between them, and then making the performed operations visible.

To maximize test coverage in combinational units, available ATPG tools can be fruitfully used to generate a sequence of stimuli on limited parts of the logic. Such sequences need then to be brought to the unit interface by means of microprocessor instructions or external interaction, and then test results have to be propagated to observable points. It may not be always possible to apply any pattern to inner circuitry: this will be further discussed in Subsect. 3.3.

Regular sequential units such as counters need to be approached taking into account the fact that their test can be quite time-consuming. For this reason, it can be useful to concentrate on applying transitions on the output of each sequential element and propagating them towards observable points, exploiting programmable features. For instance, a 32-bit programmable counter can be set to count in different shorter ranges to activate transitions in all register bits without waiting for 2^{32} clock cycles: this can be accomplished by targeting the elementary increment/decrement operations with the related generation and propagation of carry/borrow bits. Similarly, when testing a data buffer, it is needed to know its characteristics (byte/word accessibility, LIFO/FIFO architecture, etc.) and its implementation in order to develop the most suitable sequence of write and read operations.

3.2   Test Coverage Evaluation

The evaluation of test coverage requires the fault simulation process, i.e., a gate-level simulation reproducing the effect of faults and enabling to determine if the applied stimuli produce a difference between the good and the faulty circuitry. Fault simulation can be performed by suitably instrumenting a model in a logic simulator, and commercial tools are also available. Functional fault simulators aimed at validating fault-tolerant designs and at evaluating the effectiveness of test sets are becoming increasingly popular. A fault simulator may require to provide the sequence of input/output signals at the periphery of the module under test (e.g., in the form of a value change dump – vcd – file), and hence a previous functional simulation run is needed; others may directly handle the complete simulation of the testbench and any other circuit parts not currently addressed for the computation of fault coverage. The latter case, represented by, to name but a few, Cadence Incisive Safety Simulator, Z01X by Synopsys and Silvaco HyperFault, is more convenient for the problem described in this work.

Due to the potentially large number of faults within the logic under test and the non-direct logic monitoring of SBST procedures, which may require many clock cycles to propagate fault effects to observable points, the management and the running time of fault simulation can get critical also when using state-of-the-art tools.

The key factors are the number of observation points and the timing when these are actually sampled. In fact, the simulator will check the observation points only in certain instants (decided by the designer). The more frequent is the check, the larger is the time required by the simulation. On the other hand, a more frequent check may detect a larger number of faults, which may increase the overall speed of the process. This is linked to the algorithm used by the fault simulator: generally, once a fault is excited, the fault simulator creates a new simulation instance to keep track of all the evolutions of the faulty circuit. This simulation instance will be closed once the fault is detected, freeing the resource allocated for that instance (fault dropping). The larger the number of simulation instances is, the higher the amount of resources required by the fault simulator is and, consequently, the slower the fault simulation is. A similar discussion can be done regarding the number of observation points. The larger their number is, the slower the simulation is, but the higher the chance to detect a fault is. It is important to recall that, in the end, the observation point must be chosen in order to get a coverage indication as close as possible to the real test application; different solutions may be employed within the same flow in order to get a fast albeit approximate information when designing the test and a more precise one at the end. As an example, it may be useful to run experiments while sampling data on all flip-flops, even if they may not be directly observable, to iteratively evaluate the effectiveness of the pattern set in exciting faults (controllability); then, switch to more realistic approaches to improve fault propagation to monitorable points (observability), possibly with minor changes on the test.

Another important point to take into account is related to how to model circuit timing. When simulating the pure logic functionality of a circuit, or when evaluating delay-independent fault models such as the stuck-at or transition delay, zero-delay models are sufficient. In this case, the circuit states are usually updated with an event-driven approach at each clock front, resulting in a relatively low computational effort and therefore in a fast simulation. When verifying timing performance of specific operations, to complement static timing analysis, or when verifying immunity or coverage of delay-dependent faults, such as path delay or small delay defects, precise timing simulation are required. This approach implies the use of timing data (SDF) and a more complex event scheduler, which, as it will be shown later on, may have a relevant impact on simulation performance.

3.3 Functional Testability

To correctly assess test coverage on a circuit, an important concept has to be introduced. A fault is physically testable if there exists a test for the fault which can be applied on the hypothesis of full accessibility to all circuit nets. Even when using full-scan test approaches, not all input sequences can be applied to the combinational parts of the circuit: therefore, not all faults are testable even under full-scan. For example, a delay fault may not be testable, because no one of the vector pairs able to test it can be applied to the inputs of the combinational block where it is located using LoC and LoS techniques. A fault is functionally testable if there exists a functional test for exciting that fault: when delay testing a circuit using SBST (or during the normal behavior of the system), the signals feeding the addressed path are determined by the program running on the processor and on the stimuli on the interfaces. These impose temporal and spatial correlations among registers/flip-flops and thus among inputs/outputs of the addressed logic. These correlations result in a smaller set of testable faults (Fig. 3).

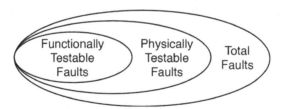

Fig. 3. Fault testability categorization.

Functionally untestable (redundant) faults cannot be activated and/or observed during normal operations of the circuit, therefore they have no impact on circuit behavior and performances. SBST focuses on functionally testable faults, intrinsically avoiding overtesting the circuit's redundant logic [11]. Two definitions are hence used: *fault coverage* is the ratio between tested faults and the total number of faults; *test coverage* is computed using the number of testable faults as denominator.

The identification of functionally untestable faults is still an open problem; however, during the analysis of the peripheral under test and during the generation of the SBST set, the fault list can be pruned to exclude parts of the logic that cannot be functionally operated, e.g., modules deactivated due to hardwired configuration values, any DfT structures that cannot be activated in functional mode, such as scan chain-related signals, or error-handling logic (e.g., redundant paths).

When considering small delay defects, the computation of effectiveness metrics such as DE should take into account the actual possibility of functionally activating the required transition along the minimum slack path, thus increasing the complexity of the problem.

4   Case Study

To demonstrate the feasibility of the functional approach and to analyze its performance with respect to stuck-at and delay faults, a communication peripheral based on the System Power Management Interface (SPMI^{SM}) specifications by the MIPI Alliance is used as a case study. The peripheral can handle two-wire serial communications up to 26 MHz and includes functions such as bus arbitration, data serialization, error detection and an automated ack/nack protocol.

4.1   Case Study Description

The selected peripheral acts as request-capable slave, i.e., a slave which can initiate sequences on the two-wire SPMI bus (SCLK and SDATA). Figure 4 shows its basic architecture. The processor system is connected by means of the AMBA AHB bus, and the master/slave AHB interface (equipped with a FIFO mailbox) handles communications. The Control and Status Register (CSR) module includes byte-addressable registers used to control and monitor the peripheral functions. Two finite state machines (FSMs) manage the arbitration (Request FSM) and the general peripheral behavior.

The synthesized peripheral counts about 21,500 equivalent gates and is equipped with full-scan. We underline that scan chains are not used when applying SBST.

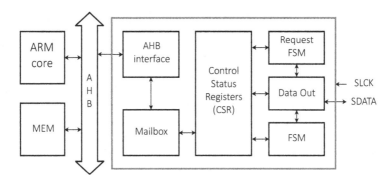

Fig. 4. Architecture of the case study.

4.2   SBST Test Suite

The complete test set is composed of a series of small program/external stimuli sequence pairs, each targeting some specific functionalities or modules within the peripheral:

- *Reset, write 0/1 and read 0/1* (Reset). This segment is operated by the microcontroller, which requests a peripheral reset and then reads the registers. After this, a comprehensive sequence of 0-to-1 and 1-to-0 write operations is done on the CSR, each followed by the needed reads, as in the following pseudo-code

```
// The MCU resets the peripheral (all flip-flops=0)
mcu.SPMI_reset();
for each register in CSR {// write 1 in each register bit
  mcu.ahb.write(reg_addr, 0xFF); // 0->1 transition
  mcu.ahb.read(reg_addr); // read register content and
                    // store the value in RAM
}
for each register in CSR {// 1->0 transition
  mcu.ahb.write(reg_addr, 0x00);
  mcu.ahb.read(reg_addr);
}
for each register in CSR {
  mcu.ahb.write(reg_addr, 0xFF);
  mcu.ahb.read(reg_addr);
}
mcu.SPMI_reset();
for each register in CSR {
  mcu.ahb.read(reg_addr);
}
```

- *Mailboxes test* (WR-fifo and RD-fifo). For each FIFO buffer (from AHB and from the outside), a sequence of write and read operations is performed to stimulate 0-to-1 and 1-to-0 transitions in the registers, and the "flush" operations are tested as well.
- *Request commands* (Request). In this segment, bus access request commands are programmed to be executed by the peripheral under test, while the external tester will emulate other peripheral on the SPMI bus.
- *All commands* (Commands). In this case, the external tester acts as a bus master and sends a sequence of all possible commands to the peripheral. For read and write commands, all possible payload sizes (1 to 16) are used, and addresses are selected so as to stimulate each bit in the address field with both 0 and 1 values. When writing to the CSR module some care has to be taken to avoid requesting unwanted peripheral operations, by carefully selecting write register addresses and data words

(e.g., when writing to *Register 0*). Tests for the authentication mechanism and for activating all states of the state machine are also applied.

- *AHB access control test* (AHB access). This part of the test targets the AHB interface, whose accessible addresses can be programmed. Read/write operations are used aiming at stimulating the address comparators within the module.
- *Counters*. The last part of the test aims at activating the embedded timers for protocol management and timeout condition evaluation.

The results of each segment are read by the CPU, compressed using a software Multiple-Input Signature Register (MISR) sequence and stored in the system memory; then, they are read from the tester with a Read transaction on the SCLK/SDATA pins.

4.3   Fault Simulation

For the case study, Z01X by Synopsys was employed as fault simulator. In general, the tool can be used for two purposes: functional safety assurance, i.e., to check the efficacy of robust design strategies, and for manufacturing assurance, i.e., to evaluate the effectiveness of a functional test set. The synthesized or post-layout circuit netlist in Verilog can be directly simulated using testbenches (also in RTL), libraries and macro models in Verilog and SystemVerilog, thus resorting on the same simulation environment used for design validation.

Three different fault monitoring (strobe) methodologies were compared for coverage and speed:

- *All flip-flops*. Coverage values are computed while monitoring all flip-flops at each clock cycle, as well as the peripheral external I/Os. These data are overestimated since they do not take into account the whole process of fault effect propagation to an observable output, but help evaluating the effectiveness of the test in terms of fault controllability.
- *RAM bus*. Coverage is computed while monitoring transactions on the system RAM, where results are stored after each test operation, and the peripheral external I/Os. The obtained coverage is a good approximation of the one obtainable on the ATE, and the running time is reduced.
- *SDATA*. Coverage is computed monitoring what is sampled by the ATE (i.e., external bus transactions); some coverage is lost with respect to the previous approaches due to the reduced fault observability of the method. This is, however, the slowest and the most memory-intensive methodology.

Regarding the modeling of circuit timing, as most logic simulators, Z01X allows the user to choose how it is handled between the following options:

- *delay mode zero*, ignoring all module path delay information and setting to zero all delay expressions in the code;
- *delay mode unit*, ignoring all module path delay information and converting all non-zero structural and continuous assignment delay expressions to a unit delay of one simulation time unit;

- *delay mode distributed*, ignoring all module path delay information and using distributed delays on nets, primitives and continuous assignments;
- *delay mode path*, deriving timing information from *specify* blocks within the libraries.

Stuck-at and transition delay faults can be analyzed resorting to the simplest timing models, hence increasing fault simulation speed. However, higher precision is needed to handle small delay defects. More realistic data can be derived from static analysis tools, which export cell and path delays taking into account the circuit structures and parasitic elements in SDF files. When importing an SDF file, the simulation complexity increases substantially. Z01X enables setting the size of the delay when injecting transition delay faults with the +trans+delay+<value> parameter.

4.4   Experimental Results

Table 1 presents the application time required for each of the previously described SBST test segments. The most time-consuming ones are the AHB access test, requiring the application of a large number of patterns for thoroughly testing the combinational logic, and the counter test.

Table 1. Duration of each SBST test segment

Test segment	Duration [ms]
Reset	0.926
WR-fifo	0.760
RF-fifo	1.154
Request	1.284
Commands	1.513
AHB access	11.630
Counters	128.390
Total	145.658

Table 2 reports fault simulation results on the stuck-at fault set, which includes 80,640 faults. Among these, at least 11,963 are deemed as functionally untestable, belonging to IP circuitry that cannot be functionally activated in this SoC context, and thus removed from *test coverage* computation. The test segments are applied sequentially on the fault list, with fault dropping. The *CPU time* column reports the duration of fault simulation, performed on an Intel Xeon CPU clocked at 3.00 GHz (a single core is used), while the *Detected* column shows the number of faults covered by the test set. When a test is applied to a sequential circuit, certain faults produce an unknown state at the output when a deterministic result is expected in the fault-free circuit. This condition is known as *potential detection* (numbers in parentheses) and each fault belonging to this category is weighted 0.5 for coverage computation.

It is noteworthy to observe that a significant number of faults produce internal effects on the flip-flops, but cannot be observed on the external circuit outputs, and thus remain undetected. Moreover, the selection of different strobe methodologies may significantly affect the required fault simulation computational effort. The observation on the RAM bus provides a reasonable compromise between accuracy and required CPU time.

Table 3 reports the same data for transition delay faults. In this case, 80,632 faults are considered, out of which 15,452 are functionally untestable. Interestingly, a number of untestable transition delay faults belong to finite state machines, and specifically to transitions from functional to "safe" states corresponding to the *default* branch of case statements of hdl languages, which can be taken only in presence of errors in the circuit behavior.

In order to provide a comparison about the coverage achievable by scan and SBST, another experiment was performed. A scan pattern set was generated with TetraMAX by Synopsys for transition delay and stuck-at faults. The scan test application takes about 120 ms with 10 MHz shift frequency and at-speed launch/capture, considering a single scan chain entirely committed to the peripheral under test. Fault coverage is provided for the scan pattern set in the *Scan chains* row of Table 4. In the following rows we report fault coverage for SBST and for the application of both test methodologies in sequence. The total number of stuck-at faults is 80,640, while transition delay faults are 70,207: faults on clock or scan-enable logic are not considered in the latter case, since it is not meaningful to test faults in such logic at functional speeds with scan-based patterns.

Fault simulation shows that the SBST test set uniquely covers 1,335 (1.66%) stuck-at faults and 4,631 (6.60%) transition delay faults in addition to the ones detected by the scan tests. Regarding transition delay faults, the scan test has a higher overall coverage, detecting 9,337 more faults than SBST, but only 6,538 out of these have been classified as functionally testable. Conversely, of the 59,032 detected faults, 5,972 belong to the functionally untestable category.

Results show that, even covering a lower number of faults, the SBST set obtains a better test coverage on transition delay faults in a comparable time. The reader must also note that most of the SBST application time is taken by the Counters segment, which contributes with 2,824 faults to the SBST set coverage, or 361 faults if run after the scan test. In other words, if the SBST set is applied after the scan test excluding the Counters segment, it is possible to increase fault coverage by more than 6% (or test coverage by 7%) in 17.27 ms.

SBST test is especially effective, obtaining higher fault coverage than the scan test, on the AHB interface, on the FSMs, on the logic that connects the peripheral to the external world and on the logic used by the Request commands.

By further inspection it is possible to see that most of the logic covered only by the functional test procedure is directly linked to clock gating circuitry or to other functions that are not available while the circuit is in scan-test mode. As a matter of fact, due to the unpredictable functional behavior during shift and capture operations, the circuit is usually brought by hardware to a "safe" state for the application of the scan test, isolating the digital logic from the external world and analog circuitry in mixed-signal devices, and avoiding possible critical configurations of system registers (whose output may be set to fixed values during test). SBST can be fruitfully employed to extend the coverage range of scan test in such cases, even after the circuit is manufactured.

Table 2. SBST stuck-at coverage results with different strobe methodologies

Strobe methodology	CPU time [s]	Detected (potentially)	Fault coverage	Test coverage
All flip-flops	72,151	65,720 (1,928)	82.69%	97.10%
RAM bus	32,915	59,796 (1,345)	74.99%	88.05%
SDATA	1,429,180	59,494 (1,346)	74.61%	87.61%

Table 3. SBST delay fault coverage results with different strobe methodologies.

Strobe methodology	CPU time [s]	Detected (potentially)	Fault coverage	Test coverage
All flip-flops	88,933	63,142 (73)	78.35%	96.93%
RAM bus	35,968	57,099 (302)	71.00%	87.83%
SDATA	1,761,990	56,748 (310)	70.57%	87.30%

Table 4. Fault coverage of scan, SBST and both tests (strobe on SDATA).

Test	Stuck-at faults		Transition delay faults		
	Detected (pot.)	Fault coverage	Detected (pot.)	Fault coverage	Test coverage
Scan chains	78,562 (0)	97.42%	59,032 (0)	84.08%	81.40%
SBST	59,494 (1,346)	74.61%	56,748 (310)	70.57%	87.30%
Both	79,897 (67)	99.12%	63,663 (42)	90.71%	88.57%

The coverage of small delay defects was evaluated for one of the SBST test segments, *Commands*, which is the one obtaining the highest transition delay test coverage, as it can be seen in Table 5. Obviously, the total coverage is not the simply the sum of the coverage obtained by each segment, since each fault can be covered by more than one test. The following analysis is done using the strobe on the RAM bus and the peripheral external I/Os.

Table 5. Transition fault coverage of each SBST test segment, and according to each strobe methodology.

Test segment	Transition delay test coverage/strobe methodology		
	All flip-flops	RAM bus	SDATA
Reset	44.24%	36.99%	36.15%
WR-fifo	39.07%	30.63%	30.12%
RF-fifo	36.93%	29.71%	29.23%
Request	38.15%	28.24%	27.41%
Commands	51.82%	44.97%	44.09%
AHB access	38.07%	27.83%	27.02%
Counters	38.49%	31.95%	31.43%
Total	96.93%	87.83%	87.30%

As aforementioned, a small delay defect on a logic path can be detected only when its size is larger than the minimum slack. Figure 5 reports the distribution of minimum slack values on the paths where the faults are located. The histogram shows two distinct peaks, due to paths related to the two different clocks used by the module under test: one corresponds to the AHB clock frequency, synchronizing the control state machines that interact with the rest of the SoC, and the other to the external SPMI clock which runs at a lower speed.

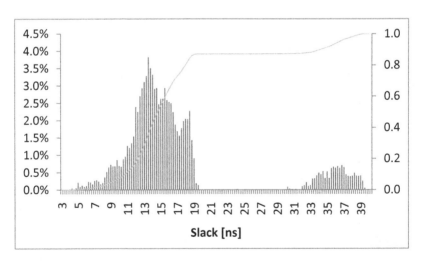

Fig. 5. Minimum slack histogram on the fault paths and cumulative distribution (in red). (Color figure online)

Transition delay and SDD coverages, with varying defect sizes, are reported in Table 6. As expected, test coverage rises with larger delay fault sizes; it must be noted that the maximum achievable value with the analyzed test is 44.97%, corresponding to the indefinitely large transition delay fault model. Defect Effectiveness is at all times larger than test coverage; however, its value decreases after the 20 ns delay size. This effect can be due to two causes. Firstly, while test coverage is computed on a fixed number of faults for the all experiments, the DE denominator grows together with fault size, and this can lead to a lower effectiveness even when the absolute number of covered faults is larger. Secondly, since SDDs are emulated in a timing simulation, the presence of hazards and glitches may in some occasions mask the effect of a fault when changing the defect size [28].

CPU time for a fault simulation run is on the order of 12 min for transition delay faults, while it rises up to 1.5 h for small delay faults. This is due to the need of performing more accurate timing simulations using SDF data.

Table 6. Small delay defect coverage of the *commands* test; the strobe is on the RAM bus.

	SDD fault size					Transition faults
	10 ns	15 ns	20 ns	25 ns	30 ns	
Detected	1,497	5,315	13,924	14,480	14,554	29,057
Pot. detected	335	339	370	426	427	515
Not detected	78,800	74,978	66,338	65,726	65,651	51,060
Fault coverage	2.06%	6.80%	17.50%	18.22%	18.31%	36.68%
Test coverage	2.55%	8.41%	21.65%	22.54%	22.66%	44.97%
Defect effectiveness	3.81%	17.79%	27.93%	26.34%	25.97%	–

5 Conclusions

This chapter describes a case study corresponding to a peripheral module within a SoC, for which tests targeting both stuck-at and transition delay faults have been developed resorting to the scan approach and to a functional one, based on SBST. We outlined a specific approach to develop the latter test targeting both stuck-at and transition delay faults. Extensive results have been presented, showing that the two methods have different and complementary characteristics. While scan test generation is fully automated, the functional test must be manually built. The fault coverage achieved by scan is higher, but some faults (especially numerous when considering delay faults) are only detected resorting to the functional approach. Moreover, we showed that some of the faults which are only detected by scan are functionally untestable. Hence, scan is likely to produce a higher degree of overtesting. We also reported some preliminary experimental results about the coverage that the functional approach can provide with respect to Small Delay Defects. Our results may allow test engineers to better understand the impact of functionally untestable faults on the achieved yield, reliability and quality of the product. We discussed the above points, providing examples for each category.

Work is currently being done in order to further improve the method to develop functional test programs targeting delay defects. Moreover, we are working to devise solutions to identify functionally untestable faults, extending to peripheral modules some of the ideas proposed in [29].

Acknowledgements. The authors wish to thank Andrea Casalino and Calogero Brucculeri for helping in the setup of the experimental campaigns.

References

1. Psarakis, M., Gizopoulos, D., Sanchez, E., Reorda, M.S.: Microprocessor software-based self-testing. IEEE Des. Test Comput. **27**(3), 4–19 (2010)
2. Bernardi, P., Cantoro, R., De Luca, S., Sanchez, E., Sansonetti, A.: Development flow for on-line core self-test of automotive microcontrollers. IEEE Trans. Comput. **65**(3), 744–754 (2016)
3. Shaheen, A.-U.-R., Hussin, F.A., Hamid, N.H., Ali, N.H.Z.: Automatic generation of test instructions for path delay faults based-on stuck-at fault in processor cores using assignment decision diagram. In: IEEE International Conference on Intelligent and Advanced Systems (ICIAS), pp. 1–5 (2014)
4. Singh, V., Inoue, M., Saluja, K.K., Fujiwara, H.: Instruction-based delay fault self-testing of processor cores. In: IEEE International Conference on VLSI Design, pp. 933–938 (2004)
5. Hage, N., Gulve, R., Fujita, M., Singh, V.: On testing of superscalar processors in functional mode for delay faults. In: IEEE International Conference on VLSI Design and International Conference on Embedded Systems (VLSID), pp. 397–402 (2017)
6. Psarakis, M., Gizopoulos, D., Hatzimihail, M., Paschalis, A., Raghunathan, A., Ravi, S.: Systematic software-based self-test for pipelined processors. IEEE Trans. Very Large Scale Integr. (VLSI) Syst. **16**(11), 1441–1453 (2008)
7. Christou, K., Michael, M.K., Bernardi, P., Grosso, M., Sanchez, E., Reorda, M.S.: A novel SBST generation technique for path-delay faults in microprocessors exploiting gate- and rt-level descriptions. In: IEEE VLSI Test Symposium, pp. 389–394 (2008)
8. Wen, C.H.-P., Wang, L.-C., Cheng, K.-T., Yang, K., Liu, W.-T., Chen, J.-J.: On a software-based self-test methodology and its application. In: IEEE VLSI Test Symposium, pp. 107–113 (2005)
9. Lai, W.-C., Krstic, A., Cheng, K.-T.: Functionally testable path delay faults on a microprocessor. IEEE Des. Test Comput. **17**(4), 6–14 (2000)
10. Fukunaga, M., Kajihara, S., Takeoka, S.: On estimation of fault efficiency for path delay faults. In: IEEE Asian Test Symposium, pp. 64–67 (2003)
11. Bernardi, P., Grosso, M., Sanchez, E., Reorda, M.S.: A deterministic methodology for identifying functionally untestable path-delay faults in microprocessor cores. In: IEEE International Workshop on Microprocessor Test and Verification, pp. 103–108 (2008)
12. Goel, S.K., Chakrabarty, K.: Testing for Small-Delay Defects in Nanoscale CMOS Integrated Circuits. CRC Press, Boca Raton (2017)
13. Grosso, M., Rinaudo, S., Casalino, A., Reorda, M.S.: Software-based self-test for transition faults: a case study. In: IEEE International Conference on Very Large Scale Integration (VLSI-SoC), pp. 76–81 (2019)
14. Nigh, P., Gattiker, A.: Test method evaluation experiments & data. In: IEEE International Test Conference, pp. 454–463 (2000)
15. Park, E.S., Mercer, M.R., Williams, T.W.: Statistical delay fault coverage and defect level for delay faults. In: IEEE International Test Conference, pp. 492–499 (1988)
16. Mattiuzzo, R., Appello, D., Allsup, C.: Small-delay-defect testing. EDN (Electr. Des. News) **54**(13), 28 (2009)

17. Metzler, C., Todri-Sanial, A., Bosio, A., Dilillo, L., Girard, P., Virazel, A.: Timing-aware ATPG for critical paths with multiple TSVs. In: IEEE International Symposium on Design and Diagnostics of Electronic Circuits and Systems, pp. 116–121 (2004)
18. Yilmaz, M., Tehranipoor, M., Chakrabarty, K.: A metric to target small-delay defects in industrial circuits. IEEE Des. Test Comput. **28**(2), 52–61 (2011)
19. Uzzaman, A., Tegethoff, M., Li, B., Mc Cauley, K., Hamada, S., Sato, Y.: Not all delay tests are the same - SDQL model shows truetime. In: IEEE Asian Test Symposium (ATS), pp. 147–152 (2006)
20. Bushnell, M., Agrawal, V.: Essentials of Electronic Testing for Digital, Memory, and Mixed-Signal VLSI Circuits. Kluwer Academic Publisher, Dordrecht (2000)
21. Cheng, K.-T., Chen, H.-C.: Classification and identification of nonrobust untestable path delay faults. IEEE Trans. Comput. Aided Des. Integr. Circuits Syst. **15**(8), 845–853 (1996)
22. Liu, X., Hsiao, M.S.: On identifying functionally untestable transition faults. In: IEEE International High-Level Design Validation and Test Workshop, pp. 121–126 (2004)
23. Zhang, Y., Peng, Z., Jiang, J., Li, H., Fujita, M.: Temperature-aware software-based self-testing for delay faults. In: IEEE Design, Automation & Test in Europe Conference & Exhibition (DATE), pp. 423–428 (2015)
24. Touati, A., Bosio, A., Girard, P., Virazel, A., Bernardi, P., Reorda, M.S.: Improving the functional test delay fault coverage: a microprocessor case study. In: IEEE Computer Society Annual Symposium on VLSI (ISVLSI), pp. 731–736 (2016)
25. Touati, A., Bosio, A., Girard, P., Virazel, A., Bernardi, P., Reorda, M.S.: Microprocessor testing: functional meets structural test. World Sci. J. Circuits Syst. Comput. **26**(8), 1–18 (2017)
26. Floridia, A., Sanchez, E., Reorda, M.S.: Fault grading techniques of software test libraries for safety-critical applications. IEEE Access **7**, 63578–63587 (2019)
27. Apostolakis, A., Gizopoulos, G., Psarakis, M., Ravotto, D., Reorda, M.S.: Test program generation for communication peripherals in processor-based SoC devices. IEEE Des. Test Comput. **26**(2), 52–63 (2009)
28. Wang, J., Li, H., Min, Y., Li, X., Liang, H.: Impact of hazards on pattern selection for small delay defects. In: IEEE Pacific Rim International Symposium on Dependable Computing, pp. 49–54 (2009)
29. Cantoro, R., Carbonara, S., Floridia, A., Sanchez, E., Reorda, M.S., Mess, J.-G.: An analysis of test solutions for COTS-based systems in space applications. In: IFIP/IEEE International Conference on Very Large Scale Integration (VLSI-SoC), pp. 59–64 (2018)

On Test Generation for Microprocessors for Extended Class of Functional Faults

Adeboye Stephen Oyeniran$^{(\boxtimes)}$, Raimund Ubar, Maksim Jenihhin, and Jaan Raik

Centre for Dependable Computing Systems, Department of Computer Systems, Tallinn University of Technology, Akadeemia 15a, 12618 Tallinn, Estonia
{adeboye.oyeniran,raimund.ubar,maksim.jenihhin,jaan.raik}@taltech.ee
http://www.ttu.ee/institutes/department-of-computer-systems/

Abstract. We propose a novel strategy of formalized synthesis of Software Based Self-Test (SBST) for testing microprocessors with RISC architecture to cover a large class of high-level functional faults. This is comparable to that used in memory testing which also covers a large class of structural faults such as stuck-at-faults (SAF), conditional SAF, multiple SAF and bridging faults. The approach is fully high-level, the model of the microprocessor is derived from the instruction set and architecture description, and no knowledge about gate-level implementation is needed. To keep the approach scalable, the microprocessor is partitioned into modules under test (MUT), and each MUT is in turn partitioned into data and control parts. For the data parts, pseudo-exhaustive tests are applied, while for the control parts, a novel generic functional control fault model was developed. A novel method for measuring high-level fault coverage for the control parts of MUTs is proposed. The measure can be interpreted as the quality of covering the high-level functional faults, which are difficult to enumerate. We apply High-Level Decision Diagrams for formalization and optimization of high-level test generation for control parts of modules and for trading off different test characteristics, such as test length, test generation time and fault coverage. The test is well-structured and can be easily unrolled online during test execution. Experimental results demonstrate high SAF coverage, achieved for a part of a RISC processor with known implementation, whereas the test was generated without knowledge of implementation details.

Keywords: Microprocessor testing · High-level functional fault model · Test generation · High-level fault coverage

1 Introduction

The growing density of integration in the semiconductor industry make today's chips more sensitive to faults while the mechanisms of the latter become more complex. New types of defects need to be considered in test generation to achieve high test quality. Similar to memory testing, broader classes of faults dependent on the neighboring logic, should be used as test targets in case of general

© IFIP International Federation for Information Processing 2020
Published by Springer Nature Switzerland AG 2020
C. Metzler et al. (Eds.): VLSI-SoC 2019, IFIP AICT 586, pp. 21–44, 2020.
https://doi.org/10.1007/978-3-030-53273-4_2

logic circuits. To make the tests less independent on particular implementation details, functional fault models and functional test approaches provide a good perspective to make the test development more efficient and to achieve higher test quality.

Software-Based Self-Test (SBST) [1–16] is an emerging paradigm in the test field. The major problem with SBST is usually the not sufficient test quality, measured by the single Stuck-at-Fault (SAF) coverage, let alone considering broader fault classes.

The quality of SBST is mainly affected by test data used in test programs. One of the ways to obtain test data is executing an Automated Test Pattern Generator (ATPG) [17,18]. In [17] it was shown that the processor can be divided into Modules under Test (MUT) to ease the task of ATPG. The difficulties arise from the need of guiding ATPGs by functional constraints to produce functionally feasible test patterns. The method [18] requires enforcing constraints during ATPG test generation. The run-time for generating test using the complete set of SBST constraints is, however, high. An alternative is to use random test patterns for MUTs [3]. However, these approaches need the knowledge about implementation.

SBST can be structural and functional. Structural approaches [4–6] use information from lower level of design, whereas functional approaches use mainly information of instruction set architecture (ISA). Hybrid SBST was proposed for combining deterministic structural SBST with verification-based test [4,5,19,20]. In addition to Hybrid SBST [7,21], there are methods that achieve comparable results and improved scalability when generating SBST using only RTL [4–6]. The structural approach cannot be used when structural information about the processor is not available. In [7], for high-level generation of SBST, the implementation details are not required, however, the low-level fault cover is not sufficiently high.

One of the first ISA based methods, using pseudo-random test sequences was proposed in [22]. Another solution, FRITS (Functional Random Instruction Testing at Speed) [23], was based on test generation using random instruction sequences with pseudo-random data. Alternative cache-resident method for production testing [24,25] using random generation mechanism proves that high cost functional testers can be replaced by low-cost SBST without significant loss in fault coverage. Another approach, based on evolutionary technique was proposed in [26]. Test is being composed of the most effective code snippets with good Stuck-at-fault (SAF) coverage, which were distinguished by constant reevaluation. The method needs structural information. Later research has been concentrated on developing dedicated test approaches for specific processor parts like pipeline, branch prediction mechanism [11,21], caches [22,23].

The drawbacks of the known methods vary in the need of knowledge about implementation details, fault coverage is measured traditionally only with respect to SAF, without considering broader fault classes, and no attempts have been made to evaluate the test coverage regarding multiple faults.

In this paper, to cope with the complexity of gate or RT level representations of microprocessors (MP), we consider the SBST generation with focus on modeling functional faults fully at the behavioral-level using only high-level information. We propose a deterministic high-level test generation method for SBST of processor cores, based on a novel implementation-independent high-level functional fault model. To compare the results with state-of-the-art, the quality of tests is measured by single SAF cover, however, at the same time, we target broader class of faults than single SAF, considering structural logic level faults such as conditional SAF [27,28], bridging and multiple faults, as well as the functional fault classes used traditionally in memory testing. For formal high-level functional fault modeling and test generation we use the idea of representing the instruction set and architecture of the microprocessor in form of High-Level Decision-Diagrams (HLDD) [29,30]. The HLDDs can be used as well for trading off different test characteristics such as test length, test generation time and fault coverage.

We generate tests separately for MUTs and in each MUT separately for its control and data parts [31]. The main contribution in the paper is related to test generation for the control parts, whereas for testing the data parts independently of the implementation details, we use the known pseudo-exhaustive test approach [32], not considered here in details.

The rest of the paper is organized as follows. In Sect. 2, we propose a novel concept of considering the control parts of the modules under test as generic abstract multiplexers, and in Sect. 3 we elaborate a concept of the novel high-level test generation for the control parts of processor modules. In Sect. 4, we develop a new general high-level functional fault model for control parts of modules. Section 5 describes a general scheme of test execution flow for the control parts of MUT. In Sect. 6, we compare the test flow with traditional memory March test, and introduce relationships between the proposed fault model with known functional and structural fault classes. In Sect. 7, we introduce High-Level Decision Diagrams for formalization of test generation and test optimization. Sections 8 is devoted to demonstrating of experimental results, and Sect. 9 completes the paper with conclusions.

2   High-Level Representation of Microprocessors

The main concept of the proposed method is based on partitioning the processor under test into functional entities – MUT, representing them as disjoint control and data parts. In this paper, we focus on the executing module and the pipeline forwarding unit as such entities, however showing that the approach is more general, and can be used always, when the MUT can be functionally represented as a set of well-defined functions.

In Fig. 1, a part of the pipelined structure of the miniMIPS microprocessor [33] is depicted. In yellow colour, the executing unit is highlighted, whereas the rest on the figure shows the main components of the pipeline architecture – pipeline registers, hazard detection circuitry, and the forwarding unit shown in grey colour. We consider the selected modules as consisting of disjoint control (decoder with MUX-s) and data parts, presented as hypothetical structures without knowing their implementation details.

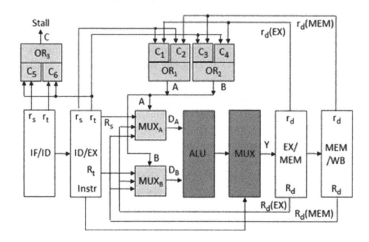

Fig. 1. A part of a RISC type microprocessor with executing unit in the pipeline and data forwarding environment (Color figure online)

The executing module in Fig. 1 (shown in yellow) consists of the data part concentrated into the ALU/MULT block, whereas the control functions are located in the decoder/multiplexer block MUX. The data part of the pipeline circuitry consists of the pipeline registers separating the different pipeline stages: instruction fetch (IF), instruction decoding (ID), executing module (EX), memory access (MEM), and write back stage (WB). The control part of the pipeline forwarding unit (shown in gray) consists of two multiplexer modules, MUX_A and MUX_B, which are fed by 4 comparators C1–C4 for calculation the values of control signals of multiplexers. The comparators C5 and C6 are used for hazard detection in case of "load-use" situations in pipeline circuits [34].

Note, the high-level functionality of the ALU/MULT module (the set of executable functions) is derived from the instruction set of the microprocessor, whereas the high-level functionality of the forwarding unit is derived from the description of the architecture of the microprocessor – a set of executable functions, which will be selected by the multiplexers MUX_A and MUX_B. In this paper, we concentrate on the ALU/MULT module.

We classify two types of high-level functional faults for the modules: control faults (for control part), and data faults (for data part). We do not consider data faults explicitly, rather we apply for data manipulation functions bit-wise pseudo-exhausting tests, which guarantee high fault coverage of a broad class of faults, whereas knowledge of implementation details is not needed.

For the high-level control faults, we introduce a novel functional fault model, as a general model, which covers a broad set of possible low-level structural faults, and also a set of traditional high-level functional fault models used in memory testing.

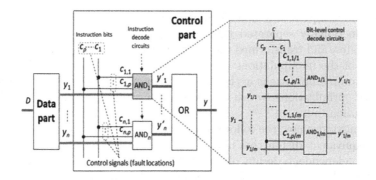

Fig. 2. Generic DNF based control structure of the executing unit

For developing the high-level functional control fault model, we introduce a generic representation of the control part in a form of high-level multiplexer. Consider the executing unit, shown in yellow in Fig. 1, and in detailed view in Fig. 2, where implementation details are abstract.

Assume, the data part in Fig. 2 executes n different functions $y_i = f_i(D_i)$ controlled by a set $F = \{F_i\}$ of instructions (functions), where D is the set of given data operands to be manipulated with $f_i \in F$. The length of data word is m, and the number of control signals p must satisfy the constraint

$$\log_2 n \leq p \leq n \tag{1}$$

and hence, depends on how the instructions are coded. However, the number of $1 - bit$ control signals p and the mapping of control vector signals to n instructions, where $n = |F|$, is considered as unknown. Let us keep for a while the coding of the control signals and the value of p in the model of MUTopen.

The control part consists of the multiplexer MUX, p control lines controlling the MUX, and an unknown circuit for mapping the instruction operation codes into the functional signals p. The high-level n AND blocks in MUX have each p control and a single m-bit data input, whereas the OR block in MUX has n data inputs from the outputs of AND blocks. Each AND block consists of m AND gates with p control inputs, and a single 1-bit data input. Hence, the described control module, represented in a form of a high-level multiplexer, consists of m different 1-bit logic level AND-OR multiplexers, used for decoding the instructions, and for extracting the results of executed instructions.

As it can be seen from Fig. 2, the border between the control part and the data part is determined by the AND gates, where the 1-bit control signals and 1-bit data signals are joining. The number of the AND gates on this border is equal to

$$n \times m \times p \tag{2}$$

By introducing the described hypothetical MUX-based executing module, we have functionally separated the data and control parts by the border of $n \times m \times p$ gates, and transformed the function of the control block from "active" controlling of the manipulations in the data part to "passive" selection of the results of data manipulations in the data part. In other words, we have neglected all possible optimizations, which may have been carried out during the design of the execution unit.

Let us introduce now the following abstraction, in accordance to Fig. 2, as a set of m equivalent disjunctive normal forms (EDNF) representing an implementation independent design of the MUT at the expense of possible over-dimensioning the real logic design. The disjoint presentation of the control and data parts allows to create an implementation-independent high-level functional control fault model.

The justification of the proposed abstraction results from the fact that a test T_{EDNF} developed for detecting all non-redundant faults in the EDNF, will detect also all faults in the real optimized circuit of the executing unit [35]. On the other hand, if the implementation details of the real circuit equivalent to EDNF were known, then the test T_{RC} of the real circuit, in general case, may have shorter length than T_{EDNF}.

The second abstraction will concern the control signal decoding, which, in general, is highly depending on the details of implementation. To allow the test generation for the control part be implementation independent, and as simple as possible, we introduce the one-to-one coding between the control signals and instruction, so that to each functions $f_i \in F$ the control signal c_i will correspond, and $C = \{c_i\}$, where $|F| = |C|$, will represent the full set of control signals. In this case, each control signal $c_i \in C$ selects the related function $f_i \in F$. In other words, by this way, we have introduced a hypothetical and simple coding scheme of int ructions, where $p = n$, which represents, according to (1) the higher bound of the value p. On the other hand, it provides the minimal length $n \times m$ for the border between the control and data parts of the MUT, determined by (2).

This second abstraction allows to overcome the problem of illegal instruction codes and to make easier the identification of redundant faults in any of the further real implementations of the control part.

The justification of the proposed abstractions will be given in the next section, where we introduce the new control fault model.

3   Basic Concepts of Generating High-Level Tests

Consider a simplified MUT in Fig. 3a, derived using the two described above abstractions, and consisting of the data and control parts. Figure 3a presents a $k - th$ bit slice of the m-bit control module, where m is the width of the data word carrying the value of f_i. The data manipulation block (e.g. ALU) executes n different functions f_i, selected by the control codes c denoted by symbolic integers $c_i, i = 0, 1, \ldots n$.

Each bit-slice of the control part consists of MUX with n control lines (control inputs to each AND). The $1 - bit$ data lines from the data manipulation module (ALU) are the data inputs to each AND. The OR gate has n data inputs.

Consider testing of the MUX in Fig. 3. Let us concentrate on testing the control code for the $k-th$ bit slice, which selects from ALU the result of the high-level defined operation $f_{i,k}$, producing the expected output value $y_k = f_{i,k}, (D)$. Consider the high-level symbolic (pseudo) control signals $c_{i,k}$, which may be applied $(c_{i,k} = 1)$ or not applied $(c_{i,k} = 0)$ as Boolean variables. From $c_{i,k} = 1$, it follows $c_{j,k} = 0$ for all $j \neq i$ due to the mutual exclusion of each other.

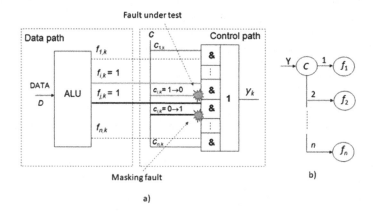

Fig. 3. A module consisting of data and control parts and its HLDD

The graph in Fig. 3b represents a High-Level Decision Diagram (HLDD) which describes the mapping "if $C = i$ then $y = f_i$", meaning that if $c_i = 1$ then $y = f_i$. About the role of using the HLDD model for representing the MUT we discuss in Sects. 7.

Definition 1. *Introduce a test T_i^* as a structure $T_i^* = (I_i, D_i)$ where I_i is an instruction, which performs the function $f_i \in F$ in the MUT represented by a set of functions F, and Di is a set of data operands used by the instruction Ii. The data Di may consist of one or more patterns $d \in D_i$. If D_i will consist of t patterns, the instruction Ii will be repeated in the test T_i^* for each pattern $d \in D_i$.*

Definition 2. *Let us introduce a notation $T_{i,k}^* = \{c_{i,k}, f_{i,k}\}$, where $c_{i,k} \in \{0,1\}$ and $f_{i,k} \in \{0,1\}$, for a single bit test, in accordance to Fig. 3.*

Consider a test $T_{i,k}^* = \{c_{i,k} = 1, f_{i,k} = 1\}$, which targets the detection of stuck-at-0 faults $c_{i,k} \equiv 0$ and $f_{i,k} \equiv 0$, in other words, the test is proving that the function $f_i \in F$ is controllable by $c_{i,k} = 1$, in the $k - th$ bit. However, this test is targeting the detection of single faults only, and the test may fail in proving the controllability of $f_{i,k}$, if there exists any multiple fault of type $\{c_{i,k} \equiv 0, c_{j,k} \equiv 1\}$, $j \neq i$, because of mutual masking of these two faults. This masking situation is illustrated in Fig. 3a.

Lemma 1. *There will be no masking of the fault $c_{i,k} \equiv 0$ by any other fault $c_{j,k} \equiv 1$, $j \neq i$, if the test $T_{i,k}^* = \{c_{i,k} = 1, f_{i,k} = 1\}$ will be applied under the constraints $f_{j,k} = 0$, for all $j \neq i$.*

Proof. The expected value of y_k for the test $T_{i,k}^*$ in case of no faults will be $y_k = 1$. In case of a single fault $c_{i,k} \equiv 0$, the value of $f_{i,k} = 1$ will not propagate to the output y_k, due to $c_{i,k} \equiv 0$ and all $c_{j,k} = 0$, $j \neq i$, causing in such a way response $y_k = 0$, which means that the fault $c_{i,k} \equiv 0$ is detected. The response $y_k = 1$ would be the proof, that the function $f_{i,k}$ is controllable. However, this proof will be valid only for the case of assuming the single fault $c_{i,k} \equiv 0$. In case of any double fault $\{c_{i,k} \equiv 0, c_{j,k} \equiv 1\}$, $j \neq i$, instead of $f_{i,k} = 1$, which is blocked by $c_{i,k} \equiv 0$, the value of another function $f_{j,k} = 1$ is propagated by $c_{j,k} \equiv 1$ to the output y_k. Hence, as the response to the test, we will get the same value $y_k = 1$ as expected, which means that the fault $c_{i,k} \equiv 0$ is masked by $c_{j,k} \equiv 1$, and we still will not know if the function $f_{i,k}$ is controllable by the signal $c_{i,k}$ or not.

Let us introduce a notation for multiple faults of type $\{c_{i,k} \equiv 0, c_{j,k} \equiv 1\}$, where $j \neq i$, and $\{c_{j,k} \equiv 1\}$ represents any subset of faults $c_{j,k} \equiv 1$ for different combinations of $j \neq i$.

Lemma 2. *To detect any multiple fault of type $\{c_{i,k} \equiv 0, \{c_{j,k} \equiv 1\}\}$ in the MUT represented by a set of functions F, a test T_i^* must be generated, so that the constraint $f_{j,k} = 0$ were satisfied for each $f_j \in F$, $j \neq i$, by at least one pattern $d \in D_i$ in T_i^*.*

Proof. Since from $c_{i,k} = 1$ the value $c_{j,k} = 0$ follows for all $j \neq i$ due to the mutual exclusion of control signals, we have satisfied automatically the conditions of sensitizing the faults $c_{j,k} \equiv 1$ on the lines $j \in i$. On the other hand, the constraint $f_{j,k} = 1$ for all $j \neq i$ will serve as the condition of propagating the faults $c_{j,k} \equiv 1$, $j \neq i$, to the output y_k, to make all control faults $c_{j,k} \equiv 1$ detectable.

There may be two border cases in generating the test T_i^*. First, a single data operand $d \in D_i$ may be generated, which allows detection of all possible multiple faults of type $\{c_{i,k} \equiv 0, \{c_{j,k} \equiv 1\}\}$ in the same time by the same data $d \in D_i$. In this case, the pattern d has to satisfy the constraints $f_{j,k} = 0$ simultaneously for all $j \neq i$, which may be a seldom case. Second, as a general case, a set of data D_i must be generated, so that each constraint $f_{j,k} = 0, j \neq i$, was satisfied at least by one pattern d in the set of data D_i.

From Lemma 1 the following corollary directly results.

Corollary 1. *The test T_i^* generated in accordance with conditions of Theorem 1 for all bits k, detects the control faults $c_{i,k} \equiv 0$, and the data faults $f_{i,k} \equiv 0$, which both belong to the fault class of SAF. The functional high-level meaning of the test T_i^* is that it proves that the function f_i, is controllable by the control signals $c_{i,k}$ in all bits k without masking due to possible additional faults $c_{j,k} \equiv 1$ on other control lines $j \neq i$.*

The added value of test $T_{i,k}^* = \{c_{i,k} = 1, f_{i,k} = 0\}$ that, a lot of data part faults, causing the change of the value of $f_{i,k}$, $1 \to 0$, will also be detected.

From Lemma 2 the following corollary directly results.

Corollary 2. *A test $T_{i,k}^* = \{c_{i,k} = 1, f_{i,k} = 0\}$, which targets the detection of the data fault $f_{i,k} \equiv 1$, will detect simultaneously also all control faults $c_{j,k} = 1$, $j \neq i$, if the constraints $f_{j,k} = 1$ for all $j \neq i$, will be satisfied at least by one pattern $d \in D_i$ in T_i^*.*

The added value of the test $T_{i,k}^* = \{c_{i,k} = 1, f_{i,k} = 0\}$, which has the goal of detecting the SAF $c_{j,k} \equiv 1$ on other control lines $j \neq i$, detects also a lot of data part SAF, which cause the change of the value of $f_{i,k}$, $0 \to 1$.

Table 1. SAF faults detection of 1-bit control signals

Test				Detected faults	Proof
ci, k	fi, k	cj, k	fj, k		
1	1	0	0	$ci, k \equiv 0$ (with no fault masking)	Corollary 1
	0		1	$c_{j,k} \equiv 1$ (of any multiplicity)	Corollary 2

From the previous discussion, it follows, that it would be very easy to test the control part of MUT if it would be implemented according to the proposed abstract model, represented by EDNF and using direct mapping $c_i \to f_i$. By the proposed two methods, the both types of SAF faults can be detected: $c_{i,k} \equiv 0$, using Corollary 1, and $c_{i,k} \equiv 1$, using Corollary 2. This result is illustrated also in Table 1.

In the following, in Sects. 4, 5 and 6, we show that Corollary 2 can be extended for a very broad class of faults and used as the basis for developing an implementation-independent test generation method for the control part of MUT.

4   A New High-Level Functional Control Fault Model

From Lemmas 1–2 and Corollaries 1–2, a strategy of testing follows. When applying the test $T_{i,k}^* = \{c_{i,k} = 1, f_{i,k} = 1\}$, it is recommended to generate data operands for applying the values $f_{j,k} = 0$ for as many $j \neq i$ as possible, to avoid mutual masking of $c_{i,k} \equiv 0$ by multiple faults $c_{j,k} \equiv 1$. On the other hand, when applying the test $T_{i,k}^* = \{c_{i,k} = 1, f_{i,k} = 0\}$, it is recommended to apply the values $f_{j,k} = 1$ for all $j \neq i$ to increase the efficiency of testing the faults $c_{j,k} \equiv 1$.

In functional testing, if two arguments or functions in the MUT model will due to physical defects interfere, then the resultant value of the interference can be calculated either by AND or OR function, depending on the technology.

Assume for the further discussion that we have OR-technology.

Definition 3. *Introduce a high-level functional control fault* $f_{i,k} \rightarrow (f_{i,k}, f_{j,k})$, *which means that instead of the function* f_i, *in the* $k-th$ *bit of the data word, both functions* $f_{i,k}$ *and* $f_{j,k}$ *will be selected and executed simultaneously. In case of the OR –technology, the result of activation of the function* f_i *in the presence of the fault* $f_{i,k} \rightarrow (f_{i,k}, f_{j,k})$ *in the* $k-th$ *bit will be* $y_k = f_{i,k} \vee f_{j,k}$.

Lemma 3. *To detect the fault* $f_{i,k} \rightarrow (f_{i,k}, f_{j,k})$ *in a MUT, represented as mapping* $(c_i \in C) \rightarrow (f_i \in F)$, *a test pattern* $T_i^*(c_i = 1, d)$ *must be applied with constraint* $f_{i,k}(d) < f_{j,k}(d)$, *where* $d \in Di$.

Proof. The proof results directly from Definition 3, because only if $f_{i,k}(d) = 0$, and $f_{j,k}(d) = 1$, the expected result $f_{i,k}(d) = 0$ and the faulty result $f_{i,k}(d) \vee f_{j,k}(d) = 1$ will be distinguishable.

Definition 4. *Introduce modifications of the high-level functional fault introduced in Definition 3, such as*

1. $f_{i,k} \rightarrow f_{j,k}$, *where instead of a function* $f_{i,k}$ *another function* $f_{j,k}$, $j \neq i$, *will be selected and executed, and*
2. $f_{i,k} \rightarrow \{f_{j,k}\}$, *where instead of a function* $f_{i,k}$, *a group of functions* $f_{j,k}$ *will be selected and executed.*

From Lemma 3 and Definitions 3 and 4, the following corollaries result:

Corollary 3. *To detect the fault* $f_{i,k} \rightarrow (f_{j,k})$, *a test pattern* $T_i^*(c_i = 1, d)$ *must be applied with constraint* $f_{i,k}(d) < f_{j,k}(d)$, *where* $d \in D_i$.

Corollary 4. *To detect the fault* $f_{i,k} \rightarrow \{f_{j,k}\}$, *a set of test patterns* $T_i^*(c_i = 1, d)$, $d \in D_i$ *must be applied, so that for each* $f_{j,k} \rightarrow \{f_{j,k}\}$, *a data pattern* $d \in D_i$ *exists, where* $f_{i,k}(d) < f_{j,k}(d)$.

Definition 5. *Let us call the set of all high-level functional control faults* $CF = \{f_{i,k} \rightarrow (f_{i,k}, f_{j,k})\}$, *for all pairs of* $f_{i,k}, f_{j,k} \in F$, *as functional control fault model of the MUT, represented as mapping* $(c_i \in C) \rightarrow (f_i \in F)$. *The size of the fault model is* $|CF| = (n-1)^2 \times m$. *Let us call the subset* $CF(f_{i,k}) \subset CF$ *as functional control fault model of the function* $f_i \in F$.

Theorem 1. *To detect all functional faults introduced in Definitions 3 and 4, for each function* $f_i \in F$, *a set of data operands must be generated, which satisfy the constraints:*

$$\forall k \in (1, m) \exists d \in D_i \left(f_{i/k}(d) < f_{j/k}(d) \right) \tag{3}$$

The proof of theorem results from Lemma 3 and Corollaries 3 and 4.

Definition 6. *Introduce a high-level control fault table* $R = \|r_{i,j/k}\|$ *as a 3-dimensional array for a given set of data patterns* D, *where the entries* $r_{i,j/k}$ *represent k-bit vectors and* $r_{i,j/k} = 1$, *if there exists a pattern* $d \in D_i$, *which satisfies the constraint* $f_{i,k}(d) < f_{j,k}(d)$, *otherwise* $r_{i,j/k} = 0$. *The size of the fault model* R *is equal to the size* $|CF| = (n-1)^2 \times m$.

The high-level control fault coverage is measured by the ratio of 1-s in the array to the size of R.

Calculation of the high-level fault coverage can be carried out by high-level fault simulation with the goal of checking if the constraints (3) are satisfied or not.

5 Test Structure and Test Execution

Denote by D_i the test data generated for detection the fault model $CF(f_i)$. Based on the data D_i, and according to Lemma 1, the following test structure results, as shown in Algorithm 1.

Algorithm 1. Test Execution Structure

---

1 **for** *all $f_i \in F$* **do**
2   **for** *all $d \in D_i$* **do**
3   apply test for $f_i(d)$

According to Algorithm 1, all tests for exercising the functions $f_i \in F$, are executed one by one, each of the tests in a loop using one by one the data $d \in D_i$ which satisfy the constraints (3). A test is a subroutine which initializes the data $d \in D_i$, executes an instruction (or a sequence of instructions) responsible for realizing the function $f_i(d)$, and performs the observation of the test result $y = f_i(d)$.

From the algorithm in Algorithm 1, the following structure of test execution can be derived: the full test T consists of a sequence of test modules $T_i, i = 1, 2, \ldots n$, where each i-th module consists of test patterns $T_{i,t}$, where each pattern $T_{i,t} \in T_{i,t}$ satisfies, a subset of constraints (3).

For each test pattern $T_{i,t} \in T_i$, including the data operand $d \in D_i$, and for each data bit k of the functions $f_i \in F$, the set $F = \{f_i\}$ can be partitioned for each k into two parts F_k^0 and F_k^1, so that

$$F_k^0 = \{f_{i,k}|f_{i,k}(d) = 0\}, and\ F_k^1 = \{f_{i,k}|f_{i,k}(d) = 1\}.$$

Such a test pattern covers all the constraints $f_{i,k}(d) < f_{j,k}(d)$, according to (3), where $f_{i,k} \in F_k^0$ and $f_{j,k} \in F_k^1$.

Such a test execution according to Algorithm 1 is depicted in Fig. 4. The unrolled test sequence consists of n test modules T_i, each of them consisting of a sequence of test patterns $T_{i,t}$ for testing a function $f_i \in F$. The behaviour of the MUT is highlighted for the $k - th$ bit of the test pattern $T_{i,t}$, showing the subset of constraints satisfied by the pattern. As an example of error detection is shown, where the expected value of $f_{i,k}$ is changed from 0 to 1 due to a fault in the control part of MUT.

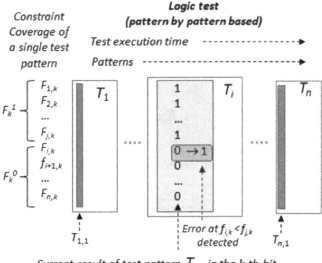

Fig. 4. Unrolled test execution evolving in time

6   Extension of the Fault Class Beyond SAF

The ideas of the proposed fault model in Sect. 4, and the test concept in Sect. 5 are adopted from the known methods of memory testing, particularly from March test [36]. The motivation was driven by the purpose to extend the fault class, to be covered by test, to that of used in case of memories.

Let us consider an example of the March test depicted in Fig. 5, and compare it with the test flow developed for a logic MUT shown in Fig. 4. The analogy between the memory test and logic test is in similar handling of addressing the cells in the memory and controlling the functions of $f_i \in F$ in logic MUTs. In case of memories, testing of cells (data part) and the addressing logic (control part) can be easily joined in the same test, whereas in the proposed approach, testing of data part and control part proceeds separately.

In case of memory, the initialization of constraints (writing $1s\,(W1\uparrow)$ into cells) can be done once for all cells in a single cycle. Then, having these constraints stored, the following test cycle $(r/w0\downarrow)$ and observation cycle $(r1)$ can be carried out.

In the proposed method, the constraints cannot be stored, rather they have to be produced "on-line" at each test pattern. In Fig. 4, a test pattern $T_{i,t} \in T_i$ including test data $d \in Di$, is illustrated, showing the values it produces on-line for the $k - th$ bit of all functions $f_i \in F$, simultaneously. All functions for the bit k are partitioned by the data $d \in D_i$ into two groups F_k^0 and F_k^1, as explained in Sect. 5. We see, that this particular test pattern with data d covers only a subset of constraints for $f_{i,k}\,(d) < f_{j,k}\,(d)$, where $f_{i,k} \in F_k^0$ and $f_{j,k} \in F_k^1$.

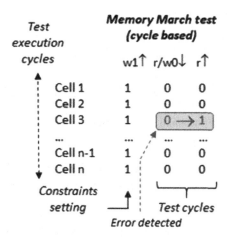

Fig. 5. Illustration of the March test for memories

In case of memory, in each step of the test cycle $(r/w0 \downarrow)$, when reading the Cell i, all constraints [Cell i] < [Cell j] are covered by a single run through all the cells. Here, [Cell i] means the value stored in the Cell i. In case of the proposed method of testing a logic MUT, the test for $f_i \in F$, has to be repeated with other data d till all the constraints (3) have been satisfied for all pairs of functions $\{f_{i,k}, f_{j,k}\}$.

The comparison of the proposed data constraints based test method with March test for memories reveals the possibility of applying the proposed approach, not only for the combinational MUTs like ALU, but also for sequential MUTs. If in sequential MUTs, a part of data $d \in D$ belongs to the registers or memory, the test must include proper initialization sequence.

Consider a MUT, represented by a set of mappings:

$$(c_i \in C) \rightarrow (f_i \in F),$$

where C is a set of mutually exclusive control signals (instructions) produced by the control part of MUT, and F is the set of operations (data manipulations) taking place in the data part of MUT.

By test data generation, used in the March test for memories and in the proposed test method for logic MUTs, the coverage of the following functional fault classes by the proposed method results [36]:

CL-1: With a certain instruction $(c_i \in C)$, no activity f_i in F will happen.
CL-2: There is no instruction (c_i), which can activate a function $f_i \in F$. A certain function is never accessed.
CL-3: With a certain instruction (c_i), multiple functions $\{f_i, f_j, \ldots\} \in F$ are activated simultaneously.
CL-4: A certain function $f_i \in F$ can be activated with multiple instructions $\{f_i, f_j, \ldots\} \in F$.

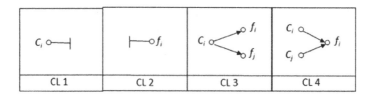

Fig. 6. Functional control fault classes CL 1–CL 4

The fault classes CL-1–CL-4 are illustrated in Fig. 7 [36]:

It is easy to realize that these high-level functional fault classes cover also SAF (CL-5) and bridging (CL-6) fault classes, i.e. these faults can be collapsed, and do not need to take into account any more, except when the fault coverage of these faults for given implementations is under interest (Fig. 6).

As shown in [37], address decoders built out of CMOS gates can exhibit CMOS stuck-open faults [CL-7]. The effect of such faults is that the combinational instruction decoder will behave as a sequential circuit for certain control signals. The consequence of such a fault is that another instruction will be decoded and executed. However, this fault can be also collapsed, because it will be covered by the faults of CL-4.

Any multiple low-level structural fault CL-8 (SAF or shorts), in the particular implementation, will cause a change of an instruction $c_i \rightarrow c_j$, which in turn can be considered as the fault from class CL-4, and hence, be collapsed.

Regarding other general fault classes, such as conditional SAF (CL-9) [28], called also as functional faults [38], pattern faults [39], fault tuples [40] or cell-internal defects (CL-10) [41], will manifest themselves as a change of instruction code $c_i \rightarrow c_j$, and are covered by the fault class CL 4.

We have shown, that the structural fault classes CL-5–CL-10 are collapsed by the implementation-independent high-level functional fault classes CL-1–CL-4, which are used in memory testing and are covered by the March test [36]. On the other hand, in Sect. 5, we have shown, that the test for microprocessor MUT, which satisfies the constraints (3), and is executed in accordance with the test flow in Algorithm 1, will cover the same fault classes CL-1–CL-4 used in memory testing. Finally, from Theorem 1, it follows, that the fault classes CL-1–CL-4 can be represented by a single fault class $CF = \{f_{i,k} \rightarrow (f_{i,k}, f_{j,k})\}$, as stated in Theorem 1.

The relationships between iterative fault collapsing are shown in Fig. 7: first, collapsing of structural faults (CL-5–Cl-9) by functional faults used in memory testing (CL-1–CL-4) [36], and thereafter, collapsing of the faults (CL1–CL4) by the general high-level control fault CF, developed in the paper.

In this paper, we do not consider testing of the faults in data part, however, we propose to use here testing of all instructions separately by using pseudo-exhaustive test (PET) data operands [32]. It is well-known that PET provides also a good fault coverage for a broad fault class.

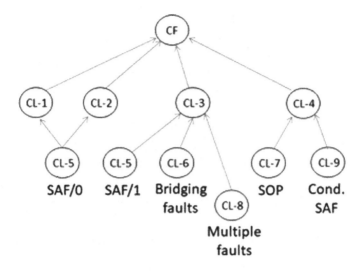

Fig. 7. Fault collapsing relationships

7   High-Level Decision Diagrams and Functional Test

The problem with the proposed functional fault model is a low scalability, because when the size n of the set of functions F is growing, the number of high-level faults $|CF| = (n-1)^2 \times m$ is growing very fast. This is actually the same problem as with memory testing: the broader class of faults is desired the longer test is needed.

From that a question follows, which is how to cope with the complexity explosion by looking for tradeoffs between some test characteristics like fault coverage, test length, test generation time etc. One possibilities is to partition the sets of F into smaller subsets, and consider high-level test generation for subsets of F separately.

High-level Decision Diagrams (HLDDs) [29,30] can be used as a uniform approach for extracting and solving the constraints (3) in test generation for the modules of microprocessors.

Consider in Fig. 8, a HLDD for a subset of 20 instruction of the MiniMIPS microprocessor [33] which represents a subset of function of the ALU. The single non-terminal decision node of the HLDD is labelled by the control variable c (denoted by the operation code of the instructions) having n control values labelling the output edges of the node c. The terminal nodes are labelled by data manipulation functions fi to be used for creating the data constraints (3).

The HLDD in Fig. 8 can be regarded as a MUX of the control part of the MUT, whereas terminal nodes describe the functions of the data part. Denote the HLDD as $G = 1$, meaning that the graph has 1 decision node. The size of the fault model for this subset of functions, $n = 20$ is $|CF| = (n-1)^2 \times m = 11552$, assuming the data word length is $m = 32$.

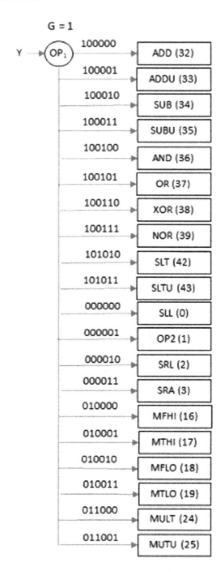

Fig. 8. HLDD with a single decision node for representing 20 MiniMIPS instructions

Depending on different partitioning of the set of control functions, HLDDs may have more than one non-terminal nodes. If the HLDD has more than one internal nodes, then for each non-terminal node m, the test is generated separately, where the subset of functions $F(m) \subset F$ related to the node m under test is set up from the HLDD, so that to each output edge of the node m, a terminal node m^T in HLDD (having a path from m to m^T) with related function f_j is mapped and included into F(m).

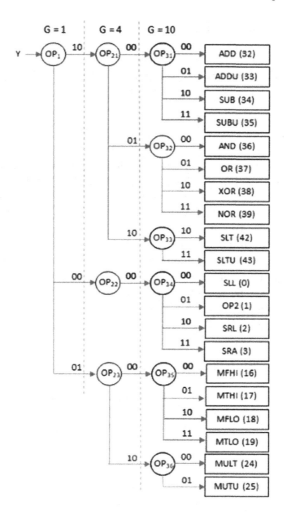

Fig. 9. HLDD for a subset of instructions of MiniMIPS (Color figure online)

To reduce the complexity of the model of the MUT, we can partition itera-tively the set of functions by adding internal nodes into the HLDD.

Consider now another version of the HLDD in Fig. 9, which represents the same subset of 20 instructions of the MiniMIPS, but has now 10 decision nodes. Each decision node represents a partitioning, and the number of edges of the decision node corresponds to the size of the related subset of functions F.

We can imagine three versions of HLDDs for this subset of 20 functions (separated by red dotted lines):

1. $G = 1$ as a HLDD with a single internal node and 20 terminal nodes with $N = 12160$ functional faults (Fig. 8),

2. $G = 4$ as 4 subgraphs with decision nodes OP1, OP21, OP22 and OP23, and with 3, 10, 4 and 6 terminal nodes, respectively, resulting in $N = (6 + 100 + 12 + 30) \times 32 = 3904$ functional faults,
3. $G = 10$ i.e. the current HLDD in Fig. 7 with Fig. 8 decision nodes, resulting in $N = (6 + (6 + 12 + 2) + (12 + 12 + 2) + (12 + 2)) \times 32 = 2112$ functional faults (Fig. 9).

We have generated tests for these three versions of HLDD models with the following results

Using these results, we see opportunities for optimization of the test, trading off different parameters like test length (number of test patterns), achieved SAF fault coverage and test pattern generation time. We see that the result of the minimization of the complexity of the fault model due to the partitioning of the set of functions under test, the number of functional faults taken into account reduces dramatically from 12160 to 2112 (7 times), which has of course impact of the quality of testing the extended class of functional faults. In the same time, the SAF coverage does not change significantly, it decreases only from 99.03% to 99.61%, despite of the reduction of the test length from 143 to 79 (nearly 2 times). As the complexity of the fault module decreases, then the test generation time as well decrease (Table 2).

Table 2. Example of scalabilities for three versions of HLDDs

HLDD	No of patterns	Number of high-level faults N	SAF FC (%)	Time (s)
$G = 1$	143	12160	99.03	0.33
$G = 4$	100	3904	98.77	0.27
$G = 10$	79	2112	99.61	0.23

8   Experimental Results

We have carried out test generation experiment with two goals, first, to investigate the possible tradeoffs between the complexity of the high-level fault model, and the characteristics of generated tests such as test length, SAF coverage, and test generation time, and second, to compare the SAF coverage of gate-level, achieved by the proposed method with state-of-the-art methods. However, it should be mentioned, that in the latter case, the proposed method has additional advantage regarding the coverage of the extended functional fault class, that has not been taken into account in the state-of-the-art methods.

We carried out experiments on Intel Core i7 processor at 3.4 GHz and 8 GB of RAM. The target was to investigate the efficiency of the new high-level implementation independent SBST generation method for microprocessors by measuring both the high-level functional fault coverage, and the gate-level fault coverage

(FC). As research objectives of the experiments, the executing and forwarding units of MiniMIPS [33] were chosen.

For investigating the possibilities of tradeoffs between the complexity of the high-level functional control fault model and the characteristics of generated tests the executing unit was used. It consists of adder and 2 multiplication modules MULT0 and MULT1. We targeted 28 instructions out of MiniMIPS 51, as the basis for the set of functions $F = \{f_i\}$ to be tested. The results are depicted in Table 4 and in Table 5. In Table 4 we show the SAF simulation results for only the control test, whereas in Table 5, we show the results of SAF simulation of the integrated control and data part tests. The latter experiment was needed to demonstrate the additional impact of the data part test to the control test, for the special case of SAF coverage.

Table 3. Test generation for different fault model complexities (only control part test is SAF simulated)

HLDD nodes	Test patterns	Functional faults N	SAF FC%		Time (s)
			ALU	EX unit	
1	161	23328	99.07	98.06	131.0
3	146	12160	99.04	98.03	82.8
6	103	6400	98.79	97.78	45.8
12	83	4032	98.67	97.65	32.9

Table 4. Test generation for different fault model complexities (both control and data part tests are SAF simulated)

HLDD nodes	Test patterns	Functional faults N	SAF FC%		Time (s)
			ALU	EX unit	
1	161	23328	99.32	98.33	131.0
3	146	12160	99.30	98.31	82.8
6	103	6400	99.11	98.13	45.8
12	83	4032	99.01	98.03	32.9

In Tables 3 and 4 we see, that the SAF coverage is very little depending on the size of the set of high-level functional faults used. We see also increase of the SAF coverage, if we simulate the full test including both control and data part tests. This is natural, because the control test is not targeting at all the data part. On the other hand, we see that the control test indirectly covers a huge amount of SAF faults in the data part (as added value of using the proposed high-level functional control fault model).

The reasons of not covering of all SAF in the gate-level simulated circuits may be twofold: (1) the faults are not detectable, or (2) the set of functions, used as the target for test generation, may not cover the full circuit, which was selected for SAF simulation (the circuit may be responsible for other functions, not included into the set of functions, which was used for high-level test generation).

The second part of experiments consisted in comparing the results with state-of-the art methods, using for comparison only the gate-level SAF coverage, which however was not the target of the proposed method, which had the target to generate an implementation-independent test.

In Table 5, we compare our high-level approach with a commercial ATPG, where we showed that the latter had to use huge time when struggling with test generation for a sequential part of the circuit (8 h), whereas the high-level approach for solving the combinational data constraints used less than a minute.

In Table 6, the fault coverage fault coverage and simulation times are given for the forwarding unit (FU), first, when applying only the ALU test, and then the dedicated test for only FU, and thereafter, combining both tests. The tests for FU were generated without knowing gate-level implementation detail, we relied only on general information of the MiniMIPS pipeline architecture, which includes the number of stages and forwarding paths.

In Table 7, we compare our results for 3 different MiniMIPS modules with 3 other test generators. Our approach is similar to [7] in the sense that the gate-level implementation details are not required, but it shows almost 5% improvement in FC compared to [7]. Although the method in [19] shows 1% improvement over the proposed method, it is based on requiring of structural information. Method in [18] requires enforcing set of constraints during ATPG test generation, requiring also gate-level information. Differently from state-of-the-art methods, where single SAF cover is the target, the proposed method targets extended class of faults including conditional and multiple SAF.

Table 5. Execute unit test

Method	Experiments		#Faults	FC (%)	Stored patterns	Executed patterns	ATPG time
Proposed high-level method	High-level ATPG		756	100	166	4818	47 s
	Gate-level simulation	Adder	2516	99.92			
		MULT0	95188	99.52			
		MULT1	91810	99.16			
Commercial gate-level ATPG		Adder	2516	99.96	957	957	8 h 27 min
		MULT0	95188	97.40			
		MULT1	91810	97.71			

Table 6. Fault coverage of forwarding unit by different tests

Module/unit	ALU test (%)	Forwarding test (%)	Combined (%)	Improvement (%)
Forwarding unit	89.71	97.84	98.03	8.32
Time (s)	808	48	460	

Table 7. Comparison with other methods

Module/unit	#faults	Gate-level implementation details are exploited		Gate-level implementation independent	
		ATIG [19]	SBST [18]	SBST [7]	Proposed
ALU	203576	98.67%	n.a.	97.85%	99.06%
PPS_EX	211136	97.62%	96.20%	84.12%	98.37%
Forwarding module	3738	99.00%	99.68%	93.64%	98.03%

9   Conclusions

In this paper, we propose a novel implementation independent SBST generation method for the modules of RISC type microprocessors, which produces high gate-level single fault coverage, comparable with the methods which use the knowledge of implementation details. However the main target of the paper is to propose a method which covers an extended class of structural faults including high-level functional faults used in memory testing.

The main idea of the method is to generate tests separately for modules under test (MUT) and in each MUT separately for its control and data parts. The main contribution in the paper is related to test generation for the control parts, whereas for testing the data parts independently of the implementation details, we use the well-known pseudo-exhaustive test approach, not considered here in detail.

A generic high-level functional fault model was developed, represented as a set of constraints to be satisfied by data operands, for the control parts of MUT. The fault model covers a broad set of low-level structural faults, and differently from state-of-the-art, a set of traditional functional fault models used in memory testing. We showed the possibility of focusing a large number of structural and functional fault classes into a single measurable high-level functional fault model.

Based on this representative fault model, a novel measure of high-level control fault coverage is proposed, and a method of evaluating the test quality using this measure, which can indirectly assess the capability of the test to cover a large class of faults beyond SAF.

The data constraints based fault model, and the introduced analogy of testing with March test flow for memories revealed the possibility of applying the proposed approach, not only for the combinational MUTs, but also for sequential ones. We introduced High-Level Decision Diagrams, as a means to be used for formalization of high-level test generation and optimization of test programs by trading off different test characteristics, such as the fault model complexity versus test length, test generation time and well measurable SAF coverage.

For comparison of our results with state-of-the-art we used the measure of SAF coverage. Experimental results demonstrate higher SAF coverage compared to other existing implementation-independent test generation methods for microprocessors. The added value of the proposed approach, compared with state-of-the-art, is the proof of covering extended fault class beyond SAF.

Acknowledgments. The work was supported by EU H2020 project RESCUE, Estonian grant IUT 19-1, and Research Center EXCITE.

References

1. Gizopoulos, D., Paschalis, A., Zorian, Y.: Embedded Proecessor-Based Self-Test. Kluwer Academic Publisher, New York (2004)
2. Gizopoulos, D.: Advances in Electronic Testing. Springer, New York (2014). https://doi.org/10.1007/0-387-29409-0
3. Chen, L., Dey, S.: Software-based self-testing methodology for processor cores. IEEE Trans. CAD IC Syst. **20**(3), 369–380 (2001)
4. Kranitis, N., Gizopoulos, D., Xenoulis, G.: Software-based self-testing of embedded processors. IEEE Trans. Commun. **54**(4), 369–380 (2005)
5. Gurumurthy, S., Vasudevan, S., Abraham, J.A.: Automatic generation of instruction sequences targeting hard-to-detect structural faults in a processor. ITC (2006)
6. Chen, C., Wei, T., Gao, H., Lu, T.: Software-based self-testing with multiple-level abstractions for soft processor cores. IEEE Trans. Very Large Scale Integr. VLSI Syst. **15**(5), 505–517 (2007)
7. Gizopoulos, D., et al.: Systematic software-based self-test for pipelined processors. IEEE Trans. Very Large Scale Integr. VLSI Syst. **16**(11), 1441–1453 (2008)
8. Psarakis, M., Gizopoulos, D., Sanchez, E., Sonza, R.M.: Microprocessor software-based self-testing. IEEE Des. Test Comput. **27**(3), 4–19 (2010)
9. Di Carlo, S., Prinetto, P., Savino, A.: Software-based self-test of set-associative cache memories. IEEE Trans. Comput. **60**(7), 1030–1044 (2011)
10. Schölzel, M., Koal, T., Roder, S., Vierhaus, H.T.: Towards an automatic generation of diagnostic in-field SBST for processor components. In: 14th Latin American Test Workshop - LATW, Cordoba, pp. 1–6 (2013)
11. Changdao, D., et al.: On the functional test of the BTB logic in pipelined and superscalar processors. In: 14th Latin American Test Workshop - LATW, Cordoba, pp. 1–6 (2013)
12. Bernardi, P., et al.: On the functional test of the register forwarding and pipeline interlocking unit in pipelined processors. In: 14th International Workshop on Microprocessor Test and Verification, Austin, TX, pp. 52–57 (2013)
13. Bernardi, P., et al.: On the in-field functional testing of decode units in pipelined RISC processors. In: IEEE International Symposium on Defect and Fault Tolerance in VLSI and Nanotechnology Systems (DFT), Amsterdam, pp. 299–304 (2014)
14. Sanchez, E., Reorda, M.S.: On the functional test of branch prediction units. IEEE Trans. Very Large Scale Integr. VLSI Syst. **23**(9), 1675–1688 (2015)

15. Bernardi, P., Cantoro, R., De Luca, S., Sánchez, E., Sansonetti, A.: Development flow for on-line core self-test of automotive microcontrollers. IEEE Trans. Comput. **65**(3), 744–754 (2016)
16. Riefert, A., Cantoro, R., Sauer, M., Sonza Reorda, M., Becker, B.: A flexible framework for the automatic generation of SBST programs. IEEE Trans. Very Large Scale Integr. VLSI Syst. **24**(10), 3055–3066 (2016)
17. Chen, L., Ravi, S., Raghunathan, A., Dey, S.: A scalable software-based self-test methodology for programmable processors. In: 40th Annual Design Automation Conference (DAC), pp. 548–553 (2003)
18. Riefert, A., Cantoro, R., Sauer, M., Sonza Reorda, M., Becker, B.: On the automatic generation of SBST test programs for in-field test. In: Design, Automation & Test in Europe Conference & Exhibition (DATE), pp. 1186–1191 (2015)
19. Zhang, Y., Li, H., Li, X.: Automatic test program generation using executing-trace-based constraint extraction for embedded processors. IEEE Trans. Very Large Scale Integr. VLSI Syst. **21**(7), 1220–1233 (2013)
20. Kranitis, N., Merentitis, A., Theodorou, G., Paschalis, A., Gizopoulos, D.: Hybrid-SBST methodology for efficient testing of processor cores. IEEE Des. Test Comput. **25**(1), 64–75 (2008)
21. Lu, T., Chen, C., Lee, K.: Effective hybrid test program development for software-based self-testing of pipeline processor cores. IEEE Trans. Very Large Scale Integr. VLSI Syst. **19**(3), 516–520 (2011)
22. Shen, J., Abraham, J.A.: Native mode functional test generation for processors with applications to self test and design validation. In: International Test Conference 1998 (IEEE Cat. No. 98CH36270), pp. 990–999 (1998)
23. Parvathala, P., Maneparambil, K., Lindsay, W.: FRITS - a microprocessor functional BIST method. In: International Test Conference, Baltimore, MD, USA, pp. 590–598 (2002)
24. Bayraktaroglu, I., Hunt, J., Watkins, D.: Cache resident functional microprocessor testing: avoiding high speed IO issues. In: IEEE International Test Conference, Santa Clara, CA, pp. 1–7 (2006)
25. Acle, J.P., Cantoro, R., Sanchez, E., Reorda, M.S.: On the functional test of the cache coherency logic in multi-core systems. In: IEEE 6th Latin American Symposium on Circuits & Systems (LASCAS), Montevideo, pp. 1–4 (2015)
26. Corno, F., Sanchez, E., Reorda, M.S., Squillero, G.: Automatic test program generation: a case study. IEEE Des. Test Comput. **21**(2), 102–109 (2004)
27. Ubar, R.: Fault Diagnosis in Combinational Circuits with Boolean Differential Equations, pp. 1693–1703. Plenum Publishing Corporation, New York (1980)
28. Holst, S., Wunderlich, H.: Adaptive debug and diagnosis without fault dictionaries. In: 12th IEEE European Test Symposium (ETS 2007), Freiburg, pp. 7–12 (2007)
29. Karputkin, A., Ubar, R., Raik, J., Tombak, M.: Canonical representations of high-level decision diagrams. Est. J. Eng. **16**(1), 39–55 (2010)
30. Ubar, R., Tsertov, A., Jasnetski, A., Brik, M.: Software-based self-test generation for microprocessors with high-level decision diagrams. In: 5th Latin American Test Workshop - LATW, Fortaleza, pp. 1–6 (2014)
31. Oyeniran, A. S., Ubar, R., Jenihhin, M., Raik. J.: Implementation-independent functional test generation for RISC microprocessors. In: 2019 IFIP/IEEE 27th International Conference on Very Large Scale Integration (VLSI-SoC), Cuzco, Peru, pp. 82–87 (2019)
32. Oyeniran, A.S., Azad, P.Z., Ubar, R.: Parallel pseudo-exhaustive testing of array multipliers with data-controlled segmentation. In: IEEE International Symposium on Circuits and Systems (ISCAS), Florence, pp. 1–5 (2018)

33. MiniMIPS Instruction Set Architecture: Opencore. https://opencores.org/
34. Patterson, D., Hennessy, J.: Computer Organization and Design. Elsevier, New York (2015)
35. Armstrong, D.B.: On finding a nearly minimal set of fault detection tests for combinational logic nets. IEEE Trans. Electron. Comput. **15**(1), 66–73 (1966)
36. van de Goor, A.J.: Semiconductor Memories: Theory and Practice. Wiley, New York (1991). pp. 512
37. Miczo, A.: Digital Logic Testing and Simulation. Wiley, New York (2003). pp. 668
38. Ubar, R.: Fault diagnosis in combinational circuits by solving Boolean differential equations. Autom. Telemech. **11**, 170–183 (1979). (in Russian)
39. Keller, K.B.: Hierarchical pattern faults for describing logic circuit failure mechanisms. US Patent 5546408, 13 August 1994
40. Dwarakanath, K.N., Blanton, R.D.: Universal fault simulation using fault tuples. In: Proceedings 37th Design Automation Conference, Los Angeles, CA, USA, pp. 786–789 (2000)
41. Happke, F., et al.: Cell-aware tests. IEEE Trans. CAD IC Syst. **33**(9), 1396–1409 (2014)

Robust FinFET Schmitt Trigger Designs for Low Power Applications

Leonardo B. Moraes[1(✉)], Alexandra Lackmann Zimpeck[1],
Cristina Meinhardt[2], and Ricardo Reis[1]

[1] Instituto de Informática - PGMicro/PPGC, Universidade Federal do Rio Grande
do Sul - UFRGS, Porto Alegre, Brazil
{lbmoraes,reis,cmeinhardt}@inf.ufrgs.br, alexandra.zimpeck@ucpel.edu.br
[2] Departamento de Informática Aplicada e Estatística, Universidade Federal
de Santa Catarina - UFSC, Florianópolis, Brazil

Abstract. The IoT development alongside with the more pronounced impact of process variability in modern technology nodes, is the central reason to control variability impact. Given the broad set of IoT devices running on battery-oriented environments, energy consumption should be minimal and the operation reliable. Schmitt Trigger inverters are frequently used for noise immunity enhancement, and have been recently applied to mitigate radiation effects and variability impact. Yet, Schmitt Trigger operation at nominal voltage still introduces high deviation on power consumption. Thus, the main contribution of this work is to identify the relationship between transistor sizing, supply voltage, energy, and process variability robustness to achieve a minimal energy consumption circuit while keeping robustness. On average, scenarios with a lower supply voltage applied on layouts with a smaller number of fins, presented adequate robustness in high variability scenarios. Exploring voltage and transistor sizing made possible a reduction of about 24.84% on power consumption.

Keywords: Process variability mitigation · Schmitt Trigger · Low power · FinFET technology

1 Introduction

Ultra-low Power (ULP) circuits are widely applied in various portable electronics applications such as cellular phones, bio-medical assistance devices and sensing networks. The ULP designs rise, alongside battery technology improvements, have provided us with portable, powerful and useful equipment for our daily routine, with wireless communication making information available anytime and anywhere [1,2]. One of the most proeminent ULP applicants is the Internet of Things (IoT) industry, determining technology development and industry tendencies.

As IoT devices emerged new kinds of applications have surfaced as well. From improving maintenance for all sorts of facilities, to sensor in remote areas

© IFIP International Federation for Information Processing 2020
Published by Springer Nature Switzerland AG 2020
C. Metzler et al. (Eds.): VLSI-SoC 2019, IFIP AICT 586, pp. 45–68, 2020.
https://doi.org/10.1007/978-3-030-53273-4_3

and even automobile applications. However IoT applications still depend on an energy source, with battery-oriented applications being the most prominent. Given the limited life cycle of batteries, self-sufficient systems have appeared in order to alleviate the power consumption dilemma [2]. Given so, an IoT application will always be restricted by its power budget, with devices that can perform their functionality under heavy power constraints being essential [3]. The ideal circuit for ULP applications is the one that can perform a given task while consuming the least amount of energy. Such circuits might be achieved under transistor sizing and supply voltage tuning, being technology and application-dependent [2].

Nevertheless, the technology advance over transistor sizing has increased the density of chips and the challenges related to the manufacturing process, for example, the process variability and aging effects, the higher power consumption due to larger leakage currents, and the increase in the radiation-induced soft errors [4]. Multigate devices, as the Fin Field Effect Transistor (FinFET), have been proposed to help overcome some of those issues. The structure of Fin-FETs shows superior channel control due to the reduced short-channel effects (SCE) and diminished Random Dopant Fluctuation (RDF) effect due to the fully depleted channel [5]. However, process variability is one of the major challenges in nanometer technology, even on FinFET designs [6]. At deep nanotechnology nodes, each chip may show a distinct behavior due to process variations during the lithography steps in the manufacturing process. These variations exert influence over the metrics of the circuits such as performance and power consumption, which can bring unpredictable circuit degradation, making them unsuitable from its expected operation regime [4,7].

This work aims to explore a low power solution considering the effects of process variability in the Schmitt Trigger (ST) designs. ST circuits are widely applied on low power applications due to its noise immunity, and, recently have been considered for process variability mitigation on nanometer technologies. This set of data can provide relevant information for ULP designers, and also for other low power applications that need to manage process variability impact. Thus, the main contribution of this work is an in-depth evaluation of the influence of different factors on the ST design, considering: 1) multiple combinations of supply voltages; 2) different levels of process variability; and 3) the variable transistor sizing relation (number of fins). The experiments analysis the impact of these factors on the maximum achievable frequency within a failure threshold, the trade-off among these parameters and power consumption.

Next section aims to give more context to this work, commenting on related works and the main differences and contributions of this work in comparison. Section 3 gives a more in-depth explanation about variability and its several factors and phenomena. Section 4 introduces the FinFET technology and the variability influence over it. Section 5 the main aspects of ST are shown as well its robustness enhancing capabilities. The methodology adopted to allow all the evaluations is explained in Sect. 6. The results are discussed in Sect. 7 and finally, Section VIII presents the main conclusions.

2   Related Work

Many works evaluate the effects of Process, Voltage and Temperature (PVT) variability on circuits and devices, but few works consider the effects for ULP designs.

Some works address theses issues focusing on the yield improvement. In [4] is developed a mathematical methodology for increase the yield considering aging, and PVT variability. With such method, the circuit sizing was optimized and, obeying some performance and power constraints, it was possible to achieve an increase from about 40% to 99% yield. [8] provides a characterization of the effects of open defects on nanoscale CMOS gates and circuits. It shows the difference on output value for several circuits, technology nodes and most important under the influence of PVT variability. In [9] is shown the implication of PVT variations on subthreshold device and circuit performance metrics. It was found that a $\pm 10\%$ on several transistor parameters could introduce up to a 77% variation in Energy, or Power-Delay Product (PDP). In this context, the use of STs is being investigated as an effective method for increasing the on-to-off current ratio, and consequently, for mitigating the process variation effects [3] on subthreshold operating systems.

Other works have evaluating the impact on arithmetic circuits, mainly on Full-Adders (FA). In [10] the effects of PVT variability in different Full Adder (FA) designs are investigated. Both Transmission Gate Adder (TGA) and Transmission Function Adder (TFA) architectures showed acceptable behavior under PVT variability with the lowest power consumption sensibility amongst the tested FAs, reaching about $11\times$ smaller in comparison with Complementary Pass Transistor Logic (CPL) FA. In [11] simulations were performed on several FA circuits considering Carbon Nanotube Field Effect Transistor (CNFET) and bulk Complementary Metal-Oxide-Semiconductor (CMOS) technology. Results show that the TGA is the most robust circuit with its CNFET version providing up to $3\times$ less variations. [12] presents a study about the delay variability caused by supply variations in the TGA. The experiments were performed at layout level. It showed that lower supply voltages bring more delay variability to the circuit with the TGA presenting worse results in comparison to static logic.

Given the energy constraints of ULP applications and the variability impact on recent nodes, the ST circuit has been pointed as an circuit-level alternative. The classical ST has been employed as a key element for several ULP circuits [13–16] and for variability mitigation, mainly attenuating the deviation on the power consumption. Schmitt Trigger was applied replacing internal inverters of full adders in [17], where spreads in major metrics were successfully limited. Also, the same experiment was executed at electrical and layout levels considering FinFET technology, and showed a considerable decrease in overall variability impact on metrics [18,19]. However, with a considerable increase in delay and power consumption.

It is important to highlight that the mentioned works do not consider analysis at the layout-level in modern technology nodes. Additionally, most works do not consider such a combination of variables and even if they do, the analysis is often performed considering the circuit under the influence of only one of the variables at a time. This work presents a layout-level analysis, considering all parasitics and electrical behavior related to transistor placement and routing, as well as all considered variables exerting their influence at the same time, as would occur on a real scenario.

3   On Variability

As technology scaling advanced, decreasing the transistor dimensions, the ratio between device geometrical parameters and the atom-size itself have been shrinking. Multiple techniques have been developed to reduce the loss of precision due to the manufacturing process at different end-of-lines. However, as the quantum-mechanical limit approaches, manufacturing-induced imprecision impact rises [20].

Variability consists of characteristic deviations, internal or external to the circuit, which can determine its operational features and can be divided by three types concerning its sources: Environmental Factors - External factors to the circuits e.g. temperature and supply voltage variations [7,21], Reliability Factors - related to the aging process e.g. Negative Bias Temperature Instability (NBTI), electromigration, dielectric breakdown and Hot Carrier Injection (HCI) [7,21–25] and Physical Factors - caused by the manufacturing process, consequence of imprecision in the manufacturing process which can be systematic, design dependent or random [21,26–32]. Figure 1, depicts the transistor intrinsic variability.

Despite the multiple advantages of new technologies, the atom scale makes process variability one of the most relevant challenge. FinFET devices have been investigated about the variability impact and the next subsection introduces the main concepts about FinFET technology to understand the variability impact on this device.

3.1   FinFET Technology and Variability Impact

The FinFET main geometric parameters are the gate length (L or L_G), fin width (W_{FIN}, T_{FIN} or T_{SI}), fin height (H_{FIN}) and Oxide Thickness (T_{OX}). FinFET transistors can be built on a traditional bulk or on a Silicon on Insulator (SOI) substrate with a conducting channel that rises above the level of the insulator, creating a thin silicon structure, the gate, as shown in Fig. 2 and Fig. 3.

The channel being surrounded from three dimensions by the gate results in a superior control, reduced SCE and RDF effect due to the fully depleted channel that causes less sensitivity to process variations [34]. FinFETs also present

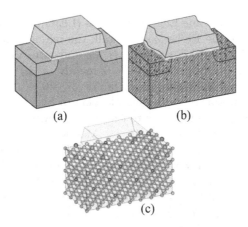

Fig. 1. Levels of abstraction from a ideal transistor towards a realistic concept. (a) Depicts a the current approach of semiconductor device simulation. (b) Depicts a 20-nm Metal-Oxide-Semiconductor FET (MOSFET). (c) Depicts a 4-nm MOSFET. [28].

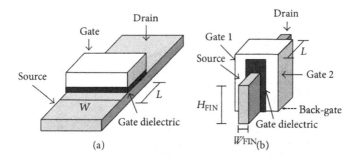

Fig. 2. Structural comparison between (a) planar MOSFET and (b) FinFET transistors. Modified from [33].

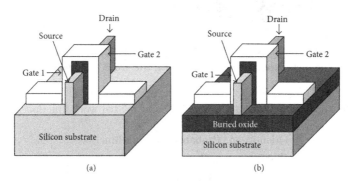

Fig. 3. Structural comparison between (a) bulk and (b) SOI FinFETs [33].

relative immunity to gate Line Edge Roughness (LER), a major source of variability in planar nanoscale FETs [35]. Overall, the major sources of variability expected for FinFETs are the L_G, W_{FIN}, H_{FIN} and gate WF [36]. Amongst all variability sources, it is shown that the V_t is mainly set by the gate WF, with fluctuations having a direct impact on its limits [37–40].

Given the challenges intrinsic to the adoption of high-k dielectrics in order tackle the increasing gate leakage due to the scaling down of gate oxide, a metal gate was adopted on FinFET devices [41–44]. Metals exist *in natura* in the form of crystals where each atom has several bonds with adjacent atoms. Although, due to defects and disorientation, several crystals are formed, with "grain boundaries" between regions of regularity (crystal grains) in the metal [45].

The electrostatic potential (e.g. V_t) varies depending on each grain boundary, as shown in Fig. 4. At Table 1 a example of possible orientation, probability and WF is given. Between several technology nodes - FD-SOI, Bulk and FinFET - the latter showed the lowest V_t variation due to the much larger gate area [45].

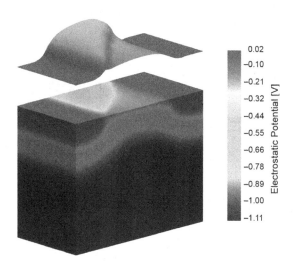

Fig. 4. Electrostatic potential in a generic 30-nm MOSFET with the surface potential shown below. The metal gate has two grains with the grain boundary diagonally across the channel [46].

Table 1. Metal orientation, probability and related work function [46].

Orientation	Probability	Work function
<200>	60%	4.6 eV
<111>	40%	4.4 eV

The main source of variability on FinFETs arises from the metal gate granularity (MGG) that provokes significant work-function fluctuations (WFF), affecting the threshold voltage and the I_{on}/I_{off} currents [6,47].

4   Schmitt Trigger for Process Variability Mitigation

Schmitt Trigger circuits present a hysteresis characteristic. Hysteresis exists in the presence of two switching threshold voltages (V_t). If the input level is inside the hysteresis interval, the ST will not switch. Such characteristic provides a higher static noise margin (SNM) in comparison to traditional inverters, ensuring a high noise immunity. Deviations in physical parameters became alarming at ultra-deep sub-micron (UDSM) nodes due to the following supply voltage scaling, making the circuits more susceptible to noise and electromagnetic interference due to the deterioration in SNM [48].

There are several ST topologies proposed in the literature. In [49], three threshold adjustable ST circuits are presented, wher two are semi-adjustable (only one threshold level can be adjusted) and one are a fully adjustable (both threshold levels can be adjusted) topology. All circuits presents small chip area, and very low static power consumption. A higher performance ST is proposed in [50] where, by a different design, a smaller load capacitor value is achieved, decreasing the slew rate of the ST internal node.

In [51] a low-power ST is proposed as well by forward body biasing, decreasing the V_t, improving performance and decreasing the short circuit current. [52] proposes a 10T ST which its hysteresis interval does not depend on transistors width/length ratios being, consequently, more robust to process variations.

In [53] a ST with a programmable hysteresis is proposed. The programmable hysteresis is achieved by adding a P and N transistors in series with the 6T ST P_F and N_F transistors, respectively, both receiving the same gate signal. A low-power ST is proposed at [54] with low short circuit current achieved by the presence of only one path to each power rail, being recommended for low power, very low frequency applications. Additionally, [55] proposes a low-power ST by having only one transistor transmitting (at stable output values), considerably reducing power consumption.

As show in Fig. 5, this work explores a traditional ST topology, where the major difference from the most popular versions is the presence of P_F and N_F transistors [56]. These transistors are responsible for a feedback system. For example, if the output is at a high level, the N_F is closed, pulling the node X to a high potential, and forcing the drain-source voltage of transistor N_I almost zero and its gate-source voltage into the negative region. This kind of arrangement reduces the leakage current N_I exponentially, increasing the I_{on}/I_{off} current ratio, minimizing the output degradation [16].

The main effect of process variability on ST circuits is a shift in the Voltage Transfer Curve (VTC) due to the threshold voltage variation. Mostly, the input voltage, where a device starts transmitting current, is directly dependent on the V_t. Given so, the variability impact onto the VTC is reduced as a result of the

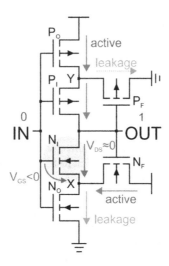

Fig. 5. ST inverter leakage suppression [16].

high influence of the gate-source voltage of the ST inner transistors (N_I and P_I) over its switching point [16].

5   Methodology

To present an broad exploration of power consumption and the process variability effects on the ST characteristics, this work evaluates: 1) ST circuit operating at multiple combinations of supply voltages; 2) the impact of different levels of process variability; 3) the influence of the transistor sizing exploring devices with different number of fins, all at the same time composing over 175 possible scenarios. The impact of these parameters on the maximum achievable frequency within a failure threshold will be analysed.

The design flow is shown at Fig. 6. The project was divided into two main steps: the layouts designing and electrical simulations. After finishing the layout design process, each layout passed through validation which consisted of a Design Rule Checking (DRC) to detect if the layout obeys the technology geometry restrictions and layer rules, Layout Versus Schematic (LVS) where layout and schematic are compared to detect their equivalence (same nodes and nets) and a Behavioral test, in order to observe if the circuit works as expected at nominal operation.

5.1   Layout Design

All ST layouts were designed on the Virtuoso tool from Cadence® with the process design kit (PDK) of 7-nm FinFET (ASAP7) from the Arizona State University in partnership with ARM [57]. This PDK was chosen due to a realistic design

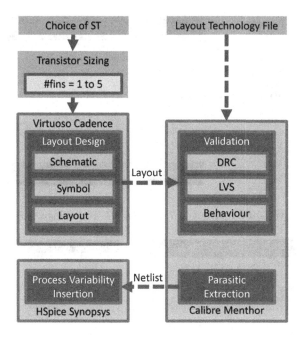

Fig. 6. Design flow of the experiments.

conjecture regarding the current design competencies and for being available for academic use. FinFET technologies present the width quantization aspect [58]. With a 27 nm fin pitch, a high-density layout is achieved with 3-fins transistors. Otherwise, for a higher fin count, there is a lower density and routing complexity [59]. The main PDK rules and lithography assumptions considered in this work are shown in Table 2. The main layers and the 3-fin ST are shown in Fig. 7.

Table 2. Key layer lithography assumptions, widths and pitches [57].

Layer	Lithography	Width/drawn (nm)	Pitch (nm)
Fin	SAQP	6.5/7	27
Active (horizontal)	EUV	54/16	108
Gate	SADP	21/20	54
SDT/LISD	EUV	25/24	54
LIG	EUV	16/16	54
VIA0-VIA3	EUV	18/18	25
M1-M3	EUV	18/18	36

This work evaluates the ST with 1 to 5 fins. For comparison, the 1 and 5-fins layouts are shown in Fig. 8. For the layouts with 1 and 2 fins, due to the minimum active area technology restriction, it was not possible to lower the cell area in

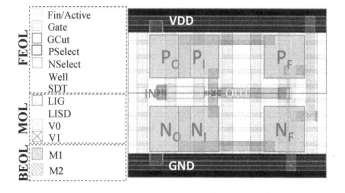

Fig. 7. 3-fins variant ST layout in 7 nm FinFET Technology (ASAP7) [60]

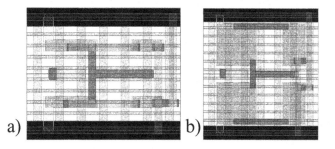

Fig. 8. a) 1 and (b) 5-fins ST layouts

comparison to the 3-fins layout. Although considering a possible scenario, the 2 and 1-fin layouts would present a 20% and 40% reduction in area, compared to the 3-fins variant, respectively. The 3, 4 and 5-fins ST area, height and area increase are shown at Table 3.

It is important to clarify that a lower fin count does not necessarily mean an area reduction. The routability could turn into a challenge and a width of height increase would be necessary.

The ASAP7 PDK contains the manufacturing process composed by front end of line (FEOL), middle of line (MOL) and back end of line (BEOL). The layouts were developed in a continuous diffusion layer with every gate surrounding another gate in the horizontal axis. The Source-Drain Trench (SDT) connects the active area to the LISD layer. The Local-Interconnect Gate (LIG) is applied to connect the gate terminal, and Local-Interconnect Source-Drain (LISD) is used to connect the source and drain of the transistors. The function of V0 is to join the LIG and LISD to the BEOL layers. The Metal 1 (M1) is used for intra-cell routing and short connections. The Metal 2 (M2) was applied to connect the P_F and N_F drains to ground and source, respectively. For the layouts with a fin count below 3, M2 was applied to connect the source/drain of the P_F and N_F transistors to the X and Y layout nodes. Given the smaller area to work

Table 3. 3, 4 and 5-fins STs area, height (in tracks of Metal 2), and the area increase corresponding to each extra fin.

#Fins	Area (nm²)	Height (M2 Tracks)	Area increase
3	131220	7.5	-
4	157464	9	20%
5	183708	10.5	40%

with, it was necessary to apply M2 in order to respect the M1 spacing rules, bringing to light one of the challenges related to a smaller layout. The M2 usage in those cases will increase the design parasitics from the neccessary extra vias connecting M1 and M2. To successfully pass the LVS step, it was necessary the addition of a TAP-cell to connect the transistors back-gates.

5.2 Electrical Simulation

The simulations were carried out in HSPICE [61] using the netlist obtained after the physical verification flow and the parasitic extraction. The reference values from ASAP7 technology for electrical simulations are shown in Table 4. For a more realistic test-bench, it was considered a scenario where the ST receives the signal from two inverters and drives a 1fF output capacitance, as shown in Fig. 9. The same supply voltage is applied in the entire testbench. Only the ST suffers from variability, and the inverters are the same (3-fins transistors) for all experiments. All designs present in the test-bench, inverters and ST, are simulated from the extracted layouts.

Table 4. Parameters applied in the electrical simulations [57].

Parameter	7 nm	
Nominal supply voltage	0.7 V	
Gate length (L_G)	21 nm	
Fin width (W_{FIN})	6.5 nm	
Fin height (H_{FIN})	32 nm	
Oxide thickness (T_{OX})	2.1 nm	
Channel doping	$1 \times 10^{22} \, m^{-3}$	
Source/drain doping	$2 \times 10^{22} \, m^{-3}$	
Work function	NFET	4.372 eV
	PFET	4.8108 eV

The process variability evaluation was taken through 2000 Monte Carlo (MC) simulations [58] varying the WF of devices according to a Gaussian distribution considering a 3σ deviation. This work explores the behavior of ST with variations from 1% up to 5%. For each step on WF variation, all simulations were carried

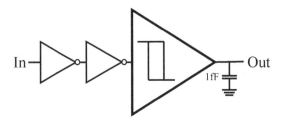

Fig. 9. Test-bench applied in all simulations [60].

from 0.1 V to 0.7 V supply voltage, with steps of 0.1 V at a nominal temperature of 27 °C. The voltage of 0.1 V shows to be the technological limit to work without the loss of the hysteresis characteristic. For all experiments, it was observed maximum values, mean (μ), standard deviation (σ) and normalized standard deviation (σ/μ) for each metric: hysteresis interval, delay, and energy, where σ/μ represents the sensibility of the cell to process variability.

Due to the variability impact a circuit may present performance degradation, given that, in order to determine the maximum frequencies for the layouts evaluated, this work considers a 10% maximum failure threshold in the Monte Carlo simulations. Failures are defined as cases where a pair of operations (high-to-low and low-to-high) propagation times do not fit into the determined frequency. In the case of a number of failures above 10%, the frequency is decreased.

6 Results and Discussion

This section is divided into three parts. First, a discussion concerning energy consumption where a scenario-specific analysis is performed, and different sets of fin count and supply voltage are recommended. A performance analysis (delays and maximum frequencies) will follow, presenting an analysis of the fin count and supply voltage over absolute and deviation values. And finally, the ST hysteresis interval values are presented in relation to the variability level and number of fins.

6.1 Energy Consumption

For each level of WFF explored in this work, there is a distinct ideal scenario for each kind of application. As shown in Table 5, considering the absolute energy consumption observed, the 1-fin layout showed, in all cases, the lowest. It is due to its smaller driving capability, resulting in smaller currents.

The supply voltage recommended for each scenario increases almost linearly in relation to the level of WFF variability. The 0.1 V regime did not prevail as the best option across all scenarios, shows the dependency of energy consumption with propagation times. Figure 10 shows an average between the each particular variability scenario related to the number of fins. It can be observed a difference

Table 5. Recommended setup by each specific scenario [60].

WFF	Lowest energy		Most robust		Cost-benefit	
	# Fins	Supply (V)	# Fins	Supply (V)	# Fins	Supply (V)
1%	1	0.1	1	0.7	1	0.7
2%	1	0.2	1	0.7	1	0.7–0.2
3%	1	0.2	5	0.3	1	0.3
4%	1	0.3	5	0.4	1	0.4
5%	1	0.4	5	0.5	1	0.5

above 100%, between maximum and minimum, showing a higher dependence of the number of fins in determining the circuits energy consumption. Results below 0.3 V did not feature the chart in order to preserve its scale, since for 0.2 V and 0.1 V there are a 1 and 2 orders of magnitude increase on energy consumption, respectively.

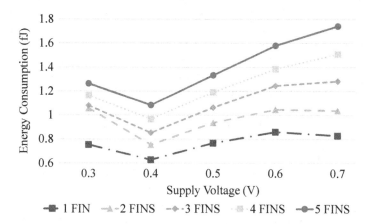

Fig. 10. Average energy consumption over supply voltage scaling [60].

Into the robustness analysis, a shift can be observed. For lower variability scenarios the setup recommended is at 1 fin layout and 0.7 V for 1% and 2% WFF. From moderate to high variability (3% to 5%), the 5 fins layout gains advantage with the supply voltage scaling linearly.

The energy robustness is mainly determined by variations in the I_{on} and, consequently, the time necessary for the circuit charging/discharging. At nominal supply voltages, the I_{on} falls into the saturation region with an exponential dependence over the V_t. Given that, variations on the V_t will result in exponential variations. With the supply voltage decrease, the I_{on} falls into the linear region, diminishing the impact of V_t variations on the I_{on}.

Thus, at low variability scenarios, close-to-nominal supply voltages will not suffer from the exponential V_t dependence, weakening its effect with high current

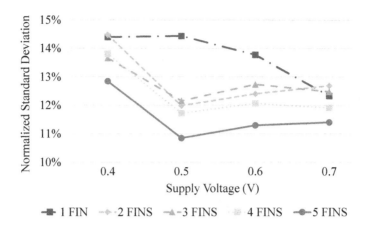

Fig. 11. Average energy consumption sensibility scaling over supply voltage [60].

peaks, small signal slopes overcharging and discharging and higher noise immunity. As variability rises, the linearity from the V_t will present an advantage, favoring smaller supply voltages. However, as variability rises again, the rise and variation in propagation times will start to determine the adequate supply voltage. Figure 11, shows the average scaling on the impact of process variability on energy consumption. It can be seen a lower than 5% discrepancy between best and worst cases, showing the minor dependence of the number of fins in determining the circuits robustness. Results below 0.4 V did not appear on the chart in order to preserve its scale. For 0.3V, 0.2V and 0.1V, maximum normalized standard deviations are 108.64%, 266.82% and 358%, respectively.

For the sake of comparison, Fig. 12 and Fig. 13 present the difference between the respective layouts with the lowest energy consumption and energy consumption variation and the traditional 3-fins layout. The highest difference was 27.85% and 14.44% for energy consumption and variability, respectively.

Considering a cost-benefit scenario, the best choice was defined by the lowest value given by the product of the energy consumption and the normalized deviation product (Energy-Deviation Product - EDP). It can be noticed a shift from a more robust layout (at 1% and 2% WFF) to a low energy layout at higher WFFs (3% to 5%). At 2% there are two supply voltages recommended since the EDP values similar. At this variability point the layout at 0.7 V presents the highest robustness and acceptable energy consumption, due to the lower propagation times, while the layout operating at 0.2 V presents the lowest energy consumption and acceptable energy deviation.

A comparison between the layouts with the lowest energy consumption, energy variability, and the best cost-benefit are shown in Figs. 14 and 15 in relation to energy consumption and energy variability, respectively. The energy variability of the lowest energy layout at 3% WFF is one example of why a cost-benefit analysis should be made since it shows an 11.5% lower energy consumption with a 582.47% higher sensibility.

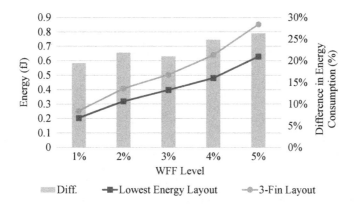

Fig. 12. Energy consumption comparison between the layout with the lowest energy consumption and the traditional 3-fins layout at the same supply voltage [60].

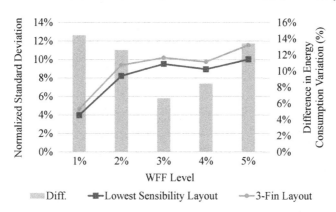

Fig. 13. Energy variability comparison between the layout with the lowest sensibility and the traditional 3-fins layout at the same supply voltage [60].

6.2 Propagation Delays and Maximum Frequencies

At performance scaling it can be observed a worsening on propagation times over the lowering of the supply voltage and fin count. The transistor driving capability is proportional to the fin count, given that with more fins there is a larger active area passing current, fastening the charging/discharging process. Given the area penalty, which will be discussed, the 4-fins layout only gives a 10% penalty on propagation times, being a good choice over area constraints in comparison to the 5-fins layout. The 3, 2 and 1 fins layouts bring a 42%, 92% and 268% delay increase on average, respectively.

In comparison to the traditional 3-fins layout, the 5 and 4-fins variants bring 20% and 13.612% decrease on propagation times while the 2-fins and 1-fin variants bring 27.24% and 107% delay increase, respectively.

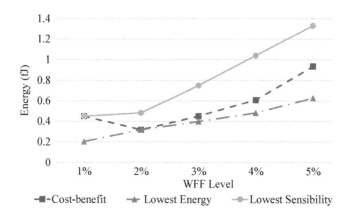

Fig. 14. Energy consumption comparison among the layouts with the best cost-benefit, lowest energy consumption and lowest variability sensibility [60].

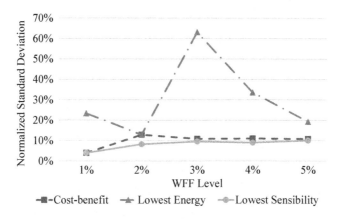

Fig. 15. Energy variability comparison among the layouts with the best cost-benefit, lowest energy consumption and lowest variability sensibility [60].

For variability impact, it can be observed a tendency of lower sensibility over higher fin count at higher supply voltages. As supply voltage scales down, a lower number of fins starts to keep up with the variability robustness, as shown in Fig. 16. It can be concluded that due to the exponential relation of drain current with gate-to-source voltage, the higher fin count is capable of providing the necessary current drive at higher supply voltages. At lower supply voltages, with the drain current decreasing exponentially, the fin count impact on variability robustness is diminished.

Maximum frequencies are shown at Table 6. The maximum frequencies are proportional to the supply voltage and fin count. The higher fin count allows faster charging and discharging due to a bigger active area driving current. On average, the 5 and 4-fins layouts were able to present 16% and 10.34% higher

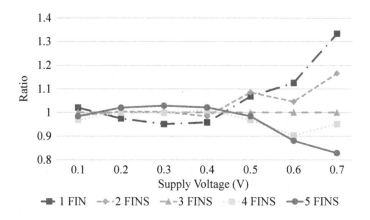

Fig. 16. Delay sensibility ratio between layouts [60].

frequencies while the 2 and 1-fin variants showed 19.18% and 44.65% lower frequencies, in comparison to the 3-fins variant.

Figure 17 and Fig. 18 show the average ratio between the different variability and circuits scenarios normalized in relation to the 1 Fin layout and 5% WFF scenario, respectively. It can be noticed a considerable 52.597 times ratio between low and high variability scenarios, being the main variable determining the circuit frequency. In comparison, the number of fins brings a maximum 3.917 times ratio between 5 and 1 fins layouts, exposing the advantage of a higher number of fins on low supply voltages.

6.3 Hysteresis Interval

Hysteresis is one of the major characteristics related to the circuit ability to filter noise. A higher hysteresis interval brings more robustness to the circuit. As a priority, the ratio between its value and the supply voltage should be as high as possible. The ST, at nominal operation (nominal supply voltage and no process variability), presented a maximum hysteresis interval of approximately 0.45 V. Given that, considering the average absolute values of the hysteresis interval, it can be observed a difference below than 5% between the best and worst cases, considering different fin counts.

At higher supply voltages of 0.6 V and 0.7 V, the difference widens up reaching up to 10.76% and 25.26% between the 5-fins and 1-fin layout, respectively. Such results come from the faster charging/discharging, which decreases the signal slopes widening the circuit hysteresis interval. At lower supply voltages, a decreased number of fins is sufficient to keep the slopes low enough, presenting high hysteresis to supply voltage ratios while at higher supply voltages a lower number of fins will increase the signal slopes.

Although, there is a hysteresis interval improvement, as shown in Fig. 19, over the WFF increase as well. Such behavior happens due to the hysteresis

Table 6. Each scenario respective maximum frequency.

WFF	# Fins	Supply Voltage (V)						
		0.1	0.2	0.3	0.4	0.5	0.6	0.7
1%	1	600 KHz	15 MHz	350 MHz	2 GHz	8 GHz	12 GHz	16 GHz
	2	1.1 MHz	25 MHz	600 MHz	4 GHz	13 GHz	19 GHz	24 GHz
	3	1.5 MHz	35 MHz	900 MHz	5 GHz	17 GHz	24 GHz	29 GHz
	4	1.75 MHz	40 MHz	1 GHz	6 GHz	19 GHz	27 GHz	33 GHz
	5	2.25 MHz	50 MHz	1.2 GHz	6 GHz	21 GHz	30 GHz	35 GHz
2%	1	200 KHz	5 MHz	150 MHz	1.5 GHz	5 GHz	11 GHz	15 GHz
	2	400 KHz	9 MHz	250 MHz	2.5 GHz	7 GHz	18 GHz	23 GHz
	3	600 KHz	12.5 MHz	300 MHz	3 GHz	9 GHz	22.5 GHz	28 GHz
	4	700 KHz	15 MHz	450 MHz	4 GHz	11 GHz	17 GHz	31 GHz
	5	900 KHz	18 MHz	500 MHz	4 GHz	12 GHz	20 GHz	25 GHz
3%	1	100 KHz	2 MHz	60 MHz	1 GHz	4 GHz	8 GHz	14 GHz
	2	200 KHz	3 MHz	100 MHz	1.5 GHz	6 GHz	11 GHz	20 GHz
	3	200 KHz	5 MHz	125 MHz	2 GHz	8 GHz	14 GHz	19 GHz
	4	300 KHz	6 MHz	150 MHz	2.5 GHz	9 GHz	16 GHz	21 GHz
	5	400 KHz	6 MHz	150 MHz	2.5 GHz	10 GHz	17 GHz	23 GHz
4%	1	50 KHz	800 KHz	25 MHz	500 MHz	3 GHz	6 GHz	13 GHz
	2	75 KHz	1.5 MHz	40 MHz	900 MHz	4 GHz	8 GHz	15 GHz
	3	125 KHz	2 MHz	50 MHz	1 GHz	6 GHz	12.5 GHz	18 GHz
	4	150 KHz	2.5 MHz	60 MHz	1.1 GHz	7 GHz	14 GHz	20 GHz
	5	150 KHz	2.5 MHz	60 MHz	1.4 GHz	7.5 GHz	15 GHz	22 GHz
5%	1	15 KHz	350 KHz	9 MHz	250 MHz	2 GHz	5 GHz	11 GHz
	2	40 KHz	600 KHz	10 MHz	350 MHz	2.5 GHz	8 GHz	14 GHz
	3	50 KHz	800 KHz	18 MHz	450 MHz	4 GHz	10 GHz	17 GHz
	4	90 KHz	1 MHz	20 MHz	500 MHz	5 GHz	12 GHz	19 GHz
	5	80 KHz	1 MHz	20 MHz	500 MHz	5 GHz	12.5 GHz	20 GHz

interval dependency over the PFET and NFET threshold voltages [56]. This means that lower WF decreases the NFET threshold, while higher WF will increase the NFET threshold, and vice-versa for PFET devices. Therefore, the ideal scenario would be with negative WFF for the PFET devices and positive WFF for the NFET devices. Though, the NFET term also depends on the β-ratio (ratio between the transistor emitter and base current) of the PFET and NFET transistors. Giving an estimate based on saturation and off-currents from [57], the NFET threshold voltage influence on the final hysteresis interval is almost 40% higher, in comparison to its counterpart.

As shown in Table 7, the only cases with considerable hysteresis worsening happens when the NFET WF is above 2%, while the subset showing improvements includes most of the possible scenarios. And since the hysteresis voltage will never be higher than the supply voltage, the average tends to the supply voltage value.

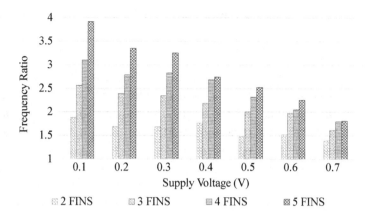

Fig. 17. Average frequency ratios between different layouts.

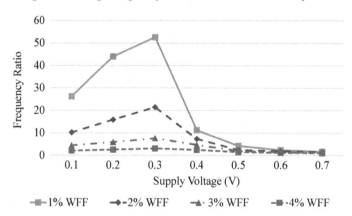

Fig. 18. Average frequency ratios between different WFF scenarios.

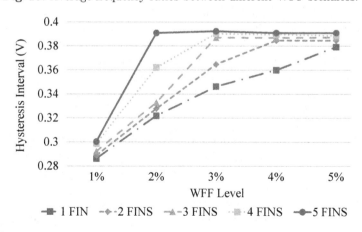

Fig. 19. Average of hysteresis interval increase over WFF scaling [60].

Table 7. Hysteresis interval ratio dependency over NFET and PFET workfunction [60].

NFET	PFET										
	5%	4%	3%	2%	1%	0%	−1%	−2%	−3%	−4%	−5%
5%	**0.30**	**0.28**	**0.28**	**0.27**	**0.26**	**0.25**	**0.26**	**0.27**	**0.28**	**0.30**	**0.32**
4%	**0.46**	**0.46**	**0.55**	**0.54**	**0.54**	**0.54**	**0.55**	**0.56**	**0.57**	**0.59**	**0.61**
3%	**0.76**	**0.76**	**0.76**	**0.78**	**0.80**	**0.81**	**0.83**	**0.84**	**0.86**	**0.87**	**0.89**
2%	**0.88**	0.90	0.92	0.92	0.95	0.97	0.99	1.00	1.00	1.00	1.00
1%	0.93	0.94	0.97	0.99	1.00	1.00	1.00	1.00	1.00	1.00	1.00
0%	0.95	0.96	0.97	1.00	1.00	1.00	1.00	1.00	1.00	1.00	1.00
−1%	0.95	0.96	0.99	0.99	1.00	1.00	1.00	1.00	1.00	1.00	1.00
−2%	0.96	0.97	0.99	1.00	1.00	0.99	0.99	0.99	0.99	0.98	0.98
−3%	0.95	0.97	0.99	0.99	0.99	0.99	0.98	0.98	0.98	0.97	0.97
−4%	0.93	0.94	0.97	0.97	0.96	0.96	0.96	0.95	0.95	0.95	0.94
−5%	0.93	0.94	0.96	0.96	0.96	0.95	0.95	0.94	0.94	0.94	0.93

7   Conclusions

An analysis over multiple scenarios considering several levels of process variability, supply voltages, and transistor sizing was performed in order to identify the adequate number of fins and supply voltage for various kinds of applications prioritizing energy consumption and the minimization of deviations.

ST is a promising circuit for variability effects mitigation and enhancement of noise immunity being fairly applied on critical applications with tight reliability constraints. The results show that fewer fins can enable considerable energy reduction. On the contrary, for the ST robustness, a higher fin count will bring an increase in the on-current, bringing noise immunity improvements.

In performance results, it could be observed up to 16% and 44.65% maximum average increase and decrease in frequency, respectively, with differences between variability impact in the layouts rising alongside the supply voltage value. The hysteresis intervals showed clear advantages over higher fin count and supply voltages with 10.76% and 25.26% better hysteresis. Considering energy consumption and variability, it was possible to achieve 24.84% and 14.44% decreases, respectively, with robust layouts taking advantage of a higher number of fins and a small decrease on the supply voltage while still maintaining very high frequencies of about 5 GHz. A cost-benefit analysis was made as well, giving an additional option in order to achieve acceptable energy consumption and variability robustness.

For future works, we expect to investigate the effects of sizing on each feedback transistor on the ST circuit independently, introduce new designs and technology nodes into the analysis, take radiation effects, on top of the variability, into account and apply such circuits into more complex projects.

Acknowledgements. This study was financed in part by the Coordenação de Aperfeiçoamento de Pessoal de Nível Superior - Brasil (CAPES) - Finance Code 001, by the Brazilian National Council for Scientific and Technology Development (CNPq), and by the Research Support Foundation of the State of Rio Grande do Sul (FAPERGS).

References

1. Miorandi, D., Sicari, S., De Pellegrini, F., Chlamtac, I.: Internet of things: vision, applications and research challenges. Ad Hoc Netw. **10**(7), 1497–1516 (2012)
2. Manoli, Y.: Energy harvesting–from devices to systems. In: 2010 Proceedings of ESSCIRC, pp. 27–36. IEEE (2010)
3. Bleitner, A., Goeppert, J., Lotze, N., Keller, M., Manoli, Y.: Comparison and optimization of the minimum supply voltage of schmitt trigger gates versus CMOS gates under process variations. In: ANALOG 2018; 16th GMM/ITG-Symposium, VDE, pp. 1–6 (2018)
4. Abbas, Z., Olivieri, M., Khalid, U., Ripp, A., Pronath, M.: Optimal NBTI degradation and pvt variation resistant device sizing in a full adder cell. In: 4th International Conference on Reliability, Infocom Technologies and Optimization (ICRITO) (Trends and Future Directions), pp. 1–6 (2015)
5. Farkhani, H., Peiravi, A., Kargaard, J.M., Moradi, F.:Comparative study of fin-FETS versus 22 nm bulk CMOS technologies: SRAM design perspective. In: 2014 27th IEEE International System-on-Chip Conference (SOCC), pp. 449–454. IEEE (2014)
6. Zimpeck, A.L., Meinhardt, C., Posser, G., Reis, R.: FinFET cells with different transistor sizing techniques against pvt variations. In: 2016 IEEE International Symposium on Circuits and Systems (ISCAS), pp. 45–48 (2016)
7. Nassif, S.: Process variability at the 65 nm node and beyond. In: Custom Integrated Circuits Conference, 2008. CICC 2008, pp. 1–8. IEEE (2008)
8. Hariharan, A.N., Pontarelli, S., Ottavi, M., Lombardi, F.: Modeling open defects in nanometric scale CMOS. In: 2010 IEEE 25th International Symposium on Defect and FaultTolerance in VLSI Systems, pp. 249–257. IEEE (2010)
9. Vaddi, R., Dasgupta, S., Agarwal, R.: Device and circuit co-design robustness studies in the subthreshold logic for ultralow-power applications for 32 nm CMOS. IEEE Trans. Electron Devices **57**(3), 654–664 (2010)
10. Ames, S.O., Zanandrea, V., Oliveira, I.F.V., Toledo, S.P., Meinhardt, C.: Investigating pvt variability effects on full adders. In: 2016 26th International Workshop on Power and Timing Modeling, Optimization and Simulation (PATMOS), pp. 155–161 (2016)
11. Islam, A., Hasan, M.: Design and analysis of power and variability aware digital summing circuit. ACEEE Int. J. Commun. **2**, 6–14 (2011)
12. Alioto, M., Palumbo, G.: Delay variability due to supply variations in transmission-gate full adders. In: Circuits and Systems, 2007. ISCAS 2007, pp. 3732–3735 (2007)
13. Kulkarni, J.P., Kim, K., Roy, K.: A 160 mv robust schmitt trigger based subthreshold sram. IEEE J. Solid-State Circ. **42**(10), 2303–2313 (2007)
14. Hays, K.I.: A 62 mv 0.13 um CMOS standard-cell-based design technique using schmitt-trigger logic (2012)
15. Melek, L., da Silva, A.L., Schneider, M.C., Galup-Montoro, C.: Analysis and design of the classical CMOS schmitt trigger in subthreshold operation. vol. 64, pp. 869–878. IEEE (2017)

16. Lotze, N., Manoli, Y.: Ultra-sub-threshold operation of always-on digital circuits for iot applications by use of schmitt trigger gates. IEEE Trans. Circ. Syst. I: Regular Papers **64**(11), 2920–2933 (2017)
17. Dokania, V., Islam, A.: Circuit-level design technique to mitigate impact of process, voltage and temperature variations in complementary metal-oxide semiconductor full adder cells. vol. 9, pp. 204–212. IET (2015)
18. Toledo, S.P., Zimpeck, A.L., Reis, R., Meinhardt, C.: Pros and cons of schmitt trigger inverters to mitigate pvt variability on full adders. In: 2018 IEEE International Symposium on Circuits and Systems (ISCAS), pp. 1–5. IEEE (2018)
19. Moraes, L.B.D., Zimpeck, A., Meinhardt, C., Reis, R.: Evaluation of variability using schmitt trigger on full adders layout. Microelectron. Reliabil. **88**, 116–121 (2018)
20. Asenov, A.: Random dopant induced threshold voltage lowering and fluctuations in sub 50 nm mosfets: a statistical 3datomistic'simulation study. vol. 10. IOP Publishing, p. 153 (1999)
21. Bernstein, K., et al.: High-performance CMOS variability in the 65-nm regime and beyond. IBM J. Res. Dev. **50**(45), 433–449 (2006)
22. Wang, W., Reddy, V., Yang, B., Balakrishnan, V., Krishnan, S., Cao, Y.: Statistical prediction of circuit aging under process variations. In: 2008 IEEE Custom Integrated Circuits Conference, pp. 13–16. IEEE (2008)
23. Young, D., Christou, A.: Failure mechanism models for electromigration. IEEE Trans. Reliabil. **43**(2), 186–192 (1994)
24. Lombardo, S., Stathis, J.H., Linder, B.P., Pey, K.L., Palumbo, F., Tung, C.H.: Dielectric breakdown mechanisms in gate oxides. J. Appl. Phys. **98**(12), 12 (2005)
25. Takeda, E., Suzuki, N.: An empirical model for device degradation due to hot-carrier injection. IEEE Electron Device Lett. **4**(4), 111–113 (1983)
26. Stine, B.E., Boning, D.S., Chung, J.E.: Analysis and decomposition of spatial variation in integrated circuit processes and devices. IEEE Trans. Semiconductor Manuf. **10**(1), 24–41 (1997)
27. Nassif, S.R.: Within-chip variability analysis. In: International Electron Devices Meeting 1998. Technical Digest (Cat. No. 98CH36217), pp. 283–286. IEEE (1998)
28. Asenov, A., Brown, A.R., Davies, J.H., Kaya, S., Slavcheva, G.: Simulation of intrinsic parameter fluctuations in decananometer and nanometer-scale MOS-FETS. IEEE Trans. Electron Devices **50**(9), 1837–1852 (2003)
29. Frank, D.J., Dennard, R.H., Nowak, E., Solomon, P.M., Taur, Y., Wong, H.S.P.: Device scaling limits of si mosfets and their application dependencies. Proc. IEEE **89**(3), 259–288 (2001)
30. Wong, H.S., Frank, D.J., Solomon, P.M., Wann, C.H., Welser, J.J.: Nanoscale CMOS. Proc. IEEE **87**(4), 537–570 (1999)
31. Frank, D.J., Wong, H.S.: Simulation of stochastic doping effects in SI MOSFETS. In: 7th International Workshop on Computational Electronics. Book of Abstracts. IWCE (Cat. No. 00EX427), pp. 2–3. IEEE (2000)
32. Brunner, T.A.: Why optical lithography will live forever. J. Vacuum Sci. Technol. B: Microelectron. Nanometer Structures Process. Measurement Phenomena **21**(6), 2632–2637 (2003)
33. Bhattacharya, D., Jha, N.K.: FinFETS: From devices to architectures. vol. 2014. Hindawi (2014)
34. Taur, Y., Ning, T.H.: Fundamentals of Modern VLSI Devices. Cambridge University Press, Cambridge (2013)

35. King, T.J.: FinFETS for nanoscale CMOS digital integrated circuits. In: ICCAD-2005. IEEE/ACM International Conference on Computer-Aided Design, pp. 207–210, November 2005
36. Saha, S.K.: Modeling process variability in scaled CMOS technology. IEEE Design Test Comput. **27**(2), 8–16 (2010)
37. Mustafa, M., Bhat, T.A., Beigh, M.: Threshold voltage sensitivity to metal gate work-function based performance evaluation of double-gate n-FINFET structures for LSTP technology (2013)
38. Hwang, C.H., Li, Y., Han, M.H.: Statistical variability in finfet devices with intrinsic parameter fluctuations. Microelectron. Reliabil. **50**(5), 635–638 (2010)
39. Mukhopadhyay, S., Lee, Y.H., Lee, J.H.: Time-zero-variability and BTI impact on advanced finfet device and circuit reliability. Microelectron. Reliabil. **81**, 226–231 (2018)
40. Meinhardt, C., Zimpeck, A.L., Reis, R.A.: Predictive evaluation of electrical characteristics of sub-22 nm finfet technologies under device geometry variations. Microelectron. Reliabil. **54**(9–10), 2319–2324 (2014)
41. Hobbs, C.C., et al.: Fermi-level pinning at the polysilicon/metal-oxide interface-part II. IEEE Trans. Electron Devices **51**(6), 978–984 (2004)
42. Gusev, E.P., Narayanan, V., Frank, M.M.: Advanced high-κ dielectric stacks with polySi and metal gates: recent progress and current challenges. IBM J. Res. Dev. **50**(4.5), 387–410 (2006)
43. Gusev, E., et al.: Ultrathin high-k gate stacks for advanced CMOS devices. In: International Electron Devices Meeting. Technical Digest (Cat. No. 01CH37224), pp. 20–21. IEEE (2001)
44. Datta, S., et al.: High mobility Si/SiGe strained channel MOS transistors with HfO/sub 2//TiN gate stack. In: IEEE International Electron Devices Meeting 2003, pp. 28–31. IEEE (2003)
45. Dadgour, H., De, V., Banerjee, K.: Statistical modeling of metal-gate work-function variability in emerging device technologies and implications for circuit design. In: 2008 IEEE/ACM International Conference on Computer-Aided Design, pp. 270–277. IEEE (2008)
46. Brown, A.R., Idris, N.M., Watling, J.R., Asenov, A.: Impact of metal gate granularity on threshold voltage variability: a full-scale three-dimensional statistical simulation study. IEEE Electron Device Lett. **31**(11), 1199–1201 (2010)
47. Meinhardt, C., Zimpeck, A.L., Reis, R.: Impact of gate workfunction fluctuation on FINFET standard cells. In: 2014 21st IEEE International Conference on Electronics, Circuits and Systems (ICECS), pp. 574–577 (2014)
48. Pal, I., Islam, A.: Circuit-level technique to design variation-and noise-aware reliable dynamic logic gates. IEEE Trans. Device Mater. Reliabil. **18**(2), 224–239 (2018)
49. Wang, Z.: CMOS adjustable schmitt triggers. IEEE Trans. Instrumentation Measurement **40**(3), 601–605 (1991)
50. Steyaert, M., Sansen, W.: Novel CMOS schmitt trigger. Electron. Lett. **22**(4), 203–204 (1986)
51. Zhang, C., Srivastava, A., Ajmera, P.K.: Low voltage CMOS schmitt trigger circuits. vol. 39, pp. 1696–1698 IET (2003)
52. Kim, D., Kih, J., Kim, W.: A new waveform-reshaping circuit: an alternative approach to schmitt trigger. IEEE J. Solid-State Circ. **28**(2), 162–164 (1993)
53. Pfister, A.: Novel cmos schmitt trigger with controllable hysteresis. Electron. Lett. **28**(7), 639–641 (1992)

54. Al-Sarawi, S.: Low power schmitt trigger circuit. Electron. Lett. **38**(18), 1009–1010 (2002)

55. Pedroni, V.: Low-voltage high-speed schmitt trigger and compact window comparator. Electron. Lett. **41**(22), 1213–1214 (2005)

56. Doki, B.L.: Cmos schmitt triggers. IEE Proc. G-Electron. Circ. Syst. **131**, 197–202 (1984)

57. Clark, L.T., et al.: Asap7: A 7-nm finfet predictive process design kit. vol. 53, Elsevier, pp. 105–115 (2016)

58. Alioto, M., Consoli, E., Palumbo, G.: Variations in nanometer CMOS flip-flops part II: energy variability and impact of other sources of variations. IEEE Trans. Circ. Syst. I: Regular Papers, **62**, 835–843 (2015)

59. Chava, B., et al.: Standard cell design in n7: Euv vs. immersion. In: Design-Process-Technology Co-optimization for Manufacturability IX, vol. 9427, p. 94270E (2015)

60. Moraes, L., Zimpeck, A., Meinhardt, C., Reis, R.: Minimum energy finfet schmitt trigger design considering process variability. In: 2019 IFIP/IEEE 27th International Conference on Very Large Scale Integration (VLSI-SoC), pp. 88–93. IEEE (2019)

61. The synopsys website. http://www.synopsys.com

An Improved Technique for Logic Gate Susceptibility Evaluation of Single Event Transient Faults

Rafael B. Schvittz[1], Denis T. Franco[3], Leomar S. da Rosa Jr.[1], and Paulo F. Butzen[2(✉)]

[1] Technologic Development Center, Universidade Federal de Pelotas, Pelotas, Brazil
{rb.schvittz,denis.franco,leomarjr}@inf.ufpel.edu.br
[2] Department of Electrical Engineering, Universidade Federal do Rio Grande do Sul, Porto Alegre, Brazil
paulo.butzen@ufrgs.br
[3] Engineering Center, Universidade Federal de Pelotas, Pelotas, Brazil

Abstract. Technology scaling increases the integrated circuits susceptibility to Single Event Effects. As a manner to mitigate soft errors, solutions incur significant performance and area penalties, especially when a design with fault-tolerant structure is overprotected. There are several estimation methods, as Probabilistic Transfer Matrix, Signal Probability Reliability, and SPR Multi-Pass, to evaluate circuit reliability. Theses methods use probabilistic transfer matrices (PTM) of the logic gates as the starting point. Few works explore the accurate generation of these matrices. This chapter briefly reviews the reliability concepts and some circuit estimation methods that explore PTM concept and presents a method to provide gate susceptibility matrices considering faults in the stick diagram level. The proposed method enriches the logic gates probabilistic matrices creation taking into account the characteristics of the logic gates to evaluate gate reliability more precisely. The results present the importance of the proposed approach. They are shown in the mean and standard deviation of the susceptibility calculated. In terms of standard deviation, high values indicate that the cell is highly sensitive to pin assignment. A good pin assignment alternative can result in 40% reduction in susceptibility for the same logic function.

Keywords: Microelectronics · Reliability · Single Event Effects · Single event transient · Failure rate

1 Introduction

The manufacturing precision limitations and supply voltage reduction combined with higher operating frequency and power dissipation are the primary concern for the technology scaling in nanoscale designs. These challenges severely impact the reliability of a system and consequently influence the need for reliability. The circuit reliability has been pointed out as one of the major challenges in deep

© IFIP International Federation for Information Processing 2020
Published by Springer Nature Switzerland AG 2020
C. Metzler et al. (Eds.): VLSI-SoC 2019, IFIP AICT 586, pp. 69–88, 2020.
https://doi.org/10.1007/978-3-030-53273-4_4

sub-micron CMOS circuits [1]. Meanwhile, with the omnipresence of electronics in our daily lives, there is even more demand for reliable system design. Despite these difficulties and the fact that the chips cannot be retested at the factory, users expect the system to remain reliable and to continue to deliver the rated performance [2].

These limitations in the fabrication process may increase the number of faults in circuits, reducing their reliability. To mitigate the problem above, it is explored different kinds of redundancy. These redundancy guarantees circuits that produce correct outputs even in the presence of errors [3]. However, they are usually based on redundancy in time, hardware, and/or information [4]. Although any redundancy-based strategy would impose extra overhead, it is still of high interest since the fabrication yield is predicted to become extremely low in nanoscale designs [5].

To avoid the overdesign and guarantee the best option in the fabricated circuit, many reliability evaluation methods may be used. An accurate method is the Probabilistic Transfer Matrix (PTM) [6], and it is the basis for other methods, as the Signal Probability Reliability Multi-Pass (SPRMP) [7]. Since the test of a circuit is a high-cost task, the probabilistic methods used to estimate the reliability of a circuit based on the reliability of the gate are even more highlighted. Besides, these methods are prone to reliability analysis under multiple faults scenario. It is known that the limitation of these methods is the simplification of the assumption of the same error probability values for all logic gates. The work proposed in [8] shows a method in transistor-level to create the logic gate probabilistic matrices. The matrices created shown that it is essential to observe the transistor arrangements to produce more accurate matrices for the logic gates that feed the probabilistic methods.

The models for evaluating the reliability of logic gates made so far consider transistor arrangement information to calculate the reliability of a gate given a type of fault. As the transient fault occurs on the sensitive nodes of the gates, stick diagram information becomes necessary for an accurate estimation. Therefore, this work proposes a probabilistic method capable of evaluating the susceptibility of logic gates concerning SET without the need for electrical simulations. It is important to emphasize that the evaluation is independent of technology since the stick diagrams are evaluated according to the number of sensitive areas. Another important point is that the specific effects of charge sharing in the transistors are not considered, always being observed the presence of the fault at the affected node, given the incidence of the particle.

This chapter is organized as follows: Sect. 2 presents a brief overview of basic reliability concepts and introduce three methods that explore PTMs to estimate the circuit reliability. Section 3 introduces Single Event Transient effect and its definitions. In Sect. 4, the methodology proposed to calculate the susceptibility of a logic gate described as a stick diagram is explained as well as a case study using a two-input NAND. Section 5 presents results and characteristics of the impact of the layouts in the single event transient susceptibility. Finally, in Sect. 6, the conclusions are presented.

2   BackGround

This section initially introduces reliability metrics and the PTM concept. Later, three reliability estimation methods are discussed. These methods have been chosen due to accuracy or runtime. They are chosen since all of them explores the PTM concept to estimate the circuit reliability.

2.1   Reliability Concepts

Metrics. The reliability (R or Q) of a circuit is defined as the probability of a circuit operates correctly during a time interval. Therefore, its complement, the probability of a failure, is defined as fault probability (P), as shown in Eq. 1.

The failure rate (λ), calculated using Eq. 2, is one of the metrics used for digital circuit reliability estimation. This failure rate indicates the number of failures that a circuit can present in one hour of operation. Similarly, the Mean Time Between Failures (MTBF) is used to represent the, as the name indicates, the time between failures in the evaluated circuit. Equation 3 presents as this metric is obtained. Once the MTBF value corresponds to the mean time between failures, as higher this value more reliable is the circuit. Both are important metrics used to compare reliabities of different systems, calculated using.

$$P = 1 - R \tag{1}$$

$$\lambda = -ln(R) \tag{2}$$

$$MTBF = \frac{1}{\lambda} \tag{3}$$

Probabilistic Transfer Matrix. The probabilistic transfer matrix, abbreviated as PTM, aim to represent the probability of success or failure of each input vector given a logic gate. This representation is very important in reliability analysis since it is used in several circuit estimation methods, as the three that are discussed later. This matrix maps the possible inputs and the respective outputs of a given circuit. To understand how the PTM is generated it is necessary to know the ideal transfer matrix (ITM) that represents the behavior of a logic gate or circuit in a fault-free scenario.

Through the truth table of a given logic gate, it is possible to determine the ITM matrix and consequently the output that supposed to be the correct, correlating this to the chosen probability the PTM is fill. In the presence of faults, there are conditions that the correct output not always occurs. If we know how frequently it happens, it is possible to map all possible conditions of this gate by using a PTM. Figure 1 shows how to generate a PTM of two-input NAND gate based on it is truth table and ITM matrix. In this case, the PTM considers that the correct output occurs with probability "q". At the same way, the erroneous output can also occurs with a probability represented by the complement of q, defined as "1-q".

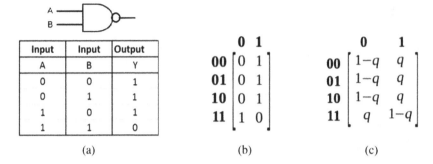

Fig. 1. NAND PTM relation to ITM and Truth Table: a) Truth table b) Ideal Transfer Matrix (ITM) c) Probabilistic Transfer Matrix (PTM)

2.2 Circuit Reliability Estimation Methods

With the basic reliability concepts reviewed, this section is dedicated to introduce three circuit reliability estimation methods. All three methods explores the PTM concept. The first one uses the same name of the concept. To avoid misunderstandings, we always used "PTM Method" to refer to the estimation method and only PTM to refer to the concept.

Probabilistic Transfer Matrices Method - PTM Method. Many methods to estimate the reliability of a circuit have been proposed in the literature [9]. The Probabilistic Transfer Matrix Method (PTM Method), proposed by Patel et al. [6], is able to produce an exact reliability evaluation of a logic circuit, in a straightforward process [10]. The method was extensively explored by Krishnaswamy et al. [11]. In the PTM Method, the reliability of a circuit is obtained by a combination of the individual gates reliability and the circuit's topology. The individual gates reliability and the circuit's reliability are represented by PTM and ITM matrices.

In a simplified way, each gate can be modeled by a PTM, and the PTM of larger circuits can be computed by multiplying the PTMs of series logic functions and applying the Kronecker tensor in the PTMs of logic gates that are in the same deep level of the circuit. The circuit reliability is extracted according to the Eq. 4, where $p(i)$ denotes the probability of input vector i [12]. If all input vectors have the same probability, the Eq. 4 can be simplified in Eq. 5.

The main limitation of the PTM Method is the size of the matrices that must be stored and manipulated. Each level in a logic circuit is represented by a PTM. The size of a PTM is a function of the number of inputs and outputs that are being modeled. The number of rows in a PTM is equal to 2^n, where n is the number of inputs in the circuit level. The number of columns in a PTM is equal to 2^m, where m is the number of outputs in the circuit level. Then for a circuit level with 24 inputs and 12 outputs, for example, the dimensions of the PTM of the level will be 2^{24} rows by 2^{12} columns, or 512 GB of storage space for 8 bytes floating point representation of probabilities. Given this scenario, the application of the PTM is limited to small size circuits, even with techniques that improve the efficiency of the method [12]

$$R_c = \sum_{ITM_c(i,j)=1} p(j|i)p(i) \tag{4}$$

$$R_c = \frac{1}{2^n} \sum_{ITM_c(i,j)=1} p(j|i) \tag{5}$$

Signal Probability Reliability - SPR. The SPR method is another method that explores PTM and ITM matrices to map the reliability behavior of logic gates in a circuit. The method proposed by [13] introduce the concept of Signal Probability matrix. This new concept avoid the generation of large matrices to represent the intermediate circuit states as in PTM Method.

The signal probability matrix is a 2×2 matrix. It represents the 4 possible states of a signal: a correct 0 ($\#_0$), a correct 1 ($\#_3$), an incorrect 0 ($\#_2$) and an incorrect 1 ($\#_1$) as shown in Fig. 2. The probability matrix of an output gate signal is easily computed through the simple multiplication of the input signals probabilities matrices by the logic gate PTM. From this assumption, it is possible to affirm that the SPR complexity is linear to the number of gates [14]. This makes the method scalable and can be applied to circuits with thousands of logic gates.

$$SIGNAL_4 = \begin{bmatrix} signal_0 & signal_1 \\ signal_2 & signal_3 \end{bmatrix}$$

$$P_{2 \times 2}(signal) = \begin{bmatrix} P(signal = correct\ 0) & P(signal = incorrect\ 1) \\ P(signal = incorrect\ 0) & P(signal = correct\ 1) \end{bmatrix}$$

Fig. 2. Matrix representation of a four-state signal probabilities [13]

The reliability of the entire circuit RC can be extracted according Eq. 6, where Rj is the reliability of each circuit output signal and m is the amount of circuit output [13]. Despite these advantages, the SPR method doesn't takes into account the probability dependence of reconvergent signals, producing reliability values that are inaccurate, depending on the number of reconvergent fanout signals in the circuit [15].

$$R_c = \prod_{j=0}^{m-1} R_j \tag{6}$$

Signal Probability Reliability Multi-Pass - SPR-MP. Considering the accuracy limitations of the SPR method, which is a straightforward algorithm, an alternative of the SPR method based on multiple passes of probabilities propagation was also proposed by [7], and was referred to as the SPR Multi-pass, or SPR-MP. In the SPR-MP method, the probabilities associated to each reconvergent signal are propagated 4 times, with a single signal state being propagated at a time. The values computed at each pass of the algorithm are accumulated to produce the final value.

As with the SPR method, there is no memory limitation associated with the SPR-MP method, but processing time is dependent on the number of reconvergent fanout signals [15]. Equation 7 represents the number of passes of the algorithm to compute the reliability of a circuit with F reconvergent fanouts. The main advantage of the SPR-MP method is the possibility to restrict the number of fanouts (and so, the number of passes of the algorithm) to be considered in the reliability computation. This characteristic allows a tradeoff between processing time and accuracy, leading to a better scalability than the PTM method and a better accuracy than the SPR method [16].

$$R_c = \sum_{f=1}^{4^F} R_c \tag{7}$$

3 Single Event Transient

Many advances in the integrated circuits are achieved due to technology scaling. The fabrication of even more capable computing architectures has been enabled by smaller, faster, and cheaper fundamental microelectronic building blocks. However, voltage scaling has dropped lower and lower. It results in a reduction in the amount of charge that represents stored information, increasing the sensitivity of CMOS devices to single-particle charge collection transients. Also, the higher frequency achieved by the circuits can intensify the soft errors due to the reduction in the timing masking.

In the case of Single event transient (SET), it is caused by the generation of charge due to a single particle passing through a sensitive node in the combinational circuit. This strike in a sensitive node within a combinational logic circuit can produce a wrong output value during a time interval. The pulse generated by the particle strike can have a positive or negative magnitude, depending on whether the particle hits at the sensitive node of the NMOS or PMOS transistors.

In the literature, the consideration of a sensitive node for CMOS circuits has some misunderstands. For example, in [17,18], and [19], it is considered as a sensitive node the drain of the OFF transistors, considering an inverter gate as an example. This assumption is not mistaken for the example, as shown in Fig. 3. The inverter gate biased with the logic value "1" presents as the only sensitive node, the drain of the PMOS OFF-transistor, as illustrated herein. Then, it is possible to affirm that the sensitive PN junction of the gate is the drain of the OFF-transistor (just in case of the inverter). However, the ideal affirmation is that a sensitive node is the reverse-biased PN junction [20, 21]. When these particles hit the silicon bulk, the minority carriers are created. If collected by the source/drain diffusion regions, the change of the voltage value of those nodes occurs [22].

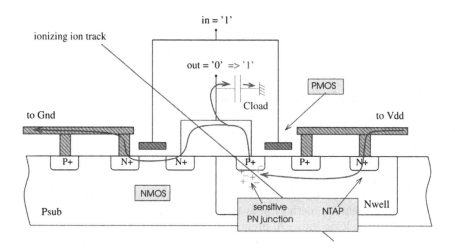

Fig. 3. Single Event Transient Mechanism: Inverter example of a particle strike at a sensitive node [23]

Besides, considering the NAND2 gate as an example shown in Fig. 2. The output node G, which belongs to the transistor M1 is sensitive when the input vector DE = "10" is applied, albeit it is an ON-transistor. Furthermore, as the behavior of the SET faults is different for a PMOS/NMOS particle strike, it is assumptive that the primary condition for reverse-biased PN junctions is satisfied with the complementary OFF-plane of the gate, instead of in the OFF-transistors.

Moreover, some internal nodes of a gate are not always sensitive to the particle strike. The pulse generated due to the particle strike in an internal node may not propagate if there is not a logical sensitized path to the output. Then, the pulse propagation from a sensitive node to the output depends on the state of the inputs [18]. Figure 4 shows an example of a sensitive node and pulse propagation in a NAND gate. When DE = "10", then there is a sensitive path between N3 and G, making N3 a sensitive node for this specific input vector. However, the input vector "11" also makes a sensitive path between N3 and G, although, in this condition, the node is not reverse biased.

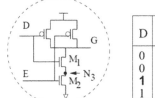

D	E	N_3 Sensitive	N_3 to G Propagation
0	0	No	No
0	1	No	No
1	**0**	**Yes**	**Yes**
1	1	No	Yes

Fig. 4. Node sensitive analysis in a NAND gate (adapted from [18])

4   SET Susceptibility Analysis

The reliability concept of a circuit is related to the probability of this circuit to perform the function to which it was designed, under certain conditions during a given time interval [24]. The results for error probability (EP) in [8] indicate that the equal EP values of logic gates traditionally used in reliability evaluation underestimate the real logic gates EPs, and consequently the circuit reliability. This chapter presents a method able to evaluate Single Event Transient fault susceptibility in a logic gate. A preliminary version of our work appeared in [25]. The previous work was extended providing a more detailed evaluation of stick diagram level and also a electrical validation of the results. The method proposed in [8], which evaluates logic gates at transistor-level, does not evaluate precisely when parallel transistors association results in two or more nodes in layout level. Also, it is known that a logic cell can be designed in different ways, then the need for a stick level analysis is highlighted.

This section presents the method proposed to evaluate the susceptibility of logic gates to transient faults. At first, a definition of fault as a probabilistic event is presented, which is the base to the method that analyzes stick diagrams.

4.1   Definition of Fault as a Probabilistic Event

A logic gate is defined as X, which has a set of nodes N. Considering that the probability of a particle incidence in a node $i \in N$ is defined as p. Then the probability is obtained considering $P(i) = p$.

The probability of a particle occurrence on a specific logic gate, in this case, is an independent event. It means that it is necessary to calculate the probability of this same particle to cause an error as the probability of the particle strike any sensitive node, given an input vector. The main reason a particle incidence in a node is considered an independent event is defined through the concept of probability theory. When two events are said to be independent of each other, it means that the probability that one event occurs does not affect the probability of the other event occurring.

Therefore, considering that a logic gate has k sensitive nodes, the output error probability is defined as the union of the probability of a particle incidence in any sensitive node of the gate. As the definition of the probability theory of independent events, the occurrence of an event $i \in N$, being N Eq. 8 gives the total number of events that cause a fault at the output.

$$P(A_1 \cup \cdots A_n) = S_1 - S_2 + \cdots + (-1)^{n-1} S_n \tag{8}$$

where S_k is defined by Eq. 9 [26]. Note that k represents the total elements present in the equation. For instance, assuming k=2 and three events $(A_1, A_2$ and $A_3)$. The value S_k corresponds to the sum of the intersection of each pair of possible elements, for example $S_2 = A_1 \cap A_2 + A_1 \cap A_3 + A_2 \cap A_3$.

$$S_k = \sum_{1 \leq i_1 < \cdots < i_k \leq n} P(A_{i1} \cap \cdots \cap A_{ik}) \tag{9}$$

After the definition of the equation necessary to calculate the susceptibility, it is possible to apply the method considering the number of sensitive nodes in an input vector of a logic gate. The next subsections present the method to evaluate the susceptibility of logic gates that depend on the probability of a particle incidence.

4.2 Simplified Method

The stick diagram method relies on the theory previously presented for its operation. The flowchart described in Fig. 5 represents the analysis of the stick model.

Consider, for example, the stick diagram in Fig. 6 for a two-input NAND function. This diagram has six nodes in total, two connected to VDD (n1 and n3), and one connected to GND (n4). In this case, none of these nodes are considered sensitive by the method, as they are connected to the circuit power supplies. The other nodes (n2, n5, and n6) depend on the input vector to be considered sensitive. Also, consider that the probability of occurrence of a particle in a sensitive node is set to p.

For input vector AB = 00, the expected output of the logic function is the logical value "1" . It means that the gate *pull-up* plane is conducting and that the transient fault may only affect the circuit if it occurs in the *pull-down* plane. Node 6 becomes sensitive as it is reverse-biased. Node 5 is not sensitized due to the lack of a conductive path to the exit. Thus, the susceptibility is given by the probability of the incidence of a particle in node 6.

For the input vector AB = 01, the expected output of the logic function is the logical value "1" . That is, just like the previous state, the fault may only affect the circuit occurring in the *pull-down* plane. As in the previous vector, only node 6 is sensitive because it is reverse-biased. Thus, the susceptibility is given by the probability of the incidence of a particle in node 6.

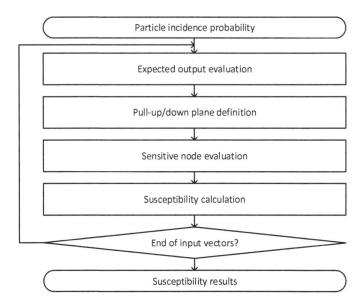

Fig. 5. Flowchart of the Simplified Method

For the input vector AB = 10, the expected output of the logic function is the logical value "1" . That is, just like the previous states, the fault may only affect the circuit occurring in the *pull-down* plane. In this vector, nodes 5 and 6 are reverse-biased and have a conductive path to the output. Thus, the susceptibility is given by the probability of the incidence of a particle at node 5 or node 6.

For the input vector AB = 11, the expected output of the logic function is the logical value "0". That is, the fault may only affect the circuit occurring in the *pull-up* plane. In this vector, node 2 is reverse-biased. Thus, the susceptibility is given by the probability of the incidence of a particle at node 2. Table 1 summarizes the values and equations for each vector.

Table 1. NAND2 analysis provided by the stick diagram model

Input vector (AB)	Sensitive node	Susceptibility
00	n6	p
01	n6	p
10	n5, n6	$2p - p^2$
11	n2	p

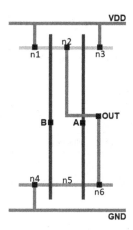

Fig. 6. Stick representation of a NAND2 logic gate

4.3   Method Validation

In this section, it is explained the methodology used to validate the proposed method. First of all, the method is based on two main rules to determine the sensitive nodes of a logic gate. To a node be sensitive, this node must present a reverse biased condition. Furthermore, a low resistance path must exist between the affected node and the output of the gate. Then, the flowchart of the method validation is presented in Fig. 7.

From the conditions mentioned above, and the Single Event Effects behavior in NMOS and PMOS transistors, it is presented the methodology to evaluate the proposed method. A total of eighteen logic gates from FREEPDK45 was used to validate. The first step performs a search for the minimum energy required ($LET_{threshold}$) to produce a bit flip in any input vector of any logic gate. The NGSPICE electrical simulator was used in this step to evaluate the gates. The search is performed to guarantee that a particle incidence on a sensitive node (node that corresponds to the two rules previously described) produces a voltage change on the output. Based on this information, it is found that the minimum LET value capable of producing an error in any logic gate found in these cells is in the output node of the NOR4 gate when ABCD = 1111, presenting a LET = 15.46 MeV. Thereby this LET value is used as particle energy to evaluate which node of the gates is sensitive.

Then, it is selected each logic gate to evaluate the sensitive nodes. The node evaluation of the gates is performed for each input vector. In this evaluation, it is analyzed the list of node candidates to be sensitive. Each node is individually evaluated. To perform the analysis, the electrical simulator software NGSPICE was used. Then, one particle incidence is performed on each sensitive node candidate at a time. For example, a logic gate containing five sensitive node candidates and three inputs is simulated $2^3 * 5$ times to evaluate each node if it is sensitive in each input vector. For each particle insertion, the output node is observed to

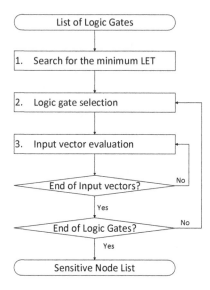

Fig. 7. Flowchart for the method validation

verify if the particle incidence has changed the output of the gate. To an error be observed at the output, it is necessary that the pulse must result in energy of 50% of the input voltage of the gate. The Fig. 8 and Fig. 9 show two conditions of the validation methodology. The first one, on the left, is the particle incidence on a node that does not fit on the specified conditions (not reverse-biased and no low resistance path to the output). The second, on the right, is the result of the same particle incidence on a reverse-biased node. For the 45 nm technology node, 50% of the respective supply voltage corresponds to 0.5V.

The NAND2 gate presented in Fig. 6 is considered to exemplify the flowchart of the validation. The gate has a total of six nodes (named n1 to n6). First of all, the nodes n1, n3, and n4 are not sensitive due to being connected to VDD or GND terminals. Then, the nodes n2, n5, and n6 could present a reverse biased condition depending on the input vector. Analyzing the NAND2 gate, when input vector AB = 00 is applied, the only sensitive node is n6, presenting a reverse biased condition. This behavior is also repeated when input vector AB = 01 is applied.

When the input vector is AB = 10, then, on the pull-down network, there are two nodes in reverse biased condition and presenting a low resistance path to the output. Then, in this input vector, the sensitive nodes that the particle strike causes a voltage change on the output are n5 and n6.

Finally, when input vector AB = 11 is applied, the only node that the particle strike produces a voltage change is the node n2. It was expected since, in the pull-up network, there is only one node that could be sensitive, because n1 and n3 are connected to VDD, and they do not present the reverse biased condition. Figure 10 presents the sensitive nodes for each input vector of this logic gate.

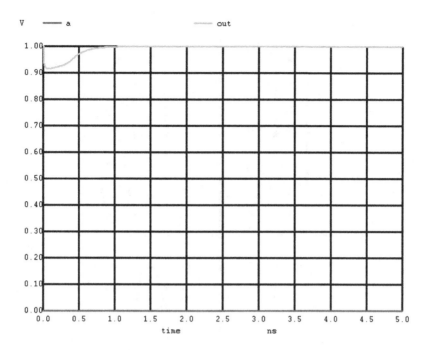

Fig. 8. Behavior of particle incidence on a PN junction not reverse-biased

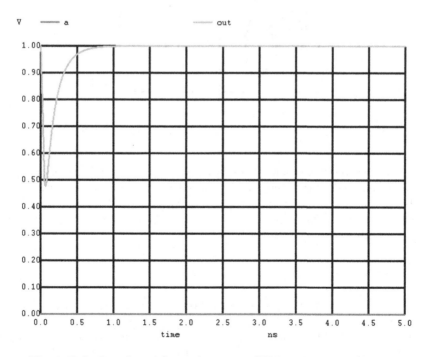

Fig. 9. Behavior of particle incidence on a PN junction reverse-biased

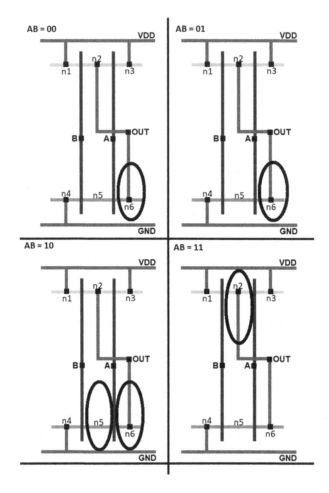

Fig. 10. Sensitive areas identified for NAND2 gate for each input vector

As expected, the validation process produced the same sensitive nodes of all logic gates analyzed by the method. This means that the defined conditions to a node being sensitive are correct. Also, the method does not need any electrical simulation to perform its analysis, resulting in the same result than the electrical simulation with less time spending.

5   Results

The results produced by the proposed method are shown considering a particle strike probability $p = 1.98e^{-6}$ was used as an estimate. This value defines the probability of the incidence of a particle in a sensitive node with sufficient energy to cause a voltage change. For the inputs of the gates, the same probability of being "1" equal to 50% was used. Then, the method was applied in a total of 19 logic gates. The results presented are a function of the mean susceptibility and even the standard deviation (σ) obtained from the values of each input vector of each function. The results obtained from the application of the method in the 45 nm library are presented in Table 2.

Table 2. Average Susceptibility (in 10^{-6}) and standard deviation (σ) calculated by the method for 45 nm library cell

	Mean	σ
Inv	1.98	0.00
NAND2	2.47	0.99
NOR2	2.47	0.99
NAND3	3.21	1.47
NOR3	3.21	1.47
NAND4	3.46	1.84
NOR4	3.46	1.84
AOI21	3.70	1.96
AOI22	3.83	2.33
AOI211	5.06	2.16
AOI221	5.12	2.35
AOI222	6.14	3.28
OAI21	3.70	1.96
OAI22	3.83	2.33
OAI211	5.06	2.16
OAI221	5.12	2.35
OAI222	6.14	3.28
OAI33	4.81	2.53
XOR2	5.93	1.61

Observing the results obtained by the proposed method, it is possible to notice that the INVERTER logic gate was the only gate that presented a zero standard deviation. It means that this gate was the only one within the cell library that showed no difference in the calculated susceptibility for its vectors.

Table 3 shows the susceptibility values obtained by applying the proposed method on the inverter logic gate. As can be observed, there is no difference in the obtained values between both input vectors of this gate, resulting in a zero standard deviation.

Another important point in the results is the behavior observed among the logic gates with complementary planes. For example, the NAND and NOR gates have complementary planes. Both gates have a network with n transistors in series, which is the sensitive network in most of the gates input vectors. Likewise,

Table 3. Susceptibility calculated for the inverter logic gate when the proposed method was applied

Input vector	Susceptibility (10^{-6})
0	1.98
1	1.98

AOI/OAI ports also exhibit this behavior. Table 4 presents the susceptibility calculated for NAND2 and NOR2. Note that the same mean obtained between both cells only occurs because the input vectors have the same occurrence probability.

Table 4. Susceptibility calculated (10^{-6}) for NAND2 and NOR2 gates for each input vector

Input vector (AB)	NAND2 Susceptibility	NOR2 Susceptibility
00	1.98	1.98
01	1.98	3.95
10	3.95	1.98
11	1.98	1.98

Finally, it is also important to note that the average susceptibility values tend to increase, according to the number of transistors in these logic gates. Another critical detail to note is the standard deviation value of these gates. Logic gates with high standard deviation values are more sensitive to different probabilities of the input vectors. A high standard deviation means that the gate has vectors in which the susceptibility can decrease or increase considerably, applying different input vectors probability.

To observe the difference between the input vectors that result in higher standard deviation values, take as an example an AOI21 logic gate. The susceptibility calculated for each input vector is shown in Fig. 11. Note that the most susceptible conditions of this gate are observed on input vectors 001, 011, and 101. Considering this information, it was performed three different scenarios considering different input vector probabilities for this logic gate. Figure 12 shows the probability for each input vector for three situations:

- a) The probability of being logical one for each input is B2 = B1 = A = 25%.
- b) The probability of being logical one for each input is B2 = B1 = 50% and A = 75%.
- c) The probability of being logical one for each input is B2 = B1 = A = 75%.

Input Vector (B2B1A)	Susceptibility (10^{-6})
000	1.98
001	5.93
010	3.95
011	5.93
100	1.98
101	5.93
110	1.98
111	1.98

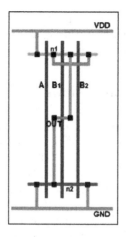

Fig. 11. Susceptibility calculated when applied the proposed method on an AOI21 logic gate

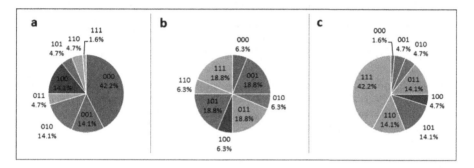

Fig. 12. Input probabilities considering three different scenarios

In the first simulation, considering 50% for the input vector probabilities, it results in a mean susceptibility of 3.70 for this logic gate. Considering the first situation presented in Fig. 12a, it results in a mean susceptibility calculated equal to 3.18. In this scenario it is possible to observe that the critical vectors have less probability wich results in less susceptibility for the gate.

The second situation present in Fig. 12b was performed to show the sensitivity to pin-assessment of the gate. When B2 = B1 = 50% and the input C = 75%. In this situation, the gate presents a mean susceptibility equal to 4.32. The small difference in the input vector probabilities causes an increase of almost 36% on the mean susceptibility of this gate.

Finally, in the last scenario presented in Fig. 12c, the inputs have probability of being logical one equal to 75%. As can be observed, this scenario results in a probability of occurrence of input 111 equal to 42%, in this input vector, the gate presents a good behavior in terms of susceptibility. Then, this scenario results in mean susceptibility equal to 3.36. This situation resulted in a difference less than

6% in susceptibility, compared to scenario "a". Observing the three scenarios, it shows that this gate can be highly dependent on the pin-assessment when calculating the mean susceptibility.

6 Conclusions

This work proposes a method to predict Single Event Transient susceptibility for logic gates. The results show that the susceptibility of a gate can be highly dependent on its implementation. Moreover, the proposed method can be used to generate probabilistic matrices for several logic gates. Also, these matrices can be used by probabilistic methods to estimate the reliability of a circuit, such as PTM or SPR-MP, for example. In the proposed method, it is not necessary to consider the possible masking conditions of SET, since they are regarded in reliability estimation techniques for circuits.

The proposed method can calculate the susceptibility of any single-stage logic function implementation, merely providing the stick diagram, input probability of being "1" and the value for particle strike probability. The susceptibility value can be an important measure for choosing the best candidate for logic functions. The results for a set of logic gates have shown the importance of considering the stick implementation in order to evaluate the logic gates susceptibility [27].

Acknowledgments. This study was financed in part by the Coordenação de Aperfeiçoamento de Pessoal de Nível Superior - CAPES, Conselho Nacional de Desenvolvimento Científico e Tecnológico - CNPq, and Fundação de Amparo a Pesquisa do Estado do Rio Grande do Sul - FAPERGS.

References

1. Borkar, S., Karnik, T., De, V.: Design and reliability challenges in nanometer technologies. In: Proceedings of the 41st Annual Design Automation Conference, p. 75 (2004)
2. Borkar, S.: Designing reliable systems from unreliable components: the challenges of transistor variability and degradation. IEEE Micro **25**(6), 10–16 (2005)
3. Vosoughi, A., Köse, S.: Leveraging on-chip voltage regulators against fault injection attacks. In: Proceedings of the 2019 on Great Lakes Symposium on VLSI, pp. 15–20 (2009)
4. Vial, J., Bosio, A., Girard, P., Landrault, C., Pravossoudovitch, S., Virazel, A.: Using TMR architectures for yield improvement. In: 2008 IEEE International Symposium on Defect and Fault Tolerance of VLSI Systems. IEEE, pp. 7–15 (2008)
5. Namazi, A., Nourani, M.: Gate-level redundancy: a new design-for-reliability paradigm for nanotechnologies. IEEE Trans. Very Large Scale Integrat. (VLSI) Syst. **18**(5), 775–786 (2009)
6. Patel, K.N., Markov, I.L., Hayes, J.P.: Evaluating circuit reliability under probabilistic gate-level fault models. In: Proceedings of the International Workshop on Logic and Synthesis, pp. 59–64 (2003)

7. Franco, D.T., Vasconcelos, M.C., Naviner, L., Naviner, J.-F.: Reliability analysis of logic circuits based on signal probability. In: 2008 15th IEEE International Conference on Electronics, Circuits and Systems, pp. 670–673. IEEE (2008)
8. Schvittz, R., Franco, D.T., Rosa, L.S., Butzen, P.F.: Probabilistic method for reliability estimation of sp-networks considering single event transient faults. In: 2018 25th IEEE International Conference on Electronics, Circuits and Systems (ICECS), pp. 357–360. IEEE (2018)
9. Xiao, R., Chen, C.: Gate-level circuit reliability analysis: a survey. *VLSI Design*, vol. 2014 (2014)
10. Pontes, M.F., Butzen, P.F., Schvittz, R.B., Rosa, S.L., Franco, D.T.: The suitability of the SPR-MP method to evaluate the reliability of logic circuits. In: 2018 25th IEEE International Conference on Electronics, Circuits and Systems (ICECS), pp. 433–436. IEEE (2018)
11. Krishnaswamy, S., Viamontes, G.F., Markov, I.L., Hayes, J.P.: Accurate reliability evaluation and enhancement via probabilistic transfer matrices. In: Proceedings of the Conference on Design, Automation and Test in Europe, vol. 1. IEEE Computer Society, pp. 282–287 (2005)
12. Cai, H., Liu, K., de Barros Naviner, L.A., Wang, Y., Slimani, M., Naviner, J.-F.: Efficient reliability evaluation methodologies for combinational circuits. Microelectron. Reliabil. **64**, 19–25 (2016)
13. Franco, D.T., Vasconcelos, M.C., Naviner, L., Naviner, J.-F.: Signal probability for reliability evaluation of logic circuits. Microelectron. Reliabil. **48**(8–9), 1586–1591 (2008)
14. Pagliarini, S.N., dos Santos, G., Naviner, L.D.B., Naviner, J.-F.: Exploring the feasibility of selective hardening for combinational logic. Microelectron. Reliabil. **52**(9–10), 1843–1847 (2012)
15. Flaquer, J.T., Daveau, J.-M., Naviner, L., Roche, P.: Fast reliability analysis of combinatorial logic circuits using conditional probabilities. Microelectron. Reliabil. **50**(9–11), 1215–1218 (2010)
16. Pagliarini, S.N., Ban, T., Naviner, L.A.D.B., Naviner, J.-F.: Reliability assessment of combinational logic using first-order-only fanout reconvergence analysis. In: 2013 IEEE 56th International Midwest Symposium on Circuits and Systems (MWSCAS), pp. 113–116. IEEE (2013)
17. Wang, F., Agrawal, V.D.: Single event upset: an embedded tutorial. In: 21st International Conference on VLSI Design (VLSID 2008), pp. 429–434. IEEE (2008)
18. Gill, B.S., Papachristou, C., Wolff, F.G., Seifert, N.: Node sensitivity analysis for soft errors in CMOS logic. In: IEEE International Conference on Test, 2005, p. 9. IEEE (2005)
19. de Aguiar, Y., Zimpeck, A.L., Meinhardt, C., Reis, R.: Permanent and single event transient faults reliability evaluation EDA tool. Microelectron. Reliabil. **64**, 63–67 (2016)
20. Baumann, R.C.: Radiation-induced soft errors in advanced semiconductor technologies. IEEE Trans. Dev. Mater. Reliabil. **5**(3), 305–316 (2005)
21. Ferlet-Cavrois, V., Massengill, L.W., Gouker, P.: Single event transients in digital CMOS-a review. IEEE Trans. Nuclear Sci. **60**(3), 1767–1790 (2013)
22. Omana, M., Papasso, G., Rossi, D., Metra, C.: A model for transient fault propagation in combinatorial logic. In: 9th IEEE On-Line Testing Symposium, 2003. IOLTS 2003, pp. 111–115. IEEE (2003)
23. Dutertre, J.-M., Bastos, R.P., Potin, O., Flottes, M.-L., Rouzeyre, B., Di Natale, G.: Sensitivity tuning of a bulk built-in current sensor for optimal transient-fault detection. Microelectron. Reliabil. **53**(9–11), 1320–1324 (2013)

24. Birolini, A.: Quality and Reliability of Technical Systems: Theory, Practice. Management. Springer, Heidelberg (2012). https://doi.org/10.1007/978-3-642-97983-5

25. Schvittz, R., Franco, D.T., Soares, L., Butzen, P.F.: A simplified layout-level method for single event transient faults susceptibility on logic gates. In: 2019 IFIP/IEEE 27th International Conference on Very Large Scale Integration (VLSI-SoC), pp. 185–190, IEEE (2019)

26. Prékopa, A., Gao, L.: Bounding the probability of the union of events by aggregation and disaggregation in linear programs. Discrete Appl. Math. **145**(3), 444–454 (2005)

27. Huard, V., Cacho, F., Federspiel, X., Arfaoui, W., Saliva, M., Angot, D.: Technology scaling and reliability: challenges and opportunities. In: 2015 IEEE International Electron Devices Meeting (IEDM), pp. 20.5.1–20.5.6, December 2015

Process Variability Impact on the SET Response of FinFET Multi-level Design

Leonardo H. Brendler[1]([✉]), Alexandra L. Zimpeck[1], Cristina Meinhardt[2], and Ricardo Reis[1]

[1] Instituto de Informática, PGMicro/PPGC, Universidade Federal do Rio Grande do Sul - UFRGS, Porto Alegre, RS, Brazil
`lhbrendler@inf.ufrgs.br, alexandra.zimpeck@ucpel.edu.br,`
`reis@inf.ufrgs.br`
[2] Departamento de Informática Aplicada e Estatística, PPGCC, Universidade Federal de Santa Catarina - UFSC, Florianópolis, SC, Brazil
`cristina.meinhardt@ufsc.br`

Abstract. Challenges were introduced in integrated circuits design due to the technology scaling. The evolution of integrated circuits has made them more susceptible to the radiation effects, besides increasing the manufacturing process variability. These challenges can lead to circuits operating outside their specification ranges. Transistor arrangement influences the performance of logic cells; complex logic gates can be used to minimize area, delay and power consumption. However, with the increasing relevance of nanometer challenges, it is necessary also to consider these factors at logic level design. This work explores different transistor arrangements for a set of logic functions at the layout level to evaluate the SET response under the process variability. The process variability is analyzed through the work-function fluctuations of the metal gate. The complex gate and the multi-level of NAND2 topologies, that implement the same function, were designed using the 7 nm FinFET ASAP7 Process Design Kit. Results show that the multi-level topology is more robust to the radiation effects at both ideal fabrication process and considering the process variability impact. The LETth value considering the multi-level topology is on average 55% higher than the values considering the complex topology. Moreover, all the logic functions analyzed independently of the topology are more sensitive to the SETs considering the impact of the process variability.

Keywords: FinFET technology · Multi-level design · Process variability · Soft errors · Single Event Transient

© IFIP International Federation for Information Processing 2020
Published by Springer Nature Switzerland AG 2020
C. Metzler et al. (Eds.): VLSI-SoC 2019, IFIP AICT 586, pp. 89–113, 2020.
https://doi.org/10.1007/978-3-030-53273-4_5

1   Introduction

The radiation-induced soft errors and the process variability are an essential reliability concern for nanotechnologies, affecting integrated circuits used for space or even terrestrial applications [1,2]. Variability is related to the random deviation, which causes an increase or decrease of typical design specifications. The primary variability issue is the uncertainty about the correct operation of the circuit. There is no guarantee that a circuit will behave as expected after the manufacturing process. Due to the variability effects, each circuit can present a different electrical behavior such as abnormal power consumption, performance deviation, or both. The unexpected behavior due to variations can stimulate circuit degradation besides make it inappropriate for your initial purpose.

Electronic circuits operating in space, especially in harsh environments, may be exposed to significant radiation doses as well as to the incidence of heavy particles from the sun or from outside the galaxy. From this exposure to radiation, changes and disturbances in the circuit can occur with high probability. Degradations that arise due to the incidence of a single particle are called Single Event Effects (SEE). If this single-particle causes a permanent failure in the circuit, it is considered a hard error. In case of an error in the system that does not cause permanent damage, it is called Single Event Transient (SET) or Non-Destructive (soft error) [3,4].

For a long time, SETs were not considered a significant reliability concern. The logical, electrical and latching window masking present in digital logic, were enough to minimize the importance of considering the phenomenon. However, with technology scaling, lower supply voltages and reduced nodal capacitances, the minimum charge required to induce a transient pulse was decreased [2,5]. Also, it is more likely that a SET generated in combinational logic will be captured at the storage element due to the higher operating frequencies. Thus, to overcome some of these problems, new device architectures and novel materials are being used.

Multigate devices have allowed the further scaling of transistors by providing better control of Short-Channel Effects (SCE), lower leakage currents and better yield [6]. On multigate devices, variability effects are mainly due to the work-function fluctuation (WFF) of the metal gate [7,8]. FinFET (Fin-Shaped Field Effect Transistor) technology is the main multigate device replacing bulk MOSFET devices in sub-22 nm technology nodes [7]. Due to its limited sensitivity volume compared to planar devices, the charge collection region is reduced in this technology [9,10], showing a better response to radiation effects, even considering the technology scaling. However, the radiation effects are not negligible on multigate devices [11].

The proper estimation of Threshold Linear Energy Transfer (LETth) along with the SET pulse width is of utmost importance for soft error (SE) mitigation and radiation-tolerant circuit design [12]. Also, few papers analyze the impact of process variability on the SET. The impact of process variability on on-state (I_{on}) and off-state (I_{off}) currents using FinFET technology in a set of technological nodes ranging from 20 nm to 7 nm is compared in [13]. The prominence is in the evaluation of Metal Gate Granularity (MGG) impact on the work-function (WF) of the gate. The results demonstrate the importance of not only evaluating variations in threshold voltage but also in other parameters and the significant influence of WFF in the threshold voltage and the I_{on} and I_{off} currents.

Regarding the radiation effects, a comparative soft error evaluation of logic gates in bulk FinFET technology using various technological nodes is presented in [9]. The main objective is allowing for estimating the SER of logic gates for ground applications, as well as for understanding the impact of voltage and drive strength through analysis of the sensitivity to soft errors. Also, similar work highlights the robustness of the 7 nm FinFET technology, considering other logic functions [14] and also majority voter circuits [15]. The latter also analyzes the impact of process variability on the SET.

In this context, this work investigates the radiation robustness, considering the process variability effects, of a set of logic functions implemented in two different transistor topologies using 7 nm FinFET technology [16]. The SET pulse width was obtained and the LETth was calculated to characterize the SET response. First, a radiation robustness analysis is performed considering only the ideal behavior, and then the process variability impact is considered. The main contributions of this work are: 1) to provide an evaluation of the SET sensitivity trends for complex logic gates, exploring the use of different transistor arrangements; 2) to consider the impact of process variability effects and radiation sensibility together on the analysis, and 3) to present a detailed investigation about the topology relation with the FinFET logic cells robustness through the LETth.

Next Section summarizes the main radiation effects, including their origins and the behavior on FinFET devices. Section 3 presents the process variability effects on FinFET technology, focusing on the WFF of the metal gate. Section 4 describes the methodology steps to observe these effects on multi-level and complex gate designs. With the set of information from the evaluations, this work discusses the results in Sect. 5 and present the main conclusions in Sect. 6.

2   Radiation Effects

The dynamic scaling alongside the low supply voltages, large transistor density, and the high-frequency operation introduce new reliability issues in integrated circuits, such as the high Single Event Effects (SEE) sensitivity and multi-charge collection [9,17]. This chapter presents the main concepts and characteristics of the radiation effects on electronic circuits. The focus is on SEEs, especially the impact of transient faults on devices. Before detailing these effects, it is important to present their origins.

Anomalies induced by the radiation effects on electronic circuits are known from the beginning of space exploration. The research aimed at the study of the radiation effects on electronic circuits was initially considered a concern of utmost relevance only in projects developed for military or space applications. The Earth is protected by the atmosphere, which acts as a semi-permeable "screen", to let throughout light and heat, while stopping radiation and ultraviolet rays (UVs) [3]. The intensity of the radiation basically increases according to the increase in altitude relative to ground level. However, due to phenomena related to the earth's magnetic field (the polar regions are an example), some regions suffer from a higher intensity of radiation even though they are located at low altitudes.

In space and the Earth's atmosphere, there is a diverse range of radiation, which is classified into two broad groups: ionizing particles and non-ionizing particles. The main particles that may cause unwanted effects in electronic circuits are electrons, protons, neutrons, muons, alpha particles and heavy ions, as well as electromagnetic radiation, such as x-rays and gamma rays [4]. At sea level, muons are the most numerous terrestrial species [18]. The primary components of radioactive phenomena encountered in space can be classified into four categories by origin: Radiation belts, solar flares, solar wind and cosmic rays [3]. Figure 1 shows the relationship between the Sun and the Earth that gave rise to these phenomena.

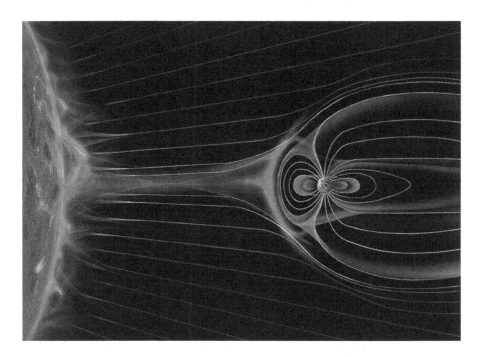

Fig. 1. Radiation effects from the Sun-Earth relationship [19].

2.1   Characterization of the Radiation Effects on Electronic Devices

The effects related to the incidence of radiation in electronic components have been studied for a long time by the international scientific community, mainly for space and military applications. The integrated circuits that experience the interaction of ionizing particles basically suffer from two types of degradation: those of singular character, occurring due to the incidence of a single particle, and those of a cumulative nature, which occur due to the accumulation of doses of ionizing radiation over the lifetime of the circuit.

Cumulative effects have their origin due to the dose of ionizing radiation accumulated over the life of the device and are classified as Total Ionizing Dose (TID). Prolonged exposure to ionizing radiation, due to accumulated (radiation-induced) electric charges, causes parts of the circuit to change in their electrical characteristics, such as a change in threshold voltage (V_{th}) and the increase in the leakage current of the device. These electrical changes impair the correct functioning of the device and may, depending on the amount of accumulated dose, permanently damage it.

The TID response of bulk silicon and SOI FinFETs are significantly different in terms of radiation-induced V_{th} and I_{off} current. Bulk silicon FinFET radiation tolerance is reduced due to an increase in I_{off}, and SOI FinFET radiation tolerance is reduced due to V_{th} shifts [20]. Bulk FinFETs have a similar TID response as planar bulk MOSFETs, that is, the buildup of oxide-trapped charge in the STI triggers a parasitic lateral transistor that modifies the electrical characteristics (higher I_{off}) [21]. Degradations that occur due to the incidence of a single particle are called Single Event Effects (SEE), these effects will be presented with more details next.

Single Event Effects. The Single Event Effects occur due to the interaction of large ionizing particles (protons, neutrons, α particles and heavy ions) that pass through insulation, semiconductor layers, or even all MOS device. These particles, when entering the silicon material, generate a transient path composed of ionized elements (electron-hole pairs - e^-/h) arranged under a radial distribution that permeates the path of the incident particle. This transient path may have sufficient mobile charge to drive a current pulse against the presence of the external electric field due to the polarization of the transistor [22].

SEEs indicate any measurable or observable change in a state or performance of a nanoelectronic device, component, subsystem or system (digital or analog) as a result of the incidence of a single energetic particle. According to the intensity and the region in which this current flows, it is capable of causing faults that may be permanent in the device structure, called destructive events (hard error), or non-destructive (soft errors), represented by the Single Event Transient (SET) and the Single Event Upset (SEU) [23]. Figure 2 presents the classification of the major SEEs in the literature. The focus of this work is the SET effect, which occurs in combinational circuits.

The most common transient effects on combinational circuits are the SETs, in which the incidence of an ionized particle produces a transient pulse that can propagate through a logic path and be latched by memory elements. The transient pulse is generated by the interaction of energetic particles near a sensitive region of a transistor when the collected charge (Q_{coll}) exceeds the critical charge (Q_{crit}). However, in sub-22 nm technological nodes other phenomena must also

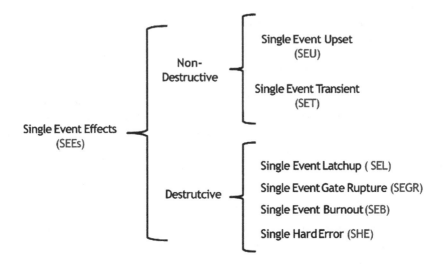

Fig. 2. Classification of major Single Event Effects. Modified from [24].

be considered in the characterization of the transient pulse. The influence of charge-sharing (charge collected by multiple transistors for a single incident particle) mechanism does not seem to have diminished for the FinFET technology. TCAD results show the extent of electrical perturbations and charge-sharing similar to what has been observed for older technologies. This effect can cause the pulse quenching in ion-induced transients, resulting in a reduced overall sensitivity of the system against SEE [25].

To quantify the SET effects, characteristics such as amplitude, shape and current pulse duration are important quantities [26]. The amplitude and duration of a SET depend on factors such as the fabrication technology, the circuit geometry, the bias voltage of the affected node, node load impedance, location of the transistor reached by the particle, in addition to factors related to the SEE itself, as the type and energy of the incident particle [26].

The energy deposited by a particle due to its ionization in silicon is an essential metric in the study of radiation effects in nanotechnologies because it is directly related to the magnitude of the generated transient pulse. Linear Energy Transfer (LET) (shown in Eq. 1) is the amount of energy that a particle releases per unit of compliance from the path traveled by it.

$$LET = \frac{\partial E}{\partial x} \tag{1}$$

The LET is dependent on the mass and energy of the particle and the ionized material, so particles with higher mass and energy ionized in denser materials have higher LETs [27]. Threshold LET (LETth) is the minimum LET to cause an effect in the circuit [11].

The disruptive nature of the FinFET structure introduces questions in terms of understanding, predicting and mitigating SEEs in circuits. The 3D structure of FinFET devices is favorable to reduce the soft error vulnerability according to several works available in the literature [10,28,29]. This reduction of the soft error vulnerability happens because the sensitive areas of FinFETs are little exposed to the charge collection region as shown in Fig. 3. FinFET technologies collect significantly less charge than conventional planar technologies. The work of [30] indicates that charge collection for semiconductor regions in FinFET technologies is approximately reduced by 70% compared to planar technologies. From a design standpoint, the accurate estimation of SEE susceptibility is crucial to ensure reliable circuits.

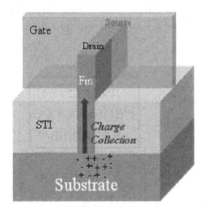 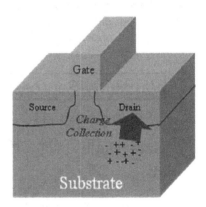

Fig. 3. Comparison of charge collection mechanism between FinFET devices and Planar CMOS technologies [29].

Although FinFET technology is more robust to soft errors than planar technologies, there are still many concerns that justify the study of this device. The process variability, one of the main challenges in sub-22 nm technologies, can modify the LETth to induce a soft error. Ultra-Low-Power (ULP) circuits are increasingly being used, and low voltages increase the probability of SE occurrence. Also, with the demand for devices increasingly faster, the operation frequency increases, also increasing the possibility of a memory element capturing a SE.

3 Process Variability Effects on FinFET Devices

The variability in electronic circuits can be divided into three different factors: environmental, reliability and physical [31]. Environmental factors appear during the circuit operation; variations in supply voltage and temperature are examples of environmental factors. Reliability factors are related to the transistor aging, due to the high electric fields presented in modern circuits. Finally, physical factors are associated with variations in electrical and geometrical parameters, which may occur due to the manufacturing process of the devices [31]. The latter is best known for process variability and is the focus of this study. This chapter details the main features of the process variability, showing its impact on FinFET devices and highlighting the most significant parameter for their effects.

The primary sources of process variability at nanometer nodes are due to the sub-wavelength lithography [31,32]. The variability on geometric parameters impact directly the transistor threshold voltage. These variations can compromise the entire blocks of cells or reduce the performance and energy efficiency of the chip. Some expected sources of variability for FinFETs are highlighted in [33]: the influence of variations in the fins height, the width variations across the double-standard layers, the variations of the fin to fin, the dependent variations the width of the pitch, the resistance of MOL (Middle of Line), and variations due to the overlap and the epitaxy. The main FinFET parameters and possible variability sources are shown in Fig. 4.

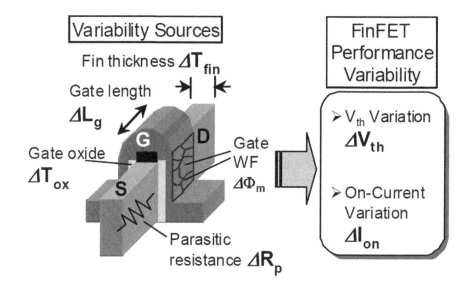

Fig. 4. Possible sources of FinFET variability [34].

For nanotechnology bulk CMOS devices, the geometric variability in the gate length has the greatest impact on the change of I_{on} current due to the random fluctuation in the dopants of the channel [35]. However, in FinFET devices, another parameter has a more significant impact. As a result of the active format of the fins, the fin channel is weakly doped to minimize variations in V_{th}. As a consequence, the V_{th} of weakly doped channels is mainly configured by the working-function of the metals adopted in the gate. The use of metal as gate material introduced some fluctuation in the work-function of the gate, mainly due to the presence of MGG.

Thus, although variations in gate length, fin height and fin width influence the electric behavior of FinFET devices, the fluctuations of the metal gate

work-function are the main source of expected variability for FinFETs sub 20 nm
[13,36,37]. Figure 5 illustrates this behavior considering the impact on the I_{on}
current.

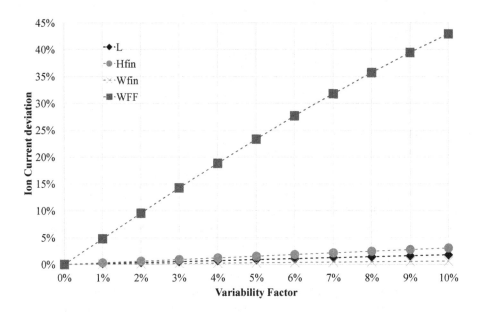

Fig. 5. Impact on I_{on} current due to work-function fluctuation [13].

In the ideal fabrication process, metal gates devices have the gates produced
with a unique metal uniformly aligned and very lower work-function deviation.
Nevertheless, in a real fabrication process, metal gate devices are generally produced with metals with different WF randomly aligned that implies in higher
WFF. WFFs are locally induced due to the polycrystalline nature of the metal
lead to potential surface variations, and it is caused by the dependency of metal
WF on the orientation of its grains, as illustrates the Fig. 6. The V_{th} fluctuation
due to MGG is close to a Gaussian distribution, and the standard deviation is
almost linearly proportional to metal-grain size [32].

4   Methodology

This work explores different transistor arrangements for a set of four logic functions (OAI21, OAI22, AOI211 and XOR) at the layout level to evaluate the
SET response under the process variability. Two different topologies of transistor
arrangement are investigated: 1) complex gate: optimized functions designed as a
complex logic gate CMOS topology; and 2) the multi-level logic of NAND2 gates:
the functions are converted using De Morgan's theorem into the only NAND2
transistor arrangements. Previous experiments also considered topologies using

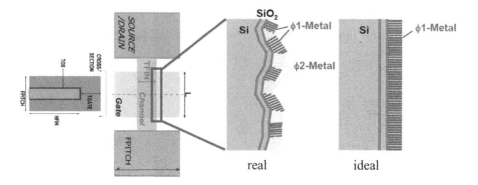

Fig. 6. FinFET devices: main geometric parameters and the random alignment of metal in real devices. Modified from [32] and [13].

only NOR2 and a mix of NAND2-NOR2-INV. However, the only NAND2 topology proved to be better, and it was chosen for this study [38]. Table 1 and Table 2 present the logic functions and the equations for the complex gate version and the converted multi-level logic composed by NAND2 version, respectively. Although they represent the same functions, the versions are intrinsically different, which is interesting, since the comparison of similar versions does not present many advantages about the variability [39]. Figure 7 presents the schematics of the OAI21 gate in its two versions highlighting all the sensitive nodes that were considered in the worst radiation sensitive case evaluation, which will be described in Subsect. 4.1.

Table 1. Complex gate functions. Modified from [40]

Logic function	Complex gate
OAI21	$Y = (A+B \cdot C)'$
OAI22	$Y = (A+B \cdot C+D)'$
AOI21	$Y = (A.B + C + D)'$
XOR	$Y = A.B' + A'.B$

All layouts were designed using the 7 nm FinFET ASAP7 Process Design Kit (PDK), developed by Arizona State University in partnership with ARM [16]. Among the different models and corners available on this PDK, this work considers the regular threshold voltage (RVT) transistor model at typical (TT) corner. Table 3 summarizes the key devices parameters of 7 nm FiFET ASAP technology. The nominal supply voltage is 0.7 V, at a typical temperature of 25 °C.

The layout of all cells adopts three fins as transistor sizing as recommended in the PDK to allow the internal routing of the cells [16]. The cell height is

Table 2. Multi-level Logic functions. Modified from [40]

Logic function	Multi-level version with NAND2 gates
OAI21	Y = (((A.A)' . (B.B)')' . C)'
OAI22	Y = (((A.A)' . (B.B)')' . ((C.C)' . (D.D)')')'
AOI211	Y = (X . X)' | X = (((A.B)'.(((C.C)'.(D.D))')'.((C.C)'.(D.D)')')'
XOR	Y = ((A . (B.B)')' . ((A.A)' . B)')'

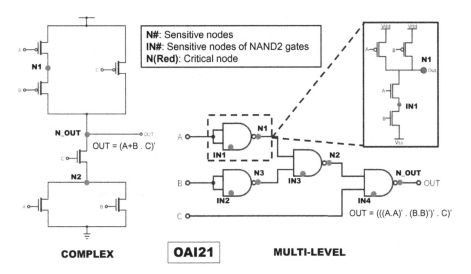

COMPLEX   **OAI21**   **MULTI-LEVEL**

Fig. 7. OAI21 schematic in complex and multi-level transistor arrangements. Modified from [40].

set to 7.5 tracks of metal 2 (M2) that correspond to 0.27 μm for all evaluated cells. The PDK assumes Extreme Ultraviolet (EUV) lithography for key layers, a decision based on its present near cost-effectiveness and resulting simpler layout rules. Non-EUV layers assume appropriate multiple patterning schemes, i.e., self-aligned quadruple patterning (SAQP), self-aligned double patterning (SADP) or litho-etch litho-etch (LELE), based on 193 nm optical immersion lithography [16]. The design rules, actual dimensions and underlying assumptions for some major layers are shown in Table 4.

The specific design rule derivation is explained for key layers at the front end of line (FEOL), middle of line (MOL) and back end of line (BEOL) of the predictive process modeled. As an example, the layout of OAI21 gate is presented on Fig. 8a and Fig. 8b in complex gate and multi-level logic topologies, respectively.

Table 3. Key parameters of 7 nm FinFET ASAP technology [16]

Parameters		7 nm
Supply Voltage		0.7 V
Gate Length (L_G)		21 nm
Fin Width (W_{FIN})		6.5 nm
Fin Height (H_{FIN})		32 nm
Oxide thickness (Tox)		2.1 nm
Channel Doping		$1 \times 10^{22} m^{-3}$
Source/Drain Doping		$2 \times 10^{26} m^{-3}$
Work	NFET	4.3720 eV
Function	PFET	4.8108 eV

All layouts were validated by Design Rule Check (DRC) and Layout Versus Schematic (LVS) steps. The extracted netlist with parasite capacitances is obtained and it was used for the radiation sensitivity evaluation. From the extracted netlist, SPICE simulations are performed. The input switching frequency is set at 500 MHz and inverters are connected to the input sources introducing realistic delays to the cells. The project flow carried out in this work can be seen in Fig. 9.

Table 4. Key layer lithography assumptions, widths and pitches [16]

Layer	Lithography	Width/drawn (nm)	Pitch (nm)
Fin	SAQP	6.5/7	27
Active (horizontal)	EUV	54/16	108
Gate	SADP	21/20	54
SDT/LISD	EUV	25/24	54[b]
LIG	EUV	16/16	54
VIA0–VIA3	EUV	18/18	25[a]
M1–M3	EUV	18/18	36
M4 and M5	SADP	24/24	48
VIA4 and VIA5	LELE	24/24	34[a]
M6 and M7	SADP	32/32	64
VIA6 and VIA7	LELE	32/32	45[a]
M8 and M9	SE	40/40	80
VIA8	SE	40/40	57[a]

[a]Corner to corner spacing as drawn.
[b]Horizontal only.

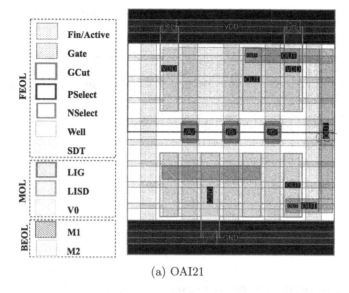

(a) OAI21

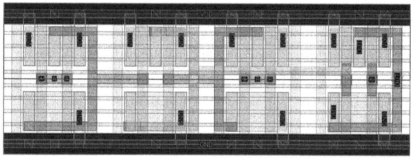

(b) OAI21_NAND

Fig. 8. OAI21 layout in the two topologies: (a) complex and (b) multi-level of NAND2 [40].

The SET fault injection is modeled as the Messenger's equation shown in Eq. 2 [41], where $Qcoll$ is the collected charge, τ_α $(1.64 \times 10^{-10}s)$ is the collect charge timing constant, τ_β $(5 \times 10^{-11}s)$ is the timing constant to establish the ion track and L $(21\ nm)$ is the charge collection depth. The values used in this work are the typical values used for simulations and experiments in silicon presented in [42], but modified to better characterize recent technologies, such as FinFET. This effect is reproduced on the SPICE simulation as a current source, simulating the SET effects on the transistors.

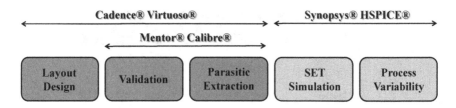

Fig. 9. Project flow for all analyzes [40].

$$I(t) = \frac{Qcoll}{\tau_\alpha - \tau_\beta}(e^{-\frac{t}{\tau_\alpha}} - e^{-\frac{t}{\tau_\beta}})$$

(2)

$$Qcoll = 10.8 \times L \times LET$$

4.1 Worst Radiation Sensitive Case

The first step in the radiation sensitivity evaluation was to identify the most sensitive node and input vector at each circuit. A fault injection campaign for a particle with LET estimated to 58 Mev. cm^2/mg was performed at each node of the circuits, as shown in Fig. 7 considering all possible input vectors. The definition of 58 Mev.cm^2/mg as the LET value used for the fault injection campaign was performed considering the highest LET that still characterizes a simulation at the ground level (LET $\leq$ 60 Mev.cm^2/mg) [43,44]. Two inverters were used for each input of the circuit and a single inverter for the output, to emulate the worst fan-out scenario, i.e. lowest fan-out (FO1). Consider the amplitude and the width of the SET pulses allow determining which node and input vector are the most sensitive [11] and characterize the worst radiation sensitive case. After the worst radiation sensitive case was obtained, each logic gate was fault injected considering this sensitive scenario, i.e., the most critical node, the sensitive input vector and the waveform of the pulse (strikes at P-type devices or N-type devices).

4.2 The SET Response at the Ideal Fabrication Process

This step evaluates the circuit under radiation effects but the effects of process variability are not considered. The LETth and the SET pulse width are used to characterize the SET response. Before starting the fault injection in the circuit, it is important to know the worst-case delay of each logic gate, which will be used to determine the LETth. Thus, the worst-case delay of each logic function considering both topologies was obtained. In this work, it is considered the SET effects, more specifically, when a transient pulse propagates to the inverter chain output. To calculate the LETth, two characteristics of the SET pulse were considered: amplitude and width. A fault in the circuit is considered when the

SET pulse amplitude exceeds half of the nominal supply voltage ($V_{DD}/2$) and the SET pulse width is greater than the circuit worst-case delay. That is, the metrics of the worst-case delay and the SET pulse width are used in obtaining the LETth, which is the primary metric used in this work. These values are used as a form of reference values to evaluate the process variability effects.

4.3   Process Variability Analysis

The analysis considering the process variability effects is performed keeping the same configurations of the previous step, however, considering the impact of the process variability through the WFF. Metal gate devices suffer from the WFF caused by the misalignment of metal grains in the gate. This fluctuation exhibits a multi-nominal distribution, which can be approximated by a Gaussian distribution if the number of grains on the surface of metal-gate is high enough (>10) [45], which corresponds to the FinFET ASAP7 model characteristics. The WFF effect due to process variation is explored through the statistical Monte Carlo simulation process, considering a Gaussian distribution with a 3-sigma deviation of 5% the WFF [13]. Two thousand simulations were run for each logic gate [45]. No correlation between different types of transistors was assumed, which means that PFET and NFET devices may come up with different variations in its parameters. Timing, SET pulse amplitude and width measurements were taken for each Monte Carlo simulation. The mean (μ) of these values is considered to calculate a new LETth, i.e., a LETth that considers the process variability impact. Also, the standard deviation (σ) of the mean values is obtained and a robustness analysis is performed using the normalized standard deviation (σ/μ) of the SET pulse width. The σ/μ is used to define how much a circuit is sensitive to process variability. The lower are the values of this ratio; the more robust to variability are the circuits.

5   Results

The worst radiation sensitive case was obtained before characterizing the SET response. The critical node, the most sensitive input vector and the transient pulse format, which compose the worst-case scenario for each logic function in both topologies are presented in Table 5.

To characterize the fault at a given node of the circuit, it is evaluated whether the SET pulse propagates to the circuit output. Thus, the probability of the critical node being the output itself is very high and this behavior is proven in the obtained results for both topologies. It can be seen that the most sensitive input vectors vary even considering the same logic function, due to the use of a different transistor arrangement. For OAI21 and AOI211 gates this difference between the input vectors is reflected in the format of the transient pulse (SET 101 or SET 010) that will be inserted in the node. Figure 10 demonstrates this behavior in more detail for the OAI21 gate.

Table 5. Worst Radiation Sensitive Case [40]

Logic function	Worst radiation sensitive case	Complex gate	Multi-level
OAI21	Critical node	OUT	OUT
	Input vector	001	011
	Transient pulse	1-0-1	0-1-0
OAI22	Critical node	OUT	OUT
	Input vector	1001	0101
	Transient pulse	0-1-0	0-1-0
AOI211	Critical node	OUT	OUT
	Input vector	0000	0101
	Transient pulse	1-0-1	0-1-0
XOR	Critical node	OUT	OUT
	Input vector	11	11
	Transient pulse	0-1-0	0-1-0

5.1   SET Evaluation Under the Ideal Fabrication Process

The worst-case propagation delays of the four logic functions in the two topologies, considering the ideal fabrication process, are shown in Table 6. In addition to presenting some differences in performance between the use of complex and multi-level topologies, the propagation times are necessary to obtain the LETth.

Table 6. Worst-case propagation delay at nominal conditions [40]

Logic function	Worst-case delay (ps)	
	Complex gate	Multi-level
OAI21	7.79	18.29
OAI22	9.63	18.48
AOI211	13.42	36.63
XOR	11.68	20.02

Figure 11 shows the SET pulse width measured when the amplitude of this same pulse exceeds half of the nominal supply voltage. To calculate the LETth of each logic gate, it is important to note that all values of the SET pulse width shown in Fig. 11 are greater than the worst-case delays shown in Table 6, characterizing the fault in the circuit output. The SET pulse width values follow much the same behavior as the delay values. The multi-level topology presents SET pulse width about 77% larger in comparison to the complex topology. This behavior does not necessarily mean a higher sensitivity of the multi-level topology to the radiation effects. The SET pulse width considering ideal fabrication

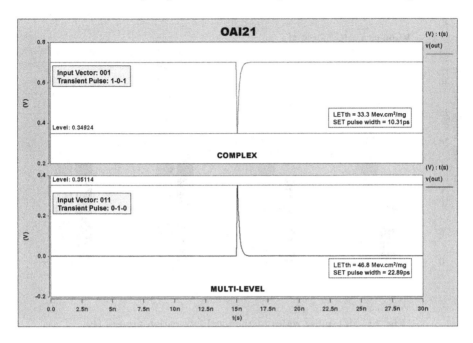

Fig. 10. The difference of transient pulse format inserted in the critical node (OUT) of complex and multi-level topologies of OAI21 gate [40].

tends to be higher for the multi-level topology since the functions implemented in this transistor arrangement are slower than the same ones implemented in the complex topology. That is, if the SET pulse width is less than the logic gate delay, the fault would be masked.

The larger SET pulse width of the multi-level topology is not reflected in the LETth calculation, as can be seen in Table 7. LETth values may seem high considering the analyzed logic gates. However, similar work highlights the robustness of the 7 nm FinFET technology, considering other logic functions [14] and also majority voter circuits [15]. NAND and NOR voters have no-fault event (at nominal supply voltage) considering a LET value of 15 Mev.cm^2/mg, for example [15]. For the OAI21 and AOI211, the LETth considering the multi-level topology is 40.54% and 72% higher than the LETth of the complex topology, respectively. XOR gate and the OAI22 gate present a difference practically null, approximately 1%. The results demonstrate that multi-level topology is more robust to the radiation effects considering the ideal fabrication process since it presents higher LETth values in comparison with complex topology. This behavior is related to the regularity of the layouts developed. The OAI22 and XOR gates, even in the complex topology, are already quite regular. Therefore, the use of multi-level topology for these functions has practically no impact.

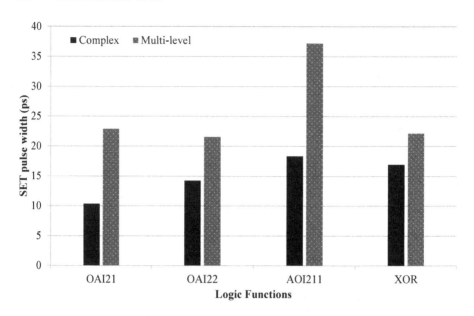

Fig. 11. SET pulse width at the ideal fabrication process [40].

Table 7. LETth at ideal conditions [40]

Logic function	LETth (Mev.cm^2/mg)	
	Complex gate	Multi-level
OAI21	33.3	46.8
OAI22	47.4	46.8
AOI211	27.5	47.3
XOR	46.8	46.9

5.2 The SET Response Under WFF

As the analysis carried out considering only the radiation effects, in the process variability analysis, the worst-case propagation delay of each logic gate is also measured but considering the WFF impact. Table 8 shows the mean (μ), standard deviation (σ) and normalized standard deviation (σ/μ) of the delays for all analyzed logic gates.

Figure 12 shows the mean of the SET pulse width for each logic function implemented in the two topologies, considering the WFF impact. Unlike the analysis under ideal conditions, on average the SET pulse width for complex topology is higher ranging from 4 ps to 9 ps of difference in comparison with the multi-level topology. Only for the AOI211 gate that this ratio is not established and the SET pulse width for the multi-level topology is still about 4 ps higher. Considering only the SET pulse width, the complex topology is more sensitive to the process variability effects.

Table 8. Worst-case propagation delay under WFF [40]

Logic gates	Worst-case delay (ps)					
	Complex gate			Multi-level		
	μ	σ	σ/μ (%)	μ	σ	σ/μ (%)
OAI21	8.43	2.56	30.37	19.21	4.00	20.83
OAI22	11.18	3.43	30.71	19.42	4.08	21.02
AOI211	14.71	4.64	31.56	38.52	7.62	19.78
XOR	12.49	2.84	22.73	20.95	4.39	20.98

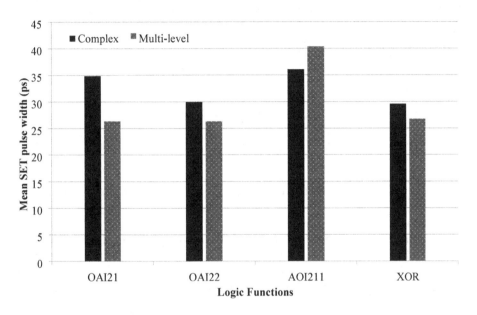

Fig. 12. Impact of WFF on SET pulse width [40].

The normalized standard deviation of the SET pulse width is shown in Fig. 13. The smaller this deviation, the more robust to the variability effects is the topology used in each logic function. Although the complex topology presents higher mean values of the SET pulse width, these values deviate less than the values considering the multi-level topology for three logic functions. This difference between the deviations is not very significant, being 2.75% for the XOR gate and approximately 19% for the OAI21 gate. As in the previous analysis, for the AOI211 gate, the behavior is inverse and the multi-level topology ends up having the smallest deviation. Although the complex topology suffers from increasing the SET pulse width due to the impact of the WFF, these values have a smaller deviation than the ones considering the multi-level topology.

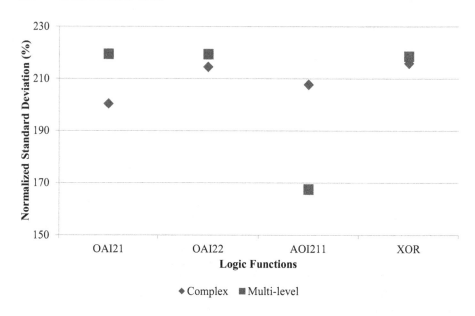

Fig. 13. Normalized standard deviation of SET pulse width [40].

In the current analysis, the deviations are normalized by the mean, i.e., a smaller value of the SET pulse width means for the 2000 Monte Carlo simulations performed, tends to a more significant deviation. Still, this analysis allows observing the quantity and how much the values deviate from the mean values presented in the previous analysis. This behavior is reflected in the probability that the WFF will more or less impact the circuit. The multi-level topology has a slightly higher probability of having a SET pulse width value greater than the mean.

After obtaining the SET pulse width mean values and confirming that they are higher than the mean worst-case delay of each logic gate, the fault characterization in the circuit output is complete. Then a new LETth can be calculated considering the WFF impact. Figure 14 shows the difference between the LETth obtained considering the ideal fabrication process and the impact of the WFF for all the logic functions in the two topologies of the study. For all logic functions regardless of the adopted topology, the LETth considering the WFF impact is smaller than the LETth at ideal fabrication process. That is, due to WFF, a smaller amount of energy transferred by the particle is required to cause a disturbance in the circuit. All evaluated circuits become more sensitive to the radiation effects. Also, in the comparison between the different transistor arrangements used in each logic gate, the multi-level topology presents the best results. For the OAI21 and AOI211 gates, the LETth considering the impact of the WFF is significantly larger in comparison with the complex topology, being 38.4% and 88% respectively. For the OAI22 and XOR gates, the LETth is smaller in the same comparison. However, signalizing a not statistically significant difference, 3.1% and 1.3%, respectively.

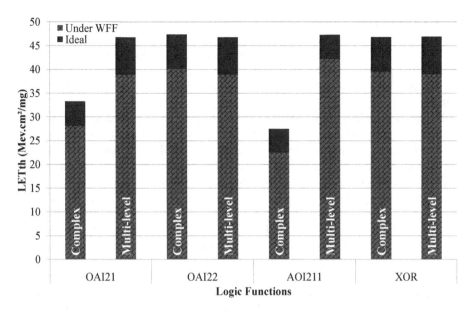

Fig. 14. Difference of LETth considering ideal fabrication process and WFF impact [40].

5.3   Area Impact

It is important to highlight one more important metric when comparing the two topologies used in this study. Table 9 shows the number of transistors and the area of each logic gate in the two topologies. All gates designed with the multi-level logic arrangement show an increase in the area used. In most cases, the area using the multi-level topology is more than three times larger than the complex gate topology. The OAI22 and AOI211 gates have the largest variation, the multi-level layout is about 4.5 times larger than the traditional layout. The XOR gate has the smallest increase in the comparison between the two topologies, approximately 67%.

Table 9. Comparison of number of transistors and area for complex gate and multi-level logic topologies

Logic function	# Transistors		Area (μm^2)	
	Complex gate	Multi-level	Complex gate	Multi-level
OAI21	6	16	0.085	0.271
OAI22	8	28	0.102	0.475
AOI211	8	28	0.102	0.475
XOR	10	20	0.203	0.339

6   Conclusion

This work evaluated the radiation robustness through the SET response, considering the process variability effects. A set of logic functions implemented in two different transistor topologies was compared using the 7 nm FinFET ASAP7 PDK.

Regarding the ideal fabrication process, the multi-level topology presents the largest SET pulse widths; however, it also shows the highest LETth values for three of the four analyzed logic functions. That is, at least considering the ideal fabrication, the SET pulse width has no direct relation to the LETth value. If the design objective is a more robust circuit to radiation effects, regardless of performance, power and area penalties, the multi-level topology is the best option.

Considering the process variability impact, the complex topology presents a large variation of SET pulse width values, even exceeding the multi-level topology values. Even with this variation, the LETth of the multi-level topology remains larger for two of the four logic functions and practically the same for the other two. This behavior confirms the conclusion of the previous analysis, in which the SET pulse width does not have a direct relation with the LETth value and the multi-level topology is the best option to deal with the SET effects.

The LETth values of each circuit can also be related to the environment where they will operate. On average, the LETth values of this study are around 42 Mev.cm^2/mg considering ideal conditions and around 36 Mev.cm^2/mg considering the WFF impact. Despite being high values, the logic functions are still susceptible to faults at the ground level. That is, the robustness of the this types of circuits must be considered even for applications that operate in a terrestrial environment.

In addition to the analysis of the behavior of each topology considering ideal fabrication and process variability, the impact of the WFF on the SET response was also evaluated. For all logic functions regardless of the topology used, the LETth value is lower, i.e., the logic gates become more sensitive to the radiation effects when considering the process variability impact. This analysis is of utmost importance because it indicates that to determine the LETth of a circuit, one must also consider other reliability factors such as process variability.

Acknowledgments. This research is partially supported by the Brazilian Coordination of Improvement of Higher Level Personnel (CAPES) - Finance Code 001, by CNPq and by FAPERGS.

References

1. Baumann, R.: The impact of technology scaling on soft error rate performance and limits to the efficacy of error correction. In: Digest. International Electron Devices Meeting, pp. 329–332. IEEE (2002)
2. Heidel, D.F., et al.: Single-event upsets and multiple-bit upsets on a 45 nm SOI SRAM. IEEE Trans. Nuclear Sci. **56**(6), 3499–3504 (2009)

3. Boudenot, J.C.: Radiation space environment. In: Velazco, R., Fouillat, P., Reis, R. (eds.) Radiation Effects on Embedded Systems, pp. 1–9. Springer, Dordrecht (2007). https://doi.org/10.1007/978-1-4020-5646-8
4. Stassinopoulos, E., Raymond, J.P.: The space radiation environment for electronics. Proc. IEEE **76**(11), 1423–1442 (1988)
5. Gadlage, M.J., et al.: Scaling trends in set pulse widths in sub-100 nm bulk CMOS processes. IEEE Trans. Nuclear Sci. **57**(6), 3336–3341 (2010)
6. Auth, C., et al.: A 22nm high performance and low-power CMOS technology featuring fully-depleted tri-gate transistors, self-aligned contacts and high density MIM capacitors. In: Symposium on VLSI Technology (VLSIT), pp. 131–132, June 2012
7. Brown, A.R., Watling, J.R., Asenov, A.: Intrinsic parameter fluctuations due to random grain orientations in high-κ gate stacks. J. Comput. Electron. **5**(4), 333–336 (2006)
8. Kleeberger, V.B., Graeb, H., Schlichtmann, U.: Predicting future product performance: modeling and evaluation of standard cells in finfet technologies. In: Proceedings of the 50th Annual Design Automation Conference, p. 33. ACM (2013)
9. Artola, L., Hubert, G., Alioto, M.: Comparative soft error evaluation of layout cells in finfet technology. Microelectron. Reliabil. **54**(9–10), 2300–2305 (2014)
10. El-Mamouni, F., et al.: Laser-and heavy ion-induced charge collection in bulk finfets. IEEE Trans. Nuclear Sci. **58**(6), 2563–2569 (2011)
11. Ferlet-Cavrois, V., Massengill, L.W., Gouker, P.: Single event transients in digital CMOS–a review. IEEE Trans. Nuclear Sci. **60**(3), 1767–1790 (2013)
12. Artola, L., Hubert, G., Schrimpf, R.: Modeling of radiation-induced single event transients in SOI finfets. In: 2013 IEEE International Reliability Physics Symposium (IRPS), SE-1, IEEE (2013)
13. Meinhardt, C., Zimpeck, A.L., Reis, R.A.: Predictive evaluation of electrical characteristics of sub-22 nm finfet technologies under device geometry variations. Microelectron. Reliabil. **54**(9–10), 2319–2324 (2014)
14. Zimpeck, A.L., Artola, L., Hubert, G., Meinhardt, C., Kastensmidt, F.L., Reis, R.: Circuit-level hardening techniques to mitigate soft errors in finfet logic gates. In: 2019 19th European Conference on Radiation and Its Effects on Components and Systems (RADECS), IEEE (2019)
15. Aguiar, Y.Q., et al.: Evaluation of radiation-induced soft error in majority voters designed in 7 nm finfet technology. Microelectron. Reliabil. **76**, 660–664 (2017)
16. Clark, L.T., et al.: Asap7: a 7-nm finfet predictive process design kit. Microelectron. J. **53**, 105–115 (2016)
17. Noh, J., et al.: Study of neutron soft error rate (ser) sensitivity: investigation of upset mechanisms by comparative simulation of finfet and planar mosfet SRAMS. IEEE Trans. Nuclear Sci. **62**(4), 1642–1649 (2015)
18. Sierawski, B.D., et al.: Muon-induced single event upsets in deep-submicron technology. IEEE Trans. Nuclear Sci. **57**(6), 3273–3278 (2010)
19. NOAA: National geophysical data center (2015)
20. Hughes, H., et al.: Total ionizing dose radiation effects on 14 nm finfet and SOI UTBB technologies. In: IEEE Radiation Effects Data Workshop (REDW). **2015**, 1–6 (2015). IEEE
21. Chatterjee, I., et al.: Geometry dependence of total-dose effects in bulk finfets. IEEE Trans. Nuclear Sci. **61**(6), 2951–2958 (2014)
22. Azambuja, J.R., Kastensmidt, F., Becker, J.: Hybrid Fault Tolerance Techniques to Detect Transient Faults in Embedded Processors. Springer, Cham (2014). https://doi.org/10.1007/978-3-319-06340-9

23. Munteanu, D., Autran, J.L.: Modeling and simulation of single-event effects in digital devices and ICS. IEEE Trans. Nuclear Sci. **55**(4), 1854–1878 (2008)
24. Chorasia, J., Jasani, K., Shah, A.: Realization of various error mitigation techniques for SRAM based FPGA. In: 2017 2nd International Conference for Convergence in Technology (I2CT), pp. 55–59. IEEE (2017)
25. Bhuva, B., Tam, N., Massengill, L., Ball, D., Chatterjee, I., McCurdy, M., Alles, M.: Multi-cell soft errors at advanced technology nodes. IEEE Trans. Nuclear Sci. **62**(6), 2585–2591 (2015)
26. Balen, T.R.: Efeitos da radiação em dispositivos analógicos programáveis (FPAAs) e técnicas de proteção. Ph.D. thesis, Universidade Federal do Rio Grande do Sul (2010)
27. Baumann, R.C.: Radiation-induced soft errors in advanced semiconductor technologies. IEEE Trans. Device Mater. Reliability **5**(3), 305–316 (2005)
28. Seifert, N., et al.: Soft error susceptibilities of 22 nm tri-gate devices. IEEE Trans. Nuclear Sci. **59**(6), 2666–2673 (2012)
29. Lee, S.: Radiation-induced soft error rate analyses for 14 nm finfet SRAM devices. In: IEEE International Reliability Physics Symposium. IEEE **2015**, 4B-1 (2015)
30. Fang, Y.P., Oates, A.S.: Neutron-induced charge collection simulation of bulk finfet srams compared with conventional planar SRAMS. IEEE Trans. Device Mater. Reliabil. **11**(4), 551–554 (2011)
31. Nassif, S.R.: Process variability at the 65nm node and beyond. In: Custom Integrated Circuits Conference, 2008. CICC 2008. IEEE, pp. 1–8. IEEE (2008)
32. Dadgour, H.F., Endo, K., De, V.K., Banerjee, K.: Grain-orientation induced work function variation in nanoscale metal-gate transistors — part II: implications for process, device, and circuit design. IEEE Transactions on Electron Devices **57**(10), 2515–2525 (2010)
33. Topaloglu, R.O.: Design with finfets: design rules, patterns, and variability. In: 2013 IEEE/ACM International Conference on Computer-Aided Design (ICCAD), pp. 569–571, IEEE (2013)
34. Endo, K., et al.: Variation analysis of tin finfets. In: Semiconductor Device Research Symposium, 2009. ISDRS 2009. International, pp. 1–2. IEEE (2009)
35. Meinhardt, C.: Variabilidade em FinFETs. Ph.D. thesis, Universidade Federal do Rio Grande do Sul (2014)
36. Henderson, C.L.: Failure analysis techniques for a 3d world. Microelectron. Reliabil. **53**(9–11), 1171–1178 (2013)
37. Saha, S.K.: Modeling process variability in scaled CMOS technology. IEEE Design Test Comput. **27**(2), 8–16 (2010)
38. Brendler, L.H., Zimpeck, A.L., Meinhardt, C., Reis, R.: Evaluating the impact of process variability and radiation effects on different transistor arrangements. In: IFIP/IEEE International Conference on Very Large Scale Integration (VLSI-SoC), pp. 71–76 (2018)
39. Zimpeck, A.L., et al.: Impact of different transistor arrangements on gate variability. Microelectron. Reliabil. **88**, 111–115 (2018)
40. Brendler, L.H., Zimpeck, A.L., Meinhardt, C., Reis, R.: Evaluation of set under process variability on finfet multi-level design. In: 2019 IFIP/IEEE 27th International Conference on Very Large Scale Integration (VLSI-SoC), pp. 179–184. IEEE (2019)
41. Messenger, G.: Collection of charge on junction nodes from ion tracks. IEEE Trans. Nuclear Sci. **29**(6), 2024–2031 (1982)

42. Carreno, V.A., Choi, G., Iyer, R.: Analog-digital simulation of transient-induced logic errors and upset susceptibility of an advanced control system. NASA Technical Memorandum **4241** (1990)
43. Javanainen, A., et al.: Linear energy transfer of heavy ions in silicon. IEEE Trans. Nuclear Sci. **54**(4), 1158–1162 (2007)
44. Hubert, G., Artola, L.: Single-event transient modeling in a 65-nm bulk cmos technology based on multi-physical approach and electrical simulations. IEEE Trans. Nuclear Sci. **60**(6), 4421–4429 (2013)
45. Alioto, M., Consoli, E., Palumbo, G.: Variations in nanometer CMOS flip-flops: Part I—impact of process variations on timing. IEEE Transactions on Circuits and Systems I: Regular Papers **62**(8), 2035–2043 (2015)

Efficient Soft Error Vulnerability Analysis Using Non-intrusive Fault Injection Techniques

Vitor Bandeira[1]([⊠]), Felipe Rosa[1], Ricardo Reis[1], and Luciano Ost[2]

[1] PPGC/PGMicro—UFRGS, Porto Alegre, Brazil
{vvbandeira,frdarosa,reis}@inf.ufrgs.br
[2] Loughborough University, Loughborough, UK
l.ost@lboro.ac.uk

Abstract. Electronic computing systems are integrating modern multicore processors and GPUs aiming to perform complex software stacks in different life-critical systems, including health devices and emerging self-driving cars. Such systems are expected to experience at least one soft error per day in the near future, which may lead to life-threatening failures. To prevent these failures, critical system must be tested and verified while under realistic workloads. This paper presents four novel non-intrusive fault injection techniques that enable full fault injection control and inspection of multicore systems behavior in the presence of faults. Proposed techniques were integrated into a fault injection framework and verified through a real automotive case study with up to 43 billions instructions. Results show that compared to traditional methods, the new techniques can increase the efficiency of fault injection campaigns during early development phase by 32.28%.

1 Introduction

Leading companies in automotive, medical, consumer electronics, and high-performance computing (HPC) industry employ general-purpose multicore processors and graphics processing units (GPUs) in their applications. The rising demand for powerful computing capacity and energy efficiency of multicore components lead to high-frequency clock operation and multiple voltage domains within the same chip. In addition to that, the increasing number of internal elements (e.g., cores, memory cells, registers) is making multicore-based systems more vulnerable to both hard and soft radiation-induced errors [1,2]. Managing the soft error occurrence is crucial to accomplishing a reliable and efficient operation in several domains. In an HPC system, an undetected soft error can impact on the efficiency of resource utilization (i.e., re-execution of applications/jobs), which may lead to financial loss. In turn, the occurrence of a soft error may cause a critical failure on a self-driving car, which can put human lives at risk.

Given trends for ever-increasing application/kernel code size and complexity, cost-effective tools to assess the soft error resilience of multicore-based systems

© IFIP International Federation for Information Processing 2020
Published by Springer Nature Switzerland AG 2020
C. Metzler et al. (Eds.): VLSI-SoC 2019, IFIP AICT 586, pp. 115–137, 2020.
https://doi.org/10.1007/978-3-030-53273-4_6

become of utmost importance to identify the most unreliable system functionalities early in the design phase. In this regard, the high cost and time inherent
to hardware-based fault injection methods make more efficient simulation-based
fault injection frameworks key to test reliability. Most fault injection simulators
available in the literature offer a restricted number of fault injection exploration
capabilities such as injection of bit-flips in memory [3], general-purpose registers and some other CPU components (e.g., load/store queue) [4,5]. However,
with the growing complexity of both processor and software architectures, more
appropriate fault injection techniques and tools are required. The underlying
techniques and tools must provide engineers with full fault injection control and
inspection of the system's behavior under the presence of faults.

This paper proposes *four novel non-intrusive* fault injection techniques
enabling engineers to perform in-depth and relevant soft error evaluation[1],
addressing the gap between the available fault injection tools and the industry requirements. These techniques consider the particularities of each software
stack component (e.g., kernel, hypervisor, or application function) running on
the target system. To maximize this research impact, we adopt a new tool called
SOFIA (S̲oft error F̲ault I̲njection A̲nalysis) [6]. SOFIA integrates the proposed fault injection techniques along with several facilities (e.g., error tracer
module), which enable to identify and classify the effects of soft errors on the
system behavior, considering both hardware and software architectures. SOFIA
is based on the Multicore Developer (M*DEV) virtual platform[2], and its implementation is highly autonomous and requires little human interaction, after its
configuration.

This work is organized as follows, in Sect. 2 we review relevant works regarding simulation frameworks and soft error analysis. Section 3 presents our tool,
its components and the simulation flow. Section 4 reviews two traditional fault
injection techniques and introduces the four novel techniques, then Sect. 5
show results that support the consistency and runtime advantages of our tool.
Sections 6 and 7 contain results of soft error analysis using SOFIA for a multicore benchmark and an automotive application, respectively. Finally, in Sect. 8
we conclude and discuss future works.

2   Related Works in Fault Injection Frameworks

Authors in [7] present the Relyzer, a hybrid simulation framework for SPARC
core using Simics [8] and GEMS [9] simulators coupled with a pruning technique to reduce the number of injected faults. The Relyzer enables the injection
of faults into architectural integer registers, and output latches of the address
generation unit. In [10], a QEMU-based fault injection framework is proposed
targeting general-purpose registers. Fault injection campaigns [10] consider an

---

[1] A soft error campaign (and thus the evaluation of said campaign) in the context
   of this paper is considered to be relevant when the result can either identify the
   existence of vulnerabilities or their source.
[2] www.imperas.com.

X86 architecture running four in-house applications on the top of RTEMS kernel. F-SEFI is another fault injection framework that relies on QEMU [11,12]. This work employs the QEMU using a hypervisor mode, i.e., it does not emulate the complete target system, which reduces both its fault injection and soft error analysis capabilities.

The authors in [3] propose the GeFIN and the MaFIN tools, which support the injection of faults in microarchitectural components such as general-purpose and cache control registers. Conducted experiments consider the execution of 10 bare metal benchmarks. Rosa *et al.* [13] propose the OVPsim-FIM framework on which several fault injection campaigns were performed in Arm processors running FreeRTOS kernel. Authors in [5] propose a gem5-based framework that allows injecting faults in different microarchitecture elements (e.g., reorder buffer, load-store queue, register file). In [5], each element is subject to small 300-long fault campaign for each of the ten applications collected from both MiBench and SPEC-Int 2006 benchmark suites. A similar gem5-based fault injection framework is described in [4].

The reviewed frameworks only support the injection of bit-flips in memory and general single-core processor components, including registers, load/store queue, among others (Table 1). Another drawback of such approaches is the lack of detailed and customizable post-simulation analysis. Reviewed works classify the detected soft errors according to the inspection of the processor architecture context (i.e., memory and registers), disregarding the impact of software components (e.g., functions and variables) on the system reliability. Further, such approaches typically report low simulation performances of up to 3 MIPS [7], which restricts the number and the complexity of fault injection campaigns. While some works consider a single ISA [7], others use only in-house applications [10] or bare-metal implementations [3–5].

Different from the above works, SOFIA offers four novel non-intrusive fault injection techniques that provide engineers with flexibility and full control over the fault injection process, allowing to disentangle the cause and effect relationship between an injected fault and the occurrence of possible soft errors, targeting a specific critical application, operating system or API structure/function. Our contribution also differs from all previous projects by allowing users to define bespoke fault injection analysis and soft error vulnerability classifications, taking into account both software and hardware components particularities and the system requirements. SOFIA framework was developed based on M*DEV simulator, and it enables to inject faults at a speed of over 3,900 MIPS while running complete software stacks, allowing fast soft error reliability assessment during early design exploration phases. Further, distinctly from other reviewed works, the promoted tool does not alter the simulator engine by using already provided extension ports to access system hardware components.

Table 1. State-of-the-art in virtual platform (VP) fault injection simulators (Sim.), where 'N/A' means 'not available'.

Ref.	VP Sim.	Kernel	Fault injection description
[3]	MARSS gem5	N/A	• General-purpose registers • L1 and L2 cache • Load/store queue
[4]	gem5	N/A	• General-purpose registers • Pipeline and functional units registers • Load/store queue
[5]	gem5	N/A	• Eleven microarchitectural components
[7]	Simics+GEMS	Open-Solaris	• General-purpose registers • Address generation latches
[10]	QEMU	RTEMS	• General-purpose registers
[11]	QEMU	N/A	• General-purpose registers • L1 and L2 cache • Physical Memory
[13]	OVPsim	FreeRTOS	• General-purpose registers • Physical Memory
This Work	M*DEV	Linux	• General-purpose registers • Physical Memory • Virtual Memory • Variables • Function Code • Function Lifespan

3 SOFIA: Fault Injection Framework

To validate and demonstrate the potential of proposed techniques, the M*DEV simulator was selected due to its support to more than 170 processor model variants (e.g., MIPS, Arm, single-core, dual-core) including state-of-the-art multicore processors and ISAs. Note that proposed techniques can be implemented in any virtual platform or simulation environment that provides access to the system memory management unit (MMU) translation tables. This section details the SOFIA fault injection framework and its main features.

3.1 Fault Model

SOFIA emulates the occurrence of single-bit-upsets (SBUs) by injecting faults into pre-selected register or memory locations during the execution of a given software stack. This paper focus on SBUs for brevity, nevertheless, the tool applies a 64 bit-wide to each target locations enabling any arbitrary multiple-bit upset fault injection. The default fault injection configuration (e.g., bit location, injection time) relies on a random uniform function, which is a well-accepted fault injection technique since it covers the majority of possible faults on a system at a low computation cost [14]. Fault injections occur during the target application lifespan (i.e., the operating system (OS) startup is not subject to faults), which includes OS system calls and parallelization API subroutines arising during this period. This approach allows identifying unexpected application execution errors (e.g., segmentation fault), which are associated with adopted OS components or API libraries.

3.2   Fault Injector Module

SOFIA incorporates a fault injector module (FIM) with five main components: (1) configuration, (2) fault monitor, (3) fault injector, (4) error analysis, and (5) exception handler. The configuration component (1) starts the simulation, reads the configuration file (i.e., fault list), and setups the monitor component (2), which is responsible for controlling the simulator flow. When the simulation reaches the injection time, the fault injector (3) is invoked, and it alters the microarchitectural elements (e.g., register file, physical memory) according to the adopted fault injection technique. After the application execution, the soft error analysis component (4) compares the simulator context against the reference execution (i.e., the application execution without fault injection) to classify the application behavior under fault presence. The analysis considers memory, register context (including the program counter), and the number of executed instructions. Additionally, component (5) automatically terminates the fault injection simulation after an execution time threshold defined by the user and captures unexpected termination events in the target application and OS .

3.3   Fault Injection Simulation Flow

The SOFIA fault injection flow (Fig. 1) comprises four phases: The faultless execution (phase 1) first cross-compiles the application source code and then simulates the target application without fault influence, aiming to verify its correctness and extract reference information, i.e., registers context and final memory state. During the simulation, SOFIA acquires additional information based on the selected fault injection technique. The second phase deploys the fault generation tool considering the injection time, the register name, and the target bit for each fault injection technique. In the third and most complex phase, the SOFIA tool starts by configuring an instruction counter event, which is defined according to the insertion time. Then, the FIM reads the fault characteristics and introduces a bit-flip according to the adopted fault injection techniques. After the application conclusion, the fault injection module compares the application outcome (e.g., the number of executed instructions, registers context, and memory state) under fault influence with the information acquired during phase 1. In the last phase, SOFIA assembles all the individual reports to create a single file, performs several statistical analysis (e.g., average, worst, and best cases) and generates individual plots.

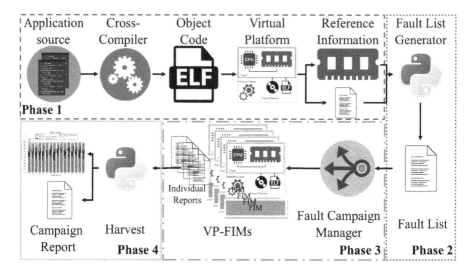

Fig. 1. SOFIA fault injection flow.

3.4   Soft Error Analysis and Classification

The *soft error analysis module* investigates the target platform software stack (i.e., application, drivers, OS under the fault injection influence) after each simulation to expose discrepancies against an identical software stack in a faultless execution. Fault injections campaigns must be followed by a customizable and flexible soft error analysis, which provides engineers with appropriate means to isolate and identify not only the occurrence but also the system characteristics (i.e., software and hardware) contributing to the error. SOFIA enables the addition of customizable inspections based on application code, execution pattern, or even final results without any modification on the original target software code. For instance, the tool can be used to check a critical variable against a predefined value or another internal variable (e.g., data duplication) ensuring the application correctness. All the soft error analysis conducted in this paper rely on a well known [15], and on a customized classification proposed by the Authors of this work.

Cho *et al.* [15] classification considers: **Vanished**, if no fault traces are left. **Application Output Not Affected** (ONA), when the resulting memory is not modified; nevertheless, one or more remaining bits of the architectural state is incorrect. **Application Memory Mismatch** (OMM), the application terminates without any error indication; however, the resulting memory is affected. **Unexpected termination** (UT), the application terminates abnormally with an error indication. **Hang**, the application does not finish, requiring a preemptive removal after a threshold execution time. Depending on the application's nature, Cho's classification may be inadequate to express possible misbehavior.

SOFIA enables the creation of new classifications to achieve a customized soft error analysis. This feature is fully explored in the Sect. 7.1, Automotive Results Analysis.

4   Fault Injection Techniques

The SOFIA framework supports six fault injection techniques (**A–F**), which are illustrated in Fig. 2. These techniques make SOFIA suitable for fast and detailed soft error vulnerability analysis at an early design space exploration stage. Obtaining early indications of soft errors enable reliability software developers to adjust the application code (or portion of it) as needed. Note that the *six* techniques target the register file or physical memory without altering the target software stack (i.e., application, OS, and related libraries).

4.1   Register File

Random register file fault injection is a well-accepted mechanism that homogeneously covers the majority of soft errors, striking both application and operating system codes. This approach ignores distinct regions of criticality (i.e., function and data structures), leading to reduced code coverage that narrows the number of errors that can be detected during the development phase. The SOFIA framework can access the processor model register file to inject faults in any visible register without altering the application under test.

4.2   Physical Memory

Another well-known fault injection technique relies on the inversion of single-bits into the system physical memory, which accurately reproduces its exposition to radiation particles. Nevertheless, the lack of correlation between the injected faults location in the physical memory and the application-level data structures may lead to inadequate error coverage. To enable this technique, SOFIA supports access to both the physical memory and the injection of bit-flips at any moment during the application execution.

Traditional fault injection frameworks only support the techniques (**A**) and (**B**), which rely on a random selection in terms of fault injection location (e.g., one bit from the complete memory range or a register) and time. Although both are well-accepted mechanisms since they cover the majority of possible faults on a system, it lacks correlation between faults and errors. Faults are arbitrary distributed throughout the execution, striking both application and operating system codes. Underlying techniques may lead to low code coverage, which restricts the identification of soft errors due to the large number of errors that are masked. Fault injection techniques (**C–F**) aim to minimize such limitation while keeping the software stack unmodified.

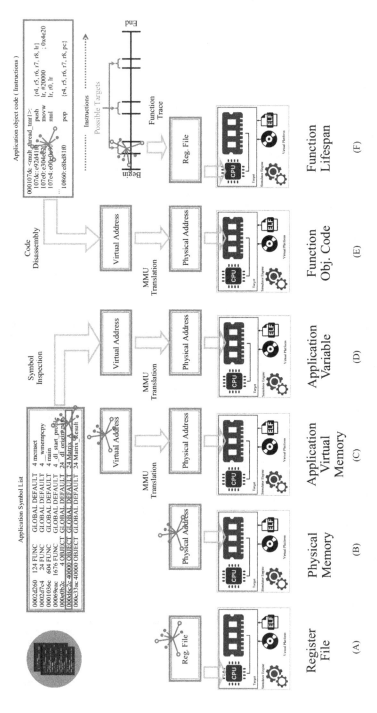

Fig. 2. Fault injection techniques targets (Sect. 4). The red mark indicates where the bit-flip occurs and the yellow arrows its propagation. (Color figure online)

4.3   Application Virtual Memory

Most operating systems abstract the physical hardware implementation of the memory from the user by making available a set of virtual address ranges while using a translation table to connect both virtual and physical ranges. The promoted technique (**C**) automatically extracts the virtual addressing ranges from the target application object code, including different segment addresses (e.g., data, code, read-only, debug) during its phase 1 (Sect. 3.3) to create an appropriated fault lists (phase 2). For each fault injection, SOFIA accesses the target OS virtual memory translation table, acquires the correspondent physical to a virtual address, and injects the bit-flip in the system physical memory representing the target application-level memory. The advantage of this technique over the purely physical memory fault injection relies on the fact that it targets the application virtual address space without affecting the OS, the execution of other applications, or libraries, reducing the number of faults campaigns that must be conducted since soft errors are more likely to manifest earlier. This approach enables the user to target a particular application running in a complex environment with multiple applications and libraries.

4.4   Application Variables and Data Structures

To precisely evaluate an application's vulnerability to soft errors the fault injection infrastructure should provide efficient means to correlate errors with particular application blocks or data structures. Technique (**D**) (Application Variable) enables the engineer to direct bit-flip injections into particular data structures, allowing to isolate and identify the most vulnerable ones with a lower number of fault campaigns and higher precision. Further, this approach allows evaluating the impact of specific application variables on the soft error reliability without affecting the application control flow. For this purpose, the user is asked to inform the target variable name, enabling SOFIA to automatically capture the variable virtual address to create a set of faults targeting the data structure virtual addressing. During any point of the application execution, the variable will suffer a single bit-flip on its physical memory representation using the translation table.

4.5   Function Object Code

To explore the impact of errors on functions assembly code, this work proposes the technique (**E**) that limits the injection spectrum to the memory region which holds the target function code—instructions and local variables. In the real world, the probability of a particular function being hit by a transient fault depends on its size (i.e., number of instructions) in comparison with the complete memory range. This technique enables the user to investigate the soft error reliability of a particular function independent of its size or execution time.

4.6 Function Lifespan

The majority of frameworks rely on a random time generation scheme where faults are scattered over the entire application and OS execution. Consequently, the number of faults per function depends on its execution time and not on its criticality level. One can argue that the critical system functions are those with the most extended execution, however, any function can produce a system malfunction that can impact on the overall system reliability. *Function Lifespan* (**F**) technique enables to reduce the fault injection spectrum by limiting the insertion time to those intervals where the target function is active—in the register context. During the simulation, the fault monitor component ((**2**), Sect. 3.2) traces the function execution at the instruction level and thus create a list of active ranges, including the processor core (s) that executed the underlying function. In this work, the lifespan technique implementation targets all the available registers: floating-point, general purposed registers (r0–r15), the program counter (PC), and the stack pointer (SP). However, this technique can be combined along with any other fault injection technique, e.g., (**C–E**), to further narrow the fault target.

5   Techniques Consistency and Performance

To validate the proposed fault injection techniques as well as to demonstrate the effectiveness of SOFIA a set of experiments are described as follows. Section 5.1 investigates the soft error analysis consistency of SOFIA concerning a cycle accurate full system simulator (gem5). Whereas in Sect. 5.2, SOFIA simulation performance is compared to the gem5 fault injection implementation. Further, Sect. 6 analysis the soft error reliability of a benchmark considering the use of a mitigation technique. In turn, in Sect. 7 a real automotive case study is used to investigate the proposed fault injection techniques.

For this section, the software stack comprises an unmodified Linux kernel (3.13) and 8 applications from the NASA NAS Parallel Benchmark (NPB) suite [16]. Each application has three versions, the base serial and two parallel implementations with different libraries (OpenMP, MPI), totaling 16 parallel scenarios. The target architecture includes an Arm Cortex-A9 processor model.

5.1   Accuracy

Aiming at evaluating the SOFIA accuracy the register file technique (**A**) has been integrated into gem5 full system mode. The gem5 simulator supports detailed cycle-accurate simulation of the system components (e.g., processor, cache, pipelines, arithmetic units), which justifies its adoption as the reference. Underlying evaluation comprises 32 fault injection campaigns (16 for each simulator) considering eight NASA benchmarks Block Tri-diagonal solver (BT), Conjugate Gradient (CG), Embarrassingly Parallel (EP), Discrete 3D fast Fourier Transform (FT), Integer Sort (IS), Lower-Upper Gauss-Seidel solver (LU), Multi-Grid (MG), and Scalar Penta-diagonal solver (SP) implemented in both MPI and OpenMP.

For each benchmark, 8,000 faults are injected in the registers of a quad-core Arm Cortex-A9 processor in random order, aiming to estimate the percentage of errors that are not masked during the execution of each benchmark. Such experiments deploy 256,000 fault injections through more than 400 thousand of simulation hours using a 5,000-core high-performance system.

Results illustrated in Fig. 3 show that the average mismatch of the SOFIA w.r.t gem5 fault injection implementation is only 5.84%, while the worst case is 23.35% for the OpenMP implementation of MG. Note that the mismatch between two fault injection campaigns is defined here as the sum of absolute differences between each soft error occurrence (e.g., ONA, OMM), divided by the total number of fault injections. Considering that the experiments have as reference a cycle-accurate simulator, which deploys a two-level detailed cache model, and eight high-performance applications implemented in both MPI and OpenMP parallelization libraries; the achieved mismatch is quite acceptable for early reliability explorations of multicore systems executing complex software stacks, specially when approximately 99% (396 h) of the simulation time was devoted to gem5 simulation.

5.2 Simulation Speed

During early design space explorations the simulation time is an important factor as a lower simulation time allows for a more thorough evaluation. This experiment evaluates the SOFIA simulation performance in terms of millions of instructions per second (MIPS) when compared to the gem5 fault injection

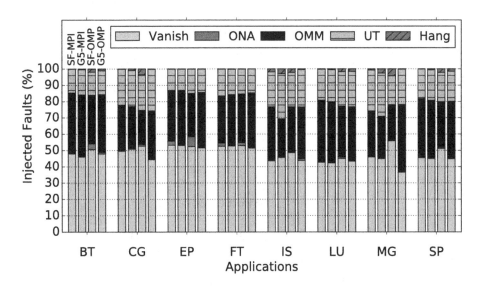

Fig. 3. Fault injection campaigns considering a quad-core processor using the SOFIA and the gem5.

implementation. Results were performed in a Quad-core Intel$^{(R)}$ Core$^{(TM)}$ i7–4790K CPU (32 GB DDR3 RAM) host machine. Figure 4 shows the simulation performance of both the SOFIA and the gem5 frameworks as we increase the number of host cores from 1 to 4 considering the 36 fault injection campaigns.

Note that both (SOFIA and gem5) fault injection flows can perform and manage parallel fault injection campaigns. Considering the most significant benchmark (i.e., EP with 87 billion instructions) and using four host cores, SOFIA achieves up to 3,910 MIPS, which is approximately 325 times faster than the reference gem5 (12.52 MIPS). The obtained results also show that the simulation speed of SOFIA w.r.t gem5 fault injection implementation increases along with the application complexity, i.e., the more instructions, the higher is the SOFIA speedup.

6   Benchmark and TMR Case Study

To showcase SOFIA's applicability, this section presents a soft error analysis for a matrix multiplication (MM) kernel. First, we compare a sequential and a parallel implementation of the same kernel in Sect. 6.1. Leveraging from acquired information on the initial analysis, this work deploys two versions of the *Triple Modular Redundancy* (TMR) mitigation technique. In this regard, results are presented according to the classic TMR approach (MM-TMR—Sect. 6.2), and a refined TMR version (MM-TMR-I—Sect. 6.3).

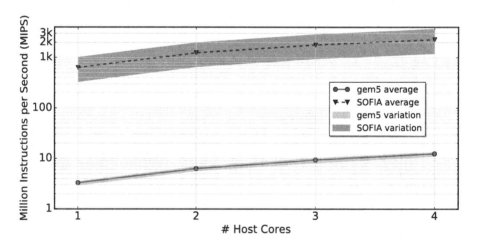

Fig. 4. SOFIA and gem5 simulation performance.

6.1   Sequential and Parallel MM

The first FI campaign deploys the MM kernel in two versions: (i) a sequential implementation, which uses a simple iteration-based algorithm, and (ii) a MM parallel kernel that relies on the Pthreads library to create two working threads. Figure 5 shows the two MM implementations subjected to 8 fault campaigns of 8,000 fault injections each totaling 128,000 simulations, considering the six FI techniques:

1. Random registers (**A**);
2. Physical memory (**B**);
3. Virtual memory (VM) entire range (**C1**);
4. VM code section (**C2**);
5. VM data sections (**C3**);
6. Result matrix (**D1**);
7. Multiplication function object code (**E1**);
8. Multiplication function lifespan (**F1**).

The sequential MM under FI shows a higher occurrence of OMMs (Fig. 5) due to dirt registers used in the multiplication, which leads to a significant number of silent data corruptions. The underlying implementations are also susceptible to UTs as consequence of incorrect memory address computation caused by registers under fault influence, which may lead to errors such as *segmentation fault*. However, the parallel MM presents a substantially more significant number of UT when compared to the sequential version. This is explained because Pthreads scheduling algorithm increases the application control flow complexity, which might incur in more wrong address computation during the MM execution.

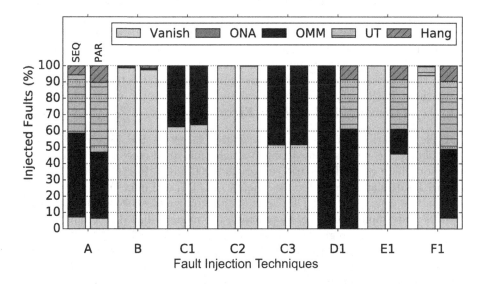

Fig. 5. Matrix multiplication soft error vulnerability analysis. Sequential (SEQ) and parallel (PAR) for a single-core processor

6.2 Triple Modular Redundancy

As identified in the previous Section, the injection of bit-flips severely impacts on the matrix multiplication kernel operation due to its simplicity and high-density code. This work deploys the TMR to improve its reliability. Such a technique combines spatial (i.e., data duplication) and temporal (i.e., concurrent execution) replication to reduce the amount of detectable silent data corruptions. The new kernel (MM-TMR) executes three independent *parallel MM* instances (i.e., six working threads), enabling one incorrect execution to be masked by a voting process at the end of MM execution (i.e., a function vote the majority from the partial results). The TMR version corrects most of the errors originated from the input and output matrices. Nevertheless, the TMR implementation using the Pthread library increases the UT occurrence.

A custom soft error analysis step was included in the fault campaign flow to demonstrate the proposed tool efficiency. This additional module compares the four matrices (i.e., each TMR replica and the voter) alongside two other error classifications considering three possible outcomes:

1. All matrices are identical, in this case, the SOFIA classifies the detected error according to one of the five default classes (e.g., Vanish, UT, Hang). Note that OMM and ONA only occur if the result matrix is correct, and thus being considered benign errors in this context.
2. If one TMR matrix does not match the other replicas, the voter will mask the error and produce the correct result. Nevertheless, in this case, the simulation diverges in terms of the number of executed instructions from the faultless run, which leads to a false-positive error (i.e., control flow error with incorrect memory) in traditional FI flows. The SOFIA classifies this execution context as **Corrected** to signal the appropriate behavior, i.e., even with the context mismatching the reference execution the final matrix is correct.
3. The third possible outcome originates from an incorrect voter execution (i.e., the three TMR matrices are identical and differ from the voter matrix) due to the FI being classified as **Voter Error**.

Table 2 describes 17 distinct FI scenarios targeting the MM-TMR, while Fig. 6 shows the results considering a single and quad-core ARM Cortex-A9 processor where each FI scenario comprises 8,000 faults. Register-based FI (**A, E, and F**) displays a considerable amount of UT (i.e., Linux OS segmentation faults in this context), around 40% due to the wrong address computation using registers under fault influence. In contrast, the memory-based technique errors depend on the stroke region, for example, targeting the 1 Gb physical memory (using technique B) would result to a minimal number of errors (i.e., masking rate of 99.95%) as the benchmark accesses a limited memory range (i.e., few dozen kilobytes). The complete VM range (**C1**) and data sections (**C3**) present a similar behavior as most of the faults hit the application 300-wide square matrices due to its size (i.e., each one possessing 360 kbytes or 20% of application size). The code section (**C2**) contains, besides the application code, hundreds of unused Linux and C libraries functions added by the compiler, leading to greater masking rate. By individually targeting the matrix replicas **(D1–3)** we exercise the TMR main functionality resulting in an almost complete error coverage. The fault campaign **(D4)** leads to a 99.9% masking rate as the final result is composed of the voter function at the application end, which incurs in a narrow sensitive window (i.e., any faults previously present in this matrix are overwritten).

Table 2. Fault injection techniques targeting the TMR-based matrix multiplication.

Ref.	Target	Ref.	Target	Ref.	Target	Ref.	Target
A	Register file	D1	Matrix 1	E1	1st replication	F1	1st replication
B	Physical memory	D2	Matrix 2	E2	2nd replication	F2	2nd replication
C1	Complete	D3	Matrix 3	E3	3rd replication	F3	3rd replication
C2	Code section	D4	Matrix result	E4	Voter	F4	Voter
C3	Data sections						

Single and quad-core processors show a similar rate of correct results (i.e., vanish, SDC, and corrected) when targeting the function object code **(E1–4)**. However, their composition diverges while the single-core processor presents a more significant SDC rate (i.e., the MM result is correct with silent data corruptions on the memory) the multicore system displays a larger masking rate. Further, the multicore system reveals a higher number of *Hangs* due to the longer and higher executions of the PTHREAD scheduling policy leading to

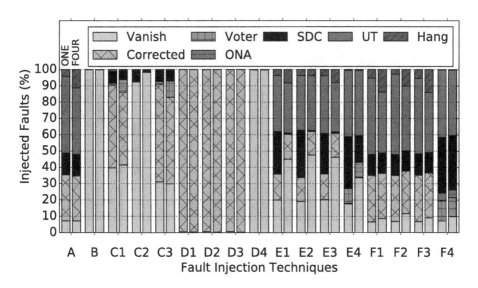

Fig. 6. Matrix multiplication soft error vulnerability analysis. MM-TMR for a single and quad-core processor

unrecoverable control flow. Random register **(A)** and Lifespan **(F1–3)** techniques show similar behaviors under FI as the MM application spends 95% on those multiplication functions. Directly targeting the voter function show a behavior not seen when targeting the complete application with random faults due to its short execution time, and thus, demonstrating the necessity of more detailed FI framework. Subjecting the voter code **(E4)** and lifespan **(F4)** to FI causes an erroneous matrix voting, which is a severe error in this context.

6.3   Improving the Triple Modular Redundancy

The initial MM-TMR solution provides complete coverage to fault injections for the replicated data (i.e., the partial matrices) while the control flows still prone to unexpected terminations. By using the promoted framework, it is possible to pinpoint the significant UT cause as OS segmentation faults in one of the thread replicas that terminates the complete application even if the other replicas had not experienced any errors. To mitigate this issue, we modified the application algorithm to include a segmentation handler for each replication, and consequently, the improved MM-TMR (MM-TMR-I) finishes correctly even if one of the replicas generates an OS segmentation fault. The experiments displayed in Fig. 7 reproduce the 17 FI scenarios mentioned above for the MM-TMR-I version using the single and quad-core processors.

The MM-TMR-I improves the MM kernel reliability by achieving of up to 90% of coverage (i.e., with correct final results) in contrast to the 50% of the traditional TMR considering register-based fault injections targeting the replicas

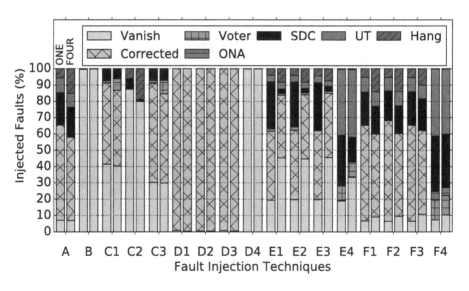

Fig. 7. Matrix multiplication soft error vulnerability analysis. MM-TMR-I for a single and quad-core processor

working threads. FI techniques (**D4, E4, and F4**) targeting the voter function and data remains unchanged without any modification being made in its code.

7 Automotive Case Study

While benchmarks can help to validate the proposed tool, a real-world application provides more useful insights in terms of functionality and applicability of the promoted techniques. To demonstrate the proposed fault injection techniques soft error analysis capabilities, we select a complex software stack to be our second case study. The experimental setup comprises a commercially available Arm Cortex-A9 processor, an unmodified Linux kernel (3.7), the Darknet framework [17] for neural networks with NNPACK float-pointing acceleration package [18], and the YOLOv3 [19] real-time object detect system. Object detection in real-time is a paramount research topic for both academia and industry to achieve SAE Level 3+ autonomous vehicles. To supply a realistic scenario, this work adopts the KITTI Vision Benchmark Suite [20], which uses challenging computer vision sets to extract data from a real-world urban environment. The YOLO algorithm takes KITTI suite images, each one measuring $1,242 \times 375$ pixels, and outputs a list of detected objects and their *confidence's degree in percentile*.

After some experiments, we identified that Cho's classification falls short when it comes to defining object detection algorithms, which produce outcomes based on probabilities, not on just absolute "yes" or "no". To improve the soft error analysis, a bespoke classification was defined according to the following conditions: **correct output** when the outputs (golden and fault injection) match, i.e., true vanished; **incorrect** if at least one object or probability is different.[3] Further, the incorrect result can be divided into **incorrect probability** when all objects are correct, but at least one has a different percentile of confidence—in most cases this would not influence the action of an autonomous vehicle; **wrong detection**, i.e., false positive or missing of an object; and **no prediction**, if no object is in the image. The last two can represent a life-threatening failure, by forcing a full stop in a highway (false positive, an object in the path) or crash (missing of an object).

We subject the selected application to multiple fault scenarios employing the fault injection techniques (see Sect. 4) targeting distinct software components alongside a customized error classification module. Each technique covers different aspects of the application considering its variables and critical functions in an isolated manner, demonstrating the importance of providing engineers with appropriate means that enable to identify not only the soft error occurrence but also the specific software characteristics that contribute more directly to their appearance.

---

[3] All input images used in this work have six to ten objects detected in the reference execution.

The fault scenarios consider commonplace techniques in the literature ((**A**) and (**B**)) as reference to evaluate the benefits and drawbacks of proposed fault injection techniques (Sect. 4): application virtual memory (**C**), two variables (**D1, D2**), and four functions—code (**E**) and lifespan (**F**). The technique (**C**) is used to target the application data structures, excluding kernel and other workloads from the system. The select two variables (**D1, D2**) for this experiment are: `colors` and `windows`; which are globally available and are used to plot the image overlay that delimit each detected object. The chosen functions represent the target application critical portions: detection and probability calculation of objects, `add_bias`, and `scale_bias`; convolutional layer creation of the neural network `make_convolutional_layer`; and matrix multiplication, as is orthogonal to this and other applications, `compute_matrix_multiplication`. Each of the individual 13 scenarios comprises three fault injections campaigns (with different input images), each campaign has 800 simulations with a single bit-flip, totaling 31,200 fault injections.

7.1   Result Analysis

This work uses traditional fault injection techniques such as targeting general propose registers (GPRs) and physical memory as a baseline for comparison. This section aims to show how these techniques can mask certain behaviors. We want to show that bespoke techniques can better guide developers towards a more efficient soft error analysis that considers the critical application elements, which reduces the number of simulations needed to extract relevant error/failure-related data.

Register File. Register file fault injection campaigns display a higher masking effect in small applications, as is the case for many benchmarks. For instance, the ArmV7 architecture has 48 registers (16 GPRs, 32 floating-point) and presents a twofold consequence: (i) bit-flips in unused registers lead to ONA as the fault remains untouched until the application ends—common in short benchmarks as they use a reduced register subset, and (ii) the usage of floating-point registers depend on the application and compiler support. Even considering a real-world application, the fault injection technique (**A**) has a masking rate of 62.32%.

The customized classification (Sect. 3.4) combined with the techniques allows more insightful investigations. While 37.68% of the campaign (**A**) has some kind of lingering difference w.r.t. Golden execution (Fig. 8), only 1.27% had their outcome affected (Figs. 9 and 10). The high number of masking and low incorrect outcomes attest to the reliability of the application. However, one can also say that 98.73% of the fault injections were "not helpfull" if the goal is to observe the behavior of the application in the presence of error.

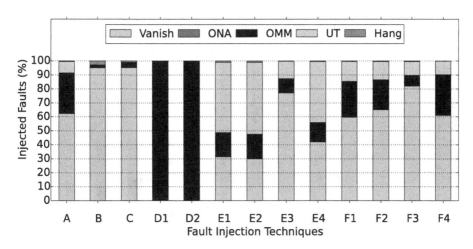

Fig. 8. Results for fault injection campaigns considering the classical (i.e., Cho's) Fault Injection classification.

Physical Memory. Physical memory fault injection masking is higher than the ones targeting the register file. There are 42.8×10^{12} targets (i.e., the number of instructions multiplied by either the register, or the memory bit count) for (**A**) versus 65.7×10^{15} in (**B**), and thus the Vanish rate increases to 95.09% (and 100% correct outcomes) due to the number of possible targets for each bit flip. This order of magnitude difference severely impacts the soft error analysis cost since longer fault campaigns are needed to extract a meaningful amount of error/failure-related data. A large number of campaigns becomes impractical

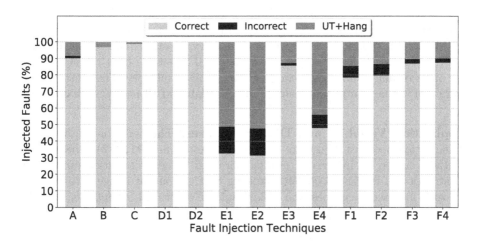

Fig. 9. Results for fault injection campaigns considering this work case study custom fault classification.

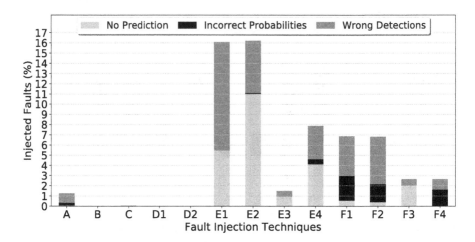

Fig. 10. Results for fault injection campaigns considering the only the incorrect results from Fig. 9.

as the complexity and size of the application increases. With this experimental setup (Sect. 7), each fault injection takes on average 10 min to execute, over 5,200 h for all campaigns in this section.

This work main objective is to explore the erroneous application behavior and not establish the number of faults when exposing the target application to a particular fluence. Bespoke techniques allow narrowing the focus on critical aspects of the application, e.g., functions, variables, data structures, and more. Further, Figs. 8, 9 and 10 also show results for campaign targeting two variables, four functions (code and lifespan).

Application Virtual Memory. The target Linux kernel (v3.7) allocates 488 MB for this application base virtual memory, mostly comprised of libraries and reserved space. This context yields 20.9×10^{15} possible fault targets, a similar order of magnitude when compared to physical memory. Thus resulting in 95.29% of the fault injection resulted in a **Vanish** and all results were **correct**.

Application Variables and Data Structures. The need for the auxiliary classification becomes even more evident for campaigns **(D1, D2)**, where 100% **OMM** leads to no **incorrect** results. Targeted variables are used during the construction of the visual output. Meaning that the output image with the box drawn is incorrect (e.g., position, color) but the algorithm output (i.e., classification) is correct.

Function Code. Fault injection on the assembly code will change the function behavior for future calls. Figure 8 shows that **E (1, 2, and 4)** have a high susceptibility to **UT**, as these functions rely on `for` loops which are sensible to wrong address (e.g., reading after a vector), and control flow (e.g., number of iterations). Further, the predominant type of prediction errors (Fig. 10), is **no prediction** and **wrong detections**. With a 32.28% reduction in the Vanished (technique (**A**) vs (**E2**)), there is more relevant data regarding erroneous application behavior. However, **E3** that creates the layers of the neural network (NN) that perform the object detection, leads to less **UT** and **incorrect** outcomes.

Function Lifespan. Even though this technique may lead to more masked faults than (**A**), it has at least twice (at most six times) the number of incorrect/wrong results. Figure 8 shows that the occurrence of **UT** is lower while **OMM** is higher than code fault injection, when considering the lifespan of a function (i.e., fault injection injected in register file only when the function is running). Considering the prediction errors (Fig. 10), the trace of the target functions are more susceptible to change the objects detected, thus **F1** is a prime candidate for fault tolerance techniques.

Techniques Evaluation/Remarks. From this experimental setup, and case study, it is possible to observe the importance of a targeted fault injection approach to finding critical elements of a given application. While fault injection in the register file shows the average behavior considering all functions, variables, and routines; it is possible to see that some variables do not change the outcome (Sect. 7.1). Furthermore, this type of analysis can improve the efficiency of the fault injection campaign. Techniques targeting Function Code and Lifespan can reduce the number of masked faults in up to 32.28%, Fig. 8. The cases where the number of vanished increased, the analysis still has more meaningful results than (**A**) as the number of **incorrect** outcomes is higher, Fig. 10. This type of analysis can show the developer where the cost×benefit of implementing a fault tolerance technique (e.g., TMR, ECC) is more profitable according to the propose of the application. Indeed, if the most crucial aspect of the application is to provide the correct object independent of its degree of confidence, protecting the function code (e.g., ECC) may yield ·better results then its execution (e.g., TMR for function lifespan).

8   Conclusion

This paper proposed the SOFIA framework, which supports detailed soft error vulnerability investigation considering complex software stacks in a non-intrusive manner. By combining novel fault injection techniques and robust analysis, the presented tool can help engineers to uncover otherwise hidden soft errors during early design space explorations. Two case studies with a resource intensive benchmark running on a quad-core platform showcase the kind of discovery and how SOFIA can aid during the early phase of development. Further, a real-world automotive application shows that SOFIA's exploration capabilities can scale beyond artificial workloads, thus validating the framework.

References

1. Baumann, R.: Radiation-induced soft errors in advanced semiconductor technologies. IEEE Trans. Device Mater. Reliab. **5**(3), 305–316 (2005)
2. Snir, M., et al.: Addressing failures in exascale computing. Int. J. High Perform. Comput. Appl. **28**(2), 129–173 (2014)
3. Kaliorakis, M., Tselonis, S., Chatzidimitriou, A., Foutris, N., Gizopoulos, D.: Differential fault injection on microarchitectural simulators. In: International Symposium on Workload Characterization, Atlanta, GA, USA, pp. 172–182. IEEE (October 2015)
4. Didehban, M., Shrivastava, A.: nZDC: a compiler technique for near zero silent data corruption. In: Design Automation Conference, Austin, Texas. ACM Press (2016)
5. Tanikella, K., Koy, Y., Jeyapaul, R., Kyoungwoo, L., Shrivastava, A.: gemV: a validated toolset for the early exploration of system reliability. In: International Conference on Application-Specific Systems, Architectures and Processors, London, United Kingdom, pp. 159–163. IEEE (July 2016)
6. Bandeira, V., Rosa, F., Reis, R., Ost, L.: Non-intrusive fault injection techniques for efficient soft error vulnerability analysis. In: International Conference on Very Large Scale Integration (VLSI-SoC), Cuzco, Peru, pp. 123–128. IEEE (October 2019)
7. Hari, S.K.S., Adve, S.V., Naeimi, H., Ramachandran, P.: Relyzer: exploiting application-level fault equivalence to analyze application resiliency to transient faults. In: International Conference on Architectural Support for Programming Languages and Operating Systems, New York, NY, USA, Association for Computing Machinery, pp. 123–134 (2012)
8. Magnusson, P., et al.: Simics: a full system simulation platform. Computer **35**(2), 50–58 (2002)
9. Martin, M.M.K., et al.: Multifacet's general execution-driven multiprocessor simulator (GEMS) toolset. ACM SIGARCH Comput. Archit. News **33**(4), 92 (2005)
10. de Aguiar Geissler, F., Kastensmidt, F.L., Souza, J.E.P.: Soft error injection methodology based on QEMU software platform. In: Latin American Test Workshop, Fortaleza, Brazil. IEEE (March 2014)
11. Guan, Q., et al.: Design, use and evaluation of P-FSEFI: a parallel soft error fault injection framework for emulating soft errors in parallel applications. In: International Conference on Simulation Tools and Techniques, Brussels, BEL, ICST (Institute for Computer Sciences, Social-Informatics and Telecommunications Engineering), pp. 9–17 (2016)
12. Guan, Q., Debardeleben, N., Blanchard, S., Fu, S.: F-SEFI: a fine-grained soft error fault injection tool for profiling application vulnerability. In: International Parallel and Distributed Processing Symposium, Phoenix, AZ, USA, pp. 1245–1254. IEEE (May 2014)
13. Rosa, F., Kastensmidt, F., Reis, R., Ost, L.: A fast and scalable fault injection framework to evaluate multi/many-core soft error reliability. In: International Symposium on Defect and Fault Tolerance in VLSI and Nanotechnology Systems, Amherst, MA, USA, pp. 211–214. IEEE (October 2015)
14. Feng, S., Gupta, S., Ansari, A., Mahlke, S.: Shoestring: probabilistic soft error reliability on the cheap. In: International Conference on Architectural Support for Programming Languages and Operating Systems, ASPLOS XV, New York, NY, USA, Association for Computing Machinery, pp. 385–396 (2010)

15. Cho, H., Mirkhani, S., Cher, C.Y., Abraham, J.A., Mitra, S.: Quantitative evaluation of soft error injection techniques for robust system design. In: Design Automation Conference, Austin, Texas. ACM Press (2013)
16. Bailey, D.H., et al.: The NAS parallel benchmarks-summary and preliminary results. In: Conference on Supercomputing, Albuquerque, New Mexico, United States. ACM Press (1991)
17. Redmon, J.: Darknet: open source neural networks in C (2016). https://pjreddie.com/darknet/
18. Dukhan, M.: Maratyszcza/NNPACK (February 2020)
19. Redmon, J., Farhadi, A.: YOLOv3: an incremental improvement. arXiv:1804.02767 (2018)
20. Menze, M., Geiger, A.: Object scene flow for autonomous vehicles. In: Conference on Computer Vision and Pattern Recognition, Boston, MA, USA, pp. 3061–3070. IEEE (June 2015)

A Statistical Wafer Scale Error and Redundancy Analysis Simulator

Atishay[1(✉)], Ankit Gupta[1(✉)], Rashmi Sonawat[1(✉)],
Helik Kanti Thacker[1(✉)], and B. Prasanth[2(✉)]

[1] DRAM Solutions, Samsung Semiconductor India Research and Development,
Bengaluru, India
{atishay.l,ankit.g2,rashmi.s,h.thacker}@samsung.com
[2] Host Software, Samsung Semiconductor India Research and Development,
Bengaluru, India
prasanth.b@samsung.com

Abstract. Manufacturing a DRAM chip involves multiple steps. External impurities, faulty deposition, or manufacturing errors in any of these steps could generate chips with faulty memory cells, rendering the chip unusable. To overcome these faulty memory cells, redundancies are included in the memory, allowing mapping of faulty memory cells to these redundant cells. The process of mapping faulty cells to redundant cells is called Redundancy Analysis (RA). Different RA algorithms have been developed and are often tested on randomly generated defect to test their efficiency and execution time. But we observed that, the defect pattern of a chip is not completely random, it follows a distribution pattern and the algorithms should be tested on chips with similar error distribution patterns. So, in this paper, we propose a Statistical Wafer Scale Error and Redundancy Analysis Simulator to generate defects on the chips similar to defects on the manufacturing line. The simulated errors on the chips are based on statistical models derived from real data. After generating defects on the chip, execution, comparison and benchmarking of algorithms based on yield and execution time is done. The simulator gives insights on algorithm behavior with different kinds of memory architectures and defect patterns. This allows designers of memory architecture and RA algorithm to simulate, predict and improve the wafer yield for different RA algorithm designs and memory architectures before manufacturing a new memory device.

Keywords: Redundancy analysis algorithm · Defect simulation · Error analysis · Statistical modeling · Wafer simulation

1 Introduction

Manufacturers have been able to keep up with the increasing semiconductor demands by producing them in large quantities on a single wafer. During manufacturing of the wafer, there might be surface flaws due to different external conditions. Since these flaws cannot be avoided, the wafer ends up with some defective chips. The increase in memory densities and the decrease in node sizes have led to an increased probability of

© IFIP International Federation for Information Processing 2020
Published by Springer Nature Switzerland AG 2020
C. Metzler et al. (Eds.): VLSI-SoC 2019, IFIP AICT 586, pp. 139–163, 2020.
https://doi.org/10.1007/978-3-030-53273-4_7

chip defects. These factors reduce the wafer yield. Along with increasing the quality of production of wafers, several measures have been taken to improve the overall yield.

Beginning with 64 Kbit generation of DRAM chips, manufacturers have included redundancies in the chips to repair them. Different operations are performed on the chip in different phases of manufacturing. Using wafer tests, the exact address of the defect can be located. This defect address is used to perform memory repair in the Laser Repair step while manufacturing. The process of memory repair is called Redundancy Analysis (RA). RA is a process of allocating spare rows and columns to the defective address detected in the chip, as illustrated in Fig. 1.

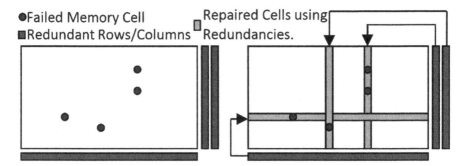

Fig. 1. Memory repair using redundant rows and columns

To a certain extent RA allows the repair of defective chips, but if the chip is unrepairable due to a large number of errors on, it would be discarded. Adding redundancies on the chip and allocating them to the defective addresses improves the yield but, the process of allocation of spares or Redundancy Analysis is an NP-complete problem [1]. So, with an increasing number of chip errors or problem size, time required to repair the chip or solve the problem using known algorithms increases exponentially. This means that only when time complexity of the algorithm is high, maximum yield can be achieved.

Some of the proposed RA algorithms have been discussed in Sect. 2, but most of these algorithms have been tested on errors that have been randomly generated, or generated based on Binomial or Polya-Eggenberger distribution. But these random defects or these distributions do not represent the defect on the chip in a wafer on the manufacturing line. These defects depend on the wafer lot, the wafer, position of the chip on the wafer and many other factors. All these dependencies have been explored in Sect. 3 along with the results of the same.

If the existing algorithms are benchmarked on random error distributions which don't take into account these factors, the yield and run time approximations are not similar to that on the manufacturing line. So, in this paper we have proposed a Statistical Wafer Scale Error And Redundancy analysis Simulator based on [13] which uses statistical models for different stages of device manufacturing to simulate chip error.It considers various factors which affect the defect distribution that allows generation of chips with error distribution similar to the actual data. It also allows to run different RA algorithms on the simulated data to provide insights on algorithm behavior with respect to various factors described in the paper.

The RA algorithm behavior insights provided by the simulator would help in designing new RA algorithms and improving the memory architecture design. The behavior insights include timing, efficiency and spare allocation of different algorithms. Wafer efficiency comparison allows analysis of yield with respect to different sizes of redundancies. The simulator would allow improvement in algorithms and memory design before the chip is manufactured which would improve the wafer yield.

The outline of the paper is as follows. Section 2 gives an explanation of Redundancy Analysis and existing Simulators and their features. Section 3 gives the detailed explanation of the statistical models used in the simulator. Section 4 describes the implementation of the simulator. Finally, Sect. 5 gives details about the experimental setup and the results are described in Sect. 5.3. In Sect. 6 conclusions are drawn from these results.

2   Background

2.1   Redundancy Analysis Algorithms

An ideal Redundancy Analysis (RA) Algorithm should find a repair solution whenever one exists, execute in a reasonable length of time and abort at the earliest sign of unreparability. The repair rate of an RA algorithm determines its ability to obtain a correct repair solution. The definitions of the repair rate and the normalized repair rate [1] are as follows:

$$R_W = C_{Repaired}/C_{Total} \tag{1}$$

$$R_{NW} = C_{Repaired}/C_{Repairable} \tag{2}$$

Where R_w is defined as the repair rate of the wafer, $C_{Repaired}$ is the number of chips repaired and, C_{Total} is the number of chips on the wafer. R_{NW} is defined as the normalized repair rate and $C_{Repairable}$ is the number of theoretically repairable chips. The total number of tested chips includes the number of chips that are unrepairable. These chips degrade the effectiveness of the RA algorithm, causing it to have a low repair rate. However, the normalized repair rate is independent of these unrepairable chips, thus making it a more appropriate for estimating the ability of an RA algorithm to obtain a correct repair solution.

Exhaustive search algorithms are required for determining if the chips are theoretically repairable. But the memory repair problem also can be solved using heuristic algorithms. Proposed heuristic algorithms like Repair-Most [2] and OSP [3] can find a solution quickly, but they may not find a solution of a theoretically repairable chip. So, the heuristic algorithms may not achieve an optimal repair rate. Whereas exhaustive search algorithms like Branch-and-Bound [1], PAGEB [1], Fault-driven [4] will certainly reach the optimal repair rate, but the time and space complexity of these algorithms grow exponentially with the number of errors. Therefore, the RA algorithm for chip repair must be chosen carefully as they provide varying yield and time complexity.

RA algorithms are generally divided into the must-repair and the final-repair phase. The must repair phase repairs the faults when there is no choice between invoking a redundant row or a column. If there are more errors in a row than spare columns, it must be repaired using a spare row. The final-repair phase analyses the remaining faults for reparability.

This paper uses the existing heuristic and exhaustive algorithms to test the repair rate and time. The time complexities of the discussed algorithms have been listed in Table 1. The Broadside Algorithm [2] is a heuristic algorithm which uses a greedy approach to perform a repair. It assigns a spare row or column based on whichever is present in excess when it repairs an error. In case of same number of spare row and column, assignment is based on the algorithm design and device requirement.

In [4] an exponential Fault Driven Comprehensive algorithm is defined. It uses a full solution tree to try all possible combinations of spare row and columns to repair an error and generates all possible solutions. In [5] a Faulty Line Covering Algorithm (FLCA) is defined. This is based on the principal that a faulty row with k faults can be covered either by a spare row or k spare columns. This eliminates branches with parents as faults which have already been repaired. Hence it is an improvement over the naive fault driven algorithm.

In [5] a Largest Effective Coefficient Algorithm (LECA) is defined. This heuristic algorithm uses Effective Coefficients (EC) to rank the rows and column of a chip in the order in which they have to be repaired. The EC considers both fault counters and complements of a faulty line.

In [3] a One Side Pivot algorithm (OSP) is defined. It uses Pivot fault properties to find repair priorities reducing the analysis time even when the error rate is high. Faults are classified into 3 types of faults Pivot faults, intersection faults and OSP faults. Where pivots fault is defined as a fault in a faulty line which is not included in any other faulty lines, an intersection fault is defined as a fault which is included in both faulty column or faulty row and one side pivot (OSP) fault is defined as a pivot fault which is not included in a faulty line which does not have an intersection fault. Row OSP faults (pivot in its column) will be solved using spare rows and column OSP faults (pivot in its row) will be solved using spare column. To repair pivot faults, if fault is pivot in its row it is solved using spare column and if fault is pivot in its column then it is solved using spare row.

Table 1. Algorithms time simulation parameters

Algorithm	Time complexity	Remarks
Broadside algorithm	$O(n)$	n is number of errors
FLCA	$O\left(2^{\left(\frac{T_F - S_F}{min} + 1\right)} - 1\right)$	T_F is number of total faults and S_F is number of single faults
LECA	$O\left(\max\{R_A, C_A\}^2 \log\max\{R_A, C_A\}\right)$	R_A is redundant row and C_A is redundant columns
OSP	$O(\max(n, n_P \cdot n))$	n_P is number of pivot fault

2.2   DRAM Manufacturing and Architecture

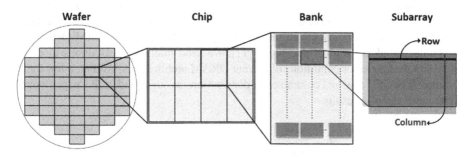

Fig. 2. Wafer, chip, bank and subarray arrangement in a DRAM chip

In Fig. 2 the relationship between the wafer, chip, bank and the subarrays has been explained. During the manufacturing process, multiple chips are manufactured on a circular wafer. Each chip contains multiple banks which is an independent two dimensional array of storage cells. In Fig. 2 each chip has 8 banks associated with it. Only one bank is accessed in a single read or write operation. Starting with DDR4 memory, banks are organized into bank groups for continuous data rate scaling without necessitating longer burst lengths.

These banks are not monolithic structures, they are divided into subarrays. Read and Writes to the DRAM are performed through row activation command which when issued, a group of storage cells gets activated in parallel. Such a group of cells is called a row, often referred to as a page. The storage cells store the binary information in the form of a charge stored on a capacitor. A row activation command caches a row or a page of memory in the sense amplifier. But the whole row is not read at a time, column or the bit line is the smallest addressable unit of memory. Row decoder extracts the row number from the address and activates the corresponding word line, and the sense amplifier compares the voltage of the bit lines to V_{ref} and thus accesses an entire word line amplifying the voltages stored in the memory cells. Then the column decoder which is a multiplexer is used to access particular bit lines.

2.3   Existing Simulators

A literature survey of some existing RA simulators has been described in this sub-section. In [6] a simulator for evaluating RA Algorithm which can calculate repair rate and allow user to manipulate memory configuration has been proposed. It uses a single Poisson, Gamma or Negative binomial distribution to find defect per dies and has fixed row, column, cluster and single fault probability. The simulator also incorporates the overhead of spare elements for evaluation of algorithms which is very useful for the user to find the better configurations of the spare elements under a certain redundancy structure and area constraint. The tool described in [6] allows the user to develop the built-in redundancy analysis (BIRA) algorithms and circuits for built-in self-repair

(BISR) of embedded memories. This work has been continued in Raisin [7] where the RTL memory behavioral model are tested with the BISR circuit.

An improved version called Raisin was proposed in [7], which also allowed development of Built-In Redundancy Analysis (BIRA) algorithms and introduced a fault detection sequence. But with the increasing DRAM sizes the DRAM memory is not implemented as a monolithic block [11], we need multiple distributions to accurately simulate the error conditions of current DRAM architectures. Adding a few more parameters like the row and column error distributions as suggested in this paper would allow more realistic results.

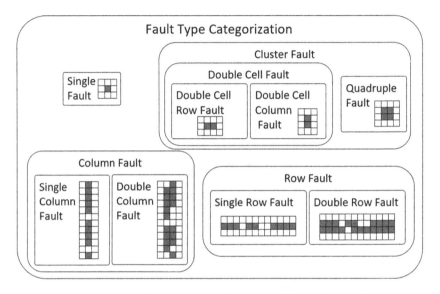

Fig. 3. Categorization of fault types used in [8]

In [8] a bank model based simulator is proposed which allows creation of realistic faults in banks. It introduces errors in the bank based on categorization of memory device such as fault-free, faulty, theoretically repairable, and repairable memories. It also, introduces various fault types as shown in Fig. 3, derived from defects that are generated statistically. It allows evaluation of RA efficiency with the help of the RA evaluation tool proposed in the paper. But the memory device categorization in [8] does not involve wafer lot distributions and wafer specific errors.

In [9] various defect models have been described. Fault analysis, combinations and distributions are used to generate faults in the wafer. Chip defects are then simulated to perform fault analysis like shorts, opens, new gate material device and open devices. Although the simulator takes into account the wafer lot and wafer simulation details, it cannot take into account newer DRAM architectures and specific chip errors.

The current simulators are either confined to a chip which hampers their ability to consider errors in the silicon wafer or do not take into account changes due to evolving DRAM architecture. Chip based simulation is one of the major drawback of the existing simulators. To the best of our knowledge, a statistical simulator with the ability to perform wafer level defect injection and chip fitting providing insights on algorithm performance has not yet been proposed.

3   Statistical Error Model

In this section we will discuss the statistical models used to determine the defects generated on the chip. These models are used to inject errors described in Sect. 4.

3.1   Wafer Lot Distribution

The manufacturing of the wafers involves cutting and polishing silicon ingots into wafers. These wafers are divided into wafer lots. Multiple distribution of errors are observed in these wafer lots because they were manufactured at different time and external conditions. So the error in a wafer is determined by wafer lot and the wafer distribution. An example of the distribution of error in a wafer lot is illustrated in Fig. 4.

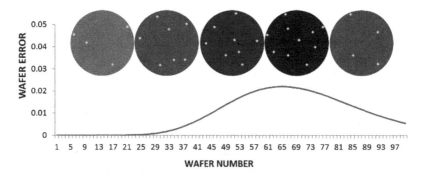

Fig. 4. Example of distribution of errors in a wafer lot

In Fig. 4, the following negative binomial distribution has been used for wafer error distribution:

$$Pr_{WL}(x = k) = \binom{\alpha + k - 1}{\alpha - 1} \left(\frac{n}{\mu}\right)^k \left(1 - \frac{n}{\mu}\right)^{n-k} \tag{3}$$

Where Pr_{WL} is defined as the defect probability among wafer lots, k is the wafer lot number, n is number of wafer lots and, μ is mean of the negative binomial distribution.

Defect distribution probability among wafers (Pr_{WF}) also follows the probability distribution described in Eq. (3). We use a two level negative binomial distribution similar to [9], for distribution of errors across wafers and wafer lots. The first level distribution allows the modelling of variance of defects among lots and the second level depicts the variance between wafers in a particular lot.

3.2 Chip Distribution

The two level negative binomial distribution used in the previous step allows us to determine the quality of wafer. Using Pr_{WL} and Pr_{WF} the wafer lot error and wafer level error are determined. Multiple chips are manufactured on a single wafer but the distribution of errors among the chips is not random.

In our experimental data, it is observed that chips near the edge of the wafer had a higher rate of failure than chips at the center. This is consistent with the Edge Effect observed in [9] and [10]. Because of different error distributions at the center and circumference of the wafer, it is difficult to fit a single distribution over the whole wafer.

So, for error distribution on chips, a Bimodel distribution has been used which was verified with Hypothesis testing of the sample data. An average p-value of 0.833 was obtained. A Bimodel distribution is observed for errors on the wafer. This distribution consists of a binomial distribution with mean at radial center and Poisson distribution at circumference of wafer with mean greater than radius of wafer.

$$Pr_A(x = k) = \binom{n}{k}\left(\frac{n}{\mu}\right)^k\left(1 - \frac{n}{\mu}\right)^{n-k} + \beta \cdot \frac{\lambda^k e^{-\lambda}}{k!} \tag{4}$$

Where Pr_A is defined as the defect probability at length k, n is normalized radial distance, μ is mean of binomial distribution, λ is mean of Poisson distribution and β is a constant, directly proportional to λ. The λ value chosen for the Poisson distribution has to be greater than n for a correct fit.

An example of the distribution described in Eq. (4) has been illustrated in Fig. 5. In this example the radial distance has been divided into 20 divisions, so each division represents error distribution in 5% of the radial length. From Eq. (4) the values used are n is 20, μ is 0.6, λ is 32 and β is 15. The radial distribution has been mirrored to represent the distribution of error on the wafer diameter. The first division, represented by R1 has a probability distribution of 0.27, calculated by keeping k value as 20. R2 represents the division with the probability distribution of 0.015 corresponding to k = 14. Similarly division R3 represents the lowest probability distribution of 4.3×10^{-6} corresponding to k = 7. R4 in the center of the chip has a probability distribution value of 0.15 corresponding to k = 0.

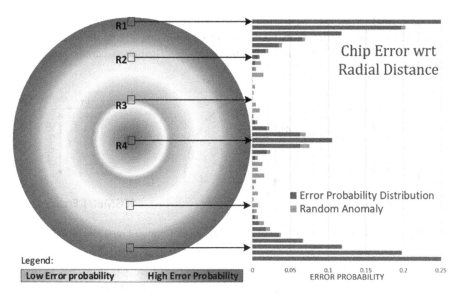

Fig. 5. Wafer error distribution example

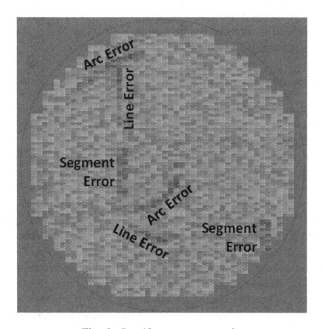

Fig. 6. Specific errors on a wafer

Other than the radial distribution, the wafer also experiences some specific faults. Specific errors consist of arc error, line error, and segment errors. Each of them have high error densities and an independent distribution. An example with all the 3 specific errors on a small wafer has been illustrated in Fig. 6. In the simulator Poisson distributions are used for specific errors which allows errors in chips lying on the line, arc or segment to have different error rates depending in the distribution parameters.

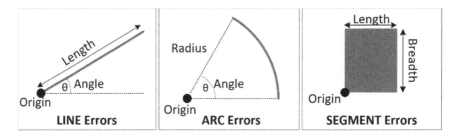

Fig. 7. Parameters used to determine specific errors simulated on a single wafer

As illustrated in Fig. 7, different parameters are used to determine the location, orientation and size of the specific errors on the wafer. For a Line Error, the origin coordinate, the angle of the line with the horizontal and the length of the line is used. For arc type error the Radius origin and the arc angle is used to determine arc errors. Segment errors are defined with an origin coordinate, length and a breadth. The parameters are defined in terms of Wafer Radius. E.g.: $0.2 \times$ Wafer Radius. Origin is defined as (x, y) coordinates and the Angle is defined in radians.

3.3   Subarray Specific Distribution

After the distribution of errors on the wafer has been decided, the quality of the chip has to be determined. This means that the number of errors on the chip is known but, on the chip, these errors are not randomly distributed.

A chip is divided into banks which are further divided into subarrays [11]. The DRAM bank is not implemented as a monolithic structure because it would require very long bit-lines and word-lines. The huge parasitic capacity of these bit-lines would severely affect the access latency. Due to this the modern DRAM bank is divided into a 2-D array of tiles [11]. An example of the tile division is shown in Fig. 8.

There is a main row decoder which drives multiple sub word line decoders which in turn drive the local memory arrays. Extra decoders might be present in between the main row decoder and the sub word line decoder depending on the architecture. In the architecture we also observe sense amplifiers which are local to each subarray. And we also have a global column decoder which allows selection of columns to be read from the memory. Multiple such decoders also might be present between these local sense amplifiers and the column decoders depending on the architecture.

In the experimental data, we observed that although the error distribution on the chip could be expressed with a Poisson equation, there were some anomalies. When these error distributions were observed, peaks in the number of errors were discovered in both row and column error count. The peak in the values were observed at multiples of the tile size. The faults on the wafer can also be in the area of the row decoder, column decoder or the sense amplifier as shown in Fig. 8. This would render the whole row or column in that tile unusable and would return incorrect values while testing.

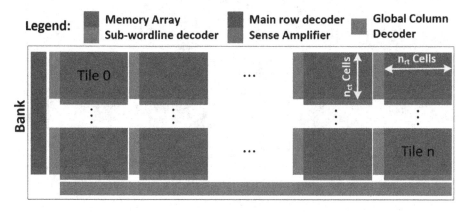

Fig. 8. Division of bank into tiles

In the examples of distribution of errors explained below, n_{rt} is number of cells in a row per tile and n_{ct} is number of cells in column per tile. We assume that the tiles are numbered from Tile 0 to Tile n for the simplicity in the explanation of the example.

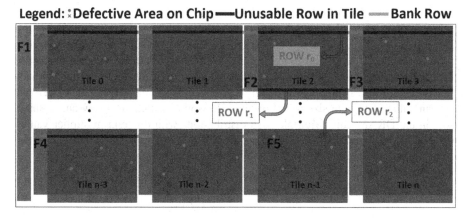

Fig. 9. Row error due to defective decoder and local row buffer

Figure 9 represents a bank with errors in different areas. Faults F_1, F_2 and F_3 are present at sub word-line decoder side which render the whole row in a tile useless. Therefore, the row error count for row r_1 will be number of cells in a row of tile 2 and tile 3 i.e., $2 \cdot n_{rt}$. Similarly row error count for row r_2 will be the sum of errors in tile n − 3 due to F_3 and the cell error F_4 in tile n − 1 i.e., $n_{rt} + 1$.

Legend: ⁝ **Defective Area on Chip** ▌**Unusable Column in Tile** ▌**Bank Column**

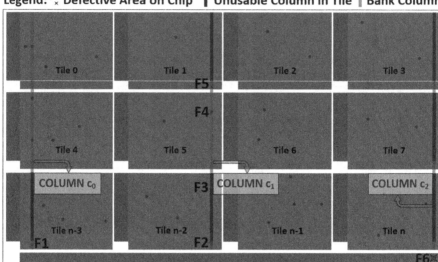

Fig. 10. Column error due to defective sense amplifier and global column decoder

Similarly column errors as represented in Fig. 10, can occur when the error on the chip is present in the local sense amplifier (F1, F2 and F5) or the row buffer (F6). Number of column errors on such a fault can be similarly calculated as $n_{ct} + 3$, $2 \cdot n_{ct} + 1$ and $3 \cdot n_{ct}$ for column c_0, c_1 and c_2 respectively.

Due to these faults, the number of row and column faults will have anomalies at $(r \cdot n_{rt}) \pm x$ and $(c \cdot n_{ct}) \pm y$ Where r and c lie between 1 and the number of tiles in a row or column of the 2D array of tiles in the bank. To the best of our knowledge, this is the first RA simulator to include tile size specific faults in the DRAM chip. This anomaly in the distribution was corrected by adding a binomial distribution with a multiplier and its mean value as the tile size to the original Poisson distribution of row and column errors in the DRAM chip. Multiple such distributions with different multiplier values can be added to the original Poisson distribution with mean values as a multiple of tile size to accurately depict the row and column error distribution.

$$Pr_{Lm}(x = k) = \frac{\lambda^k e^{-\lambda}}{k!} + \sum_{i=1}^{i=\frac{a_n}{t_n}} \gamma_i \binom{n}{k} \left(\frac{n}{\mu_i}\right)^k \left(1 - \frac{n}{\mu_i}\right)^{n-k} \tag{5}$$

Where Pr_{Lm} is defined as the defect probability of line having k faults, λ is mean of Poisson distribution, a_n is number of cells in the array, t_n is the number of cells in a tile, γ_i is damping factor of ith binomial distribution, n is tile size and μ_i is mean of ith binomial distribution. Pr_{Lm} can be the defect probability of a row or a column (Pr_{LR} or Pr_{LC}).

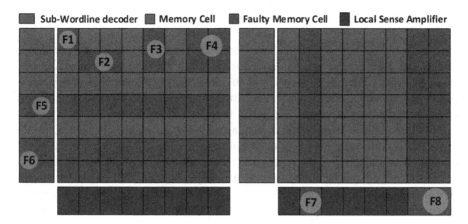

Fig. 11. Fault types in a DRAM tile

The probability distribution described in Eq. (5) allows distribution of errors on the chip in form of row and column errors in each tile. In [8], different faults occurrences have been considered at bank level, but in the simulator, faults are also considered on a tile level. Faults can occur in the DRAM due to a manufacturing defect. Faults are the reason for occurrence of errors in the memory. As illustrated in Fig. 11, the *F1* fault only introduces a single cell error in the memory array. Faults *F2* and *F3* due to their occurrence on the boundary of 2 cells, cause 2 adjacent errors. Fault *F4*, a fault of a larger size might cause an error in 4 adjacent cells. Faults *F5* and *F6*, occur in the sub-word line decoder, which causes an error in a single row or 2 adjacent rows. Similarly, faults *F7* and *F8* in the local sense amplifier might cause a single column or 2 adjacent columns to be faulty. The fault types are also a part of the error model which is incorporated into the simulator with the help of the Defect Injector described in Sect. 4.

3.4   Final Distribution

The final probability of error in the chip is calculated using the probability values of Pr_{WL}, Pr_{WF} and Pr_A which are the probability of error in a wafer lot, a wafer and a region of the wafer respectively.

These 3 values determine the probability of an error at a particular location in a wafer which decides the error in the chip that is manufactured at that location. This error probability needs to be distributed among the banks in that chip as row errors, column errors and other faults. Pr_{RN} and Pr_{CN} is the probability of occurrence of a particular number of row errors in a row or column errors in a column of a bank.

After these probabilities are decided, similar to [8] the row and column errors are divided into single and double row errors and single and double column errors respectively. Rest of the errors are divided into single, double and quad errors.

4 Implementation

The overall architecture of the simulator is described in Fig. 12. Simulator parameters can be input manually or can be derived from fitting the error distributions on processed chip errors. Change in the wafer or chip size changes the distribution parameters for the models in the Defect Injector. The distribution parameters are used by the defect injector module to define errors in a particular region of the wafer.

The chips are fit onto the wafer depending on the wafer and the chip size. Once the chip fitting is done, the defect injector module injects error in these chips by fitting the distribution parameters onto the equations described in Sect. 3. The defect injector logs the defects in the bank for future use and debugging, and the RA simulation module outputs simulation results for further analysis as described in Sect. 6. A detailed description of the chip fitting module and defect injector has been done in this section.

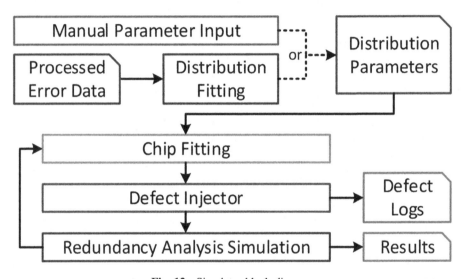

Fig. 12. Simulator block diagram

4.1 Chip Fitting

The Chip Fitting module takes into consideration parameters like wafer size and chip size to iteratively fit different memory architectures in the wafer. Defect injection is performed and RA algorithms are applied on these chips while measuring the repair rate. This results in a wafer efficiency peak with respect to different memory architectures as illustrated in Fig. 13.

For a given memory configuration and RA Algorithm, as the number of spares increases, the repair rate and the chip area also increases. Increase in chip area means a decrease in the total number of chips on the wafer. So in this paper, a solution for finding an optimized memory architecture that accounts for the repair rate and the number of chips on the wafer has been proposed.

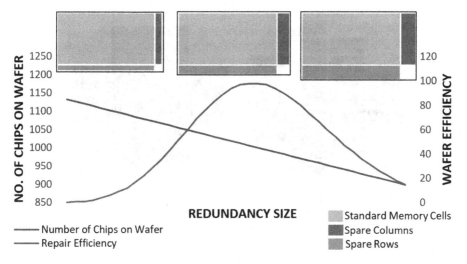

Fig. 13. Number of chips and wafer efficiency with respect to the redundancy size

The chip fitting module uses the bank and chip configuration to find out the area occupied by each chip. Chips are fit side by side optimally on the wafer taking into consideration the radius of the wafer. Figure 14 illustrates how different chip sizes lead to difference in the number of chips on the wafer. In the example illustrated in the figure, a steady decrease in the number of chips with increasing redundancies is observed. But the number of repairable chips on the wafer is not maximum when the number of chips are maximum, rather when the number of redundancies are an optimal number the number of usable chips on a wafer is maximum.

Various user adjustable mechanisms for chip fitting were introduced in the simulator to maximize the number of chips that could fit in a wafer. Initially a fixed coordinate was used to determine the starting position of the chip, but it would lead to inefficient chip placement on the wafer. Depending on the chip configuration i.e.: the number of rows, columns, spare rows and spare columns, starting coordinate of the top left chip is determined and the rest of the chips are arranged accordingly to maximize the number of chips on the wafer.

The same bank and chip configuration have been used in both the wafers but the number of spare rows and columns have been increased in (A). The specifications considered for the illustration are a chip with 8 banks in a 4 × 2 configuration. Each of the bank is 256 × 128 bits. The wafer on the left (A) has 8 spare rows and 4 spare columns with a total of 24 chips on the wafer. Even though the wafer size is small, a considerable decrease of 4 chips in the number of chips on the wafer was observed. The wafer on the right (B) has 20 chips as it has 32 and 16 spare rows and columns respectively. Although wafer (B) might have a higher yield, but it is possible that wafer (A) might have more usable chips even with lower yield.

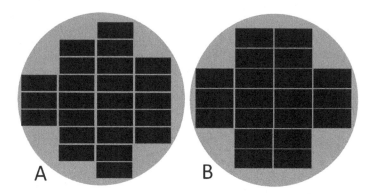

Fig. 14. Illustration of chip fitting on a wafer

4.2   Defect Injector

The Defect Injector uses the distributions described in Sect. 3 to inject errors into chips as shown in Fig. 15.

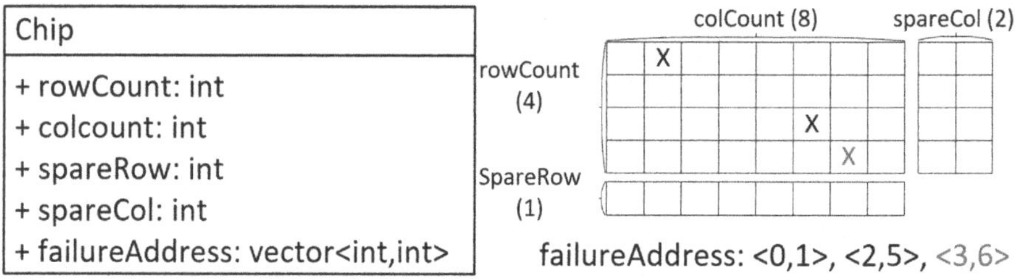

Fig. 15. Chip implementation in the Defect Injector (Color figure online)

The Chip object in the Defect Injector contains the row, column count and the number of spare rows and columns in that chip. To store the errors, a *failureAddress* vector is used which stores the failed bit addresses in form of a <row, column> pair. When a new error is generated with the help of the distributions in Sect. 3, it is added to the failed bit address vector of the chip object. As shown in Fig. 15, when a chip is created, the *failureAddress* vector is empty. For example, when a 3rd error is injected in row 3 and column 6 represented as a red X, a <3, 6> pair is added to the vector.

Due to memory constraints, the chip objects are created one at a time and tested with different RA algorithms sequentially during the simulation. After testing with RA algorithms and logging the necessary parameters, this chip object is deleted. The probability distributions used to determine the wafer lot, wafer and chip errors are stored in maps for faster access and probability value insertion.

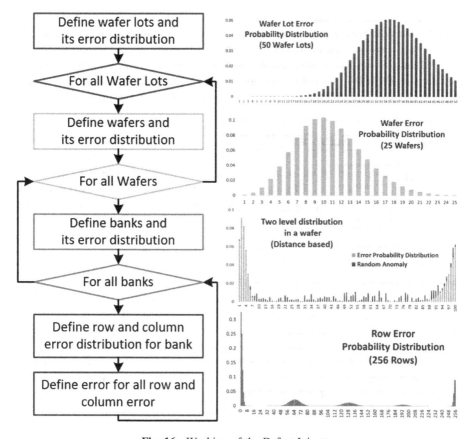

Fig. 16. Working of the Defect Injector

The Defect Injector as shown in Fig. 16 is divided into four distributions as described in Sect. 3. The Defect Injector begins by defining the error distribution in between the wafer lots. In the example shown in Fig. 16, the error is distributed among 50 wafer lots using the distribution from Eq. (3) with x as wafer lot number, α as 50, μ as 103 and n as 60. In the second step, for each of the wafer lots, errors are distributed among the wafers. In this example, 25 wafers were generated using the negative binomial distribution from Eq. (3) with x as the wafer number, α and n as 25 and, μ as 35. The distributions are stored in an error Distribution map as a <key, value> pair. The keys are the wafer lot or wafer number and the values are their respective error probabilities.

Then the error is divided among the chips which are placed on the wafer. A bi-modal distribution which takes into account the Edge Effect [10] is used for radial error distribution of chips on the wafer. Before injecting different chip errors, specific errors are also injected into the wafer which bring in some anomalies in the distribution data. The following values are used in Eq. (4): n is 150, μ is 8.3×103, β is 60 and λ is 125. The final step of the distribution is to distribute the errors in the chip. The distribution used here is described in Eq. (5). The λ value used in this equation is 1.5. It is then added to four different binomial distributions as a_n/t_n is 4. Assuming that the tile size in this example is 64 bits, the mean values for the distributions, μ_1, μ_2, μ_3 and μ_4 are 64, 128, 192 and 256 respectively which are multiples of 64. The γ_1, γ_2, γ_3, and γ_4 values used are 0.4, 0.25, 0.1 and 0.25 respectively. This allows addition of defects at row level which takes into account the tile based architecture explained in Sect. 3.

5   Experimental Setup and Results

Multiple algorithms were tested on the simulator. This included an implementation of the Broadside [2], FLCA [5], LECA [5] and OSP [3] algorithm. In the experimental setup subsection we have also discussed the data structures and optimization steps used to implement the algorithms as these impact the yield and algorithm run time results.

5.1   Experimental Setup - Algorithm

The fault address are stored in the fail bit address vector which can be decoded into the row and column addresses. This vector along with the redundancy architecture details are input to the algorithm for finding a solution. As explained in Fig. 17, one of the common operations in an algorithm is iterating and decoding the failed bit vector to row and column address, followed by the algorithms steps. Next, depending on the availability of spare rows and columns or by user preferences, spares are assigned to that faulty bit by inserting into the row and column solution vector. This helps to easily compare the performance of the algorithms on a particular chip. All algorithms invoke must-repair and also check for early abort conditions before starting their respective steps.

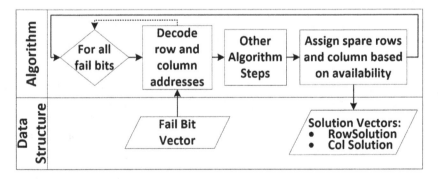

Fig. 17. General implementation of algorithms

The Broadside Algorithm was implemented as described in [2]. For each fault that has not yet been repaired, a spare row or column is assigned depending on whichever is available more at that stage of the algorithm execution.

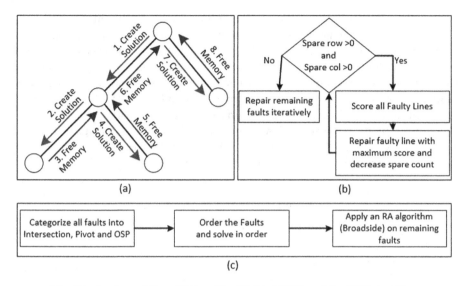

Fig. 18. Implementation details of the FLCA, LECA and the OSP algorithm

Implementation of the FLCA algorithm [5] involves an object-oriented approach where solution node object contains total errors left, spare rows, columns left and the number of single faults. To save memory, as illustrated in Fig. 18 (a), Depth First Search (DFS) is used while generating the solution tree so that objects generated can be cleared when not needed. Also, since the single faults can be solved in any manner, they are handled at the very end of the algorithm execution as mentioned in [5]. It is sometimes advantageous to find all the possible solutions for a particular configuration. But in this case since only the yield is important, we stop the execution as soon as one solution is found. This helps in further reducing the amortized time complexity over various chips because all the possibilities in the search space are not explored.

In LECA algorithm [5] implementation (Fig. 18 (b)), score maps are maintained. After one spare is allocated, the scores of some faulty lines need to be modified. Only the affected maps are renewed with each pass of the algorithm step while keeping in check the maximum score values. Counter values used to calculate the scores are maintained in vectors for faster access.

In the implementation of the OSP algorithm [3] described in Fig. 18 (c), vectors are used to classify and keep track of Pivot, Intersection and OSP faults. This allows quickly solving and removing faults based on priority. After priority based repair, any RA algorithm can be used to repair the remaining faults. Broadside algorithm was selected since it was experimentally observed that the yield improvement for the other algorithms was not justifiable, given the increase in execution time.

5.2   Experimental Setup – Defect Injector

The parameters for different simulations performed have been described in Table 2. In this table, under Wafer Lot and Wafer subsection, n_{WL} is the number of wafer lots and

n_W is number of wafers. α and μ can be referred from Eq. (3). Under chip Specification, r_n and c_n are the total number of rows and columns. sr_n and sc_n are the total number of spare rows and spare columns. n_{rt} and n_{ct} represent the total number of rows and columns in a tile. Under Wafer Area section, N represents the number of chips in a wafer and rest of the parameters are mentioned in Eq. (4). Row and column error distribution for the subarray section can be referred from Eq. (5). Here two parameters have been mentioned for row and column distribution. Some parameters in the simulation like μ in the Wafer subsection of simulation S_2 lies within a range of 15 to 20 and is not fixed. This is represented by [15, 20]. Similarly in the subarray section, row and column distributions can have different μ_i values.

Table 2. Simulation parameters

Simulation		S_0	S_1	S_2	S_3	S_4
Wafer and Wafer Lot (IIIA)	n_{WL}	–	–	9	7	–
	α_{WL}	–	–	12	20	–
	μ_{WL}	–	–	35	55	–
	n_w	–	–	21	15	–
	α_w	–	–	[10, 14]	[10, 15]	–
	μ_w	–	–	[15, 20]	[25, 35]	–
Chip specification	$r_n \times c_n$	512 × 256	512 × 256 256 × 128	1024 × 512	128 × 64	128 × 64
	sr_n	[16, 256]	[4, 256] [4, 128]	128	16	16
	sc_n	[8, 128]	[2, 128] [2, 64]	64	8	8
	$n_{rt,}\ n_{ct}$	512, 256	512, 256 256, 128	256, 256	64, 32	64, 32
Wafer Area (III B)	N		3700	1250	1200	153047
	n		270	41	7	Random chip error (mt19937)
	μ		9000	[10, 30]	[15, 50]	
	β		0	3	[2, 3]	
	λ	–	–	20	12	
Subarray (III C)	λ	–	–	1.5	1.5	Random distribution of single errors (mt19937)
	i	–	–	[1, 4], [1, 2]	2	
	μ_i	–	–	[256, 1024], [256, 512]	[64, 128], [32, 64]	
	γ_i	–	–	[0.1, 0.3]	[0.15, 0.25]	

In Simulation S_0 and S_1, only a single wafer has been simulated, so the wafer lot and wafer parameters have not been used. Here tile size is assumed to be the same as chip size as sr_n and sc_n sizes are being varied in the simulation. The number of spare rows and columns are varied in the range as described in sr_n and sc_n rows of Table 2. These values are varied in multiples of 2 and the result for the same has been discussed in the next section.

In S_2, the whole wafer lot was simulated, but since the number of errors were very high (up to 5000) FLCA was not implemented as it is an exponential algorithm. This simulation was done for runtime comparisons between OSP, LECA and Broadside algorithms. In S_3, a very small chip size was simulated with the full wafer lot simulation to see the execution time and normalized repair rate using the FLCA algorithms. In S_4 random error on the chip and random single error distribution were simulated. For comparison, the number of chips simulated were the same as simulation S_3. The chip error and the position of chip errors were determined using a Mersenne Twister pseudorandom number generator [12].

5.3   Results

In simulation S_0, a single wafer with different chip configurations was simulated to observe the pattern of usable chips on the wafer with respect to the redundancy size. The simulation was done with the Broadside algorithm, the maximum yield was obtained at 112 spare rows and 8 spare columns, as shown in Fig. 19. Similar simulations can be run by chip designers and manufacturers with their respective RA algorithm to predict the number of spares to be included in the new memory architecture. The useful insight gained from this simulation is that just increasing the number of spare rows and columns does not guarantee an improved wafer yield i.e., the number of usable chips obtained per wafer.

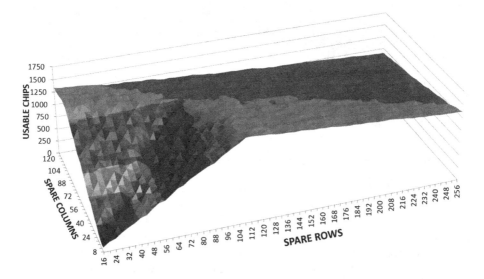

Fig. 19. Usable chips on wafer vs spare size

In Fig. 20, results of simulation S_1 with two different executions on a row and column configuration of 512×256 (Fig. 20 (a)) and 256×128 (Fig. 20 (b)) was simulated. Difference in the slope to achieve the maximum wafer yield was observed.

There was also a difference in the initial yield with low spare columns and rows where in case of a larger chip size, the number of solvable chips were close to 0.

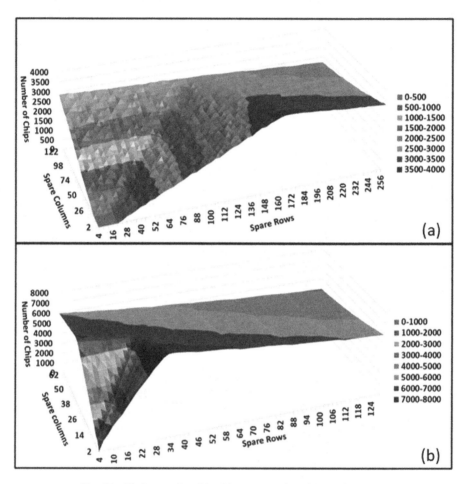

Fig. 20. Variance of usable chips on a wafer with configuration

In simulation S_2, the whole wafer lot was simulated and three algorithms were compared. The number of chips repaired and time taken by different algorithms for wafers have been plotted. The average error of the wafers for all wafer lots are also plotted in the lower part of the graph in Fig. 21. In S_2, LECA repaired 72.9% and 24.9% more chips than Broadside and OSP algorithms respectively. The Broadside algorithm had a constant execution time and was at least 15 times faster than other algorithms executed. On an average, LECA was 24.5% slower than OSP in the entire simulation.

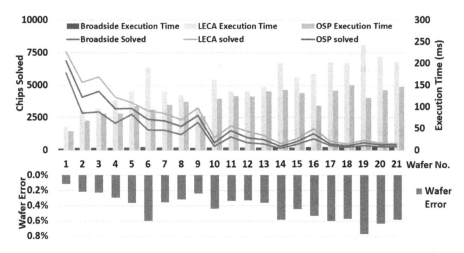

Fig. 21. Algorithm yield and wafer error

In simulation S_3, a small chips size is simulated to observe the normalized yield of the algorithms from Eq. (2). The Broadside algorithm has a 0% normalized repair rate if chip error is more than 1%, whereas LECA and OSP still maintain a normalized repair rate of ∼20% and ∼5% respectively. LECA and OSP have a high (>90%) normalized repair rate up to a chip error rate of 0.5%, so these algorithms can be used at a low error rate for determining the chip reparability.

Using S_3 a compound RA solution for a wafer can be designed which would use multiple algorithms, say LECA and OSP. This simulation would help in determining when to use the algorithms. From Fig. 22, it can be observed that till a chip error rate of 0.64%, OSP provides better normalized repair rates, but after that LECA outperforms OSP. Also, algorithms like Broadside can be included in the compound RA solution to solve chips below an error rate of 0.34%.

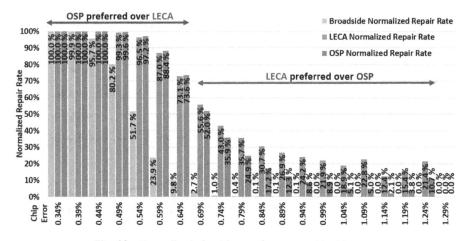

Fig. 22. Normalized algorithm performance with chip error

Figure 23 is a plot of the execution time with respect to the chip error rate. With respect to the error rate, FLCA has an exponential increase in execution time, whereas LECA and OSP have a linear increase in the execution time. A decrease is seen in FLCA execution time after 1.34% chip error because of early abort conditions being satisfied.

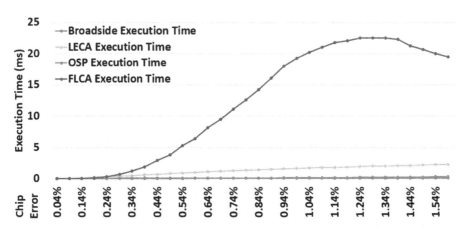

Fig. 23. Execution time with chip error

In Fig. 24, the simulation results of S_3 are compared with S_4, a random defect injector. In S_4 13.6% of the chips were repairable compared to 59.2% by this simulator in S_3. Not only is the average chip error rate constant in S_4, but also algorithms are not able to solve chips with more than 0.6% error. In S_3, exhaustive and heuristic algorithm can solve chips with a maximum error rate of 1.6% and 1.3% respectively which is much closer to real life errors.

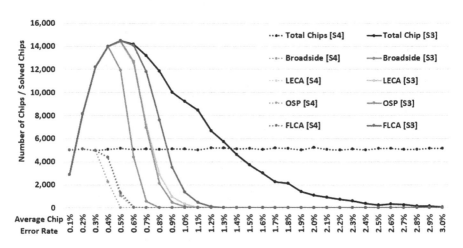

Fig. 24. Comparison of this simulator [S_3] with random defect injector [S_4]

6 Conclusion

In this paper we presented a Statistical Wafer Scale Error And Redundancy analysis Simulator, a statistical model based approach which provides various insights into RA algorithms. Algorithm designers can use these insights to simulate errors similar to those on the manufacturing line before actually manufacturing the chip and improve their algorithm design. Memory architects would be able to gain insights on the impact of memory design and RA algorithms on wafer yield, which would allow them to make changes in the memory design and improve the yield.

For upcoming DRAM technologies like DDR5 and LPDDR5, with even higher memory densities, the simulator would provide insights which would allow designers of both memory architecture and RA algorithm to simulate, predict and improve the wafer yield before actually manufacturing or finalizing the design of the new memory device.

References

1. Cho, S.K., Kang, W., Cho, H., Lee, C., Kang, S.: A survey of repair analysis algorithms for memories. ACM Comput. Surv. **49**, 1–41 (2016)
2. Tarr, M., Boudreau, D., Murphy, R.: Defect analysis system speeds test and repair of redundant memories. Electronics **29**(12), 175–179 (1984)
3. Kim, J., Cho, K., Lee, W., Kang, S.: A new redundancy analysis algorithm using one side pivot. In: 2014 International SoC Design Conference (ISOCC), Jeju, pp. 134–135 (2014)
4. Day, J.R.: A fault-driven comprehensive redundancy algorithm. IEEE Des. Test Comput. **2** (3), 35–44 (1985)
5. Lombardi, F., Huang, W.K.: Approaches for the repair of VLSI/WSI RRAMs by row/column deletion. In: International Symposium on Fault-Tolerant Computing, pp. 342–347 (1988)
6. Huang, R.-F., et al.: 'A simulator for evaluating redundancy analysis algorithms of repairable embedded memories. In: Proceedings of the IEEE International Workshop Memory Technology, Design and Testing, pp. 68–73 (2002)
7. Huang, R.-F., et al.: Raisin: redundancy analysis algorithm simulation. IEEE Des. Test Comput. **24**, 386–396 (2007)
8. Yamasaki, K., Hamdioui, S., Al-Ars, Z., Genderen, A.V., Gaydadjiev, G.N.: High quality simulation tool memory redundancy algorithms. In: ProRISC 2008, pp. 133–138 (November 2008)
9. Walker, H., Director, S.W.: VLASIC: a catastrophic fault yield simulator for integrated circuits. IEEE Trans. Comput.-Aided Des. Integr. Circuits Syst. **5**, 541–556 (1986)
10. O'Donoghue, G., Gomez-Uribe, C.A.: A statistical analysis of the number of failing chips distribution. IEEE Trans. Semicond. Manuf. **21**(3), 342–351 (2008)
11. Kim, Y., Seshadri, V., Lee, D., Liu, J., Mutlu, O.: A case for exploiting subarray-level parallelism (SALP) in DRAM. In: International Symposium on Computer Architecture, pp. 368–379 (2012)
12. Matsumoto, M., Nishimura, T.: Mersenne Twister: a 623-dimensionally equidistributed uniform pseudo-random number generator. ACM Trans. Model. Comput. Simul. **8**(1998), 3–30 (1998)
13. Atishay, Gupta, A., Sonawat, R., Thacker, H.K., Prasanth, B.: SEARS: a statistical error and redundancy analysis simulator. In: 2019 IFIP/IEEE 27th International Conference on Very Large Scale Integration (VLSI-SoC), Cuzco, Peru, pp. 117–122 (2019)

Hardware-Enabled Secure Firmware Updates in Embedded Systems

Solon Falas[1]([✉]), Charalambos Konstantinou[2], and Maria K. Michael[1]

[1] Department of Electrical and Computer Engineering, KIOS Research and Innovation Centre of Excellence, University of Cyprus, Nicosia, Cyprus
{falas.solon,mmichael}@ucy.ac.cy
[2] FAMU-FSU College of Engineering, Center for Advanced Power Systems, Florida State University, Tallahassee, FL, USA
ckonstantinou@fsu.edu

Abstract. Firmware updates on embedded systems are essential for patching vulnerabilities and improving the functionality of devices. Despite the importance of firmware updates, manufacturers and firmware developers often consider firmware security as a secondary task. As a result, firmware often turns into an alluring target for adversaries to inject malicious code into embedded devices. In this work, we present a framework that supports secure and fast firmware update delivery with minimal downtime on embedded devices. The proposed framework makes use of cryptographic primitives implemented on hardware in addition to the device's intrinsic physical characteristics acting as digital authentication fingerprints. Our implementation ensures firmware authenticity, confidentiality, and integrity. A proof-of-concept design is emulated on FPGA demonstrating high performance, strong security guarantees, and minimal hardware overhead.

Keywords: Embedded systems · Firmware updates · Hardware security

1 Introduction

Embedded devices are increasingly integrated into several Cyber-Physical System (CPS) domains such as Industrial Control Systems (ICS), home and automation networks, wireless sensing services, automobiles, etc. The deployment of these devices in mission-critical environments, however, introduces security challenges that require a different approach compared to general-purpose computing systems security [30]. Embedded systems are highly constrained in terms of performance and resources, therefore it is typically not realistic to employ similar security methods as those in general-purpose systems. Embedded device manufacturers and CPS integrators have to incorporate specialized security measures to protect these devices, and thus the CPS application they support. Studies,

© IFIP International Federation for Information Processing 2020
Published by Springer Nature Switzerland AG 2020
C. Metzler et al. (Eds.): VLSI-SoC 2019, IFIP AICT 586, pp. 165–185, 2020.
https://doi.org/10.1007/978-3-030-53273-4_8

however, have shown that these security strategies are not a priority for enterprises [22]. This is evident by the growing number of attack incidents related to microprocessor-based embedded devices [38].

A prominent example of attacks against embedded systems is the 2010 Stuxnet incident. This computer worm targeted Programmable Logic Controllers (PLCs) modifying their firmware code to perform malicious actions while also hiding its presence. Stuxnet leveraged zero-day[1] exploits in the PLCs firmware to take control over critical machinery in a nuclear power plant facility, leading to catastrophic failure [20]. Another example is the 2015 attack on Ukraine's power grid [50]. This Advanced Persistent Threat's (APT) objective was to launch a Denial-of-Service (DoS) attack on the power distribution entity's call center, disabling the Uninterruptible Power Supplies (UPS) for the control centers, and corrupting the firmware of Human-Machine Interfaces (HMI) found in Remote Terminal Units (RTU) and serial-to-Ethernet port servers. Due to the firmware corruption, circuit breakers were disabled and a power outage occurred that the customers could not report since the call centers were overloaded. A more recent large-scale attack, the Mirai botnet, was able to turn networked devices into controlled bots [23]. Mirai identified devices connected to the internet and tried to log into them using a table of more than 60 common factory default usernames and passwords. It then proceeded to infect them with the Mirai malware. The devices continued to function correctly except for some occasional sluggishness and increased bandwidth usage. These zombie devices were then directed to certain web-services to overwhelm anti-DoS software and make the service inaccessible. The fact that hundreds of thousands of networked embedded devices still use default credentials is very concerning; the effectiveness of these attacks indicates that embedded system security can no longer be an afterthought.

Firmware in embedded systems is the dedicated software that acts as an abstraction layer between bare metal hardware and software. Firmware is often residing in read-only memory, playing the role of the "operating system" in an embedded device [4,28,35], providing low-level control of the device. Due to this ability, firmware is considered a critical component of a device that has to be routinely updated and maintained in order to fix bugs, address performance-related issues, and even enhance or change the device's intended functionality. However, embedded device owners are often reluctant to update their devices' firmware due to the chance of rendering their devices inoperable in case of an error and because of the extensive downtime that they may experience [17,24]. On the other hand, manufacturers often do not provide firmware updates or support once their devices are released to the market. Even if they do, their updates typically do not conform to security principles including encryption and authentication. A recent survey proves that there have not been significant security gains in the firmware domain for the last 15 years [45]. The firmware

---

[1] "Day Zero" or "Zero-day" is the day which a vulnerability of a system is made known to its vendor or to those who should be interested in mitigating the vulnerability. Hackers discovering these vulnerabilities can exploit them well before they are mitigated. Such exploits are known as "zero-day exploits".

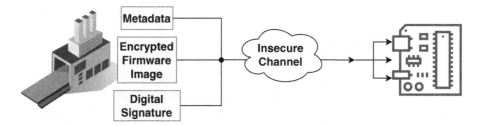

Fig. 1. An overview of the proposed approach. A firmware package is formed by combining necessary metadata, the encrypted firmware image, and the manufacturer's digital signature. The firmware package is transmitted to the embedded system through an insecure channel. The device unpacks it and verifies its source and contents utilizing hardware-implemented cryptographic primitives.

security of embedded systems is not addressed to the same level as that of general-purpose computers or BIOS security [36].

Existing industry efforts aim to secure firmware and other sensitive information stored at the device hardware in the form of secure storage and trusted execution environments. However, these methods have been proven to leak data to malicious attackers using a variety of attacks that take advantage of bugs and exploits in operating systems [39], user applications [33], and even proprietary code that aims at securing cryptographic keys and encrypted data [37]. To tackle these challenges, our work proposes the utilization of hardware-based cryptographic primitives to avoid storing secrets in non-volatile memory and alleviate reliance on software routines. Our proposed framework ensures firmware data integrity and confidentiality in a time-efficient manner by using hardware-implemented cryptographic modules while hardware-intrinsic characteristics are used as "digital fingerprints" to perform authentication procedures.

The overview of our framework is shown in Fig. 1. Firmware updates are transmitted from the manufacturer to the embedded device through an insecure channel. The proposed approach relies on hardware as a root-of-trust to attain high security levels and is motivated towards low-end embedded devices [19]. The framework is designed in a way that user intervention and device downtime are minimized. Hence, there is no need for intermediate authenticators to perform key exchange and management. The embedded device can be deployed without requiring any secure key-enrollment phase. Specifically, we employ hardware-implemented encryption and cryptographic hash functions to provide firmware confidentiality and data integrity, respectively. The means of digital fingerprinting are demonstrated via Physical Unclonable Functions (PUFs) [52]. The unclonable nature of PUFs bounds the firmware packages created by the manufacturer to a single device. If a device gets compromised, same model devices retain security. The PUF used in our proof-of-concept design is a Public PUF (PPUF), meaning that it does not rely on the secrecy of the Integrated Circuit's (IC) physical parameters since the model describing the PPUF is public.

Our framework is implemented and evaluated in an experimental setup using both software and hardware. A general-purpose computer is in charge of the firmware packaging procedure, acting as the device manufacturer. The embedded device to be updated is emulated on FPGA as a proof-of-concept hardware design. The unpacking process, involving the authentication and decryption, is carried out on the embedded device. Our security analysis of the proposed approach shows strong security guarantees while our experimental measurements demonstrate the feasibility of the approach and applicability for constrained embedded devices.

The rest of the chapter is organized as follows. Related work on firmware update security mechanisms and PUF-based authentication protocols are discussed in Sect. 2. The underlying security primitives considered in our proof-of-concept design are discussed in Sect. 3. The proposed methodology for secure firmware updates is presented in Sect. 4 alongside with the security analysis of the approach. The experimental setup and implementation details are presented in Sect. 5. Section 6 concludes the chapter.

2   Related Work

Firmware images and updates are typically provided online via vendors or manufacturers' websites. It has been shown that web crawlers can be used to gather images of critical equipment by traversing websites that host firmware [13]. These files can be accessed, downloaded, and modified due to the lack of access control measures and encryption. Firmware can also be acquired through physical access to the device [25]. By having access to the firmware image, a malicious adversary can retrieve the inner workings of a device and expose its functionality.

The information acquired from reverse engineering the firmware can lead to revealing zero-day exploits or other known vulnerabilities, that may provide an adversary an "attack path" to the system utilizing the aforementioned device. For example, access to the firmware image binary may allow adversaries to launch firmware modification attacks able to cause severe implications to a system's functionality. Recent works have demonstrated the severity of such attacks in the ICS domain when targeting devices such as PLCs and protection relays [4,26,54]. These types of attacks have also been shown to be effective against a large variety of other embedded devices such as printers, cameras, and network switches [13,14].

Efforts to secure the firmware update mechanisms on embedded devices led to secure storage and trusted execution environments, such as i-NVMM [12] and ARM TrustZone [41]. However, the design of such systems is an attractive target for both invasive and non-invasive attacks [8,27,29]. For instance, since the JTAG protocol is not designed with security in mind, the JTAG test port can provide access to secure memories allowing embedded devices to be reconfigured. Also, it has been demonstrated that attackers are able to exploit implementation-based weaknesses to leak sensitive information through covert channels [40].

To overcome these shortcomings, we propose avoiding reliance on software and pre-stored data in non-volatile memories by moving towards a hardware root-of-trust. Research works towards this end, suggest using the hardware's intrinsic properties to design and support security mechanisms. Such solutions include PUFs that leverage manufacturing variability to produce secret keys for authentication and encryption purposes. Different types of PUFs are used to produce unique identifiers that can be used in security schemes for authentication and secure code updates. Silicon-based PUFs (ring-oscillator, SRAM, arbiter, etc.) utilize manufacturing variability as an entropy source to create chip-specific identifiers. Examples of non-silicon designs include optical PUFs that exploit the random scattering of light to act as physical one-way functions. These kinds of solutions are successful in several domains such as intellectual property protection and Internet-of-Things (IoT) [9,32].

Several approaches incorporating PUFs have been proposed to address the problem of storing sensitive information in non-volatile memories. Rostami et al. propose a PUF-based authentication and key exchange protocol based on substring matching [47]. The scheme utilizes PUFs for secure communications while alleviating the need for error correction against PUF's inherent noise. In [2], an end-to-end privacy-preserving authentication protocol is described, suitable for resource-constrained devices. The protocol attempts to perform mutual authentication procedures between enrolled embedded devices and a server utilizing reverse fuzzy-extraction mechanisms for key recreation on each side. In the context of IoT, a PUF-based communication protocol is presented in [10]. Before any secure communication is initiated between two devices, each PUF-enabled party has to share its Challenge-Response Pairs (CRPs) with an intermediate server. This server coordinates the communication between the two devices by issuing a public and a private key for each party. Feng et al. demonstrate a code update protocol utilizing PUFs [21]. The protocol starts with a temporary session in a secure environment between a server and the embedded device to share symmetric keys. The enrolled device is then employed and can securely communicate and update its code using its PUF for authentication. Che et al. show how within-die path delay variations can be utilized to enable a mutual PUF-based authentication protocol [11].

Most of the proposed solutions incorporate either strong or weak PUFs[2] which are highly susceptible to a variety of attacks. For example, weak PUFs have to remain entirely secret and an attacker with physical access could easily extract the required CRPs and break the authentication protocol in place [46]. Strong PUFs are more difficult to reverse engineer or extract information from, but they are highly susceptible to modeling and machine learning attacks. Such attacks involve producing a relatively low number of CRPs from the PUF and

---

[2] The strength of a PUF depends on the number of CRPs that can be generated [34]. Weak PUFs produce very few CRPs derived from a physical characteristic. They usually act as fingerprints, e.g., a static bitstring, unique for each device due to manufacturing variability altering the IC's characteristics. Strong PUFs, on the other hand, produce a very large amount of CRP, exponential to their size, whereas weak PUFs produce a linear or polynomial number of CRPs. They are utilized as secret key providers for encryption/decryption purposes.

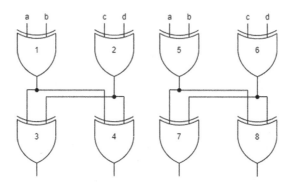

Fig. 2. An example of a small differential Public Physical Unclonable Function (dPPUF). Left (1–4) and right (5–8) circuits are the same in functionality. The challenge (abcd) is presented at both sides at the same time. However, the output of gates 3–4 and 7–8 stabilizes at different times due to manufacturing variability. The fastest propagating signals determine the corresponding response that forms the CRP.

then create a machine learning model that will be trained using the gathered CRPs. The model then can quickly derive the remaining CRPs and create a dictionary that will contain an excessive amount of known pairs [48,49,55]. The aforementioned proposed protocols also require a secure setup phase; an essential key exchange procedure that must happen in a secure environment. A number of the proposed approaches also require intermediate servers to coordinate key distribution or enable communication between embedded devices. In comparison with the existing works on hardware-based secure communication protocols, our proposed framework neither requires a secure setup phase nor intermediate authenticator servers. The public-key infrastructure of our firmware update scheme alleviates the need for the aforementioned measures due to the public-key components including PPUFs, public-key cryptography, and digital signatures.

3   Underlying Security Primitives

The proposed framework employs cryptographic primitives in hardware in order to implement securely the firmware image exchange protocol. The approach requires both a private and a public key encryption/decryption core, a cryptographic hash function, and a PPUF in order to provide confidentiality, authenticity, and integrity guarantees.

PPUFs are a category of PUFs whose IC characteristics can be made public since they do not rely on their secrecy, unlike traditional PUFs. A PPUF is designed to be fast-to-execute and slow-to-simulate [42]. In the context of this work, a differential PPUF (dPPUF) is utilized due to its characteristics of not requiring ultra-accurate timing mechanisms. For instance, traditional XOR-based PPUFs, as the one shown in Fig. 2, require a very high clock resolution to accurately "catch" the racing signals at the end of the PPUF circuit. A 256-bit

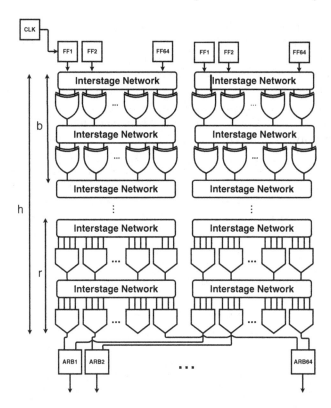

Fig. 3. The differential Public Physical Unclonable Function (dPPUF) architecture consists of consecutive layers of boosters and repressers. The two sides are identical in structure but different in inherent delays (inertial, propagation, switching, etc.). A layer of arbiters is placed at the end to capture the fastest propagating signals and according to the result, create the appropriate response bit string.

dPPUF is adopted from [43], presented in Fig. 3. PUFs are inherently noisy and therefore require error correction mechanisms to stabilize them. To alleviate for the PUF's inherent noise, in this work, and without loss of generality, we consider a Bose–Chaudhuri–Hocquenghem (BCH)-based code-offset fuzzy extractor as an effective PUF error correction mechanism [15].

In order to create a PPUF model, as required in our framework, the manufacturer has to perform gate-level characterization[3]. The measured IC characteristics form a software model that can be stored in a public repository. The software model is the "public part" of the PPUF since it does not provide any advantage to any adversary. This is because of the Execution-Simulation Gap (ESG). ESG

---

[3] Gate-level characterization is the process of characterizing each gate of an IC in terms of its physical properties using lasers, micro-probing, and simulations [31]. Typical characteristics measured include gate width and length, and properties such as leakage power and switching power.

is the time advantage the PPUF hardware owner has over a simulating attacker when calculating a CRP. A CRP is formed by the input to the PPUF's model, i.e., the challenge, and its corresponding output, i.e., the response. The procedure to produce a CRP is very fast when executed on hardware but significantly slower when done via simulation. In order to take advantage of this disparity we use the challenge as an encryption key while responding to the decrypting party. The inverse operation, i.e., deriving which challenge created the provided response, can only be completed on the actual PPUF hardware since simulating all the possible challenges to find a matching response is infeasible in simulation. Therefore, this ESG can be used as a root-of-trust and the model can be stored publicly without any security implications. ESG can also be manipulated to give as much advantage to the PPUF owner over the simulating adversary as needed. Increasing either the key width or number of challenges that need to be calculated increases the simulation effort for any attacker trying to derive the challenge of a particular response.

In order to provide confidentiality guarantees, we encrypt the firmware image. Encryption is the process of encoding plaintext data making it unintelligible and scrambled in a way that no unauthorized party can understand them. To decrypt the data, a cryptographic key is required. The key acts as a guide, helping the authorized party rearrange and reassemble the encrypted data correctly, so that access to the plaintext is possible. To address confidentiality, we employ the symmetric-key encryption algorithm Advanced Encryption Standard in Galois/Counter Mode (AES-GCM). AES-GCM is an authenticated encryption algorithm providing both data integrity and confidentiality [16]. Its hardware implementation provides a high encryption/decryption data rate while being adequately efficient in the use of hardware resources. AES-GCM is operating with 128-bit blocks and has four inputs: a 128-bit secret key, a 96-bit initialization vector, a plaintext, and optional additional authenticated data. AES-GCM generates two outputs: a message authentication code and a ciphertext. The message authentication code acts as a checksum value that enables integrity checks.

Towards ensuring that the firmware package contains undeniable truth that it originated from the manufacturer (non-repudiation) and thus protecting the device from impersonation attacks, the proposed approach utilizes digital signatures. The concept of digital signatures is depicted in Fig. 4. They are data that accompany the firmware image and provide evidence of their origin. To effectively use digital signatures, a cryptographic hash function is required along with the utilization of a public-key cryptosystem. Essentially, the sender has to hash the data payload, e.g., the firmware image, and encrypt it with a private key. In our setup, the procedure to create the manufacturer's digital signature is the following: (1) the manufacturer has to select a secret private key and (2) a public key. (3) A hash digest of the firmware image is created and encrypted by a public-key cryptosystem using the manufacturer's private key. The public-key cryptosystem utilized in our setup is RSA, also known as Rivest–Shamir–Adleman, while the cryptographic hash function employed is SHA-256, both NIST-approved cryp-

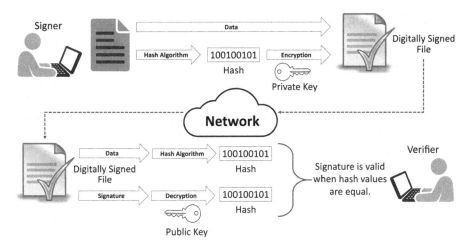

Fig. 4. Digital signature creation involves the usage of a cryptographic hash function and a public-key cryptosystem. A hash of the payload data is encrypted using the signer's private key. The verifier decrypts the digital signature using the signer's public key and hashes the payload data. The signature is considered valid if the resulting hashes match.

tographic implementations [3,44]. The verifier, in this case the device, is able to receive the data alongside the digital signature and recreate the digest on its side. Then the signature is decrypted using the manufacturer's public key and compared to that digest. If the hashes match, then the manufacturer is authenticated.

While the aforementioned cryptographic primitives are well established and widely used mechanisms in the area of cryptography and security, alternatives with similar characteristics can still be utilized in our proposed framework. Our approach is designed with modularity and flexibility in mind. Alternative cryptographic hash functions and encryption algorithms can be considered as long as they adhere to the needs of the secure firmware update protocol. For example, alternative encryption algorithms of symmetrical type can be chosen instead of AES-GCM. Examples include Simon [5], a lightweight block cipher released by the National Security Agency (NSA) and optimized for performance in hardware implementations, and Twofish [51], a symmetric key block cipher alternative to AES. The cryptographic hash function and public-key cryptosystem can also be interchanged with similar mechanisms. For instance, lighter alternatives can be used to adjust the design for even more constrained devices, such as a lightweight implementation of Keccak using only 200 permutations [7]. This flexibility gives the ability to the manufacturer to adjust their devices to certain security level constraints and available computational resources depending on each domain and application scenario.

4   Methodology

In this section, we provide the details of the proposed framework under the consideration of a malicious individual trying to manipulate the firmware updating procedure. The main objective is to encrypt a firmware image and deliver it to the embedded device through an insecure channel. An attacker observing the insecure channel should be unable to extract information from the firmware image. Only the intended device can decrypt the firmware image and verify its authenticity.

4.1   Threat Model and Countermeasures

We consider that the firmware packaging procedure from the manufacturer is an error-free process taking place in a secure facility, i.e., the firmware package is prepared correctly. The dPPUF model, however, is publicly available since accessing it does not give the attacker any advantage. The firmware package is transferred to the device over an insecure channel. The attacker can intercept packages on that channel. The attacker's goal is to uncover the firmware image binary and reverse-engineer it to place backdoors and uncover proprietary device operations. Using a malicious firmware binary the attacker tries to impersonate the device manufacturer to transfer a modified firmware package to the embedded system as the legitimate one.

In order to prevent this malicious activity, we employ several cryptographic techniques utilizing their hardware-implemented counterparts. To encrypt the firmware image and protect its binary form from unauthorized access, we use a symmetric cipher, specifically the AES-GCM. The keys required for this encryption procedure will be provided by the dPPUF and its model, making the firmware package chip-specific. In addition, the device receiving the firmware update must also have proof of the firmware package's origins in order to be secure against impersonation attacks. In order to alleviate this issue, we employ asymmetric cryptography as well in the form of digital signatures. A digital signature accompanying a payload gives proof of firmware origins while also being a checksum for integrity checks. The digital signatures in our setup utilize SHA-256 for cryptographic hashing and RSA for asymmetric cryptography.

4.2   Firmware Update Procedure

The firmware update procedure consists of two main parts, each undertaken – in sequence – by the device manufacturer and the device user. The manufacturer constructs a firmware package that contains the encrypted firmware image as well as metadata. Metadata allows the embedded device to authenticate and decrypt the firmware image without revealing useful information to any malicious entity observing the insecure channel used for data transfer. For this methodology to be successful, a combination of security primitives is utilized such as a cryptographic hash function (SHA-256), a symmetric (AES-GCM) and an asymmetric

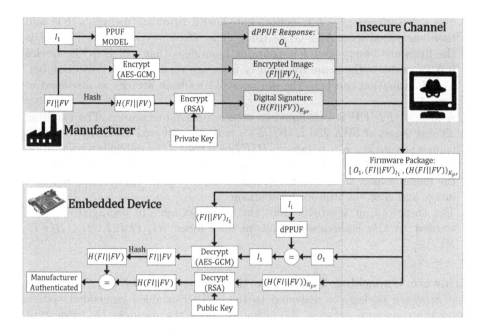

Fig. 5. The firmware package generation flow: the firmware vendor encrypts the composed image utilizing a public PUF model. The firmware unpacking process at the device level: the firmware package is decrypted, verified, and uploaded to the embedded device by utilizing public PUF's (dPPUF) intrinsic manufacturing variability.

(RSA) encryption/decryption module, and a PPUF (dPPUF). These crypto-modules are implemented on the hardware of the embedded device to avoid reliance on software routines and pre-stored data. The firmware transition, from the manufacturer packaging to the embedded device delivery, is shown in Fig. 5.

Secure Firmware Package Generation by Manufacturer: The upper half of Fig. 5 presents the steps required by the manufacturer to produce a valid and secure firmware package. The manufacturer uses a challenge to create a response from the dPPUF model, encrypts the firmware image using that challenge, and creates a digital signature. Then, these 3 output products are bundled together in a firmware package to be sent to the embedded device. In particular, the overall process involves the following:

1. The manufacturer generates a random challenge I_1. This is a 256-bit long binary that is going to be used as input to the dPPUF model. This challenge creates the 256-bit response O_1. This CRP's challenge I_1 is used to encrypt the firmware image such that only the intended device is able to decrypt it. The length of the CRP strings can be increased, if necessary, to further reduce the risk of brute force attacks.

2. The firmware image FI is concatenated with firmware metadata FV and then encrypted with AES-GCM using I_1 as the encryption key. The FI is the firmware binary and FV contains identifiers that will help the device further evaluate the firmware, namely firmware version and revision number. This information can help the device avoid rollback attacks as discussed in Sect. 4.3.
3. A hash of $FI\|FV$ is calculated to create a digital signature. The resulting 256-bit digest of SHA-256 $H(FI\|FV)$ is then encrypted using the manufacturer's private key K_{pr} to create $(H(FI\|FV))_{K_{pr}}$. The public key encryption scheme used is RSA. The digital signature allows the device to authenticate the manufacturer since it is the only one capable of decrypting the firmware image and create a hash for comparison.
4. The three output products from the manufacturer are packaged and forwarded to the embedded device in this form: $[O_1, (FI\|FV)_{I_1}, (H(FI\| FV))_{K_{pr}}]$.

Firmware Unpacking Process by the Embedded Device: The generated firmware package is delivered to the dPPUF-enabled embedded system through an insecure network. The device utilizes the response O_1 to decrypt $(FI\|FV)_{I_1}$ and authenticate the package's origins using the digital signature $(H(FI\|FV))_{K_{pr}}$. The unpacking process steps include the following:

1. The embedded device makes use of the response O_1 to recreate challenge I_1. In order to achieve it, the device iterates throughout all possible input combinations to the dPPUF until it finds a response that matches O_1. This *CRP iteration* is only feasible using dedicated hardware and it is computationally prohibitive to carry out this operation through simulation [6]. Therefore, only the correct recipient device is able to perform this operation efficiently.
2. Once I_1 is derived, the embedded device uses I_1 as the key, for the hardware-implemented AES-GCM module, to decrypt $(FI\|FV)_{I_1}$ and get $FI\|FV$. Once the FV is obtained, the device is able to check the firmware version of the update and compared it to the firmware currently installed at the device. If the firmware image FI indicates an older version of the device's existing firmware, the update operation is aborted.
3. In parallel to the previous step, the digital signature $(H(FI\|FV))_{K_{pr}}$ is decrypted with RSA using the manufacturer's public key. This operation results in $H(FI\|FV)$.
4. If the firmware image indicates a firmware update, a cryptographic hash digest of $FI\|FV$ is generated using SHA-256. The hash digest is compared to the result of the RSA decryption. If the hashes match, then the embedded device authenticates the origin of the firmware from the legitimate manufacturer.
5. If all the required authentication and decryption procedures are completed, the device can proceed with updating its firmware code.

As explained in Sect. 3, the dPPUF is a series of cascading gates which, when a challenge is introduced, a response is created. The manufacturer has access to a software model describing the dPPUF present in the device which is going to be updated. Using a software model to simulate CRPs is significantly slower than performing the same operation directly on hardware. By using the challenge as an encryption key while providing the response in plaintext, we ensure that only the intended device is be able to decrypt the firmware image in a feasible time frame. This is based on the fact that in order to find a challenge for a corresponding response requires iterating through all possible challenges until a matching response is found. Therefore, we leverage the ESG characteristic of PPUFs to keep malicious attackers from getting a plaintext version of the firmware binary. The time advantage of the dPPUF hardware during CRP iteration over an attacker, simulating the same procedure, can vary depending on the dPPUF implementation. For example, a 1024-bit implementation of the dPPUF makes breaking the protocol extremely prohibitive, according to the analysis in [6]. Our implementation focuses on constrained devices, thus the structure is based on a 256-bit design. The firmware package is also chip-specific since every device will have a different PPUF and consequently different CRPs. The manufacturer also appends a digital signature to the encrypted firmware so that the embedded device can authenticate it.

Overall, our proposed framework has the following features: (1) it does not require a secure setup phase for key exchange between the firmware sender and receiver because the decryption key is dynamically generated by the hardware, (2) a malicious attacker observing the insecure channel cannot uncover the firmware image and cannot impersonate the manufacturer, (3) the firmware can only be decrypted by the intended device, and (4) the methodology can be easily adapted to incorporate different cryptographic primitives. Encryption/decryption modules and cryptographic hash functions can be substituted with other equivalent crypto-cores without altering the overall functionality of the design.

4.3   Security Analysis

The framework is designed to adhere to certain security requirements. First, we need to ensure that adversaries eavesdropping in the communication channel and able to intercept the firmware package, cannot reveal the binary of the firmware, and thus identify code subroutines that expose the embedded device's functionality. We also need to ensure that if the firmware package is corrupted or tampered during transmission, the device would be able to detect it. The device must also have the ability to authenticate the package's origins in order to be protected against impersonation and man-in-the-middle attacks. Installing earlier versions of firmware may re-introduce bugs and thus firmware rollback should be avoided.

To fulfill the above requirements we employ hardware-implemented versions of the AES-GCM algorithm, SHA-256 cryptographic hash functions, and RSA public-key cryptosystem. Since the firmware image, alongside the necessary metadata, is encrypted using AES-GCM, an attacker cannot extract the firmware binary from the transmitted package in plaintext form without having access to the key. The key, however, is only known by the manufacturer and only the intended device can recreate it. RSA and SHA-256 are used to form the manufacturer's digital signature. The role of the digital signature is not only to act as a checksum value that allows the device to check the firmware's data integrity but also as undeniable evidence that the sender is indeed the manufacturer. Digital signatures require a hash digest which acts as a checksum value. The digest is encrypted by the manufacturer's private key. Therefore, it can only be decrypted using the manufacturer's public key, authenticating the package's origins. After completing the decryption and authentication procedures, the embedded device checks FV to determine the firmware version of the update. If it is not an update to the existing firmware, the device halts the updating operation to avoid roll-back attacks.

The aforementioned security primitives are utilized as hardware-based cryptographic modules implemented on the embedded device. These primitives alleviate the need for secure storage of secret information such as credentials and encryption keys directly on the device's non-volatile memory. Keys and other secret information are dynamically recreated on the device upon demand. The firmware update operation is also non-dependent on software-based routines, and thus less susceptible to software-based attacks [53].

The utilized dPPUF circuit inherits by design certain security guarantees. The effort to simulate dPPUF using its public model scales exponentially with the dPPUF's depth and width. A small increase in depth or width may prove prohibitive in terms of time, for pre-computing all sets of CRPs. Even with enough computing capabilities for generating CRP lookup tables, the storage requirement would be impractically high. Also, the public model of dPPUF ensures that profile characterization (e.g., power profile) of the circuit would not reveal any side-channel information.

5   Experimental Setup and Results

We implement a proof-of-concept experimental setup in order to validate and evaluate our approach. As shown in Fig. 6, both the firmware packing and unpacking phases have been implemented. The procedures performed by the manufacturer are implemented in software using a 64-bit computer with 3.2 GHz Intel Core i5-4460 quad-core processor and 8 GB RAM. The unpacking process, on the embedded device's end, is emulated utilizing a Xilinx Kintex7 FPGA with a system clock frequency of 100 MHz.

Our PPUF implementation is using multiple layers of boosters (2-input XOR gate) followed by repressers (small NAND-based circuit [43]), i.e., $b = 1$ and $r = 1$ with the height and width of the dPPUF being $h = 10$ and $w = 256$, respectively. It is implemented on hardware, using the aforementioned FPGA, using artificial transmission and switching delays at each gate, shown in Fig. 3, to emulate manufacturing variations. The delay values are generated by a pseudo-random number generator software to avoid any kind of bias. The model of the dPPUF is constructed in $C++$ as a graph, where its nodes represent the dPPUF gates and their respective delays.

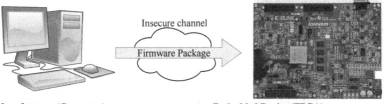

Manufacturer (Computer):
1) Creates a CRP using the C++ dPPUF model
2) Encrypts firmware and creates digital
signature using Python script
3) Append into a firmware package

Embedded Device (FPGA)
1) Unpacks the firmware package
2) Recreates decryption key using the dPPUF hardware
3) Decrypts firmware and constructs required hashes
4) Authenticates manufacturer using digital signature

Fig. 6. Experimental and evaluation setup. The hardware-implemented security primitives are developed on a FPGA in order to emulate a dPPUF-enabled device. The firmware packaging procedure are carried out on a computer which is connected to the FPGA through a serial cable.

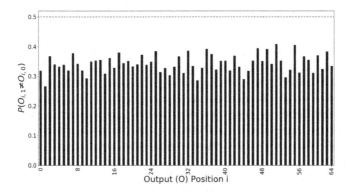

Fig. 7. Strict Avalanche Criterion (SAC) of dPPUF model. The red dashed line shows the ideal case, where $P(O_i - 1) = 0.5$ for all i. (Color figure online)

The effectiveness of a dPPUF design is determined by the entropy that it exhibits. We ensure that the responses cannot be correlated to their corresponding challenges and its CRPs are adequately random by conducting extensive tests. Specifically, we validate the dPPUF's software model with $10k$ input vectors and compare them with the resulting outputs. Then, we utilize the Strict Avalanche Criterion (SAC) to quantify the entropy. SAC is measured by calculating the correlation probability of the corresponding outputs of two input vectors that have a hamming distance equal to 1. Figure 7 presents the SAC demonstrated by our dPPUF design with an average probability of each output switching equal to 0.3425, similar to the results in the related literature [43].

Every procedure needed for completing the firmware packaging process is done in software. Firstly, the dPPUF model is utilized to create a CRP that will be used for encrypting the firmware package in a chip-specific way. The resulting response O_1 is going to be used as an unencrypted header for the firmware pack-

Table 1. FPGA resource utilization for the firmware unpacking process.

Resources	AES-GCM	SHA-256	RSA	dPPUF	Overall design
LUT(#)	2671	1330	547	766	3183
FF(#)	1568	753	527	275	3981

Table 2. Firmware unpacking timings.

Device	Firmware (kB)	Total execution (ms)
Sercos III	233	72.27308
Zelio Logic	323	72.42759
Modicon	1183	73.90583

age while its corresponding challenge I_1 is also used as a secret key to encrypt the concatenation of the firmware image and the firmware version data $(FI||FV)$ to create $(FI||FV)_{I_1}$. The manufacturer also needs to prepare a digital signature to prove the firmware's origins to the device. The procedure for creating a digital signature involves hashing the concatenation $(FI||FV)$ to create $H(FI||FV)$ and then encrypting it using the manufacturer's private key. The resulting digital signature $(H(FI||FV))_{K_{pr}}$ is appended to O_1 and $(FI||FV)$ to create the firmware package. The required cryptographic algorithms, such as encryption/decryption and hashing, are implemented in Python using the *pycryptodome* library [18]. For our experiments, we choose three commercial firmware files acquired from the vendors' websites to be tested. The firmware images are those of embedded systems designed for ICS environments. The devices are a Sercos III field bus interface module, a Zelio Logic SRA2/SR3 smart relay, and a Modicon M258 logic controller.

We use an FPGA to emulate the embedded device supporting the described hardware-implemented cryptographic primitives. The unpacking process is carried out using Hardware Description Language (HDL) to demonstrate the effectiveness of the approach when running directly on hardware. We make use of Xilinx Vivado Design Suite 2018.3. The hardware resources required for these primitives are presented in Table 1. The hardware overhead for each security primitive is shown as the hardware usage of the overall design. Synthesis and implementation algorithms provided by the HDL development tools help with optimizing the overall design in terms of area. Also, routing and placement algorithms can remove a lot of redundant hardware between these modules.

The firmware package produced by the manufacturer (e.g., the computer in our setup) is transferred at the receiving party which loads it into the memory and initiates the unpacking process. In our implementation, we first pre-load the firmware image in *block RAM* and then proceed with decryption and authentication procedures. During the unpacking process of the firmware, the dPPUF input challenge, O_1, from the firmware package header is used to recreate the key of AES-GCM, I_1. Then, the dPPUF iterates through all the possible challenges

Table 3. Comparison with previous work.

Method	Area overhead		Performance (ms)
	LUT (#)	FF (#)	
Proposed	3183	3981	73.90583
Aysu *et al.* [2]	3543	1275	61
Che *et al.* [11]	6038	1724	1250

of a given set (10^6 possible inputs in our setup), until it finds a response matching O_1. This is the CRP iteration explained in Sect. 3, utilizing the ESG to have an advantage over the attacker. Once I_1 is derived, the AES-GCM decryption core is ready to decrypt $(FI||FV)_{I_1}$ and get the plaintext $FI||FV$. In parallel, the RSA core decrypts $(H(FI||FV))_{K_{pr}}$ using the manufacturer's public key K_{pub} to uncover $H(FI||FV)$. This hash derived from the digital signature is going to be compared to the output of the SHA-256 core when the input is the plaintext $FI||FV$. If the resulting hash matches the hash uncovered from the digital signature, then the manufacturer is authenticated and the embedded device is assured of the firmware image's origin and integrity. Finally, the FV is examined to determine the firmware image's version and revision number. If it is determined to be an actual update, then the firmware update procedure can be initiated. If the version or revision number indicate a downgrade, the firmware image is rejected to avoid rollback attacks. The whole experiment is run for each one of the industrial-grade firmware images. The time to finish the decryption and authentication is measured, starting from the package's arrival to the device. The three firmware images are presented in Table 2 along with their respective total unpacking time.

Table 3 provides a comparison with relevant state-of-the-art methods in terms of area and performance overhead. The time measured by [2] and [11] is the time that the device needs to establish a secure connection with the server and authenticate it. On the other hand, we measure our performance as the time a device takes to unpack a firmware package and perform all the necessary authentication and decryption procedures. Therefore, our measurements include time-consuming decryption procedures that put us at a disadvantage when compared to the time measurements reported by [2] and [11]. The performance for the proposed methodology, reported in Table 3, is the time needed to completely unpack the Modicon firmware image and authenticate the manufacturer. In [2] and [11], PUF-based privacy-preserving authentication protocols are being considered. When we only compare area overhead, [2] is lighter; however, it exhibits several drawbacks. As discussed in Sect. 2, the proposed approach by Aysu *et al.* requires initial setup and an enrollment phase (on top of PUF hardware characterization), steps which our approach does not require. It also necessitates having a trusted third-party server to complete the authentication handshake. Also, the protocol does not take into account data integrity issues neither implements any countermeasures. In addition, the work utilizes an SRAM-based PUF which is known to be vulnerable to a variety of attacks [1,46]. An authentication protocol that provides both confidentiality and mutual authentication is presented in [11]. This protocol is utilizing a new type of PUF, the hardware-embedded path delay (HELP) PUF. This kind of PUF derives randomness from path delay variance within a hardware implementation of AES. The work shows comparable resource usage. Nevertheless, the protocol does not address data integrity. Also, our implementation performs significantly better in terms of execution time than the mechanism proposed by [11], while also requiring a lot fewer hardware resources.

6   Conclusions

In this work, we develop a flexible firmware update framework for securely updating embedded systems. The framework makes use of the unique physical characteristics of each embedded system's IC to bind firmware packages to a specific device. By utilizing hardware-implemented cryptographic primitives, we can guarantee the confidentiality and integrity of the firmware image while being transmitted through an insecure channel. Our framework's security analysis demonstrates the validity of the security measures while showing the device's protection mechanisms against impersonation and other types of attacks. A proof-of-concept implementation with a commercial-off-the-shelf firmware of an industrial embedded system verifies the practicality of the approach in resource constraint devices. The performance results show that the proposed framework not only provides security but also fast firmware updates.

Acknowledgment. This work has been supported by the European Union's Horizon 2020 research and innovation programme under grant agreement No. 739551 (KIOS CoE) and from the Government of the Republic of Cyprus through the Directorate General for European Programmes, Coordination and Development. Partial support of this research was also provided by the Woodrow W. Everett, Jr. SCEEE Development Fund in cooperation with the Southeastern Association of Electrical Engineering Department Heads.

References

1. Anagnostopoulos, N.A., Arul, T., Rosenstihl, M., Schaller, A., Gabmeyer, S., Katzenbeisser, S.: Low-temperature data remanence attacks against intrinsic SRAM PUFs. In: 2018 21st Euromicro Conference on Digital System Design (DSD), pp. 581–585. IEEE (2018)
2. Aysu, A., Gulcan, E., Moriyama, D., Schaumont, P., Yung, M.: End-to-end design of a PUF-based privacy preserving authentication protocol. In: Güneysu, T., Handschuh, H. (eds.) CHES 2015. LNCS, vol. 9293, pp. 556–576. Springer, Heidelberg (2015). https://doi.org/10.1007/978-3-662-48324-4_28
3. Barker, E., Dang, Q.: NIST special publication 800–57 part 1, revision 4. Tech. rep, NIST (2016)
4. Basnight, Z., Butts, J., Lopez Jr., J., Dube, T.: Firmware modification attacks on programmable logic controllers. Int. J. Crit. Infrastruct. Prot. **6**(2), 76–84 (2013)

5. Beaulieu, R., Shors, D., Smith, J., Treatman-Clark, S., Weeks, B., Wingers, L.: The simon and speck families of lightweight block ciphers. IACR Cryptol. ePrint Arch. **2013**(1), 404–449 (2013)
6. Beckmann, N., Potkonjak, M.: Hardware-based public-key cryptography with public physically unclonable functions. In: Katzenbeisser, S., Sadeghi, A.-R. (eds.) IH 2009. LNCS, vol. 5806, pp. 206–220. Springer, Heidelberg (2009). https://doi.org/10.1007/978-3-642-04431-1_15
7. Bertoni, G., Daemen, J., Peeters, M., Van Assche, G.: Keccak. In: Johansson, T., Nguyen, P.Q. (eds.) EUROCRYPT 2013. LNCS, vol. 7881, pp. 313–314. Springer, Heidelberg (2013). https://doi.org/10.1007/978-3-642-38348-9_19
8. Breeuwsma, M., De Jongh, M., Klaver, C., Van Der Knijff, R., Roeloffs, M.: Forensic data recovery from flash memory. Small Scale Digit. Device Forensics J. **1**(1), 1–17 (2007)
9. Brisbanne, O.M., Bossuet, L.: Restoration protocol: lightweight and secure devices authentication based on PUF. In: IFIP/IEEE International Conference on Very Large Scale Integration, VLSI-SoC 2017 (2017)
10. Chatterjee, U., Chakraborty, R.S., Mukhopadhyay, D.: A PUF-based secure communication protocol for IoT. ACM Trans. Embed. Comput. Syst. (TECS) **16**(3), 67 (2017)
11. Che, W., Martin, M., Pocklassery, G., Kajuluri, V.K., Saqib, F., Plusquellic, J.: A privacy-preserving, mutual PUF-based authentication protocol. Cryptography **1**(1), 3 (2017)
12. Chhabra, S., Solihin, Y.: i-NVMM: a secure non-volatile main memory system with incremental encryption. In: 2011 38th Annual International Symposium on Computer Architecture (ISCA), pp. 177–188. IEEE (2011)
13. Costin, A., Zaddach, J., Francillon, A., Balzarotti, D.: A large-scale analysis of the security of embedded firmwares. In: 23rd {USENIX} Security Symposium ({USENIX} Security 2014), pp. 95–110 (2014)
14. Cui, A., Costello, M., Stolfo, S.J.: When firmware modifications attack: a case study of embedded exploitation. In: NDSS (2013)
15. Dodis, Y., Ostrovsky, R., Reyzin, L., Smith, A.: Fuzzy extractors: how to generate strong keys from biometrics and other noisy data. SIAM J. Comput. **38**(1), 97–139 (2008)
16. Dworkin, M.J.: SP 800–38D, Recommendation for Block Cipher Modes of Operation: Galois/Counter Mode (GCM) and GMAC. NIST, Gaithersburg (2007)
17. Eaton, C.: Hacked: energy industry's controls provide an alluring target for cyberattacks (2017). http://www.houstonchronicle.com/
18. Eijs, H.: pycryptodome (2014). https://github.com/Legrandin/pycryptodome
19. Falas, S., Konstantinou, C., Michael, M.K.: A hardware-based framework for secure firmware updates on embedded systems. In: 2019 IFIP/IEEE 27th International Conference on Very Large Scale Integration (VLSI-SoC), pp. 198–203. IEEE (2019)
20. Falliere, N., Murchu, L.O., Chien, E.: W32. Stuxnet dossier. White Pap. Symantec Corp. Secur. Response **5**(6), 29 (2011)
21. Feng, W., Qin, Y., Zhao, S., Liu, Z., Chu, X., Feng, D.: Secure code updates for smart embedded devices based on PUFs. In: Capkun, S., Chow, S.S.M. (eds.) CANS 2017. LNCS, vol. 11261, pp. 325–346. Springer, Cham (2018). https://doi.org/10.1007/978-3-030-02641-7_15
22. ISACA: Firmware security risks and mitigation: enterprise practices and challenges (October 2016). https://cybersecurity.isaca.org/csx-resources/firmware-security-risks-and-mitigation--enterprise-practices-and-challenges

23. Kolias, C., Kambourakis, G., Stavrou, A., Voas, J.: DDos in the IoT: Mirai and other botnets. Computer **50**(7), 80–84 (2017)
24. Konstantinou, C., Chielle, E., Maniatakos, M.: PHYLAX: snapshot-based profiling of real-time embedded devices via JTAG interface. In: 2018 Design, Automation Test in Europe Conference Exhibition (DATE), pp. 869–872 (March 2018)
25. Konstantinou, C., Keliris, A., Maniatakos, M.: Taxonomy of firmware trojans in smart grid devices. In: Power and Energy Society General Meeting (PESGM), 2016, pp. 1–5. IEEE (2016)
26. Konstantinou, C., Maniatakos, M.: Impact of firmware modification attacks on power systems field devices. In: 2015 IEEE International Conference on Smart Grid Communications, pp. 283–288. IEEE (2015)
27. Konstantinou, C., Maniatakos, M.: A case study on implementing false data injection attacks against nonlinear state estimation. In: Proceedings of the 2nd ACM Workshop on Cyber-Physical Systems Security and Privacy, pp. 81–92 (2016)
28. Konstantinou, C., Maniatakos, M.: Security analysis of smart grid. Commun. Control Secur. Chall. Smart Grid **2**, 451 (2017)
29. Konstantinou, C., Maniatakos, M.: Hardware-layer intelligence collection for smart grid embedded systems. J. Hardw. Syst. Secur. **3**, 1–15 (2019)
30. Konstantinou, C., Maniatakos, M., Saqib, F., Hu, S., Plusquellic, J., Jin, Y.: Cyber-physical systems: a security perspective. In: 2015 20th IEEE European Test Symposium (ETS), pp. 1–8. IEEE (2015)
31. Koushanfar, F., Boufounos, P., Shamsi, D.: Post-silicon timing characterization by compressed sensing. In: Proceedings of the 2008 IEEE/ACM International Conference on Computer-Aided Design, pp. 185–189. IEEE Press (2008)
32. Li, W., Wang, Y., Li, H., Li, X.: P3M: a PIM-based neural network model protection scheme for deep learning accelerator. In: Proceedings of the 24th Asia and South Pacific Design Automation Conference, pp. 633–638 (2019)
33. Lipp, M., et al.: Meltdown. arXiv preprint arXiv:1801.01207 (2018)
34. McGrath, T., Bagci, I.E., Wang, Z.M., Roedig, U., Young, R.J.: A PUF taxonomy. Appl. Phys. Rev. **6**(1), 011303 (2019)
35. McLaughlin, S., et al.: The cybersecurity landscape in industrial control systems. Proc. IEEE **104**(5), 1039–1057 (2016)
36. Mocker, A.: Tuya: revised update process hacked again. https://www.heise.de/ (November 2019)
37. Moghimi, D., Sunar, B., Eisenbarth, T., Heninger, N.: TPM-FAIL: TPM meets timing and lattice attacks. In: 29th USENIX Security Symposium (USENIX Security 20). USENIX Association, Boston, MA (August 2020). https://www.usenix.org/conference/usenixsecurity20/presentation/moghimi
38. National Crime Agency UK: The cyber threat to UK business. National Cyber Security Centre (2017–2018)
39. Newman, L.H.: Windows 10 has a security flaw so severe the NSA disclosed it (January 2020). https://www.wired.com/story/nsa-windows-10-vulnerability-disclosure/
40. O'Flynn, C., Chen, Z.D.: Side channel power analysis of an AES-256 bootloader. In: 2015 IEEE 28th Canadian Conference on Electrical and Computer Engineering (CCECE), pp. 750–755. IEEE (2015)
41. Pinto, S., Santos, N.: Demystifying arm trustzone: a comprehensive survey. ACM Comput. Surv. (CSUR) **51**(6), 1–36 (2019)
42. Potkonjak, M., Goudar, V.: Public physical unclonable functions. Proc. IEEE **102**(8), 1142–1156 (2014)

43. Potkonjak, M., Meguerdichian, S., Nahapetian, A., Wei, S.: Differential public physically unclonable functions: architecture and applications. In: Proceedings of the 48th Design Automation Conference, pp. 242–247 (2011)
44. PUB, F.: Secure hash standard (SHS). FIPS Pub 180(4) (2012)
45. Roberts, P.: Huge survey of firmware finds no security gains in 15 years (August 2019). https://securityledger.com/
46. Roelke, A., Stan, M.R.: Attacking an SRAM-based PUF through wearout. In: 2016 IEEE Computer Society Annual Symposium on VLSI (ISVLSI), pp. 206–211. IEEE (2016)
47. Rostami, M., Majzoobi, M., Koushanfar, F., Wallach, D.S., Devadas, S.: Robust and reverse-engineering resilient PUF authentication and key-exchange by substring matching. IEEE Trans. Emerg. Top. Comput. 2(1), 37–49 (2014)
48. Rührmair, U., Sehnke, F., Sölter, J., Dror, G., Devadas, S., Schmidhuber, J.: Modeling attacks on physical unclonable functions. In: Proceedings of the 17th ACM Conference on Computer and Communications Security, pp. 237–249. ACM (2010)
49. Sahoo, D.P., Nguyen, P.H., Mukhopadhyay, D., Chakraborty, R.S.: A case of lightweight PUF constructions: cryptanalysis and machine learning attacks. IEEE Trans. Comput.-Aided Des. Integr. Circuits Syst. 34(8), 1334–1343 (2015)
50. Sanjab, A., Saad, W., Guvenc, I., Sarwat, A., Biswas, S.: Smart grid security: threats, challenges, and solutions. arXiv preprint arXiv:1606.06992 (2016)
51. Schneier, B., Kelsey, J., Whiting, D., Wagner, D., Hall, C., Ferguson, N.: Twofish: a 128-bit block cipher. NIST AES Propos. 15(1), 23–91 (1998)
52. Suh, G.E., Devadas, S.: Physical unclonable functions for device authentication and secret key generation. In: 44th ACM/IEEE Design Automation Conference, 2007, DAC 2007, pp. 9–14. IEEE (2007)
53. Van Bulck, J., et al.: Foreshadow: extracting the keys to the intel {SGX} kingdom with transient out-of-order execution. In: 27th {USENIX} Security Symposium ({USENIX} Security 2018), pp. 991–1008 (2018)
54. Wang, X., et al.: Malicious firmware detection with hardware performance counters. IEEE Trans. Multi-Scale Comput. Syst. 2(3), 160–173 (2016)
55. Xu, X., Burleson, W.: Hybrid side-channel/machine-learning attacks on PUFs: a new threat? In: 2014 Design, Automation & Test in Europe Conference & Exhibition (DATE), pp. 1–6. IEEE (2014)

Reliability Enhanced Digital Low-Dropout Regulator with Improved Transient Performance

Longfei Wang, Soner Seçkiner$^{(\boxtimes)}$, and Selçuk Köse

Department of Electrical and Computer Engineering,
University of Rochester, Rochester, NY, USA
{longfei.wang,soner.seckiner,selcuk.kose}@rochester.edu

Abstract. Digital low-dropout voltage regulators (DLDOs) have drawn increasing attention for the easy implementation within nanoscale devices. Despite their various benefits over analog LDOs, disadvantages may arise in the form of bias temperature instability (BTI) induced performance degradation. In this Chapter, conventional DLDO operation and BTI effects are explained. Reliability enhanced DLDO topologies with performance improvement for both steady-state and transient operations are discussed. DLDOs with adaptive gain scaling (AGS) technique, where the number of power transistors that are turned on/off per clock cycle changes dynamically according to load current conditions, have not been explored in view of reliability concerns. As the benefits of AGS technique can be promising regarding DLDO transient performance improvement, a simple and effective reliability aware AGS technique with a steady-state capture feature is proposed in this work. AGS senses the steady-state output of a DLDO and reduces the gain to the minimum value to obtain a stable output voltage. Moreover, a novel unidirectional barrel shifter is proposed to reduce the aging effect of the DLDO. This unidirectional barrel shifter evenly distributes the load among DLDO output stages to obtain a longer lifetime. The benefits of the proposed techniques are explored and highlighted through extensive simulations. The proposed techniques also have negligible power and area overhead. NBTI-aware design with AGS can reduce the transient response time by 59.5% as compared to aging unaware conventional DLDO and mitigate the aging effect by up to 33%.

Keywords: NBTI · Reliability · Aging · Steady state performance · Transient performance · Shift register · Unidirectional control

1 Introduction

Semiconductor technology that enables rapid advancements in the design and fabrication of nanoscale integrated circuits continuously improves while demanding a higher amount of power per unit area [1]. Integrating voltage regulators fully on-chip to provide robust power to the integrated circuits have been a

© IFIP International Federation for Information Processing 2020
Published by Springer Nature Switzerland AG 2020
C. Metzler et al. (Eds.): VLSI-SoC 2019, IFIP AICT 586, pp. 187–208, 2020.
https://doi.org/10.1007/978-3-030-53273-4_9

challenging design issue. Several techniques have been proposed in the literature to improve the power conversion efficiency, stability, and reliability of on-chip voltage regulators or power delivery networks as a whole [2–14]. There is also an emerging trend to leverage voltage regulators to address security concerns [15–23]. In addition to the existing challenges, bias temperature instability (BTI) induced reliability concerns have recently drawn attention especially for digital low-dropout regulators (DLDOs) [24–27]. Modern computing systems and internet of things (IoT) devices require reliable operation and long lifetime of on-chip voltage regulators [23, 25, 29]. Generating and delivering a robust output voltage under highly dynamic workload conditions have become even more difficult with the variations in the environmental conditions. These environmental conditions deteriorate the performance and lifetime of the transistors. Voltage regulators suffer from the abrupt variations in the workload and may experience serious aging phenomenon, necessitating reliability aware designs [25].

Transistor aging mechanisms such as BTI, hot carrier injection, and time-dependent dielectric breakdown have become more important with the scaling of transistor size. BTI is the major aging mechanism [30–36] where negative BTI (NBTI) induces performance degradation of PMOS transistors. Various studies have been performed to address the reliability issues of semiconductor devices [28, 37, 38]. BTI-aware sleep transistor sizing algorithms for reliable power gating design [37], integral impact of BTI and PVT variation [39], and impact of BTI variations [40] have been investigated. A conventional DLDO has a bi-directional controller which activates certain transistors frequently and leaves the others unused. This reliability unaware control scheme makes the performance degradation even worse because the activation pattern of PMOS is concentrated on certain transistors, thus causing heavy electrical stress on these transistors. The over usage of certain transistors degrades the performance significantly. Distributing the electrical stress among all of the transistors can therefore be effective. The primary literature that address the aging effects of on-chip DLDOs include a reliable digitally synthesizable linear drop-out regulator design, a digitally controlled linear regulator for per-core wide-range DVFS of Atom^{TM} cores, and mitigation of NBTI induced performance degradation in on-chip DLDOs [25, 41, 42]. To evenly distribute the workload, a decoding algorithm for DLDO is proposed in [41]. A code roaming algorithm with per-core dynamic voltage and frequency scaling method is proposed in [42]. These techniques need dedicated control algorithms to enhance the reliability of a DLDO. A unidirectional shifter is proposed for conventional DLDOs in [25] to decrease the electrical stress on transistors. A DLDO without AGS, however, suffers from slow response time when there are large transitions in the load current. The supply voltage should be robust as the operation of all of the on-chip devices are sensitive to the variations at the output of the voltage regulators. Transient performance enhancements and loop stability can be increased by utilizing a barrel shifter as discussed in [43]. A barrel shifter which can perform the switching of two or three transistors within a single clock cycle improves the transient response time significantly. A barrel shifter based DLDO design with a steady

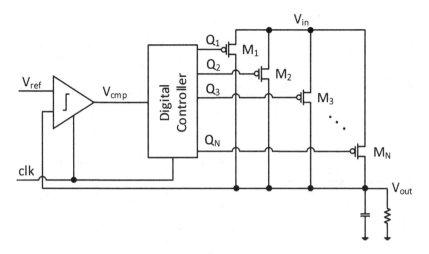

Fig. 1. Schematic of conventional DLDO.

load current estimator and dynamic gain scaling control is discussed in [44]. Although there are benefits of the aforementioned techniques, a DLDO with AGS still suffers from performance degradation due to NBTI. Additionally, a conventional DLDO with AGS also does not consider aging effect. Gain scaling using a bi-directional barrel shifter in [45,46] may not be directly applicable to add gain scaling capability for a reliability enhanced DLDO. Therefore, further research should be performed on AGS DLDO to mitigate performance degradation due to NBTI. A novel aging aware DLDO with AGS and a steady-state detection circuit to obtain fast transient response under abrupt changes in the load current is proposed in this work.

The main contributions of this work are threefold. First, an NBTI-aware DLDO with AGS is proposed. Second, a simple and effective steady state, overshoot, and undershoot detection circuit is proposed and verified. Third, extensive simulations verify that the proposed circuit works effectively.

As an extension of [47], the rest of this Chapter is organized as follows. Background information regarding conventional DLDOs, steady state and transient performance of DLDO, and BTI is discussed in Sect. 2. Existing NBTI-aware DLDO topologies are explained in Sect. 3. The proposed NBTI-aware DLDO with AGS is discussed in Sect. 4. Evaluation of the proposed technique and simulation results are discussed in Sect. 5. Concluding remarks are given in Sect. 6.

2   Background

In this section, background information on the design of conventional DLDO, steady state performance and transient performance thereof, and BTI effects are explained.

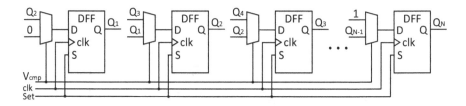

Fig. 2. Schematic of bidirectional shift register [25, 29].

Q₁	Q₂	Q₃	Q₄	Q₅	Q₆	Q₇	...	...	Q_{N-1}	Q_N
(1) Initialize: all Mᵢs turned off										
1	1	1	1	1	1	1	...	...	1	1
(2) Step k										
0	0	0	0	0	1	1	...	...	1	1
(3-a) Step k+1, if Vcmp is High: Shift right ➡										
0	0	0	0	0	0	1	...	...	1	1
(3-b) Step k+1, if Vcmp is Low: Shift left ⬅										
0	0	0	0	1	1	1	...	...	1	1

Fig. 3. Operation of bi-directional shift register.

2.1   Conventional DLDO

The schematic of a conventional DLDO [29] is illustrated in Fig. 1. The V_{ref} and clk are the inputs and V_{out} is the output of the conventional DLDO. The schematic and the operation principle of a bi-directional shift register used in the conventional DLDO are described in Figs. 2 and 3, respectively. The bi-directional shift register consists of a multiplexer and a DFF in each stage. The digital controller modulates the value Q_i based on Fig. 3. The DLDO is composed of N parallel PMOS transistors and a feedback control to adjust the output voltage. A bi-directional shift register is implemented in conventional DLDOs. M_i is the ith PMOS and Q_i is the logic output of the digital controller. i denotes the activation stage of the digital controller. The bi-directional shift register switches the state of one of the power transistors according to V_{cmp} at rising edge of each clock cycle. Q_N is the Nth output signal of the digital controller, as shown in Fig. 1. At step $k + 1$, Q_{n+1} (Q_n) is turned on (off) when V_{cmp} is high (low) and the bi-directional shift register shifts right (left), as shown in Fig. 3 where k is the activation step of the digital controller [25]. Each M_n is connected to Q_n. Since the activation scheme is bi-directional, this scheme leads to heavy usage of M_1 to M_n. DLDO performance degradation can occur due to this power transistor activation and deactivation scheme as discussed in Sects. 2.3 and 2.4.

2.2   Bias Temperature Instability

BTI includes NBTI for PMOS transistors and positive BTI (PBTI) for NMOS transistors. BTI leads to the increase of transistor threshold voltage $|V_{th}|$. NBTI increases the $|V_{th}|$ of PMOS transistors utilized in the DLDO power transistor array, leading to slower response time and the decrease of load supply capacity of the DLDO. The increase in $|V_{th}|$ is related to the traps generated in Si/SiO_2 interface at the gate when there is a negative gate voltage [48]. ΔV_{th} formula is given in (1) where C_{ox}, k, T, α, and t are the oxide capacitance, Boltzmann Constant, temperature, fraction of time when the transistor is under stress, and time, respectively. K_{lt} and E_a are the fitting parameters to comply with the experimental data [49].

$$\Delta V_{th} = K_{lt}\sqrt{C_{ox}(|V_{gs}| - |V_{th}|)}e^{-E_a/kT}(\alpha t)^{1/6} \tag{1}$$

Considering the case of DLDOs, most practical applications need less than average power, which leads to heavy utilization of certain transistors within conventional DLDOs. The undamped voltage output of DLDO causes large swings at the voltage waveform which leads to heavy use of certain transistors. The operation of the regulator causes the heavy use of M_1 to M_m and less or even no use of M_{m+1} to M_N. Alternatively, certain transistors (i.e., the ones with a lower index number) are almost always active whereas some other transistors (i.e., the ones with a greater index number) are almost never active. This activation scheme therefore induces serious non-symmetric degradation of PMOS due to NBTI.

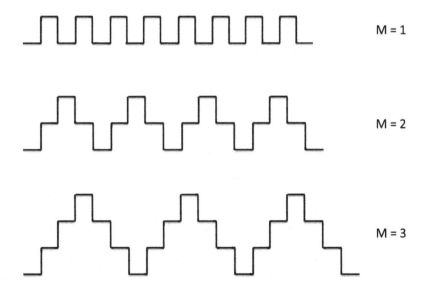

Fig. 4. Illustration of DLDO limit cycle oscillation mode.

2.3 Steady State Performance of DLDO

Under a constant load current, DLDO reaches steady state operation as V_{out} approaches V_{ref}. Due to the discrete nature of digital control loop and the corresponding quantization error, limit cycle oscillation occurs during DLDO steady state operation, which negatively affects output voltage ripple. The mode of limit cycle oscillation M can be indentified through the output of bidirectional shift register $Q(t)$ as shown in Fig. 4. The period of limit cycle oscillation (LCO) is $2MT_{clk}$, where T_{clk} is the clock period. Under a certain f_{clk}, a larger LCO mode typically leads to a larger amplitude of output voltage ripple. LCO mode and output voltage ripple amplitude are largely affected by the unit current provided by each power transistor, load capacitance, clock frequency, and load current [50–53]. As NBTI can introduce PMOS $|V_{th}|$ degradation, it can be also detrimental to the existing LCO mitigation technique detailed in Sect. 3.

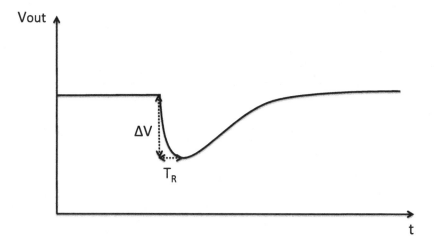

Fig. 5. Illustration of DLDO transient response.

2.4 Transient Performance of DLDO

Transient performance of a DLDO largely affects important application domains such as dynamic voltage and frequency scaling (DVFS) and near-threshold computing (NTC). A typical DLDO transient response is illustrated in Fig. 5. When the load current of the DLDO increases, the DLDO output voltage V_{out} decreases to $V_{out} - \Delta V$ before recovering, where ΔV is the magnitude of the transient voltage droop and T_R is the load response time. Smaller values of ΔV and T_R are desirable for better DLDO transient performance. ΔV and T_R can be, respectively, expressed as [25, 54–57]

$$\Delta V = R\Delta i_{load} - I_{pMOS}f_{clk}R^2Cln(1 + \frac{\Delta i_{load}}{I_{pMOS}f_{clk}RC}). \qquad (2)$$

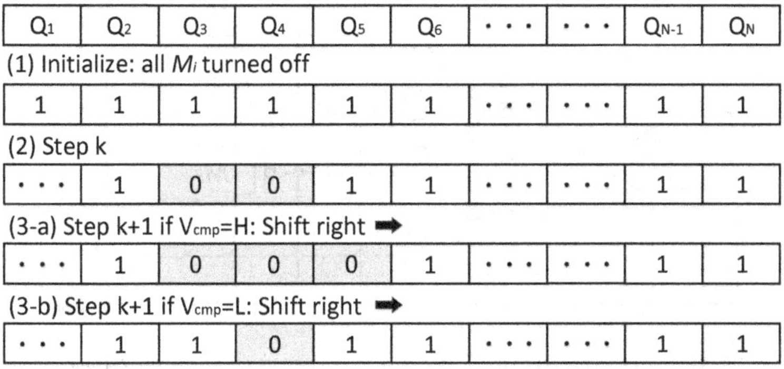

Q₁	Q₂	Q₃	Q₄	Q₅	Q₆	· · ·	· · ·	Q_{N-1}	Q_N
Q_1	Q_2	Q_3	Q_4	Q_5	Q_6	· · ·	· · ·	Q_{N-1}	Q_N
(1) Initialize: all M_i turned off									
1	1	1	1	1	1	· · ·	· · ·	1	1
(2) Step k									
· · ·	1	0	0	1	1	· · ·	· · ·	1	1
(3-a) Step k+1 if V_cmp=H: Shift right ➡									
· · ·	1	0	0	0	1	· · ·	· · ·	1	1
(3-b) Step k+1 if V_cmp=L: Shift right ➡									
· · ·	1	1	0	1	1	· · ·	· · ·	1	1

Fig. 6. Operation of the uni-directional shift register [25].

and

$$T_R = RCln(1 + \frac{\Delta i_{load}}{I_{pMOS}f_{clk}RC}) \tag{3}$$

where I_{pMOS}, Δi_{load}, C, and R are, respectively, the current provided by a single active power transistor, load current change, load capacitance, and average DLDO output resistance before and after load current change. Due to the NBTI induced $|V_{th}|$ degradation, it is demonstrated in [25] that ΔV and T_R also degrade. Such DLDO performance degradation needs to be considered when designing voltage regulators with a stringent lifetime requirement [58–60].

3 NBTI-Aware Digital Low-Dropout Regulators

Multiple NBTI-aware DLDO topologies have been proposed to mitigate steady state and transient performance degradation [24–26,38]. The working principles of these techniques are explained in this section.

3.1 NBTI-Aware DLDO with Unidirectional Shift Register

As illustrated in Fig. 3, the operation of a bi-directional shift register leads to the heavy usage of the first few power transistors, which essentially increases activity factor of these transistors and the corresponding $|V_{th}|$ degradation. To mitigate this side effect, NBTI-aware DLDO with a unidirectional shift register control is proposed in [25,61]. With minor changes of the control logic in each stage, the power transistor activation and deactivation can be realized in the same direction. In such a way, activity factor of each power transistor can be effectively reduced and the resulting DLDO performance degradation can be mitigated. Furthermore, the power and area overhead of the implementation are negligible.

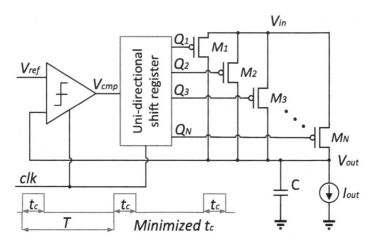

Fig. 7. Schematic of reduced clock pulse width DLDO [24].

3.2 Reduced Clock Pulse Width DLDO

During steady state operation, the LCO can be an issue for DLDO as it affects the amplitude of the output voltage ripple. It is demonstrated in [24] that BTI induced threshold voltage degradation can lead to the propagation delay degradation of the clocked comparator and shift register. Such delay degradation has a negative effect on the possible mode of LCO. Reduced clock pulse width DLDO as shown in Fig. 7 is proposed in [24] to mitigate the side effects of LCO. Minimum clock pulse width t_c considering BTI induced propagation delay degradation is adopted and a uni-directional shift register is utilized to simultaneously improve steady state and transient performance of DLDO.

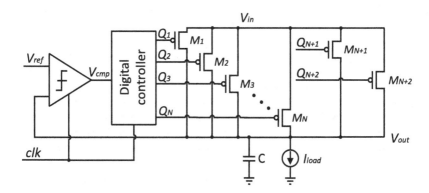

Fig. 8. Schematic of NBTI-aware DLDO with LCO mitigation [38].

3.3   NBTI-Aware DLDO with Limit Cycle Oscillation Mitigation

Due to the side effects of LCO on the DLDO steady state performance, it is desirable to achieve the minimum LCO mode or even remove LCO to reduce the steady state output voltage ripple. It is discovered in [62] that by adding two additional parallel power transistors as shown in Fig. 8, minimum LCO mode of one can be realized. However, due to NBTI induced $|V_{th}|$ increase, the current provided by a single additional power transistor deviates from that provided by the original power transistor. Such deviation gradually nullifies the effectiveness of the proposed technique. To more evenly distribute the electrical stress among all of the $N + 2$ power transistors, NBTI-aware DLDO with LCO mitigation is proposed in [38]. A dedicated digital controller is proposed to realize unidirectional control among the $N + 2$ power transistors.

Q_1	Q_2	Q_3	Q_4	Q_5	Q_6	• • •	• • •	Q_{N-1}	Q_N
(1) Initialize: all P_i turned off									
1	1	1	1	1	1	• • •	• • •	1	1
(2) Step 1									
0	1	1	1	1	1	• • •	• • •	1	1
(3) Step 2: Shift right ➡									
1	0	0	1	1	1	• • •	• • •	1	1
(4) Step 3: Shift right ➡									
1	1	0	0	0	1	• • •	• • •	1	1
(5) Step 4: Shift right ➡									
1	1	1	0	0	0	• • •	• • •	1	1
(6) Step 5: Shift right ➡									
1	1	1	1	0	0	• • •	• • •	1	1

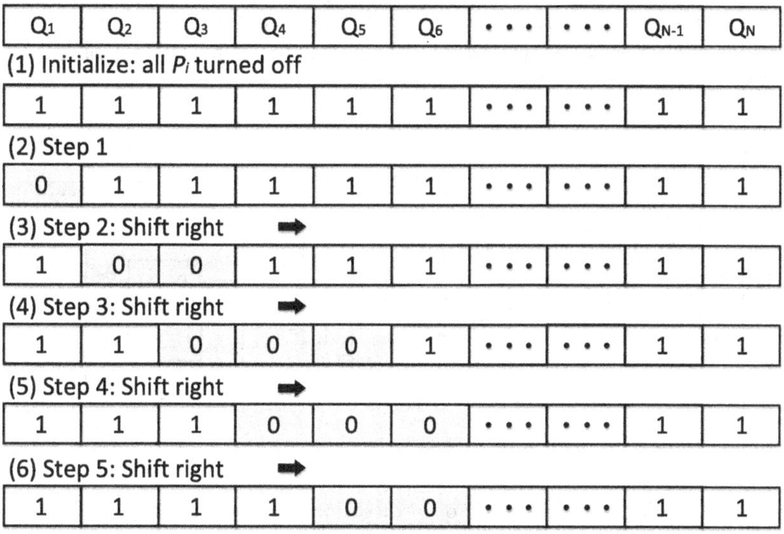

Fig. 9. Operation of the startup aware reliability enhancement controller [26].

3.4   NBTI-Aware DLDO with Improved Startup Performance

NBTI-Aware DLDO with unidirectional shift register is effective to more evenly distribute electrical stress among all of the power transistors as compared to bidirectional shift register control. However, for a special case when DLDO has to be turned off before or shortly after reaching steady state operation, the first few power transistors still undergo too much electrical stress as compared to the rest. When utilized in cyclic power gating [63], DLDOs can be periodically turned off when reaching around steady state. In this case, an unidirectional shift register functions similar to a bidirectional shift register. To mitigate this drawback and enhance the reliability of DLDO during cyclic power gating operations, NBTI-Aware DLDO with improved startup performance is proposed in [26]. The operation of the startup aware reliability enhancement controller is demonstrated in Fig. 9. When more number of power transistor needs to be turned on during startup, two more power transistors are turned and one is turned off at the same time. In such a way, electrical stress can be more evenly distributed among more number of power transistors.

4   Proposed NBTI-Aware DLDO with AGS

Although there are respective advantages of the aforementioned DLDOs, the techniques proposed in previous works cannot be directly applied to DLDOs with AGS capability [64,65]. With AGS, DLDOs can adaptively change the number of power transistor (de)activated per clock cycle to speed up the transient process. NBTI-aware DLDO with AGS capability is proposed and investigated in this work. This is the first work which designs a novel uni-directional barrel shifter with AGS control.

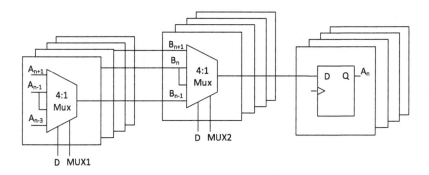

Fig. 10. Schematic of bi-directional barrel shifter.

4.1   Barrel Shifter

Barrel shifter is the main component of the control loop. A simple schematic for a barrel shifter is shown in Fig. 10. A barrel shifter can activate multiple power transistors at the same clock cycle. For example, it can shift $-3, -2, -1, 0, 1, 2, 3$ stages at the same clock cycle. The magnitude of the shift in a barrel shifter serves as a gain control knob in the forward activation pattern of a DLDO. The barrel shifter in Fig. 10, is implemented using two levels of signal multiplexing followed by a flip-flop. A is the output of D flip flop and B is the output of the first level of MUX. The first level of MUX gives $0, 2, -2$ and second level of MUX gives $0, 1, -1$ shifts to obtain $-3, -2, -1, 0, 1, 2, 3$ shifts at the output of the barrel shifter. The positive values mean a shift to the right and negative

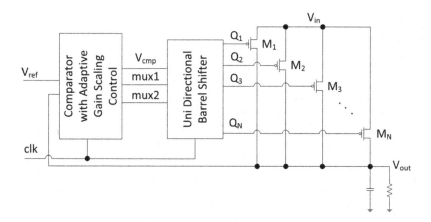

Fig. 11. Proposed NBTI-aware DLDO with AGS capability.

values to the left. $MUX1$ and $MUX2$ are used to control the barrel shifter as an output of up to three shifts. The first stage leads the input signals to the output of the 4:1 mux. D is the comparator output which determines the direction of the activation scheme. n is the stages of the barrel shifter. $n-1$ determines previous stage and $n+1$ determines forward stage similarly. The combination of D, $MUX1$, and $MUX2$ determines the gain of the barrel shifter and direction of the barrel shifter output activation scheme.

A bi-directional barrel shifter is proposed in [43] where the details can be seen in Fig. 10. This barrel shifter operates by switching a maximum of three transistors at the same clock cycle. 2N number of muxes and N number of D flip-flops are housed in the barrel shifter. The operation is maintained by adjusting the gain which can be adapted by selecting the logic inputs of the muxes. The work in [44] improves the operation of conventional DLDOs by introducing a bi-directional barrel shifter with steady-state load current estimator and a dynamic bi-directional shift register gain scaling control which adjusts the barrel shifter to obtain fast transient time. Steady-state load current estimator senses the load current and adjusts the frequency of the digital controller to get damped behavior of the voltage waveform. Dynamic bi-directional shift register gain scaling control automates the eight different gain according to the predetermined conditions which are studied in [44].

In this work, a new NBTI-aware DLDO with uni-directional barrel shifter with AGS is implemented. Therefore, the performance mitigation due to NBTI is maintained low and a good improvement in the transient response time has been achieved.

DLDO has a slow transient response under large load current changes. A trade-off exists between steady-state stability, transient response, and performance degradation due to NBTI. A new architecture is designed to reduce the NBTI induced stress and to speed up the transient response.

Q_1	Q_2	Q_3	Q_4	Q_5	Q_6	Q_7	Q_8	...	Q_{N-1}	Q_N
(1) Initialize: all M_i turned off										
1	1	1	1	1	1	1	1	...	1	1
(2) Step k										
1	0	0	0	0	1	1	1	...	1	1
(3-a) Step k+1, if Vout < Vref & mux1=L, gain=1 shift ➡										
1	0	0	0	0	0	1	1	...	1	1
(3-b) Step k+1, if Vout > Vref & mux1=L, gain=1 shift ➡										
1	1	0	0	0	1	1	1	...	1	1
(3-c) Step k+1, if Vout < Vref and Vout > Vref - Δ, gain=2 shift ➡										
1	0	0	0	0	0	0	1	...	1	1
(3-d) Step k+1, if Vout > Vref and Vout < Vref + Δ, gain=2 shift ➡										
1	1	1	0	0	1	1	1	...	1	1
(3-e) Step k+1, if Vout < Vref - Δ, gain=3 shift ➡										
1	0	0	0	0	0	0	0	...	1	1
(3-f) Step k+1, if Vout > Vref + Δ, gain=3 shift ➡										
1	1	1	1	0	1	1	1	...	1	1

Fig. 12. Operation of uni-directional barrel shifter with AGS.

Rotating the load stress among the power transistors enables the distribution of the loading evenly and reduces the NBTI induced performance degradation [66]. Furthermore, due to the steady-state gain control, settling time after the overshoots and undershoots are reduced. The transient loading effects are also minimized. As compared to a conventional DLDO, the transient loading response is improved.

A uni-directional DLDO with a barrel shifter is implemented within the proposed AGS. An enhanced AGS control manages all of the power transistors in a way that shortens settling time under severe transient loading and reduced aging for longer operation times have been achieved as compared to a conventional DLDO. The V_{cmp}, $mux1$, and $mux2$ are the control signals generated by the AGS. The details are depicted in Fig. 11.

4.2   Uni-Directional Shift Register

The activation pattern of pass transistors in a conventional DLDO is typically designed to serve bidirectional. This deactivation and activation of the PMOS scheme can be observed in Fig. 12. The one-directional activation pattern can be observed in Fig. 12 (3-a) and (3-b). The M_i represents the PMOS transistors. In the first stage, all PMOS is deactivated. In the second stage, when the digital controller reaches the k stage, the controller determines the output pattern according to $Vout$ value. In Fig. 12 (3-a), the gain is one which leads to activation of one transistor at the right boundary of the activation schema. In Fig. 12 (3-b),

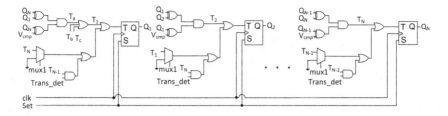

Fig. 13. Proposed uni-directional NBTI-aware DLDO with barrel shifter.

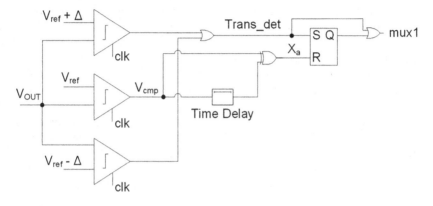

Fig. 14. Three stage adaptive gain scaling with steady state capture.

the activation of PMOS is at the left boundary of activation schema. Similarly, in Fig. 12 (3-c) and (3-d), the gain is two which activates two PMOS transistors at the same clock cycle. In Fig. 12 (3-e) and (3-f), the gain is three and causes the activation of three PMOS at the same clock cycle within the defined boundaries. This activation pattern should be modified to mitigate the NBTI induced performance degradation. Evenly distributing the electrical stress to all of the transistors can decrease the degradation in the current supply capacity of PMOS. Under transient loading, a uni-directional DLDO can activate and deactivate the PMOS due to the increased load current.

4.3 Uni-Directional NBTI-Aware DLDO with Barrel Shifter

The uni-directional barrel shifter is shown in Fig. 13. The schematic and operation of the proposed architecture are shown in Fig. 11 and Fig. 12. The Comparator in adaptive gain scaling control produces the signal of V_{cmp}, $mux1$, and $mux2$ which controls the uni-directional barrel shifter as the steady-state, gain 2 and gain 3 regions are operated. The elementary D flip-flop (DFF) and multiplexer within bi-directional shift register are replaced with T flip-flop and simple logic gates within the proposed uni-directional shift register. A multiplexer and simple logic gates are designed for uni-directional barrel shifter. A multiplexer and logic gates are added to get barrel shifter behavior in the uni-directional controller. This controller is designed to toggle a maximum of three gates at a single clock cycle, and it is the first time implementation of the uni-directional barrel shifter controller. The parallel gates remain unchanged, and uni-directional barrel shifter and AGS are added. The idea is to balance the loading of each power transistors under all load current conditions. The Q_i and Q_{i-1} are gated using XOR gate to equate the output signal switched conse-quently. V_{cmp} is gated with Q_{i-1} together with other Q_i to determine the logic T_i. Therefore, when V_{cmp} is high (low), inactive (active) power transistors at the right (left) boundary is turned ON (OFF). A uni-directional barrel shift regis-ter is realized through this activation/deactivation scheme, as demonstrated in Fig. 12. T_b and T_c are added at the logic to prevent the conflicting situations. $T_b = Q_1 \times Q_2 \times ... \times Q_N \times V_{cmp}$ and $T_c = \overline{Q_1 + Q_2 + ... + Q_N + V_{cmp}}$ [25]. During transient state, three signals V_{cmp}, $mux1$, and $Trans\_det$ are generated to adjust the gain of the barrel shifter where $mux1$ is a steady-state indicator signal that is generated by a novel steady-state detection circuit. After the system enters the steady-state, the system adjusts the gain to one. For barrel shifter, one mux and three additional gates are used in Fig. 14. Area overhead can be determined by counting the additional transistors and compared to the conventional DLDO per control stage. According to the previous definition, there is only a 4.5% area overhead. As the bi-directional shift register consumes a few μW power, the uni-directional shift register power overhear is also negligible [25,49]. Additional controllers consume low current, thus the power overhead is negligible for the proposed design.

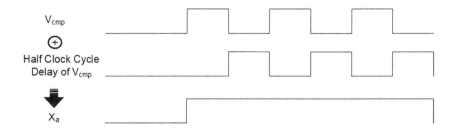

Fig. 15. V_{cmp} and half clock cycle delay of V_{cmp} XORed.

4.4   Three Stage AGS with Steady-State Detection Circuit

The schematic of a three-stage AGS with steady-state capture is shown in Fig. 14. There are three voltage comparators, two OR gates, one XOR gate, one-time delay, and one SR latch. There are two inputs and two outputs which are V_{ref}, V_{out}, $mux1$, and $Trans\_det$, respectively, for this circuit. Two comparators pro-vide overshoot and undershoot detection. One comparator senses the changes in the V_{out}. Half cycle time delayed V_{cmp} is XORed with V_{cmp} to determine the steady-state operation. AGS senses the changes in V_{cmp} during steady-state operation. The operation of uni-directional barrel shifter starts to control the oscillation at the output of DLDO due to limit cycle oscillation [67]. When V_{cmp} starts to oscillate during the steady-state operation, X_a, the output of XOR gate X_a is high, leading to the reset of SR latch. The X_a signal can be observed in Fig. 15. Thus, the output $mux1$ is low to enter a steady-state region. The variation at the output of DLDO is minimum when the gain is one because the voltage change of one PMOS activation is lower than two or more PMOS activation. If the number of parallel PMOS increases, according to Kirchhoff's voltage law, the drop-out voltage decreased. When the DLDO enters out of the steady-state region, V_{cmp} and time-delayed V_{cmp} are XORed giving logic low at X_a. Following the output of the XOR gate, SR latch's output is high which makes $mux1$ high and the gain scaling circuit operates out of steady-state mode.

The circuit operates in three different modes in three different regions. The first region is the highest gain area in which the circuit operates to provide high in $mux1$ and $Trans\_det$ and the gain is three, which means that barrel shifter switches three consecutive power transistors at the rising edge of a single clock cycle. Within the second region, the gain is two such that two power transistors will be turned on/off at the same time. This region is for fast settling of the output voltage. The third region is the gain one region where the steady state voltage variation is achieved at the output by changing the minimum amount of power transistor. For steady state operation $mux1$ and $Trans\_det$ are logic low.

4.5   Operation of the Proposed NBTI-Aware DLDO with AGS Capability

The NBTI-aware uni-directional controller with AGS capability is shown in Fig. 12. When V_{out} is lower than V_{ref}, the barrel shifter activates the power transistors at the right boundary. Similarly, when V_{out} is higher than V_{ref}, the barrel shifter deactivates the power transistors at the left boundary of the inactive/active power transistor region. Depending on the value of gain, a maximum of three active (inactive) power transistors switch inactive (active) power transistors at the boundary. The uni-directional barrel shifter always toggles the power transistors at the right of the boundary. The switching of the power transistors is always in one direction (right shift). Therefore, the stress on the power transistors evenly distributed because the operation load of each PMOS is distributed equally among each transistor. Furthermore, as compared to conventional DLDO, the steady-state performance does not change and the transient response time is decreased. During the design of the DLDO, being aware of NBTI induced performance degradation is important. The reliability of DLDO can be enhanced by implementing the method in this article. This work improves the performance of AGS with respect to other works in Table 1 since the AGS has three modes. The first mode is aggressive gain scaling. The second mode is slow settling and the third mode is steady-state mode.

Steady-State Operation. In the steady-state mode, the number of active and passive PMOS is changing dynamically. Limit cycle oscillation leads to output voltage ripple at steady-state. The number of active/inactive transistors are the same for both NBTI-aware DLDO with AGS and conventional DLDO but the gain is different while transient state resulting in faster settling time. In Fig. 12 (3-a) and (3-b), the operation of steady-state operation can be observed. The PMOS at the right boundary changes its activity one transistor at each clock cycle.

Slow Settling Operation. In the slow settling mode, the barrel shifter gain is two, meaning that PMOS transistors change their activity two transistors at each clock cycle. The operation is quite different from conventional DLDO since the gain of conventional DLDO is one in every loading case. The advantage of this mode is that it reduces the overshooting and undershooting under transient loading. In Fig. 12 (3-c) and (3-d), the slow settling operation can be observed. The PMOS at the boundary changes its activity two transistors at each clock cycle. Depending on V_{out}, the transistors at the left boundary or at the right boundary change their operation from inactive to active.

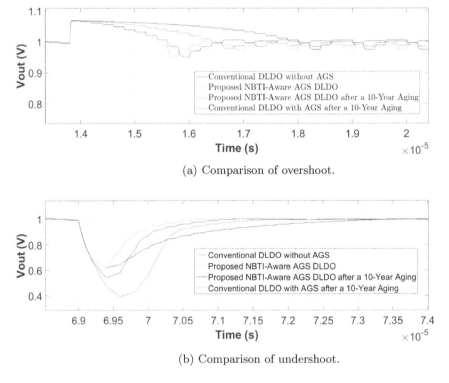

(a) Comparison of overshoot.

(b) Comparison of undershoot.

Fig. 16. Comparison of transient loading among aging-aware and aging-unaware DLDOs.

Aggressive Gain Scaling. In the aggressive gain scaling mode, the barrel shifter gain is three. The advantage of this operation is that it reduces the settling time significantly [44,68]. Under transient loading, the load current changes significantly. In Fig. 12 (3-e) and (3-f), the operation of aggressive gain scaling can be observed. The active PMOSs (shaded region) change their operation to inactive depending on the V_{out}. The consecutive three transistors change their operation in the same clock cycle.

5   Evaluation of the Proposed Circuit

In order to validate the effectiveness of the 1.1 V to 1.0 V DLDO, this on-chip circuit is designed in a 32 nm standard CMOS process. The proposed DLDO can supply a maximum of 124 mA current. The transient output voltage waveform from 20 mA to 60 mA step load change and comparison of the results of the conventional DLDO without AGS, the proposed NBTI-aware DLDO with AGS, the proposed NBTI-aware DLDO with AGS after 10-year aging and the conventional DLDO with AGS after 10-year aging are shown in Fig. 16. 1 MHz clock frequency is applied and aging induced degradation is evaluated under 100 °C. The settling time after load decrease is 4.5 μs and the settling time after load increase is 4.2 μs for the conventional DLDO without AGS. The proposed NBTI-aware AGS DLDO has 2.4 μs settling time after an overshoot and 1.7 μs settling time after an undershoot. The proposed NBTI-aware DLDO with AGS after 10-year aging has 2.8 $μs$ settling time after an overshoot and 2.1 μs settling time after an undershoot. The conventional DLDO with AGS after a 10-year aging has 3.4 μs settling time after overshoot and 2.8 μs settling time after undershoot. The results for conventional DLDO with AGS without aging is the same as the results of proposed NBTI-aware DLDO with AGS. There is 46.7% decrease in the settling time of overshoot of the proposed DLDO with AGS as compared to the conventional DLDO. There is also a 59.5% decrease in the settling time of undershooting of the proposed DLDO with AGS as compared to the conventional DLDO. Furthermore, the settling time for the proposed DLDO with AGS after 10-year aging is decreased by 59.5% as compared to the conventional DLDO with AGS after 10-year aging.

Previous works are compared with this work in Table 1. The power overhead in [41] is negligible since added decoders have little power consumption with respect to power PMOS. Similarly, the power overhead in [42] and [25] is negligible because the modifications add negligible power consumption. The works in [41] and [42] have AGS capability.

Table 1. Comparison with previous aging-aware on-chip DLDOs

	[41]	[42]	[25]	This work
Year	2015	2017	2018	2019
Broad load range	Yes	Yes	Yes	Yes
Additional controller	Yes	Yes	No	No
Added overhead	Multiple decoders	Decoder	Modification of original controller	Modification of conventional DLDO
Topology	Row rotation scheme	Code roaming algorithm	Uni-directional shift controller	Uni-directional shift controller with barrel shifter
Adaptive gain scaling capability	Yes	Yes	No	Yes

6 Conclusion

In this work, an NBTI-aware DLDO with the AGS control is proposed to diminish the aging effect and to reduce the settling time. The settling time is reduced by 46.7% and 59.5% for overshoot and undershoot without aging aware design, respectively. The proposed circuit is NBTI-aware, thus, performance degradations due to NBTI are reduced. A novel uni-directional shift register with barrel shifter is proposed to distribute the electrical stress among the power transistors evenly. The proposed NBTI-aware DLDO with AGS control is efficient because the settling time is reduced by 33% after 10-year aging.

References

1. Vaisband, I., et al.: On-Chip Power Delivery and Management, 4th edn. Springer, Heidelberg (2016). https://doi.org/10.1007/978-3-319-29395-0
2. Köse, S., Friedman, E.G.: Distributed on-chip power delivery. IEEE J. Emerg. Sel. Topics Circuits Syst. **2**(4), 704–713 (2012)
3. Uzun, O.A., Köse, S.: Converter-gating: a power efficient and secure on-chip power delivery system. IEEE J. Emerg. Sel. Topics Circuits Syst. **4**(2), 169–179 (2014)
4. Köse, S., Friedman, E.G.: An area efficient fully monolithic hybrid voltage regulator. In: Proceedings of the IEEE International Symposium on Circuits and Systems, pp. 2718–2721, May/June 2010
5. Köse, S., Friedman, E.G.: On-chip point-of-load voltage regulator for distributed power supplies. In: Proceedings of the ACM/IEEE Great Lakes Symposium on VLSI, pp. 377–380, May 2010
6. Köse, S., Friedman, E.G.: Distributed power network co-design with on-chip power supplies and decoupling capacitors. In: Proceedings of the ACM/IEEE International Workshop on System Level Interconnect Prediction (SLIP), pp. 1–6, June 2011
7. Köse, S., Tam, S., Pinzon, S., McDermott, B., Friedman, E.G.: An area efficient on-chip hybrid voltage regulator. In: Proceedings of the IEEE International Symposium on Quality Electronic Design (ISQED), pp. 398–403, March 2012

8. Wang, L., et al.: Efficiency, stability, and reliability implications of unbalanced current sharing among distributed on-chip voltage regulators. IEEE TVLSI **25**(11), 3019–3032 (2017)
9. Wang, L., Kuttappa, R., Taskin, B., Köse, S.: Distributed digital low-dropout regulators with phase interleaving for on-chip voltage noise mitigation. In: Proceedings of the ACM/IEEE International Workshop on System Level Interconnect Prediction (SLIP), pp. 1–5, June 2019
10. Khatamifard, S.K., et al.: ThermoGater: thermally-aware on-chip voltage regulation. In: Proceedings of the ISCA, pp. 120–132 (2017)
11. Köse, S.: Thermal implications of on-chip voltage regulation: upcoming challenges and possible solutions. In: Proceedings of the IEEE/ACM Design Automation Conference (DAC), pp. 1–6, June 2014
12. Vaisband, I., Price, B., Köse, S., Kolla, Y., Friedman, E.G., Fischer, J.: Distributed power delivery with 28 nm ultra-small LDO regulator. Analog Integr. Circuits Signal Process. **83**(3), 295–309 (2015)
13. Köse, S.: Regulator-gating: adaptive management of on-chip voltage regulators. In: Proceedings of the ACM/IEEE Great Lakes Symposium on VLSI, pp. 105–110, May 2014
14. Uzun, O.A., Köse, S.: Regulator-gating methodology with distributed switched capacitor voltage converters. In: Proceedings of the IEEE Computer Society Annual Symposium on VLSI, pp. 13–18, July 2014
15. Wang, L., Khatamifard, S.K., Karpuzcu, U.R., Köse, S.: Exploring on-chip power delivery network induced analog covert channels. IEEE Tech. Comm. Cyber-Phys. Syst. (TC-CPS) Newslett. **1**(7), 15–18 (2019)
16. Khatamifard, S.K., Wang, L., Köse, S., Karpuzcu, U.R.: A new class of covert channels exploiting power management vulnerabilities. IEEE Comput. Archit. Lett. (CAL) **17**(2), 201–204 (2018)
17. Vosoughi, A., Wang, L., Köse, S.: Bus-invert coding as a low-power countermeasure against correlation power analysis attack. In: Proceedings of the ACM/IEEE International Workshop on System Level Interconnect Prediction (SLIP), pp. 1–5, June 2019
18. Khatamifard, S.K., Wang, L., Das, A., Köse, S. Karpuzcu, U.R.: POWERT channels: a novel class of covert communication exploiting power management vulnerabilities. In: Proceedings of the IEEE International Symposium on High-Performance Computer Architecture (HPCA), pp. 291–303, February 2019
19. Wang, L., Köse, S.: When hardware security moves to the edge and fog. In: Proceedings of the IEEE International Conference on Digital Signal Processing (DSP), pp. 1–5, November 2018
20. Köse, S., Wang, L., Demara, R.: On-chip sensor circle distribution technique for real-time hardware trojan detection. In: Government Microcircuit Applications and Critical Technology Conference (GOMACTech), pp. 1–4, March 2017
21. Roohi, A., Demara, R., Wang, L., Köse, S.: Secure intermittent-robust computation for energy harvesting device security and outage resilience. In: IEEE Conference on Advanced and Trusted Computing (ATC), pp. 1–6, August 2017
22. Yu, W., Köse, S.: Security-adaptive voltage conversion as a lightweight countermeasure against LPA attacks. IEEE Trans. Very Large Scale Integr. (VLSI) Syst. **25**(7), 2183–2187 (2017)
23. Yu, W., Köse, S.: Time-delayed converter-reshuffling: an efficient and secure power delivery architecture. IEEE Embed. Syst. Lett. **7**(3), 73–76 (2015)

24. Wang, L., Khatamifard, S.K., Karpuzcu, U.R., Köse, S.: Exploiting algorithmic noise tolerance for scalable on-chip voltage regulation. IEEE Trans. Very Large Scale Integr. (VLSI) Syst. **27**(1), 229–242 (2019)
25. Wang, L., Khatamifard, S.K., Karpuzcu, U.R., Köse, S.: Mitigation of NBTI induced performance degradation in on-chip digital LDOs. In: Proceedings of the Design, Automation & Test in Europe, pp. 803–808, March 2018
26. Wang, L., Köse, S.: Startup aware reliability enhancement controller for on-chip digital LDOs. In: Government Microcircuit Applications and Critical Technology Conference (GOMACTech), pp. 1–4, March 2020
27. Wang, L., Köse, S.: Reliable on-chip voltage regulation for sustainable and compact IoT and heterogeneous computing systems. In: Proceedings of the ACM/IEEE Great Lakes Symposium on VLSI (GLSVLSI), pp. 285–290, May 2018
28. Giering, K., et al.: NBTI degradation, and recovery in analog circuits: accurate and efficient circuit-level modeling. IEEE Trans. Electron Devices **66**(4), 1662–1668 (2019)
29. Okuma, Y., et al.: 0.5-V input digital LDO with 98.7% current efficiency and 2.7-uA quiescent current in 65 nm CMOS. In: Proceedings of the IEEE Custom Integrated Circuits Conference, pp. 1–4, September 2010
30. Mahmoud, M.M., Soin, N., Fahmy, H.A.H.: Design framework to overcome aging degradation of the 16 nm VLSI technology circuits. IEEE Trans. Comput.-Aided Des. Integr. Circuits Syst. **33**(5), 691–703 (2014)
31. Chan, T., Sartori, J., Gupta, P., Kumar, R.: On the efficacy of NBTI mitigation techniques. In: Proceedings of the Design, Automation & Test in Europe, pp. 1–6, March 2011
32. Parihar, N., Goel, N., Chaudhary, A., Mahapatra, S.: A modeling framework for NBTI degradation under dynamic voltage and frequency scaling. IEEE Trans. Electron Devices **63**(3), 946–953 (2016)
33. Parihar, N., et al.: Resolution of disputes concerning the physical mechanism and DC/AC stress/recovery modeling of Negative Bias Temperature Instability (NBTI) in p-MOSFETs. In: Proceedings of the IEEE International Reliability Physics Symposium, pp. XT-1.1–XT-1.11 (2017)
34. Parihar, N., Sharma, U., Southwick, R.G., Wang, M., Stathis, J.H., Mahapatra, S.: Ultrafast measurements and physical modeling of NBTI stress and recovery in RMG FinFETs under diverse DC-AC experimental conditions. IEEE Trans. Electron Devices **65**(1), 23–30 (2018)
35. Parihar, N., Goel, N., Mukhopadhyay, S., Mahapatra, S.: BTI analysis tool–modeling of NBTI DC, AC stress and recovery time kinetics, nitrogen impact, and EOL estimation. IEEE Trans. Electron Devices **65**(2), 392–403 (2018)
36. Parihar, N., Southwick, R., Wang, M., Stathis, J.H., Mahapatra, S.: Modeling of NBTI time kinetics and T dependence of VAF in SiGe p-FinFETs. In: IEEE International Electron Devices Meeting, pp. 7.3.1–7.3.4 (2017)
37. Wu, K., Lin, I., Wang, Y., Yang, S.: BTI-aware sleep transistor sizing algorithm for reliable power gating designs. IEEE Trans. Comput.-Aided Des. Integr. Circuits Syst. **33**(10), 1591–1595 (2014)
38. Wang, L., Köse, S.: Reliability enhanced on-chip digital LDO with limit cycle oscillation mitigation. In: Government Microcircuit Applications and Critical Technology Conference, March 2019
39. Agbo, I., et al.: Integral impact of BTI, PVT variation, and workload on SRAM sense amplifier. IEEE Trans. Very Large Scale Integr. (VLSI) Syst. **25**(4), 1.444–1.454 (2017)

40. Fang, J., Sapatnekar, S.S.: The impact of BTI variations on timing in digital logic circuits. IEEE Trans. Device Mater. Reliab. **13**(1), 277–286 (2013)
41. Patra, P., Muthukaruppan, R., Mangal, S.: A reliable digitally synthesizable linear drop-out regulator design for 14 nm SOC. In/: Proceedings of the IEEE International Symposium on Nanoelectronic and Information Systems, pp. 73–76, December 2015
42. Muthukaruppan, R., et al.: A digitally controlled linear regulator for per-core wide-range DVFS of AtomTM cores in 14nm tri-gate CMOS featuring non-linear control, adaptive gain and code roaming. In: Proceedings of the IEEE European Solid State Circuits Conference, pp. 275–278, August 2017
43. Nasir, S.B., Gangopadhyay, S., Raychowdhury, A.: All-digital low-dropout regulator with adaptive control and reduced dynamic stability for digital load circuits. IEEE Trans. Power Electron. **31**(12), 8293–8302 (2016)
44. Lin, J., et al.: A digital low-dropout-regulator with steady-State Load Current (SLC) estimator and Dynamic Gain Scaling (DGS) Control. In: Proceedings of the IEEE Asia Pacific Conference on Circuits and Systems, pp. 37–40, January 2016
45. Nasir, S.B., Raychowdhury, A.: On limit cycle oscillations in discrete-time digital linear regulators. In: Proceedings of the IEEE Applied Power Electronics Conference and Exposition, pp. 371–376, March 2015
46. Pathak, D., Homayoun, H., Savidis, I.: Smart grid on chip: work load-balanced on-chip power delivery. IEEE TVLSI **25**(9), 2538–2551 (2017)
47. Seçkiner, S., Wang, L., Köse, S.: An NBTI-aware digital low-dropout regulator with adaptive gain scaling control. In: Proceedings of the IFIP/IEEE International Conference on Very Large Scale Integration (VLSI-SoC), pp. 191–196, October 2019
48. Alam, M.A., Mahapatra, S.: A comprehensive model of PMOS NBTI degradation. Microelectron. Reliab. **45**(1), 71–81 (2005)
49. Rossi, D., et al.: Reliable power gating with NBTI aging benefits. IEEE Trans. Very Large Scale Integr. (VLSI) Syst. **24**(8), 2735–2744 (2016)
50. Geng, J., et al.: Modeling digital low-dropout regulator with a multiple sampling frequency circuit technology. In: Proceedings of the IEEE 13th International Conference on Anti-counterfeiting, Security, and Identification, pp. 207–210 (2019)
51. Lim, C., Mandal, D., Bakkaloglu, B., Kiaei, S.: A 50-mA 99.2% peak current efficiency, 250-ns settling time digital low-dropout regulator with transient enhanced PI controller. IEEE Trans. Very Large Scale Integr. (VLSI) Syst. **25**(8), 2360–2370 (2017)
52. Maeng, J., Shim, M., Jeong, J., Park, I., Park, Y., Kim, C.: A sub-fs-FoM digital LDO using PMOS and NMOS arrays with fully integrated 7.2-pF total capacitance. IEEE J. Solid-State Circuits **55**, 1624–1636 (2019)
53. Reddy, K.K., Rao, P.S.: Digital low drop-out regulator-power dissipation modeling and reliability modeling. In: International Conference on Smart Systems and Inventive Technology, pp. 764–766 (2019)
54. Chang, K., Tsai, C.: Transient performance estimation of DLDO by building model in MATLAB simulink. In: Proceedings of the IEEE Asia Pacific Conference on Postgraduate Research in Microelectronics and Electronics, pp. 57–60 (2017)
55. Bernardo, D.D., Lopez, J.L., Lopez, M.D., de Leon, M.T., Rosales, M., Alarcon, L.P.: 0.5 V output digital low dropout voltage regulator with VCO-based digital feedback loop. In: Proceedings of the IEEE Region 10 Conference, pp. 505–509 (2017)

56. Huang, M., Lu, Y., Seng-Pan, U., Martins, R.P.: 20.4 an output-capacitor-free analog-assisted digital low-dropout regulator with tri-loop control. In: Proceedings of the IEEE International Solid-State Circuits Conference, pp. 342–343 (2017)
57. Leitner, S., West, P., Lu, C., Wang, H.: Digital LDO modeling for early design space exploration. In: Proceedings of the IEEE International System-on-Chip (SoC) Conference, pp. 7–12 (2016)
58. Tsou, W., et al.: 20.2 digital low-dropout regulator with anti PVT-variation technique for dynamic voltage scaling and adaptive voltage scaling multicore processor. In: Proceedings of the IEEE International Solid-State Circuits Conference, pp. 338–339 (2017)
59. Cheah, M., Mandal, D., Bakkaloglu, B., Kiaei, S.: A 100-mA, 99.11% current efficiency, 2-mVpp ripple digitally controlled LDO with active ripple suppression. IEEE Trans. Very Large Scale Integr. (VLSI) Syst. **25**(2), 696–704 (2017)
60. Krishna Chekuri, V.C., Singh, A., Dasari, N., Mukhopadhyay, S.: On the effect of NBTI induced aging of power stage on the transient performance of on-chip voltage regulators. In: Proceedings of the IEEE International Reliability Physics Symposium (IRPS), pp. 1–5 (2019)
61. Chen, Y., Lin, Y.: NBTI-aware digital LDO design for edge devices in IoT systems. In: Proceedings of the IEEE China Semiconductor Technology International Conference, pp. 1–3, March 2019
62. Huang, M., Lu, Y., Sin, S., Seng-Pan, U., Martins, R., Ki, W.: Limit cycle oscillation reduction for digital low dropout regulators. IEEE Trans. Circuits Syst. II **63**(9), 903–907 (2016)
63. Çakmakçi, Y., Toms, W., Navaridas, J., Luján, M.: Cyclic power-gating as an alternative to voltage and frequency scaling. IEEE Comput. Architect. Lett. **15**(2), 77–80 (2016)
64. Song, H., Rhee, W., Shim, I., Wang, Z.: Digital LDO with 1-bit modulation for low-voltage clock generation systems. IEEE Electron. Lett. **52**(25), 2034–2036 (2016)
65. Yang, F., Mok, P.K.T.: A nanosecond-transient fine-grained digital LDO with multi-step switching scheme and asynchronous adaptive pipeline control. IEEE J. Solid-State Circuits **52**(9), 2463–2474 (2017)
66. Ahn, Y., Jeon, I., Roh, J.: A multiphase buck converter with a rotating phase-shedding scheme for efficient light-load control. IEEE JSSC **49**(11), 2673–2683 (2014)
67. Liang, C., Liang, L., Wang, Z.: A fully integrated digital LDO with voltage peak detecting and push-pull feedback loop control. IEICE ELEX **15**(15), 20180611 (2018)
68. Li, D., Qian, L., He, X., Sang, J., Xia, Y.: A transient-enhanced digital low-dropout regulator with bisection method tuning. In: Proceedings of the IEEE Asia Pacific Conference on Circuits and Systems, pp. 50–52 (2018)

Security Aspects of Real-Time MPSoCs: The Flaws and Opportunities of Preemptive NoCs

Bruno Forlin[1(✉)], Cezar Reinbrecht[1], and Johanna Sepúlveda[2]

[1] Federal University of Rio Grande do Sul,
Av. Paulo Gama, 110 - Farroupilha, Porto Alegre, RS, Brazil
bruno.eforlin@inf.ufrgs.br
[2] Airbus Defence and Space GmbH, Willy-Messerschmitt-Straße 1,
82024 Taufkirchen, Germany
johanna.sepulveda@airbus.com

Abstract. Multi-Processor System-on-Chips (MPSoCs) is a standard platform used in time-critical applications. These platforms usually employ Priority-Preemptive NoCs (PP-NoCs), a widely used real-time on-chip interconnection structure that offers communication predictability. A deep analysis of the PP-NoC parameters and their impact on system security is required. Moreover, countermeasures that can protect the system while guaranteeing the real-time capabilities should be proposed and evaluated. To this end, this paper explores and evaluates the impact of the PP-NoCs parameters on system security; exploits PP-NoCs vulnerabilities and demonstrates for the first time two very powerful attacks; and proposes and integrates three new security countermeasures: RT-blinding, RT-masking, and RT-shielding. Results show that PP-NoCs are vulnerable to attacks and that is possible to uncover victim's information with high accuracy (up to 96.19%). On the other hand, protection techniques were able to harden the system, effectively and efficiently mitigating the vulnerabilities while maintaining deterministic behavior.

Keywords: Network-on-Chip · Secure MPSoC · Timing side-channel attacks

1 Introduction

Real-time applications (RTA) are becoming very popular as more embedded systems enter in daily life. Examples include health care equipment, automotive safety mechanisms, smart greenhouses, agriculture, avionics, and aerospace technology. Most of these systems require a powerful and efficient hardware platform, where Multi-processor Systems-on-Chips (MPSoCs) are the *status quo*. Current MPSoCs already support RTAs through ad-hoc solutions, such as real-time processors [1], operating systems for critical applications [2] and Networks-on-Chip

© IFIP International Federation for Information Processing 2020
Published by Springer Nature Switzerland AG 2020
C. Metzler et al. (Eds.): VLSI-SoC 2019, IFIP AICT 586, pp. 209–233, 2020.
https://doi.org/10.1007/978-3-030-53273-4_10

(NoCs) with Quality-of-Service (QoS) [3–5]. Although all these components perform RTAs successfully, the techniques, architectures, and implementations used to ensure their predictability create security vulnerabilities. Consequently, any security issue in these critical systems will also be critical. Security backdoor can be easily exploited to affect the safety-related characteristics of the systems. Therefore, to ensure the development of safety-critical systems, it is mandatory to understand and to guarantee the security of these systems. In this work, we contribute by identifying and discussing the flaws and opportunities in designing secure real-time MPSoCs. In particular, we focus on this work in the on-chip communication structure based on NoCs.

Recent works have shown the effectiveness of Priority-Preemptive NoCs (PP-NoCs) in guaranteeing real-time requirements and support mixed-critically traffic [4–7]. The works of [6] and [7] demonstrated that low priority traffic at PP-NoCs can affect the high priority traffic behavior. Furthermore, these works elaborate on a mathematical model able to estimate such effects in terms of packet latency. Despite these accurate models were developed to support the design of predictable communication structures for critical applications, they also provide a means for attackers to successfully retrieve sensitive data from the MPSoCs. An adversary, for example, may use this information to perform the so-called NoC timing attacks [8–10]. These attacks exploit the microarchitecture of the NoC, the shared communication nature and the main role of the communication in the system operation to passively gather information during the normal operation of the system [11]. A processor inside the MPSoC can be infected (i.e., an external malicious application with hidden functionalities or backdoors) and then, it may start to inject dummy packets in the network. In this scenario, the attacker aims to collide its traffic with a victim's traffic. In the absence of collisions, the attacker throughput is maximal. However, the degradation of throughput sensed by the attacker reveals the presence of collisions. Sensitive information, such as communication affinity (to whom the victim communicates most), communication rates and size of packets, may be extracted using this technique. In addition, this information may be used to further enhance powerful attack (e.g., cache attacks), as described in [12,13]. The identification of vulnerabilities and further exploitation of cover channels on the real-time NoCs, like PP-NoCs, are still unexplored.

Previous attacks were demonstrated in a wide variety of NoC architectures. However, NoC attacks on real-time MPSoC have been not widely explored. For the best of our knowledge, our previous work in [14] is the only study in this direction. This work introduced two attacks named *Direct Interference* and *Back-Pressure*. These attacks exploit two MPSoC vulnerabilities. First the traffic predictability and shaping of sensitive applications. Second, the shared memories. As a protection mechanism to circumvent potential attacks, this former work proposed two NoC countermeasures. In this paper, we further extend the work in [14] by providing a refined and deep analysis of the PP-NoCs vulnerabilities. We explore the different design parameters that define the configuration of a PP-NoC and evaluate their impact on the overall MPSoC security. Also, we propose a new countermeasure, which tunes the PP-NoCs parameters at design time to avoid the main known vulnerabilities. In summary, the contributions of the paper are:

- Vulnerability exploration of preemptive NoCs through the evaluation of the impact of the PP-NoCs configuration parameters on the MPSoC security;
- Optimization of the previous two PP-NoCs attacks: *Direct-Interference* and *Back-Pressure*; and
- Design, implementation and evaluation of three new protection techniques for PP-NoCs: i) RT-Blinding; ii) RT-Masking and; iii) RT-Shielding.

This paper is organized as follows. Section summarizes existing NoC attacks in literature. Then, Sect. 3 describes the Priority-Preemptive Network-on-Chip concept, as well as, our hardware implementation of it. In Sect. 4, we show how to exploit the analytical models of PP-NoCs to elucidate NoC vulnerabilities. Thereafter, two attacks are described in Sect. 5. Then, security countermeasures and their impact are presented in Sect. 6. Section 7 presents the experiments and evaluation results. From the results a discussion is made in Sect. 8. Finally, conclusions are drawn in Sect. 9.

2 Related Works in NoC Attacks and Protections

In this section, we describe the previous works that deal with the NoC vulnerability exploration and security integration. The NoC-timing attack was the first attack against NoCs mentioned in scientific articles [8,10]. These works described for the first time the exploitation of NoC covert channels. A malicious agent (attacker) inside the MPSoC can elicit channel leakage by the evaluation of the throughput of the own injected packets (attacker packets). As routers are shared, different packets must compete for the resources when they are being communicated simultaneously. The communication collisions between the attacker packets and sensitive traffic cause latency perturbations. Thus, affecting the attacker communication throughput. This effect is shown in Fig. 1, where the attacker traffic is represented as λ_O while victim traffic as λ_V. As a result, this congestion reveals the sensitive traffic information of the victim. Examples of characteristics that can be extracted by this attack are mapping, topology, routing, communication pattern and volume of communication. The collisions are sensed by the attacker due to the reduction of throughput to inject new packets in the network.

The first demonstration of NoC timing attacks was presented in [12]. In this work, the authors show the effectiveness of the classical NoC timing attack and of a powerful variation: Distributed NoC Timing Attack (DNTA). It uses two or more attackers inside an MPSoC to better tune the MPSoC congestion and thus to maximize the attacker observation capabilities. It was demonstrated that DNTA was immune to the NoC countermeasures proposed in [10] and [15]. In order to avoid NoC timing attacks and DNTA, the authors proposed Gossip NoC, a security enhanced NoC able to identify traffic anomalies and avoiding attacks through the on-chip traffic distribution. Each NoC router included a

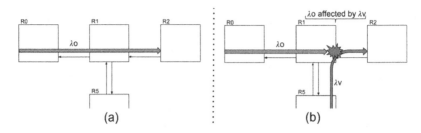

Fig. 1. Attack scenarios: (a) attacker traffic λ_O only; (b) attacker traffic λ_O blocked by victim traffic λ_V.

monitor to detect possible points of attack. This information was used to adapt the routing of packets. The attack was executed in an FPGA MPSoC prototype. Similar approach was used in [16]. Despite the effectiveness of the detection and protection mechanisms, these secure NoCs cannot meet hard communication deadlines and only offer best-effort communication services.

Recently, the NoC timing attack has been used to enhance the capabilities of dangerous cache attacks, creating extremely powerful attacks such as the NoC Prime+Probe [17] and Earthquake [11]. In [17], the authors propose the NoC Prime+Probe attack which uses the NoC timing attack to extract information regarding the communication behavior between a cryptographic IP core and a shared cache, a usual configuration of secure MPSoCs. By using the NoC timing attack, it is possible for the attacker to detect, in a non-intrusive way, the optimal point in time to probe the shared cache[1]. For a system that implements the AES (Advanced Encryption Standard) symmetric cryptography based on a transformation table (T-Table) implementation, the best attack point (increases the efficiency of the attack) to probe the shared cache is at the end of the first AES round. By using the NoC Prime+Probe, the authors retrieved 12 of the 16 key bytes after 80 AES encryptions.

In the Earthquake attack of [11], the authors use the NoC timing attack to collect the time where the third round of AES starts. Earthquake manipulates the input of the cryptographic IP core to force several cache collisions (i.e., cache hits) until the third round of AES, thus causing faster encryptions/decryptions. The faster results can be used to break the key. Since the important timing information resides within the first three rounds, the NoC timing attack allows the attacker to sample effectively (less noise) the time. This work presented the first practical implementation of timing attacks.

Although NoC timing attack has been studied in different NoC configurations and scenarios, attacks to real-time NoCs, specifically Priority-Preemptive NoCs, have been not widely explored yet. For the best of our knowledge, the only works that address attacks to real-time NoCs are [19] and [14]. The work of Indrusiak

---

[1] Following the classical cache attack, Prime+Probe from Osvik et al. [18], the best moment to probe a cache is when all the accesses to the cache depends only on the value of the secret key used for encryption.

et al. [19] showed the impact of the NoC routing in the security of the system. As a protection mechanism, the authors proposed a packet route randomization mechanism to increase NoC resilience against side-channel attacks. The route randomization was based on an evolutionary optimization approach for effectively controlling the impact on hard real-time performance guarantees. In our previous work in [14], we have demonstrated for the first time an attack that exploits preemptive NoC-based MPSoCs. Also, two countermeasures were proposed.

The protection against NoC timing attacks has been addressed in the works of [10, 20–22] and [15]. The works of Yao and Suh [20] and Wassel et al. [21] proposed the integration of hard Quality-of-Service (QoS) mechanisms to isolate the sensitive information. They included temporal network partitioning based on different priorities arbitration: high priority [20] and bounded priority [21]. The work of Sepúlveda et al. [22] presented a secure enhanced router architecture that dynamically configures the router memory space according to the communication and security properties of the traffic. Furthermore, the work of Sepúlveda et al. [10] proposed random arbitration and adaptive routing as protection techniques. The work of Stefan and Goossens [15] introduced the usage of multiple path communication for sensitive flows. The work of Reinbrecht et al. [12] showed the Gossip NoC, an NoC architecture with a distributed protection mechanism that changes the routing algorithm in the presence of abnormal traffic.

3   Priority Preemptive NoCs

Priority Preemptive NoCs (PP-NoCs) allow that high priority communication flows preempt low priority packets on the NoC router. Thus, higher priority packets are preferentially communicated while lower priority packets remain stored inside the router buffers. High priority traffic is assumed to be either periodic or sporadic, as to avoid starvation of low priority packets due to continuous high priority interference. This chapter presents the target MPSoC platform (architectural scenario) used to demonstrate the attacks and the security of the countermeasures. The on-chip communication structure is a parameterizable PP-NoC. The architecture overview and functionality are further detailed.

3.1   Target MPSoC Platform

The MPSoC platform allows performing the practical study of the PP-NoCs vulnerabilities. In such environment, the proposed PP-NoCs attacks and countermeasures (Sects. 5 and 6, respectively) can be evaluated. In this work, we use the Glass MPSoC, a parameterizable hardware platform presented in [11] and which has been already used to evaluate logical side-channel attacks. To evaluate the PP-NoC vulnerabilities, the Glass NoC was modified to support the priority-preemptive flow control.

Glass MPSoC is presented in Fig. 2. It integrates 16 tiles (from IP_0 to IP_15) through 4×4 mesh-based PP-NoC. It supports several layers of memory hierarchy. The MPSoC tiles include an inclusive shared cache (64 KB, 16-way set-associative cache L2) at IP_0, serial UART interface at IP_3 and 14 RISC-V processing elements. We used a verified and functional RISC-V distribution called RI5CY core, from the Pulpino Platform [23]. Besides the processor, each of the 14 processing tiles integrates local instruction and data memories (8 KB, direct-mapped cache L1), a cycle-accurate timer and a network interface to communicate with the NoC. The NoC routers implement credit-based flow control with four virtual channels (each one at a different priority level) and Priority-Preemptive routers.

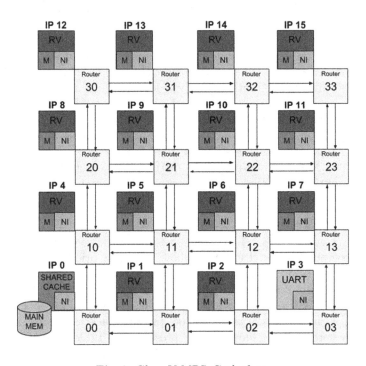

Fig. 2. Glass-V MPSoC platform

3.2 Priority-Preemptive (PP) NoC Architecture and Functionality

To guarantee different real-time and mixed-critically requirements, communication on-chip is prioritized. That is, communication flows that are characterized by tight delay requirements are granted the highest communication priority. A preemptive policy allows a higher priority packet to anticipate (preempt) an already progressing lower-priority packet. To support the preemptive communication technique, routers should be enhanced through the integration of virtual channels. These additional structures are capable of storing a packet blocked during its communication. When packets with the same priority-level dispute a communication resource (collision), any arbitrary decision algorithm can be applied, such as Round-Robin [3] or aging [5].

The structure of the packets of the PP-NoC follows the typical packet organization. It includes a header flit, N payload flits and a trailer flit, where N can reach a maximum of 1024 flits per packet. Besides these flits, nine control bits are present in the links: header/trailer identification (1 bit), packet priority (2 bits), handshake (2 bits) and credit information (4 bits). A detailed description of the router is given in the following paragraphs.

Priority-Preemptive (PP) Router: The proposed PP-router is defined to support four different priority levels. It uses credit-based virtual channels to handle different priority messages simultaneously (each virtual channel is a different priority lane). Since the preemption of low priority packets by higher priorities is allowed, this router supports packet interleaving. The PP-router integrates six components as shown in Fig. 3:

1. *Priority multiplexer:* It is responsible for monitoring the packet priority and selecting the proper input buffer.
2. *Routing computing unit:* It defines the output port of each packet.
3. *Virtual channel (PP) allocator:* It selects the active priority level at the output port.
4. *Switch allocator:* It is a unit included for each priority level. It is used to attend each request (of the same priority) using a Round-Robin arbiter to cope with resource conflicts.
5. *Crossbar:* Also included for each priority level. It is used to connect the defined input and output of the router.
6. *Virtual channel demultiplexer:* It links the active priority crossbar with the output of the router.

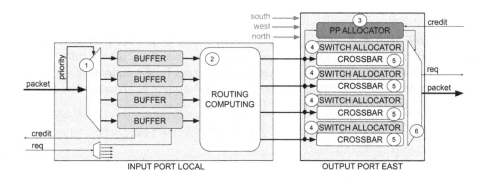

Fig. 3. Priority-Preemptive router architecture

When a packet arrives at the input port, the priority information in the control bits defines which input buffer will be used. This information is used for referring the packet to the proper virtual channel. The buffers request the proper output port for each packet being handled, where the virtual channel allocator (VA Allocator) at the output port decides which virtual channel will be granted by the crossbar. Hence, VA Allocator is responsible for providing the preemption feature. The output port always chooses the higher priority packet to perform the data commutation. When different input ports dispute the same output port and the level of priority is the same, the Round-Robin arbitration takes place. It is implemented in the Switch Allocator of Fig. 3.

4 Exploiting Priority-Preemptive Models for Security

In this chapter, we show how the priority-preemptive models can be used to evaluate vulnerabilities of the Preemptive Network-on-Chip (PP-NoC). First, we present the existing models in the literature that predicts in detail the traffic behavior. Thereafter, we use the *IBN* model to explore the PP-NoC vulnerabilities to NoC timing attacks. Also, we explore the impact that the PP-NoC parameters have on the overall system security.

4.1 Priority-Preemptive Models

Scheduling of real-time systems requires the calculation of upper-bounds for packet transmission delay. To evaluate if the system can meet the application deadlines, analytic models can be used. Although these models were elaborated to support designers to validate the real-time constraints, in this work we use them as an important tool to evaluate vulnerabilities and elaborate NoC timing attacks.

The Priority-Preemptive models allow estimating the worst-case latency for different flows of packets in the NoC. We define flow i as λ_i, where the flow represents the first flit leaving the origin node until the last flit arrives at the destination node. In the sequence, three models developed in previous works are here described: i) SB model; ii) XLWX model; and iii) IBN model.

SB Model: The work of [6] presents the *SB model* to predict packet network latency. It is based on direct and indirect interference from other traffic flows and calculates the upper-bound interference suffered by a communication flow. When no flow interferes with λ_i, the worst-case latency is given by the flow's zero-load latency (C_i), given by Eq. (1):

$$C_i = RouteL * (route_i - 1) + LinkL * (route_i) + LinkL * (L_i - 1) \qquad (1)$$

Where $RouteL$ is the router latency in cycles, $route_i$ is the contention domain of λ_i in hops, $LinkL$ is the link latency in cycles and L_i is the number of flits in each packet of λ_i. The direct interference presented in this model can be seen in Eq. (2). The worst-case response R_i is quantified by the summation of two components: the flow's zero-load latency (C_i) and the worst possible delays resulting from blocking and preemption caused by higher priority packets.

$$R_i = C_i + \sum_{\lambda_j \in S_i^D} \left\lceil \frac{R_i + J_j}{T_j} \right\rceil C_j \qquad (2)$$

The worst-case delay is the summation of the effects of all interfering flows on the contention domain (cd_{ij}), defined as the interference Set S_i^P, which is the path λ_i intersects with the interfering higher priority λ_j. This equation is a recurrent ceiling function that depends on the relation between release jitter (J) in cycles, the period of the flow (T) in cycles, and the flow latency (R), also in cycles. The equation is calculated until the result converges.

XLWX Model: Xiong et al. [24] presented the *XLWX model*. The work extended the *SB model* to support Multi-point Progressive Blocking (MPB) for downstream indirect interferences. MPB takes place when a flow λ_i is preempted by a flow λ_j by more than its base latency C_j. This scenario usually occurs when a third flow λ_k interferes with λ_j downstream from the link that λ_j interferes with λ_i. The model can be represented by Eq. 3.

$$R_i = C_i + \sum_{\lambda_j \in S_i^P} \left\lceil \frac{R_i + J_j + J_j^I}{T_j} \right\rceil (C_j + I_{ji}^{down}) \tag{3}$$

Where $J_j^I = R_j - C_j$ is used to calculate the effects of upstream interference of λ_j, I_{ji}^{down} is the number of hits suffered by λ_j from every λ_k in the downstream indirect interference Set of λ_i, given by Eq. (4):

$$I_{ji}^{down} = \sum_{\lambda_k \in S_{I_i}^{down_j}} \left\lceil \frac{R_j + J_k}{T_k} \right\rceil (bi_{ij}) \tag{4}$$

Where $bi_{ij} = buf \cdot LinkL \cdot |cd_{ij}|$ is the maximum buffered interference over the contention domain cd_{ij}, R_j is the worst-case latency experienced by λ_j, buf is the routers FIFO buffer size, and T_k is the release period of packets for λ_k.

IBN Model: The work of Indrusiak et al. [7] proves that the analysis proposed by Xiong et al. [24] for downstream indirect interference is overly pessimistic since it treats all interferences as direct interference. The authors improve the *XLWX model* by presenting an upper-bound analysis. In order to find R_i, two cases are considered when calculating the upper-bound for downstream interference I_{ij}^{down}. First, when interference is caused by flows that do not suffer from upstream and downstream interference. Second, when interference is caused by flows that do suffer from upstream interference. The first case is described by Eq. 5. It includes the effects of the maximum buffered interference (bi_{ij}) and the high priority flows downstream. The latter case is identical to the analysis proposed by Xiong et al. [24].

$$I_{ji}^{down} = \sum_{\lambda_k \in S_{I_i}^{down_j}} \left\lceil \frac{R_j + J_k}{T_k} \right\rceil min(bi_{ij}, C_k + I_{kj}^{down}) \tag{5}$$

Even though these models give guarantees regarding the system's ability to meet the deadlines, the predictability of the system allows an attacker to take advantage of the additional information about the system behavior, especially packet delay times. This data could be used to create a refined NoC timing attack (exploiting thresholds), allowing an attacker to skip the costly attack setup and tune phases as showed in [12]. These phases usually are dedicated to monitor the throughput in order to find a value that allows an attacker to have a communication sensibility such that sensitive packets are efficiently and effectively detected (attack threshold). The details regarding the estimation of the latency experienced by preempted packets will be explored in the next Sect. 4.2. We show that it is possible for an attacker to further extract information of the sensitive flow (victim's flow), such as packet sizes. We refer to the improved version of the *XLWX model* as the *IBN* model, and it will be used for the rest of this paper.

4.2   PP-NoC Vulnerabilities

The analytical model used to predict the behavior of the PP-NoCs can reveal information regarding the system operation that can be exploited by an attacker. As described in [14], two vulnerabilities can be found at PP-NoCs: *Direct-interference* and *Back-pressure*.

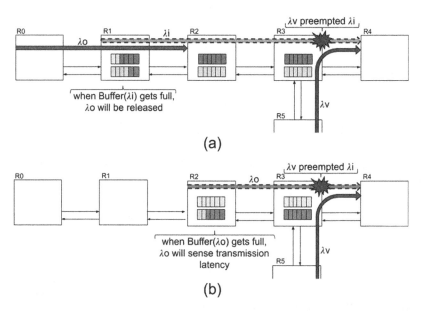

Fig. 4. Flow representation of the discussed vulnerabilities: (a) back-pressure (b) interference

Direct-Interference Vulnerability. It takes place when two flows with different priorities dispute the same output port, such as in Fig. 4.b. The flow λ_o is preempted by a higher priority flow λ_v and a contention occurs at router R_3. Direct measurements of transmission latency times can be used to retrieve predicted access times of secure flows. In this case, only direct interference was considered. We call the preemption caused by high priority messages as interference, and since high priority messages can occur all over the system, we consider this feature as a vulnerability only when the attacker and the victim can be placed close enough to avoid external interference (caused by a third IP core communication flow). In the case of an attacker be placed distantly from victim traffic, the interference behavior from higher priority packets can be used as a protection technique, since it becomes a source of noise in the attacker measurements. As a result, a high amount of false-positive sensitive packet detection is caused to the attacker.

Back-Pressure Vulnerability. This vulnerability is based on the MPB scenario. It considers three communication flows λ_v, λ_i and λ_o, originating from routers R_5, R_1 and R_0, ordered from highest priority to lowest, respectively. In this scenario, represented in Fig. 4.a, the flow λ_i preempts all packets from λ_o. However, when the high priority flow λ_v is injected, a contention occurs at R_3 and λ_i is preempted. Then, packets start to accumulate on the upstream routers from R_3 until all buffer space in the upstream path is used. As a result, all of the buffer credits from λ_i are expended, allowing λ_o to take over the transmission in the path. Based on Eq. (3), it is noticed that when λ_v stops transmitting, λ_o gets preempted by more than λ_i baseline latency, due to the accumulation in the cd_{ij} buffers.

4.3   Exploiting PP-NoC Through IBN Model

To evaluate the vulnerabilities of the PP-NoC, the *IBN model* can be used. In this case, the impact of each PP-NoC parameter of the IBN model on the security of the system is explored. The multiple parameters described by the equations in the previous sections can be classified into three different categories: i) Network Interface (jitter); ii) Router (Buffer size); and iii) Application parameters (transmission period and packet size). As described in Subsect. 4.1, each of the analyzed flows (λ_v, λ_o, and λ_i) has a set of proprieties as: zero-load latency (C) in cycles, worst-case latency (R) in cycles, and packet period (T) in cycles. Also, the network itself has parameters that influence the latency of packets, such as router buffer-size in (buf) flits, packet release jitter (J) in cycles, link latency ($LinkL$) in cycles, and the contention domain cd_{ij} (e.g., the routers where two flows intersect). The range of values explored for each one of the parameters of the PP-NoC is shown in Table 1.

Direct Interference Evaluation. Each PP-NoC configuration is obtained after defining the values of the different PP-NoC parameters. The previously discussed IBN model can be used to further understand the behavior of the system. The Eq. (2) can be used with the corresponding PP-NoC values. Initially, an oscillation of the resulting value R_i is observed and by using recursively this mathematical expression, until a stable value is reached. However, for some PP-NoC configurations the stable value is never reached (the equation diverging to

Table 1. Selected parameters for network interface, router and application.

Parameters	Values					
Router buffer size (flits) ($LinkL$)	4	8	16	32	64	
Packet transmission period (% of 1000 cycles)	10%	20%	30%	40%	50%	
Release jitter (cycles)	4	8	16	32	64	128
Flow packet size (flits)	4	8	16	32	64	128

infinity). These scenarios lead to stalls and they are not considered nor evaluated in this paper. Table 2 presents 10 different PP-NoC configurations considered as representative candidates of all possibilities evaluated.

Table 2. Different configurations of parameters for direct interference.

Parameter	Config 1	Config 2	Config 3	Config 4	Config 5	Config 6	Config 7	Config 8	Config 9	Config 10
Jitter (Cycles)	4	4	4	4	8	16	32	128	64	64
λ_v Period (Cycles)	200	200	500	300	200	200	200	500	500	200
λ_o Size (Flits)	4	128	128	128	128	16	64	128	64	64

The Direct-interference vulnerability may be used to exploit the PP-NoC as a cover channel. By manipulating specific communication flows, the information of a victim flow can leak. In the Direct-Interference case, the victim v is a high priority flow that will directly affect the low-priority attacker o. Figure 5 presents the impact of the victim's packet size on the attacker's flow delay. Results show that some PP-NoC configurations exhibit a greater latency sensibility when the packet size increase. This evaluation has not been presented before and the results allow the designer to identify potential leakages in PP-NoCs. Consequently, there are configurations that mitigate the observation of a potential attack. The strategy uses this benefit to protect the MPSoC will be further discussed and presented in Sect. 6.

Figures 6(a) and 6(b) present the difference in latencies for all considered configurations. Each area represents the delta for subsequent packet sizes, meaning that there is an expressive difference in terms of the latency when the packet size is increased. Some configurations (e.g., Dif 16–32) raise this difference even further (an increase of almost 400%). When the difference is large enough, the attacker is able to easily differentiate the victim's packet size.

Back-Pressure Vulnerability Evaluation. In order to evaluate the Back-Pressure vulnerability (or indirect interference), Eqs. (3) and (5) must be used. These calculations involve a wide variety of variables. As a consequence, the exploration space is wider, that is, there are a wide variety of PP-NoC configurations. In this paper, a representative set of this design space was selected. Table 3 presents the 10 different PP-NoC configurations selected for the study.

Figure 7 shows that the victim's packet size does not produce a linear influence for all configurations of the PP-NoCs. For some PP-NoC configurations,

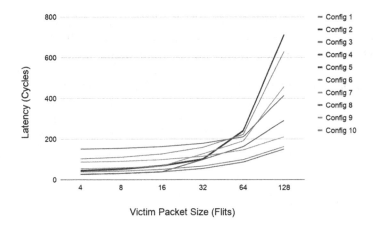

Fig. 5. Interfering packet size effect in direct interference latency.

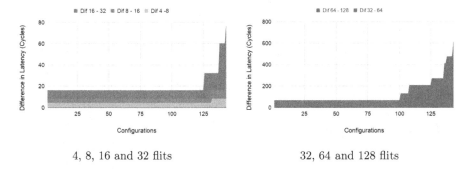

4, 8, 16 and 32 flits   32, 64 and 128 flits

Fig. 6. Value of the difference in latency between packet sizes of interfering flow

Table 3. Different configurations of parameters for back-pressure.

Parameter	Config 1	Config 2	Config 3	Config 4	Config 5
Injector packet size (flits)	4	4	8	8	8
Observer packet size (flits)	4	4	4	8	32
Injector period (cycles)	100	300	100	300	500
Victim period (cycles)	100	300	200	500	300
Jitter (cycles)	4	8	8	64	8
Buffer size (flits)	4	16	4	64	4
Parameter	Config 6	Config 7	Config 8	Config 9	Config 10
Injector packet size (flits)	16	16	32	32	128
Observer packet size (flits)	8	32	64	128	32
Injector period (cycles)	500	300	200	500	300
Victim period (cycles)	200	300	100	100	500
Jitter (cycles)	32	64	16	4	4
Buffer size (flits)	32	32	8	32	8

such as *Config 2* and *Config 5*, the packet size does not influence at all on the latency experienced by the observer. In contrast, for some PP-NoC configurations, such as *Config 8* and *Config 9*, the packet latency is not easily predictable. As a conclusion, for some PP-NoC configurations, the Back-Pressure attack could not yield information about packet sizes, even if it could detect them.

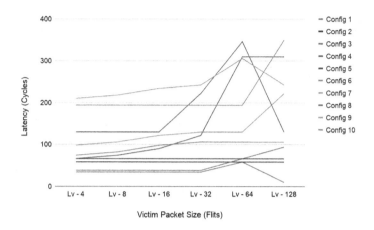

Fig. 7. Interfering packet size effect in indirect interference latency.

5 Proposed Attacks

This section presents two attacks based on the vulnerabilities already presented.

5.1 Direct-Interference Attack

This attack explores the interference vulnerability and it is performed in three phases. In the first phase, the latency upper and lower-bounds are calculated based on the different parameters (PP-NoC configuration and attacker's flow). This generates a range of values of the expected latency for the observer's packets being preempted. This information can be used to increase the precision of the NoC timing attacks. In the second phase, an IP core is infected (through a malicious software or the trigger of a Trojan), in order to create the λ_o flow from the attacker through the secure flow's path (see Fig. 4(b)). The Direct-Interference attack requires a close engagement of the attacker on the secure traffic observation. The attack applies measurement of the interference from the secure flow close to the target path while trying to avoid at maximum interference from non-victim flows (also called indirect interference). The third and final phase employs a mathematical algorithm to correlate the timing results collected by the attacker's monitor to infer an unknown key or private information. From this point, the attacks presented in [25] or [26] can be performed to retrieve secret information.

Attack Conditions: In order to execute this attack on a PP-NoC, the following conditions are required:

- The attacker can infect at least one IP in the MPSoC with malicious software or any other infection technique.
- This IP has to be, at most, one-hop away from the secure flow.
- The attacker knows where the target elements are located in the NoC (logical addresses).
- The attacker knows the topology and routing algorithm of the communication infrastructure.

Attack Optimization: This attack can be optimized in a way that can retrieve not only the victim's traffic pattern but also the size of the messages exchanged. The size of the packets provide important information that can be correlated with the sensitive application running. For example, it can reveal if the AES cryptography uses T-table (32-bit information) or S-Box (8-bit information) implementation. In addition, it may reveal the bit width of the keys distributed in the system. Finally, by knowing the granularity of the information and the moments of data transfers, more sophisticated and efficient attacks can be elaborated.

In order to achieve this, modifications are performed in the phases of the Direct-Interference attack. In the first phase, a range of values for R_o and C_o is calculated, based on the jitter, attacker packet size, and possible victim period and packet size. The attacker will then monitor the latency of it's packets and filter configurations that lead to an R_o value smaller than the one measured. For example, assuming a NoC with a Jitter of 4 cycles, if the attacker chooses a large packet size (e.g., 128 flits), there will be a discernible difference in R_o for victim packet sizes (e.g., 710 cycles for 128 flits, 98 cycles for 32 flits, and 42 cycles for 4 flits), as it can be seen in *Config 2* in Fig. 5. Therefore, an attacker can distinguish with less effort the size of victim's packet.

5.2   Back-Pressure Attack

This attack explores back-pressure vulnerability. It uses the same first and third phases of the Direct-Interference attack. In contrast with the previous attack, the second phase of the Back-Pressure attack requires the infection of two IPs: an injector IP and an observer IP. The injector IP is responsible for creating traffic interfering with the observer IP, λ_i flow as shown in Fig. 4(a). The λ_i flow intends to accumulate back pressure until the buffers are filled. When the priority flow (victim flow), λ_v, preempt the injector, the observer flow, λ_o, will be released to proceed. Therefore, the observer understands that the secure flow has been communicated through the increase of its transmission throughput. Besides, the observer can use Eq. (3) to calculate specific features of the secure flow, such as message size.

The predicted advantages of this type of attack are its ability to infer sensitive information of high priority packets indirectly, while not being necessarily close to the target path of the secure flow. This allows more flexibility for the attacker and expands the range of MPSoC configurations that could be targeted. In the same manner as the previous attacks, from this point, different methodologies can be applied to successfully perform a complete logical Side-Channel attack.

Attack Conditions: In order to execute this attack on a PP-NoC, the following conditions are required:

- The attacker can infect at least two IPs in the MPSoC with malicious software.
- The attacker knows where the target elements are located in the NoC (logical addresses).
- The attacker knows the topology and routing algorithm of the communication infrastructure.
- The attacker is able to create low and medium priority messages.

Attack Optimization: In the same manner as the previous attack, this attack can be optimized to retrieve other characteristics of the victim's traffic rather than pattern. To retrieve the granularity of the packets, modifications are preformed to the Back-Pressure attack.

Before describing the optimized methodology, note that Back-Pressure vulnerability is affected by much more parameters of the NoC than direct-interference. Hence, it is more difficult to guarantee the attacker knows or can infer all required information. However, once the attacker knows the parameters, the optimized attack is possible. Therefore, the attacker has first to conduct an exploration of the NoC parameters, and then evaluate the best configuration of attacker packet sizes and period to match with the victim's behavior. For example, in an MPSoC with jitter of 64 cycles and buffer size 64 flits, if the attacker applies an injector period of 300 cycles, and packet sizes of 8 flits, the latency experienced by the observer would be 310 cycles for 128 flit packets, 122 cycles for 32 flits, and 66 cycles for 4 flits. As observed, the differences allow the attacker to distinguish the size of the messages.

6   Proposed Countermeasures

Our proposed attacks depend heavily on the preemption caused by secure flows. Hence, we propose three main strategies to mitigate the risk of a successful attack on PP-NoCs: a) RT-Blinding, b) RT-Masking and c) RT-Shielding.

6.1   RT-Blinding

The blinding strategy relies on the timely delivery of payloads by the secure IP. The Back-Pressure attack identifies high priority flows and assumes they are sensitive flows being exchanged through the PP-NoC. One possible way to avoid detection is to use dummy high priority payloads intentionally. Delivered at predefined intervals, these payloads could be replaced by an actual secure packet when needed. In this scenario, the victim has fixed time slots to send it's high priority secure packages. Since the attacker has no way to differentiate between a secure flow and a simple high priority flow, the attacker would not be able to determine whether it is an actual payload.

This interval would be determined by calculating the maximum acceptable delay that the secure application could endure. This application-dependant value is then used as a baseline for all high priority transmissions. The secure application must calculate it's zero-load latency C, with Eq. 1. The drawback of this approach is the increase in traffic in the NoC, which, in turn, may compromise the overall system performance. However, since secure flows are intended to be sporadic, it is expected that the average time defined in the time slots will be high enough to avoid performance penalties.

6.2 RT-Masking

The masking strategy proposes the saturation of the channels when a *high priority (secure) flow* is passing. Our proposed protection technique, nicknamed as Distraction, employs several high priority dummy packages sent prior and after the actual secure package to pad the channel. In this scenario, the secure flow is extended to have a random number of dummy packets sent with the secure packet. This would effectively mask the actual timestamp of the packet and message size, as each secure package would be sent in a random position of this enlarged secure flow. When the high priority flows are replaced by *normal priority flows*, our proposed protection technique, nicknamed as Avoidance, can be triggered. It masks the secure flow with the saturation of the normal priority channels.

An IP, defined at design time, would be responsible for generating a random series of large normal priority packets directed to the sensitive path of the target IP. The goal of this technique is to generate interference with the normal priority attacker packets which will be defined by the round-robin arbiter. Thus, the secure packets could be sent to the defined router, where they would preempt both the attacker's traffic and the companion normal priority buffered traffic.

6.3 RT-Shielding

Both of the previous countermeasures could be employed at the application level or with little modification to the design. The RT-Shielding strategy uses instead the models, described in Sect. 4.2, to build a NoC that makes the distinction of victim traffic by the attacker more arduous. It accomplishes this by setting the routers or the network interface with a specific set of parameters (i.e., buffer size, jitter). In this manner, the attacker would not be able to attack since by definition of the models certain configurations do not present interference in low priority packets. Furthermore, if the most security-critical paths in the system can be established at design time, only few routers and network interfaces require adjust, reducing the overall costs of choosing this strategy.

The RT-Shielding strategy relies on the redesign of NoC parameters, such as jitter and buffer sizes to prevent any possible interference to be used by an attacker. The direct interference equations only use jitter parameter, so an exhaustive analysis for different configurations was elaborated, where 17 of these different configurations can be seen in Fig. 8. It is clear on Fig. 8 that jitter has an effect on Latency at higher values, while maintaining a more constant behavior at lower settings. Hence, to avoid direct interference in the system, the IPs considered as victim in the system should have network interfaces with fast injection times (reduced jitter). In practice, this means to design a network interface with a small size of buffers, as they increase the delay to inject a packet in the network. Based on our results, we consider any value below 32 cycles as secure.

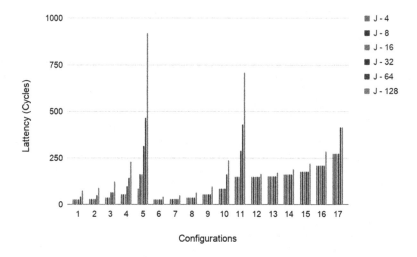

Fig. 8. Effect of jitter in different configurations.

For indirect interference, buffer sizes of the routers and the jitter have to be taken into account. The impact of these parameters was evaluated by calculating all possible configurations of Router, Network Interface, and applications. As with direct interference, some configurations resulted in infinite latencies, so these were filtered, only leaving the viable sets. The plot of all these configurations can be seen in Fig. 9. On the other hand, in Fig. 9, it is possible to see the impact of the buffer size of the routers by itself, and how this size emphasizes other variables, creating new spikes of latency. This effect is probably caused by buffered interference, as the accumulated flow λ_i will take longer to dissipate. In the case of the indirect interference vulnerability, large buffer sizes between the observer and the injector are detrimental to the attack, as there is plenty of time for victim behavior to be obfuscated. Therefore, for a secure NoC, Buffer Sizes outside critical paths should aim for higher values.

7   Experiments and Results

This section presents the setup of all experiments, the results of the efficiency of the attacks, and the decrease of attack efficiency under countermeasures.

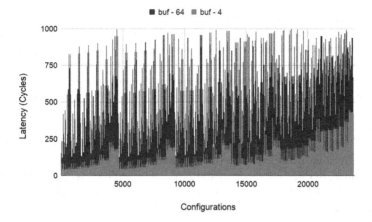

Fig. 9. Latencies for all viable configurations, when comparing 4 flit buffer and 64 flit buffer.

7.1 Setup of Experiments

In this subsection, the scenarios considered and metrics used to evaluate the attack's efficiency are presented. All experiments were executed through RTL MPSoC Glass simulations. The Routers were configured to have a buffer size of 32 flits and a jitter of 64 cycles.

Scenarios. Two scenarios were elaborated and mapped into the target platform. The first scenario (*Scenario 1*) uses IP_{13} as a trusted RISC-V that provides encryption services. This processor runs the AES-128 encryption as a T-Table implementation [13], whose algorithm uses huge tables that must be accessed in the shared cache located at IP_0. In the second scenario (*Scenario 2*), IP_1 and IP_{13} exchange messages to perform the Diffie-Hellmann (DH) key establishment protocol. DH protocol requires intense communication, therefore, three message sizes (packet granularity) were evaluated in our experiments: 32 flits (KEY32), 64 flits (KEY64), and 128 flits (KEY128). The following paragraphs describe the preparation and execution of the attacks.

Evaluation Metrics. To evaluate the effectiveness of the attacks, three metrics are defined:

- *False Positives* (FP), which measures the percentage of wrong guesses among all guesses of the attacker. Note that these guesses represent the victim's traffic occurrence time
- *Observation Efficiency* (OBS), which refers to the percentage of correctly guessed (observed) by the attacker of the total victim's traffic occurrence times
- *Attack Efficiency*, that relates the FP and OBS. It is described by Eq. (6). Note that the FP shows the quality of the information collected and OBS shows the sensitivity of the attack observation

$$Efficiency = Obs * (100\% - FP) \tag{6}$$

Direct-Interference Attack Execution. To perform the Direct-Interference attack in the *Scenario 1* the three phases are executed. During the first phase, IP_5 is infected and the desired flow configuration (packet size and injection rate) is calculated so to maximize the attacker's observation. We desire to calculate the attacker latency R_a for direct interference, therefore we use Eqs. (1) and (2). The system parameters needed by the attacker are all queryable by the attacker in the infected IP.

During the second phase, IP_5 starts to inject a high volume of small packets (4 flits) to the IP_9 (at low priority). Meanwhile, the encryption runs at IP_{13}. When a cache miss occurs at the local L1 memory of IP_{13}, a request to the L2 shared cache is performed through the NoC. The shared cache L2 responds to IP_{13} request with high priority flow. Such flow preempts the attacker's flow at IP_5 at the *Router* 11.

For *Scenario 2*, the key exchange application, the same behavior of preemption takes place. IP_1 and IP_{13} exchange a high volume of high priority messages, which are intersected by the attacker's flow at *Router* 11. The attacker records all latencies of the transmission. Any increase in latency above the calculated threshold C_a is marked as a sensitive traffic point.

Back-Pressure Attack Execution. The execution of the Back-pressure attack at *Scenario 1* is performed in three phases. First, IP_6 and IP_7 are infected, becoming the observer (low-priority) and the injector (medium-priority), respectively. Then, the attacker calculates a range of expected latency values for the defined attacker flow.

In contrast with the Direct-Interference attack, Eqs. (3) and (5) are used to calculate the indirect interference from the injector. In the second phase, the planned flow is executed. Injector IP generates large packets (128 flits) addressed to the IP_9. Meanwhile, the observer sends data to IP_5 (4 flits). The encryption is performed at IP_{13}, provoking cache misses. As a result of the cache hierarchy handling, the shared cache responds to the data requests with high priority flows. This traffic preempts the flow from IP_6 at the *Router* 11. Thus, IP_6 flow gets buffered on the route. Hence, the flow of IP_7 is now free to transmit its packets downstream.

For *Scenario 2*, the cores exchanging key information are IP_1 and IP_{13}. Since this operation also uses high priority messages, the injected packets of the attacker at IP_6 are also preempted at *Router* 11. This condition releases observer traffic. Any delay of the observer latency at the execution stage, based on the threshold found in phase 1, is considered as the identification of a sensitive packet. For our experiments, the injector packet's were sized so to guarantee that any interference always generates maximum back-pressure.

7.2   Evaluation of Attacks

Table 4 shows the results for the Direct-Interference attack, in which the attacker acts as the injector and observer. Small packets are not able to fill the buffer space in the route fast enough for contention to occur. On the other hand, bigger packets take longer time to be generated, and therefore, sensitive information can be lost in the meantime. Especially, when dealing with smaller packets as in an AES execution, where the victim received packages of 16 flits from the shared memory. The results for the Back-Pressure attack show an overall lower detection capacity in comparison with the Direct-Interference attack. However, these strategies were able to correctly detect smaller packets, such as the packets generated by the AES encryption. The main reasoning behind this is that since the observer is constantly starved, the liberation of its flow is almost instantaneous, while the smaller packets guarantee a faster observation in the increase of the throughput. This occurs even in the case where the injector flow is preempted for a very small period. We can also observe that in general, bigger packets are easier to detect in the NoC. As in the cases of key exchanges with larger granularity.

Table 4. Evaluation results of the attacks under unprotected MPSoC in two scenarios.

| | No protection | | | | | |
| | DI attack | | | BP attack | | |
	FP	Obs.	Efficiency	FP	Obs.	Efficiency
Scenario 1 - AES	0%	71.29%	71.29%	0%	72.07%	72.07%
Scenario 2 - KEY32	0%	93.53%	93.53%	0%	80.43%	80.43%
Scenario 2 - KEY64	0%	93.95%	93.95%	0%	81.25%	81.25%
Scenario 2 - KEY128	0%	96.19%	96.19%	0%	87.18%	87.18%

7.3   Evaluation of Countermeasures

The objective of the countermeasures is either distracting the attacker or avoiding the attacker through false traffic. The countermeasures added 2% of overhead in performance, which is related to the setup time to activate the defense mechanisms. Note that the elaboration of countermeasures also took into account the IBN model. As a result, all real-time constraints were met. Table 5 shows the results of both countermeasures under both scenarios.

RT-Blinding: The RT-Blinding strategy pad the sensitive information with high priority packets. These padding packets are sent from the victim's IP in a time table-fashion. In addition, they are identical in terms of size and destination. Therefore, without a frame of reference, the attacker could not identify which of these packets (the sensitive packet or the padding packets) is the actual secure message. In this test scenario, one of each four packages is a real secure packet. In our test system, these values were defined as maintaining a latency below an arbitrary threshold. In a real system, this would be defined at design time, based on the critical application and the hard time constraints. In both attacks, the result of the countermeasure is a plummet of efficiency values through all of the scenarios. This comes at the cost of having four times as many secure packages on the NoC, possibly preempting other flows beside the attackers.

RT-Masking: The RT-Masking strategy saturates the attacker with low-priority packages. To accomplish this, without undermining performance for the secure process, we employ another IP (Defender IP) which sends medium-sized (32 flits) and low priority packages at random intervals (pseudo-randomness achieved by a Linear Feedback Shift Register function). For the *Scenario 1*, this dedicated IP is defined as IP_1 at design time, and ideally, it would be placed as close as possible to the cache memory, as the attacks target the returning message of the cache. For the *Scenario 2*, the Defender IP is placed at IP_2, and in other scenarios should be placed as close as possible to the secure processor. As observed in Table 5, the effects of this strategy in the Direct-Interference Attack are closely related to the package size of the secure flow. When the size of the Defender's IP package is equal or close to the secure package, there is a heavy loss of efficiency. This is a consequence of the inability of the attacker to differentiate the latencies caused by the congestion of the same priority packets (Defender) and the high priority packets (Victim). However, larger secure packages produce a higher effect on preemption, thus turning easier to distinguish the latency thresholds. The Back-Pressure attack remains unaltered by the countermeasure. This is the result of the utilization of the sensitive path by the Defender IP, whose packets are exchanged with low priority to avoid important performance penalties. Since the Back-Pressure attack uses medium priority in the sensitive traffic path, the defender IP will not affect this attacker.

RT-Shielding: The RT-Shielding strategy avoids direct interference and back-pressure interference by designing the NoC properly. It has large enough buffers to sustain the throughput of potentially malicious traffic while providing a structure to quickly transmit sensitive packets. This approach can be theoretically guaranteed by applying the IBN model equations discussed in Sect. 4.2. In our experiments, the four routers in the sensitive path (i.e., routers 11, 12, 21 and 22) had its buffers increased. Two configurations were evaluated, using 64 flits and 128 flits. To decrease the time to propagate sensitive packets in the system, the sensitive IPs (i.e., IP 13 and IP 1) were configured with low jitter - 4 cycles - Network Interfaces. To guarantee a minimal difference between the jitter of trusted and non-trusted IPs, the other network interfaces were configured with a jitter of 32 cycles, especially for IP 5, IP 6, IP 9, and IP 10. In addition, to comprise a scenario where a jitter of 4 cycles would affect the performance of the sensitive IPs, we also tested the system with 32 cycles as low jitter (for sensitive IPs), and 128 cycles as high jitter (for other IPs). In total, four different PP-NoCs were evaluated under both Direct-Interference and Back-Pressure attacks. As expected, the attacks did not experienced latency degradation, obtaining zero observability in the system.

Note that RT-Shielding provides a very efficient countermeasure that avoids any performance issue. However, it imposes several limitations as a protection mechanism. First, it increases the hardware considerably. Second, it is tailored to specific attacks; thus it is not guaranteed that variations of these attacks can be avoided as well. And finally, since this is defined at design time, there is no flexibility concerning the applications running.

Table 5. Evaluation results of the attacks under RT-Blinding and RT-Masking countermeasures (S1 - *Scenario 1*; S2 - *Scenario 2*)

	Masking countermeasure						Blinding countermeasure					
	DI attack			BP attack			DI attack			BP attack		
	FP	Obs.	Efficiency	FP	Obs.	Efficiency	FP	Obs.	Efficiency	FP	Obs.	Efficiency
S1.AES	72.38%	71.29%	19.69%	0%	72.07%	72.07%	75%	71.29%	17.82%	75%	72.07%	18.02%
S2.KEY32	91.85%	93.53%	7.41%	0%	80.43%	80.43%	75%	93.53%	23.38%	75%	80.43%	20.11%
S2.KEY64	88.08%	93.95%	11.20%	0%	81.25%	81.25%	75%	93.95%	23.49%	75%	81.25%	20.31%
S2.KEY128	20.75%	96.19%	76.23%	0%	87.18%	87.18%	75%	96.19%	24.05%	75%	87.18%	21.79%

8 Discussion

In this section, we clarify why the assumptions used for the attacks are practical. Regarding having a malicious IP inside the MPSoC, mobile and embedded systems allow external software to run on the devices (under low privileges). These external applications may hide malicious code (also known as Trojans), which configures a system or IP infection. Another way to have an attacker in the system is when a hidden functionality is embedded in a third-party hardware IP (also known as Hardware Trojan). Regarding the knowledge of the logical location (i.e., mapping in the NoC), typically the Operating System provides an API that points system services to logical addresses. Even if the IP is in another processor, there will be some logical identification by the system manager. Sometimes, the documentation clarifies the logical (or even the physical) addresses of the system components. About topology and routing knowledge, if the technical documentation of the device does not disclose this information, it is possible to infer it by injecting traffic into the NoC and observing the physical behavior (power, timing). Regarding the application privilege levels, note that the attacks do not require a high priority level. It is expected, that any application will have a minimum of privilege in the real-time service (at least two levels of privileges). For the one-hop location requirement, the attacker does not need to know the distance. The drop in attack efficiency will reveal to the attacker that this condition is not met. This allows location tuning by the attacker.

9 Conclusion

In this paper, we have shown that Priority-Preemptive NoCs are vulnerable to logical side-channel attacks. The accurate analytical model developed for these systems to prove their demanding time constraints may be used to develop powerful attacks. The predictability of such systems provides the attacker with accurate information before the chip infection. We create two three-phase attacks: Direct-Interference and Back-Pressure. These attacks exploit two MPSoC vulnerabilities: i) the traffic predictability and shaping of sensitive applications. These attacks may detect key updates in the MPSoC. Key refreshing in sensitive applications is a common practice and it is usually performed through a key exchange protocol that presents a very specific traffic pattern. This can be exploited to determine the attack's momentum; and ii) the shared memories, which is a very common practice in MPSoCs. The time or access of the cache can be integrated with NoC timing attacks to reveal the secret key. We show that critical time systems must consider security already during the design stage. We demonstrated that providing lightweight security to critical systems while guaranteeing the time constraints is feasible.

References

1. Sapra, D., Altmeyer, S.: Work-in-progress: design-space exploration of multi-core processors for safety-critical real-time systems. In: 2017 IEEE RTSS, pp. 360–362 (December 2017)
2. Rockwood, M., Joshi, V., Sullivan, K., Goubran, R.: Using a real-time operating system for multitasking in remote patient monitoring. In: 2014 IEEE MeMeA, pp. 1–5 (June 2014)
3. Bolotin, E., Cidon, I., Ginosar, R., Kolodny, A.: Qnoc: Qos architecture and design process for network on chip. J. Syst. Archit. **50**, 105–128 (2004)
4. Lo, S., Lan, Y., Yeh, H., Tsai, W., Hu, Y., Chen, S.: Qos aware binoc architecture. In: 2010 IEEE IPDPS, pp. 1–10 (April 2010)
5. Nikolić, B., Petters, S.M.: EDF as an arbitration policy for wormhole-switched priority-preemptive NOCs - myth or fact? In: 2014 EMSOFT, pp. 1–10 (October 2014)
6. Shi, Z., Burns, A.: Real-time communication analysis for on-chip networks with wormhole switching. In: Second ACM/IEEE International Symposium on Networks-on-Chip (NOCs 2008), pp. 161–170 (April 2008)
7. Indrusiak, L.S., Burns, A., Nikolić, B.: Buffer-aware bounds to multi-point progressive blocking in priority-preemptive NOCs. In: 2018 DATE, pp. 219–224 (March 2018)
8. Yao, W., Suh, E.: Efficient timing channel protection for on-chip networks. In: NOCS 2012 Proceedings of the 2012 IEEE/ACM Sixth International Symposium on Networks-on-Chip, Lyngby, Denmark, pp. 142–151. IEEE (May 2012)
9. Daoud, L., Rafla, N.: Analysis of black hole router attack in network-on-chip. In: 2019 IEEE 62nd International Midwest Symposium on Circuits and Systems (MWSCAS), pp. 69–72 (August 2019)
10. Sepúlveda, J., Diguet, J.P., Strum, M., Gogniat, G.: NoC-based protection for SoC time-driven attacks. IEEE Embed. Syst. Lett. **7**(1), 7–10 (2015)
11. Reinbrecht, C., Forlin, B., Zankl, A., Sepúlveda, J.: Earthquake - a NoC-based optimized differential cache-collision attack for MPSoCs. In: 2018 DATE, Dresden, Germany, pp. 1–7. ACM (March 2018)
12. Reinbrecht, C., Susin, A., Bossuet, L., Sepulveda, J.: Gossip NoC - avoiding timing side-channel attacks through traffic management. In: IEEE Computer Society Annual Symposium on VLSI (ISVLSI 2016), Pittsburgh, USA, pp. 601–606. IEEE (July 2016)
13. Sepúlveda, J., Gross, M., Zankl, A., Sigl, G.: Exploiting bus communication to improve cache attacks on systems-on-chips. In: IEEE Computer Society Annual Symposium on VLSI (ISVLSI 2017) (July 2017)
14. Forlin, B., Reinbrecht, C., Sepúlveda, J.: Attacking real-time MPSoCs: preemptive NoCs are vulnerable. In: 2019 IFIP/IEEE 27th International Conference on Very Large Scale Integration (VLSI-SoC), pp. 204–209 (October 2019)

15. Stefan, R., Goossens, K.: Enhancing the security of time-division-multiplexing networks-on-chip through the use of multipath routing (2011)
16. Chaves, C.G., Azad, S.P., Hollstein, T., Sepulveda, J.: A distributed dos detection scheme for NoC-based MPSoCs. In: 2018 IEEE Nordic Circuits and Systems Conference (NORCAS): NORCHIP and International Symposium of System-on-Chip (SoC), pp. 1–6 (October 2018)
17. Reinbrecht, C., Susin, A., Bossuet, L., Sigl, G., Sepulveda, J.: Side channel attack on NoC-based MPSoCs are practical: NoC prime+probe attack. In: 29th Symposium on Integrated Circuits and Systems Design (SBCCI), Belo Horizonte, Brazil, pp. 1–6. IEEE (August 2016)
18. Osvik, D.A., Shamir, A., Tromer, E.: Cache attacks and countermeasures: the case of AES. In: Pointcheval, D. (ed.) CT-RSA 2006. LNCS, vol. 3860, pp. 1–20. Springer, Heidelberg (2006). https://doi.org/10.1007/11605805_1
19. Indrusiak, L.S., Harbin, J.R., Reinbrecht, C., Sepúlveda, M.J.: Side-channel protected MPSoC through secure real-time networks-on-chip. Microprocess. Microsyst. **68**, 34–46 (2019)
20. Yao, W., Suh, E.: Efficient timing channel protection for on-chip networks. In: 2012 Sixth IEEE/ACM International Symposium on Networks on Chip (NoCS), pp. 142–151 (2012)
21. Wassel, H., et al.: Networks on chip with provable security properties. IEEE Micro **34**(3), 57–68 (2014)
22. Sepulveda, J., Florez, D., Soeken, M., Diguet, J., Gogniat, G.: Dynamic NoC buffer allocation for MPSoC timing side channel attack protection. In: Network-on-Chip, Timing, Side Channel Attack (LASCAS), Florianópolis, Brazil, pp. 91–94. IEEE (March 2016)
23. Traber, A., Stucki, S., Zaruba, F., Gautschi, M., Pullini, A., Benini, L.: Pulpino: a RISC-V based single-core system. In: ORCONF2015, October 9–11, 2015, Geneva, Switzerland (2015)
24. Xiong, Q., Wu, F., Lu, Z., Xie, C.: Extending real-time analysis for wormhole NoCs. IEEE Trans. Comput. **66**(9), 1532–1546 (2017)
25. Reinbrecht, C., Susin, A., Bossuet, L., Sigl, G., Sepúlveda, J.: Timing attack on NoC-based systems: Prime+Probe attack and NoC-based protection. Microprocess. Microsyst. **51**, 556–565 (2017)
26. Reinbrecht, C., Forlin, B., Sepúlveda, J.: Cache timing attacks on NoC-based MPSoCs. Microprocess. Microsyst. **66**, 1–9 (2019)

Offset-Compensation Systems for Multi-Gbit/s Optical Receivers

László Szilágyi$^{(\boxtimes)}$, Jan Pliva, and Ronny Henker

Chair of Circuit Design and Network Theory,
Technische Universität Dresden, 01069 Dresden, Germany
{laszlo.szilagyi,jan.pliva,ronny.henker}@tu-dresden.de

Abstract. Offset compensation (OC) systems are indispensable parts of multi-Gbit/s optical receiver (RX) frontends. Effects of offset are addressed in this chapter. The analytical expression for the highest lower-cut-off frequency of the OC with minimum impact on the sensitivity is found. Existing OC solutions are discussed. Then, a novel mixed-signal (MS) architecture is introduced which uses digital filtering of the signal, and current-digital-to-analog converters to compensate the static offset in the limiting amplifier. In the transimpedance amplifier both static and dynamic offset are compensated. By using two feedback loops and a continuous tracking the presented solution offers more functionality than other existing MS architectures. Three RX implementations, with RC, switched-capacitor (S-C) and with the MS-OC architectures, in the same 28 nm bulk-CMOS are compared quantitatively with measurements. The presented MS design reaches a lower-cut-off frequency of under 9 kHz, a dynamic range of over 1 mA, 3.2 µA residual input offset-current and it is compensating the RX via two feedback loops. The presented system offers a higher flexibility and functionality in implementation, as well as a very good compromise between area, precision and performance over the commonly used RC-filter and S-C filter based solutions.

Keywords: Optical receiver · Offset · Offset compensation · Mixed-signal control loop · Residual offset · Lower-cut-off frequency · Transimpedance amplifier (TIA) · Limiting amplifier (LA)

1 Introduction

Optical links provide a cost- and power-efficient alternative to copper-based electrical interconnects for multi-Gbit/s ($\times 10$ Gbit/s), short-range (<100 m) applications [1]. In board-to-board or rack-to-rack communications vertical-cavity surface-emitting laser (VCSEL) based multi-mode fiber (MMF) interconnect is the preferred choice over modulator with single-mode fiber. The reason behind is that the VCSEL driver power consumption is lower, voltages can be handled by CMOS technologies, while assembly and alignment efforts as well as costs are less in comparison to modulator-based transmission. In order to achieve the best

© IFIP International Federation for Information Processing 2020
Published by Springer Nature Switzerland AG 2020
C. Metzler et al. (Eds.): VLSI-SoC 2019, IFIP AICT 586, pp. 235–255, 2020.
https://doi.org/10.1007/978-3-030-53273-4_11

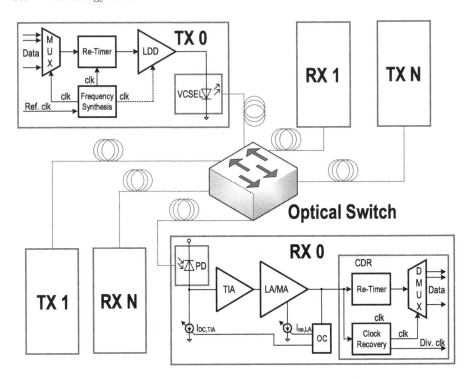

Fig. 1. Optical communication link in a network.

performance at the lowest cost, full integration of the analog frontend, together with the digital data processing and switching core [2], and in future the photonic device as well [3], in the same highly scaled CMOS technology is aimed.

Such a short/medium range link is described in Fig. 1. It consists of VCSEL-based transmitters (TX). Parallel data streams at lower speed are multiplexed (MUX) to a single signal with high data-rate. It is then enhanced to a high amplitude by the re-timer, synchronized to the MUX by the frequency synthesis loop. The laser diode driver (LDD) transforms the digital signal into a high-power signal, with impedance matching to the VCSEL diode. Equalization can be used to cope with the bandwidth limitation of the VCSEL device [4,5]. The optical signal reaches the receivers (RX) through MMF and optical switches. The RX itself uses a photo diode (PD) to convert the light into an electrical current. This is amplified and converted to a voltage by the transimpedance amplifier (TIA). The small voltage is further amplified and conditioned into a digital signal by the limiting amplifier (LA) or main amplifier (MA) with very high and sometimes variable gain. Next, the clock-data recovery (CDR) circuit extracts the clock from the signal and de-multiplexes (DMUX) the information in parallel streams, to the speed of standard digital logic. Additional circuits such as the offset compensation (OC) loop reduce the offset in the LA and sink the unwanted dc current of the PD.

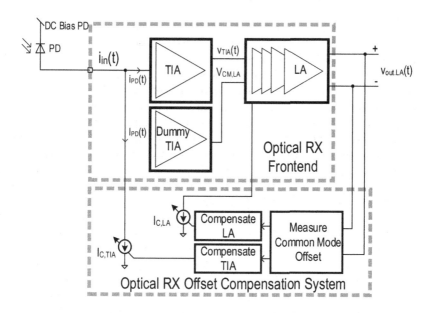

Fig. 2. Offset compensation system in an optical RX frontend.

Another field for short/medium optical links is in consumer electronics, with the spread of fiber-to-home. Its purpose is to provide very high speed internet at low cost. This can be achieved for example via passive optical networks (PON), where a passive optical switch is used instead the optical/electrical conversion, switching of the electrical signal then conversion back to the optical domain. This kind of network and system is illustrated in Fig. 1. It can be seen that for the same RX, TXs placed at different distances will transmit data packages in bursts of impulses. It results that different packages reach the RX with different optical power. This burst-mode RX needs to set the offset and common-mode compensation very fast so the data is received correctly. In this case analog loops reaction speed is too slow, therefore mixed-signal based compensation systems need to be used after taking the measures for the system to settle quickly.

2   State-of-Art Offset Compensation

The received signal in VCSEL-transmitter based links suffers from a strong dc component created by the limited extinction-ratio of the optical signal [6]. This current needs to be removed by the RX, which needs to deal with variations of optical power and mismatch created offset as well. Little attention is given in the available literature to the offset and dc-current compensation (OC) systems in optical RXs. In Sect. 3, OC systems and the most important parameters of the design process are addressed. An analytic expression for the maximum lower-cut-off frequency is obtained for a given data rate (DR) bit pattern and allowed sensitivity deterioration [7]. At present, the most common OC system is based on RC low-pass filter (LPF) [8–12], that suffers from several drawbacks such as extremely high area, power consumption dependent residual offset, stability and fixed lower-cut-off frequency. Some of these issues are dealt by the switched-capacitor (S-C) LPF based systems [8,13,14]. Their area is significantly smaller and the lower cut-off frequency is adjustable. Section 3 gives the analytical dependency between the low-pass frequency of the LPF and lower cut-off frequency of the RX. These conventional architectures are discussed in Sect. 4. A fully flexible system can be implemented in a digital CMOS process by using mixed-signal (MS) control loops with digital-to-analog converters (DAC). Such OC system was implemented in [3] using a 7 bit current-DAC (IDAC) which is used for calibration, compensating for the static offset. In [2] an IDAC with successive approximation register (SAR) is used to calibrate for the dc current at the input of the RX at every burst cycle.

A novel MS OC architecture is introduced in Sect. 5 that uses digital filtering and compensates with an IDAC the static offset of the LA stage of the RX and a second IDAC with SAR algorithm reduces the dc current at the input of the TIA. Then, this second IDAC, in contrast to [2] continuously tracks and compensates the offset during operation. This architecture was implemented and presented briefly in [15]. In [16] further details regarding the digital algorithms, the IDACs, measurements and comparison of the different systems is described. This chapter reveals further theoretical and modeling issues, and extends the scope of MS systems into burst-mode RXs for PONs. A 28 nm bulk-CMOS process is used to implement a RX with the proposed MS OC system [15], one with RC-LPF OC [9] and one with the S-C OC [14]. Advantages of the MS OC over the other two systems are discussed. Superiority of the proposed architecture is proven when measurement results are compared in Sect. 6.

3   Offset Compensation in Optical Receivers

The optical RX system, as depicted by Fig. 2, consists of the RX frontend and the OC system. The useful signal $i_{PD}(t)$, part of $i_{in}(t)$, is a current generated by the PD amplified by the TIA and converted in a voltage $v_{TIA}(t)$. A dummy TIA provides the common mode at the differential input of the LA $V_{CM,LA}$. Several LA stages further amplify the signal into $v_{outLA}(t)$ that will go to the next blocks in the signal processing chain [13].

Process spread and mismatch causes static offset in the LA [12]. At the TIA input $i_{in}(t)$ also contains a dc current which can slowly change with time, $I_{PD}(t)$ caused by the finite extinction ratio of the transmitter laser diode [6]. This causes $V_{TIA}(t)$ to drift. Furthermore, temperature variation and changes in the input optical power will cause dynamic offset seen as difference between $V_{CM,LA}$ and $V_{TIA}(t)$. As the RX chain, especially the LA, has a very high gain, a small offset in the RX can cause saturation of the output stages, thus result in the impairment of functionality. For this reason an OC system is used that has the block diagram depicted by Fig. 2. The difference between the common-mode of the two output polarities is measured. Then, $I_{C,LA}$ compensates for the static offset of the LA. Meanwhile $I_{C,TIA}(t)$ sinks the dc current coming from the PD,

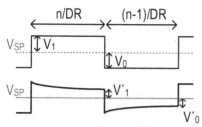
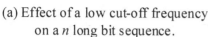

(a) Effect of a low cut-off frequency on a *n* long bit sequence.

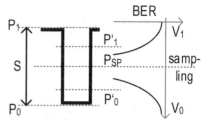

(b) Relation of sampling level, sensitivity, P_1 and P_0 to the BER.

Fig. 3. Low cut-off frequency effect on the signal, sensitivity and BER.

$I_{PD}(t)$, which also compensates for the variation of optical power at the input. Offset between the common modes of the TIA and dummy TIA is also reduced by $I_{C,TIA}(t)$.

The offset compensation loop, which cancels the dc component of the signal behaves as a high-pass filter in the signal path. Not only the dc component is extracted, but in reality there is a low-pass frequency, mainly limited by technological considerations, therefore a significant amount of components in frequency domain are canceled. This causes a high-pass effect called "dc-wander" [17]. Figure 3a shows how an n-bit long run of 1's with DR and V_1 amplitude will decrease to V_1'. The same can be observed for a long run of 0's. In order to avoid this, either the number of consecutive same-state bits (run length) or the lower cut-off frequency f_{LCO} has to be reduced [17]. Since the run length is defined in the transmission standard, the f_{LCO} needs to be decreased accordingly.

A common signal-pattern standard used in wire-line communications is the pseudo-random bit sequence (PRBS) with the length of $2^n - 1$ bits. A PRBSn has a run length of n 1's and $n - 1$ 0's. For simplicity, however n will be used for both 1's and 0's.

The decay of voltage from $V_{1/0}$ to $V_{1/0}'$, shown in Fig. 3a can be expressed as

$$V'_1 = V_1 \cdot \exp\left(\frac{-2\pi n_1 f_{LCO}}{DR}\right). \tag{1}$$

The sensitivity, S is one of the most important measures of a RX and is the smallest input signal power that can be amplified error-free. In optical communications this signal is quantified by the optical modulation amplitude (OMA) of the signal. As it can be seen in Fig. 3b, $S = P_1 - P_0$. The $P_{SP} = (P_0 + P_1)/2$ in Fig. 3b is the level with the lowest bit error-rate (BER), therefore it is chosen as the sampling level and is meanwhile the common-mode or symmetry level of the signal $P_{CM} = P_{SP}$. So, dc-wander causes P_1 to decrease into P_1', while P_0 increases to P_0', thus S to worsen with the long 0 and 1 run, causing an asymmetry by shifting P_{SP}, thus a "decision offset" [18]. The new sensitivity will be now $S' = P_1' - P_0'$. A power-penalty of the sensitivity PP_S can be defined, that accounts for dc-wander effect on both levels

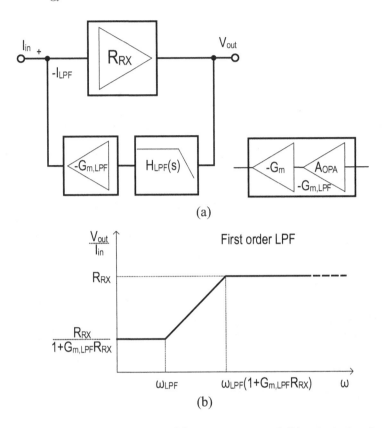

Fig. 4. Lower cut-off frequency f_{LCO} (a) system view and (b) calculation for a first order LPF.

$$PP_S = S - S' = P_1 - P_0 - P_1' + P_0'. \tag{2}$$

By fixing $P_{SL} = P_{SL}'$, thus the sampling takes place at the same level in both cases, results

$$P_1 - P_1' = P_0 - P_0'. \tag{3}$$

Introducing (3) into (2) the power penalty can be further written as

$$PP_S = 2(P_1 - P_1'). \tag{4}$$

To express P_1', Eq. (1) is used, considering a fixed resistance. Next, $n_1 = n_0 = n$ is considered for simplicity in (1). This is introduced in (4) so the power penalty can be expressed in dB $PP_S(dB)$ as

$$PP_S(dB) = 40\pi \frac{n f_{LCO}}{DR} \log_{10} 2e. \tag{5}$$

In the following, a PRBS31 signal is used to evaluate the performance of RXs and $PP_S < 0.01$ dB is aimed, meaning an insignificant sensitivity deterioration. With Eq. (4), f_{LCO} of 70 kHz can be calculated for a DR of 20 Gbit/s.

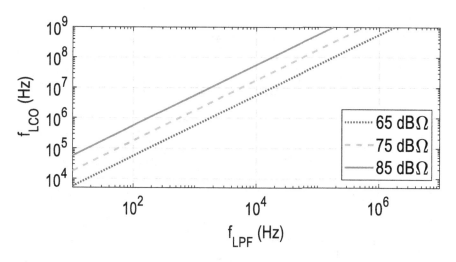

Fig. 5. Lower cut-off frequency f_{LCO} dependence on f_{LPF} at different RX gains.

It can be concluded that an OC system is needed for an optical RX in order to ensure its error-free functionality. Furthermore, the lower cut-off frequency must be low enough so the sensitivity at an error-free detection is not degraded with a given run-length of the input data at the desired DR.

4 Conventional Low-Pass Filter Based Offset Compensation

The most straightforward way to implement an OC loop is by using a LPF in a negative feedback loop, as depicted by Fig. 4a. The RX with transimpedance gain of R_{RX}, output voltage V_{out} is passed through the high-pass filter with output voltage $H_{LPF}(s)$. This has a negative transconductance gain of output voltage $-G_{m,LPF}$ and creates a feedback current $-I_{LPF}$ added to I_{in}. $-G_{m,LPF}$ will be implemented practically as shown in Fig. 4a from an operational amplifier (OPA) with voltage gain A_{OPA} and a transconductance $-G_m$, for instance a current-sink transistor. The loop can be described with as

$$V_{out} = R_{RX}\left[I_{in} + V_{out}G_{m,LPF}H_{LPF}(s)\right]. \tag{6}$$

From Eq. (6) the lower cut-off characteristic $H_{LCO}(s)$, dependent on the LPF can be expressed as

$$H_{LCO}(s) = \frac{V_{out}}{I_{in}} = \frac{R_{RX}}{1 + R_{RX} \cdot G_{m,LPF}H_{LPF}(s)}. \tag{7}$$

Equation (7) gives a generalized formula for $H_{LCO}(s)$. When a first-order LPF is used, such as an RC LPF the transfer characteristic can be expressed in a more specific manner, such as depicted in Fig. 4b. A zero is created in $-\omega_{LPF}$, while

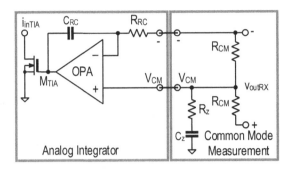

Fig. 6. Conventional RC low-pass filter based offset compensation schematic.

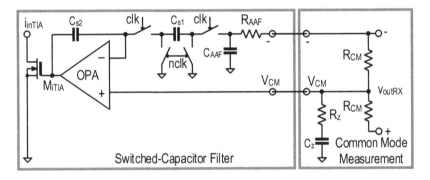

Fig. 7. Conventional S-C low-pass filter based offset compensation schematic.

a pole appears in $-\omega_{LPF}(1 + R_{RX} \cdot G_{m,LPF})$. The dc offset and low frequency signal will be suppressed to $R_{RX}/(1 + R_{RX} \cdot G_{m,LPF})$ leading to the conclusion that $G_{m,LPF}$ should be made as high as possible. However, if f_{LCO} is expressed depending on f_{LPF}

$$f_{LCO} \approx R_{RX} \cdot G_{m,LPF} f_{LPF}, \tag{8}$$

it can be seen that increasing $G_{m,LPF}$ results in increasing f_{LCO} that will require larger LPF elements in order to keep the same f_{LCO}. This is illustrated in Fig. 5, where it can be seen how changing f_{LPF} impacts f_{LCO}. The simulation is done with different, common RX transimpedance gains of 65, 75 and 85 dBΩ. Gain in the feedback is kept constant, with a customary A_{OPA} of 50 dB and 1 mS one-transistor current sink $G_{m,LPF}$.

It can be concluded from Fig. 5 that f_{LPF} needs to be significantly lower than the required f_{LCO} resulting in extremely large elements for the filter, implicitly a very area inefficient circuit topology.

As the lower-cut-off frequency needs to be in the kHz domain, the LPF needs a capacitor in the nano-Farad region, which cannot be realized on-chip. This method, although still found in [1] has become rather obsolete. A simple on-chip RC filter is used in [19]. However, it needs a 13 MΩ resistor and 150 pF capacitor which occupy an unacceptably large area for the highly scaled RX designs from today. A very common implementation [9–12] is the active RC filter where the Miller effect is used to multiply the capacitance to $C_{Mill} \approx A_{OPA} C_{RC}$ as also depicted by Fig. 6. This solution offers a low complexity circuit on a reasonable area. The cut-off frequency of the LPF can be approximated as

$$f_{LPF,RC} = \frac{1}{2\pi R_{RC} C_{RC} A_{OPA}}. \tag{9}$$

The biggest disadvantage of this method is that the f_{LCO} is fixed by the resistor and capacitor and need to be sized, according to Eq. (5) to the lowest DR and longest run length which results in an increased area.

This disadvantage can be overcome by implementing a tunable filter. The S-C filter has a clear area advantage over the RC LPF thus it has been chosen in [8] and [13]. The switches and C_{s1} in Fig. 7 emulate a large resistor. The cut-off frequency of the LPF can be expressed as

$$f_{LPF,S-C} = f_{clk} \frac{C_{s1}}{C_{s2}}. \tag{10}$$

It can be seen in (10) that $f_{LPF,S-C}$ can be adjusted with f_{clk}. A S-C LPF needs additionally an anti-aliasing filter (AAF) with a cut-off frequency of at least $f_{clk}/2$ [8]. This results in a compromise that needs to be done when choosing the clock frequency, C_{s1}/C_{s2} ratio which can be limited by the smallest capacitor in a given technology and the accuracy of the ratio when the smallest value is used and finally f_{AAF} as this additional filter directly impacts the area needed by the OC loop.

A major drawback of LPF based offset compensation loops is the residual offset. For the conventional systems from Fig. 6 and 7 residual offset current $I_{os,rez}$ can be expressed as

$$I_{os,rez} = \frac{2I_{os,RX}}{A_{RX} \cdot A_{OPA}} - \frac{2V_{os,OPA}}{A_{RX} \cdot R_{T,RX}}. \tag{11}$$

Equation (11) shows how $I_{os,rez}$ is influenced by several factors. In order to decrease this unwanted current the gain of the OC loop, namely A_{OPA} needs to be as high as possible. This can cause stability issues as well as burn a significant amount of power.

5 Novel Mixed-Signal Offset Compensation

5.1 System Considerations

An offset compensation with digital core is proposed. Figure 8 shows the block diagram of the mixed-signal OC loop. An RC AAF isolates the output of the RX from the clock of the digital core. f_{AAF} is chosen 2 MHz. A comparator follows, which decides if there is a difference between the negative RX output − and V_{CM}. The comparator results are accumulated in a digital integrator with 1024

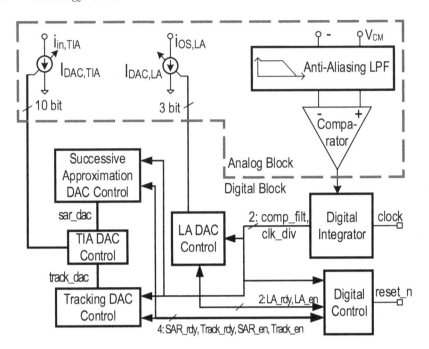

Fig. 8. Block diagram of the mixed-signal offset compensation system.

samples. The result *comp_filt* indicates whether the majority of the samples was positive or negative. By building an average, the high frequency components are suppressed similar to a conventional LPF. This is described by the signal flow in Fig. 9a. This block divides the clock as well, so for every decision of *comp_filt* there is a clock edge on *clk_div*.

5.2   Digital Design

The following blocks are controlled by the finite state machine (FSM) or digital control block. Figure 9b shows the state diagram of the FSM. After the reset signal *rst_n* the 3 bit *LA DAC* will overcompensate roughly the offset in the LA, until *comp_filt* = 1. Then, after the *LA_rdy* signal the FSM hands over control to the SAR TIA DAC. As visible in Fig. 9b, the *SAR TIA DAC Control* will use the SAR algorithm to compensate for the input offset current and dc current generated by the average light power of the PD. After 10 bits the process is handed over to the *Track TIA DAC Control*. Figure 9c shows how the tracking works. When the current at the input changes, first the direction is detected, if the current increased the DAC will be stepped one bit up, if it decreased one bit down, until full compensation is achieved. In case of reset *rst_n* the FSM returns to the *LA_DAC* state. The common-mode offset is continuously tracked and compensated by increasing or decreasing the current at the TIA DAC in a thermometric manner.

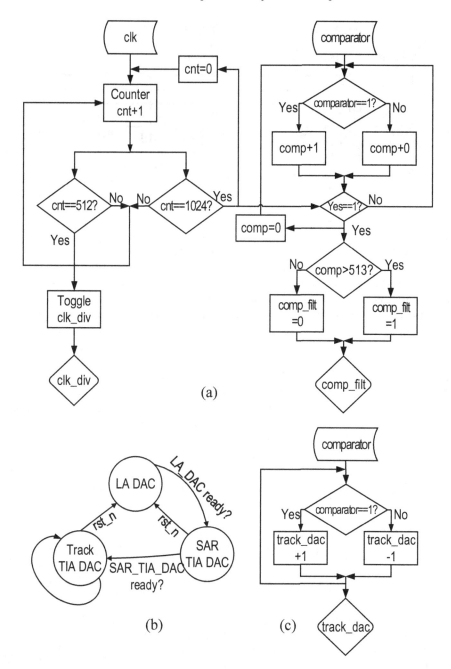

Fig. 9. Mixed-signal offset compensation system: (a) digital integrator signal flow; (b) finite-state-machine; (c) tracking algorithm flow.

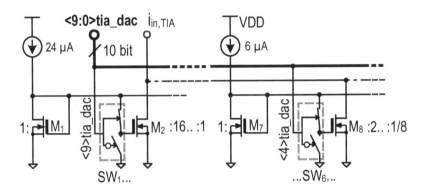

Fig. 10. Schematic of the TIA current DAC (IDAC TIA).

The digital integrator and the controlling state machine were synthesized using a custom 14-Track 1 V standard cell library. The digital library consists of 133 standard cells and its design is described in [20]. The lack of prior hardware testing was one of the reasons to keep the clock frequency low at 2 MHz. With a hardware proven library, the clock frequency could be set significantly higher, which would allow significantly faster convergence.

5.3   The Digital-to-Analog Converters

The schematic of the IDAC TIA is shown in Fig. 10. It is a binary weighted DAC split in two, sub-DACs. This is done in order to maintain a reasonable aspect ratio between very large and very small transistors, thus maintaining a reasonable matching. It follows, that $24\,\mu A$ are injected into the reference M_1, while M_7 sinks $6\,\mu A$. Turning on and off the current sources is done by toggling between the reference voltage or ground of the gate of transistors M_2 to M_6 and M_8 to M_{12}. IDAC LA is implemented in a similar way with only 3 bits.

5.4   Scalability

A major motivation for the MS approach is its scalability. The lower cut-off frequency of the loop can be easily adjusted by means of the digital clock frequency. While only low-frequency digital clock has been implemented out of reliability concerns, clock frequencies in the order of GHz are feasible for hardware proven standard-cell libraries. Since the dynamic properties of the proposed offset compensation loop are proportional to the clock period, there are extremely high prospects for improvements of the transient behavior. With additional changes to the successive approximation algorithm, a convergence in the order of 20 ns can be achieved as shown in Fig. 11 in comparison with a conventional RC-low pass filter with the low cutoff frequency of 70 kHz. Such dynamic behavior would be suitable for burst-mode operation.

The digital circuits can be easily modified and extended without major design effort, unlike the analog implementations. Similarly, the porting to a different

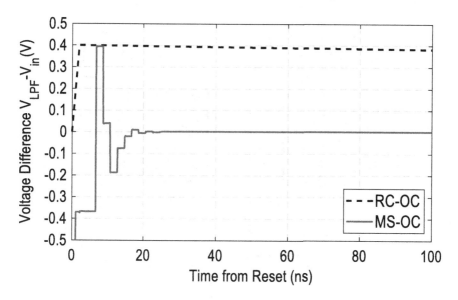

Fig. 11. Simulated turn-on time with an RC and MS loop with fast SAR algorithm.

technology is easier and more reliable, since the behavior of the loop is determined by the clock frequency and RTL description, which are technology-independent.

On the other hand, the presented approach shares the challenges typical for system-on-a-chip (SoC) designs. A wider tool-set as well as standard cell IP are required for the design. Supply separation and supply noise rejection might be gradually predominant with increasing clock frequency of the OC loop and the complexity of the digital block.

5.5 Burst-Mode Operation

Another argument supporting MS approach to OC is their suitability for burst-mode operation and therefore usage in PON systems as described in Sect. 1. Adaptive systems are another opportunity for burst-mode receivers [15]. In the current state-of-the-art, optical transceivers usually operate in full speed mode constantly. While the VCSEL cannot be completely turned off due to long power-on time, considerable power-savings can be achieved by powering down other parts of the transceiver. As shown in [21] and [22], up to 50% power consumption can be saved by disabling parts of opto-electronic transceivers while maintaining acceptable power-on time for burst-mode operation.

Fast power-on times are required to allow acceptable latency and avoid the necessity for large memories to store the data during the power-up time. The settling time of a conventional OC loop is inversely proportional to the lower-cut-off frequency of the LPF and therefore results in considerable wake-up time. The bandwidth of a MS signal OC loop can be controlled dynamically using its FSM to allow fast settling at wake-up as well as sufficient dc rejection during

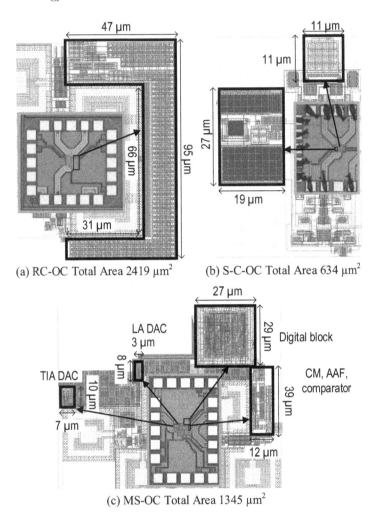

(a) RC-OC Total Area 2419 μm²   (b) S-C-OC Total Area 634 μm²

(c) MS-OC Total Area 1345 μm²

Fig. 12. Offset compensation implementations: (a) RC filter, (b) S-C filter (c) mixed-signal.

regular operation. While a dynamic LPF adjustment can be achieved using analog techniques as well, as shown in [2], the MS loop also has better retention and can maintain its value with minimum power consumption as long as supply is active.

6   Measurements and Comparison

For comparison of the three systems, two previously implemented RX chips, one with RC filter [9] and one with S-C filter [14] and a new design with mixed-signal OC system [15] were designed and fabricated in the same 28 nm bulk-CMOS digital process.

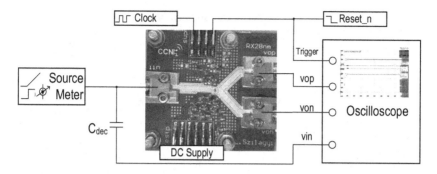

Fig. 13. Measurement setup.

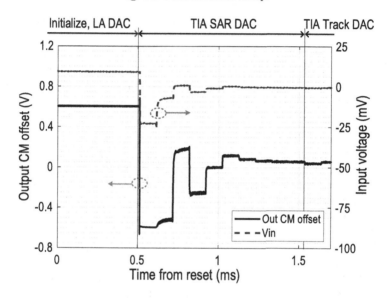

Fig. 14. Oscilogram of the MS OC, output CM offset and input signal.

Figure 12a shows the RC filter based OC system. A capacitor C_{RC} of 15 pF and R_{RC} 3.6 MΩ are used as in the schematic from Fig. 6. These large passive devices increase the area of the RC-LPF based OC to over 2400 μm^2. The S-C-LPF OC system implementation is shown in Fig. 12b. The corresponding values to the components in Fig. 7 are C_{AAF} of 2.2 pF and R_{AAF} 400 kΩ for the AAF and C_{s1} of 35 fF, C_{s2} of 4.4 pF for the SC LPF. f_{clk} is 5 MHz in this case. The total area is only 634 μm^2. The middle value of 1345 μm^2 is needed for the MS-OC system from Fig. 12c. The digital block occupies 783 μm^2, the rest is occupied by the AAF, comparator and DACs.

The setup in Fig. 13 is used to show the functionality of the MS-OC system. For stable measurements the chip is bonded to dc and signal connections on a PCB. A 5 MHz square wave clock with 50% duty cycle and 1 V amplitude

dx: 10 ps/div dy: 60 mV/div

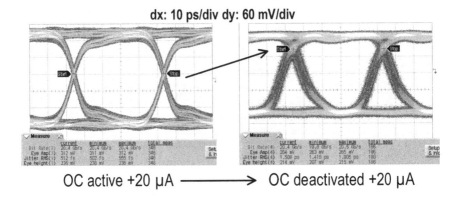

OC active +20 μA ⟶ OC deactivated +20 μA

Fig. 15. Eye diagram at 20 Gbit/s +20 μA offset with OC active and de-activated.

is used for the following measurements. The *reset_n* is used as a trigger for the oscilloscope, that visualizes the output and input voltages as well. Next, a source meter is used to inject a current ramp or step.

In order to measure the residual offset, a dc current of 100 μA is injected in the input. The output common-mode offset $V_{os,CM,out} = V_{vop} - V_{von}$ are visualized and measured in Fig. 14. At the start of the sequence more than 600 mV initial offset is measured at the output. Until around 0.2 ms the digital block is initialized and the LA DAC started. It can be seen that after bit 2, the offset changes its sign. The OC procedure is handed over to the *SAR TIA DAC*. Then, the SAR algorithm can be clearly seen until around 1.6 ms. Finally, the TIA DAC toggles the current at the input by the least significant bit up/down to sense a change on the dc current. The final average output offset voltage is 18 mV. Knowing the RX has a transimpedance gain $R_T(\mathrm{dB}\Omega) = 74\,\mathrm{dB}\Omega$ [15], the residual, input-referred offset current of 3.2 μA can be estimated.

Next, the effect of offset on the transmitted signal and functionality of the OC is demonstrated. Additionally to the setup in Fig. 13 a PRBS signal current with 20 Gbit/s is injected to the input of the RX. The outputs are connected to a high-speed sampling oscilloscope. The source meter will inject 20 μA of dc current. It can be seen in Fig. 15 that a correctly balanced eye diagram can be captured at the output of the RX. Next, the clock is deactivated. It can be seen that already such a small current causes the crossing point of the signal shifting up by more than 100 mV. This results in a signal that cannot be detected error-free anymore. This experiment simulates the changes in optical power of the received signal. Furthermore, it demonstrates the necessity of an OC system as the correct functionality of the presented circuit.

The second important comparison point is the f_{LCO}. For this measurement a Rhode & Schwarz, ZVL6 network analyzer with 9 kHz lowest frequency is used. A short-open-load-through calibration is done with a standard kit. Figure 16 shows the transfer functions of the three RX up to 1 MHz. Since the chips have different gain, the normalized transfer function is used. It can be seen that the

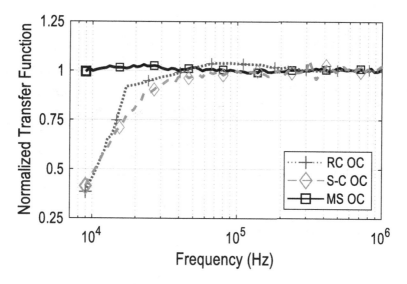

Fig. 16. Measurement of the lower cut-off frequency f_{LCO}.

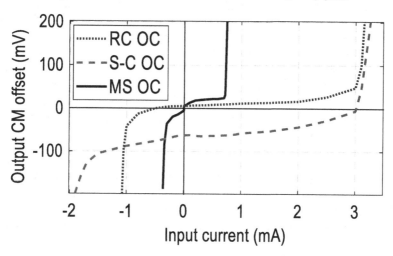

Fig. 17. Measured dynamic range of the OC architectures.

RX using RC and S-C LPF OC system have a similar f_{LCO} of approximately 20 kHz (with f_{clk} of the S-C LPF of 5 MHz). The MS OC system has on the other hand f_{LCO} which is much lower than the instrument can measure, when $f_{clk} = 5$ MHz. This is around 4.9 kHz.

The dynamic range of an OC loop (I_{DR}) can be defined as the difference between the highest and lowest dc current that can be applied at the input which will cause a negligible offset voltage at the output, $V_{OS,CM,out}$. A value of 10% of the single-ended output swing is chosen as limit for offset, that is approximately

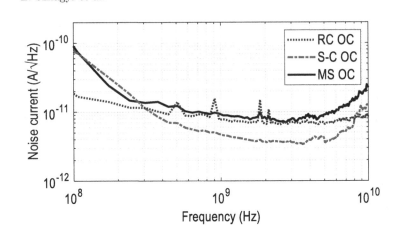

Fig. 18. Measurement of the input referred noise current.

30 mV for the MS OC. This parameter depends on the size of the compensation current source, or in case of the MS-OC, on the dynamic range of the IDAC. It was measured using the setup from Fig. 13, by injecting a slow current ramp in the RX. The output CM offset exceeded 30 mV for 0.72 mA input current, that corresponds to 1.58 dBm optical power with a 0.5 A/W responsivity PD. By using a second IDAC (LA DAC), that has an opposite sign to the TIA DAC, negative input current of up to −0.34 mA can be compensated. Figure 17 shows the dynamic range measurement results. It can be seen that, although the S-C OC has the highest dynamic range, its residual offset is large, −49 mV at the output. In case of the MS OC, the I_{DR} can be adjusted precisely according to the design requirements by increasing the LSB current or the number of bits for the TIA IDAC, meanwhile for the other two architectures only a vague forecast can be made. In addition, these implementations of the LPF based systems use a complementary PMOS to M_{dTIA} in order to compensate also negative currents. By this, a constant quiescent current of about 1 mA is constantly drawn from the supply that is present even if no dc current from the PD is sourced. The MS OC on the other hand does not have this disadvantage.

Although the noise spectral density (NSD) depends strongly on the gain and bandwidth of the complete RX, the input referred noise current of the three receivers was measured, plotted in Fig. 18 and the NSD calculated in Table 1. It is found that by using a proper AAF, clocked OC loops (S-C and MS) have no negative influence on the noise performance and input sensitivity of the RX.

Table 1 compares the three OC systems discussed in this chapter. It can be seen that the MS system offers the best trade-off between area, f_{LCO} and residual offset current. The RC and S-C LPF based OC in these implementations compensate the offset only at the input of the TIA and for the dc input current. On the other hand the proposed MS OC reduces the static offset of the LA in addition to the TIA input and dc current at the input. The biggest advantage of the proposed system is its flexibility. By reducing the sample number at the

Table 1. Comparison of the offset compensation systems.

Parameter	Unit	[9]	[14]	This work [15]
Architecture		RC LPF	S-C LPF	MS
Area	(μm^2)	2419	634	1345
$I_{os,res}$	(μA)	1.7	24.4	3.2
I_{DR}	(mA)	3.3	3	1.06
f_{LCO}	(kHz)	20	20	<9
f_{LCO} adjustable	Y/N	No	Yes	Yes
NSD	$(pA/\sqrt{Hz})$	73	43	84
Compensated blocks		TIA	TIA	TIA & LA

digital integrator, the loop speed can be increased so the system can be used in burst-mode RX as in [2].

7 Conclusion

The function of offset compensation in optical receivers is addressed. The lower-cut-off frequency is defined and a calculation method is given for the highest frequency that does not impact the RX performance. An analytical relation between the lower cut-off frequency and low-pass frequency for filter-based systems is defined. Therefore, this chapter presents a complete modeling tool for offset compensation in optical receivers. Existing offset compensation solutions are discussed. Then, a novel mixed-signal architecture is introduced which uses digital filtering of the signal, an IDAC to compensate the LA, and a second IDAC for the TIA. The second IDAC first reduces static offset with the SAR algorithm and then continuously tracks and compensates the offset at the input of the TIA. The presented solution differs from other previous implementations that it reduces the offset using two DACs and from other mixed-signal solutions that it not only calibrate for the static offset but continuously tracks the changes in offset and compensates them. The system is extended for burst-mode receivers suitable for PON systems.

The quantitative differences to the commonly used architectures based on RC-filter and S-C filter are shown also by comparing measurements on three RX implementations each with one of the mentioned offset-compensation system, in the same 28 nm bulk-CMOS technology. The comparison is done in terms of area, residual offset current, dynamic range, lower cut-off frequency and noise spectral density. System considerations as adjustable lower cut-off frequency and the compensated RX blocks are also taken in consideration. It is found that the presented system offers a higher flexibility and functionality in implementation and a very good compromise between area precision and performance over the other existing solutions.

Acknowledgment. This work was supported in part by BMBF program Zwanzig20 FAST in sub-project fast-bits (contract 03ZZ0525D).

References

1. Pan, Q., Wang, Y., Lu, Y., Yue, C.P.: An 18-Gb/s fully integrated optical receiver with adaptive cascaded equalizer. IEEE J. Sel. Top. Quantum Electron. **22**(6), 361–369 (2016)
2. Rylyakov, A., et al.: A 25 Gb/s burst-mode receiver for low latency photonic switch networks. IEEE J. Solid-State Circuits **50**(12), 3120–3132 (2015)
3. Saeedi, S., Menezo, S., Pares, G., Emami, A.: A 25 Gb/s 3D-integrated CMOS/silicon-photonic receiver for low-power high-sensitivity optical communication. J. Lightwave Technol. **34**(12), 2924–2933 (2016)
4. Belfiore, G., Khafaji, M., Henker, R., Ellinger, F.: A 50 Gb/s 190 mW asymmetric 3-Tap FFE VCSEL driver. IEEE J. Solid-State Circuits **52**(9), 2422–2429 (2017)
5. Khafaji, M.M., Belfiore, G., Pliva, J., Henker, R., Ellinger, F.: A 4 × 45 Gb/s two-tap FFE VCSEL driver in 14-nm FinFET CMOS suitable for burst mode operation. IEEE J. Solid-State Circuits **53**(9), 2686–2695 (2018)
6. Goswami, S., Silver, J., Copani, T., Chen, W., Barnaby, H.J., Vermeire, B., Kiaei, S.: A 14 mW 5Gb/s CMOS TIA with gain-reuse regulated cascode compensation for parallel optical interconnects. In: Proceedings of the IEEE International Solid-State Circuits Conference - Digest of Technical Papers, pp. 100–101, 101a, February 2009
7. Szilagyi, L.: Transceiver Front-ends for high-speed short-range optical communications integrated in complementary-metal-oxide-semiconductor technologies, Ph.D. thesis (2018)
8. Szilágyi, L., Belfiore, G., Henker, R., Ellinger, F.: Area-efficient offset compensation and common-mode control circuit with switched-capacitor technique in an 18 Gbps optical receiver in 80 nm CMOS. In: IEEE 2015 Optical Interconnects Conference (OI), pp. 58–59. IEEE (2015)
9. Szilagyi, L., Schoeniger, D., Henker, R., Ellinger, F.: Optical receiver amplifier with adaptive power and bandwidth for up to 30 Gbit/s in 28 nm CMOS. In: 2016 11th European Microwave Integrated Circuits Conference (EuMIC), pp. 105–108. IEEE (2016)
10. Honda, K., Katsurai, H., Nada, M., Nogawa, M., Nosaka, H.: A 56-Gb/s transimpedance amplifier in 0.13-μm SiGe BiCMOS for an optical receiver with −18.8-dBm input sensitivity. In: Proceedings of the IEEE Compound Semiconductor Integrated Circuit Symposium (CSICS), pp. 1–4, October 2016
11. Li, D., et al.: A 25 Gb/s 3D-integrated silicon photonics receiver in 65 nm CMOS and PIC25G for 100GbE optical links. In: Proceedings of the IEEE International Symposium Circuits and Systems (ISCAS), pp. 2334–2337, May 2016
12. Schow, C.L., et al.: Low-power 16 x 10 Gb/s bi-directional single chip CMOS optical transceivers operating at ≪5 mW/Gb/s/link. IEEE J. Solid-State Circuits **44**(1), 301–313 (2009)
13. Palermo, S., Emami-Neyestanak, A., Horowitz, M.: A 90 nm CMOS 16 Gb/s transceiver for optical interconnects. IEEE J. Solid-State Circuits **43**(5), 1235–1246 (2008)
14. Szilagyi, L., Belfiore, G., Henker, R., Ellinger, F.: 20–25 Gbit/s low-power inductorless single-chip optical receiver and transmitter frontend in 28 nm digital CMOS. Int. J. Microw. Wirel. Technol. **9**(8), 1667–1677 (2017)

15. Szilagyi, L., Pliva, J., Henker, R., Schoeniger, D., Turkiewicz, J.P., Ellinger, F.: A 53-Gbit/s optical receiver frontend with 0.65 pJ/bit in 28-nm bulk-CMOS. IEEE J. Solid-State Circuits **54**(3), 845–855 (2019)
16. Szilagyi, L., Pliva, J., Henker, R., Ellinger, F.: A mixed-signal offset-compensation system for multi-Gbit/s optical receiver frontends. In: Proceedings of the IFIP/IEEE 27th International Conference on Very Large Scale Integration (VLSI-SoC), pp. 46–51, October 2019
17. Razavi, B.: Design of Integrated Circuits for Optical Communications. Wiley, Hoboken (2012)
18. Aznar, F., Pueyo, S.C., López, B.C.: CMOS Receiver Front-ends for Gigabit Short-range Optical Communications. Springer, Heidelberg (2012). https://doi.org/10. 1007/978-1-4614-3464-1
19. Galal, S., Razavi, B.: 10-Gb/s limiting amplifier and laser/modulator driver in 0.18-μm CMOS technology. IEEE J. Solid-State Circuits **38**(12), 2138–2146 (2003)
20. Pliva, J., et al.: Design of a custom standard-cell library for mixed-signal applications in 28 nm CMOS. In: 2017 IEEE International Workshop of Electronics, Control, Measurement, Signals and their Application to Mechatronics (ECMSM), pp. 1–6. IEEE (2017)
21. Khafaji, M., Pliva, J., Henker, R., Ellinger, F.: A 42-Gb/s VCSEL driver suitable for burst mode operation in 14-nm bulk CMOS. IEEE Photonics Technol. Lett. **30**(1), 23–26 (2018)
22. Pliva, J., Khafaji, M., Szilagyi, L., Henker, R., Ellinger, F.: Opto-electrical analog front-end with rapid power-on and 0.82 pJ/bit for 28 Gb/s in 14 nm FinFET CMOS. In: Proceedings of the 30th IEEE International System-on-Chip Conference (SOCC), pp. 253–257, September 2017

Accelerating Inference on Binary Neural Networks with Digital RRAM Processing

João Vieira[1(✉)], Edouard Giacomin[2], Yasir Qureshi[3], Marina Zapater[3],
Xifan Tang[2], Shahar Kvatinsky[4], David Atienza[3],
and Pierre-Emmanuel Gaillardon[2]

[1] INESC-ID, Instituto Superior Técnico, University of Lisboa, Lisbon, Portugal
joaomiguelvieira@tecnico.ulisboa.pt
[2] LNIS, University of Utah, Salt Lake City, USA
[3] ESL, Swiss Federal Institute of Technology Lausanne (EPFL),
Lausanne, Switzerland
[4] Andrew and Erna Viterbi Faculty of Electrical Engineering,
Technion, Israel Institute of Technology, Haifa, Israel

Abstract. The need for efficient *Convolutional Neural Network* (CNNs) targeting embedded systems led to the popularization of *Binary Neural Networks* (BNNs), which significantly reduce execution time and memory requirements by representing the operands using only one bit. Also, due to 90% of the operations executed by CNNs and BNNs being convolutions, a quest for custom accelerators to optimize the convolution operation and reduce data movements has started, in which *Resistive Random Access Memory* (RRAM)-based accelerators have proven to be of interest. This work presents a custom *Binary Dot Product Engine*(BDPE) for BNNs that exploits the low-level compute capabilities enabled RRAMs. This new engine allows accelerating the execution of the inference phase of BNNs by locally storing the most used kernels and performing the binary convolutions using RRAM devices and optimized custom circuitry. Results show that the novel BDPE improves performance by 11.3%, energy efficiency by 7.4% and reduces the number of memory accesses by 10.7% at a cost of less than 0.3% additional die area.

Keywords: Machine Learning · Embedded systems · Binary Neural Networks · RRAM-based Binary Dot Product Engine

1 Motivation

Machine Learning (ML) is the field of *Artificial Intelligence* (AI) that studies algorithms and statistical models aiming at teaching computer systems to perform specific tasks based on information inferred from patterns on datasets.

J. Vieira—At the time of this work, João Vieira was affiliated with the University of Utah.

© IFIP International Federation for Information Processing 2020
Published by Springer Nature Switzerland AG 2020
C. Metzler et al. (Eds.): VLSI-SoC 2019, IFIP AICT 586, pp. 257–278, 2020.
https://doi.org/10.1007/978-3-030-53273-4_12

A class of such algorithms is *Convolutional Neural Networks* (CNNs), which is applied to a vast diversity of fields, from image processing to natural language processing [1]. On the one hand, CNNs are versatile and can be used for numerous purposes, from teaching a machine how to play chess [2] to having an embedded system with a camera recognizing objects in real-time [3]. On the other hand, CNN-driven algorithms are costly both on computing power and energy demand. While having a machine or a cluster of machines learning how to play chess in a data warehouse may not be time-, compute-, or power-bounded, using an embedded system to detect objects in frames in real-time has all those constraints. Therefore, it is important to find efficient implementations of CNNs targeting embedded systems.

CNNs are composed of phases called layers. Each layer of a CNN can be seen as an independent function that takes inputs, applies a set of mathematical operations and exports an output. The output of a layer may be used as the input of another layer. Usually, each layer has a significant amount of inputs and outputs that may have to be transferred multiple times from and to the memory subsystem throughout the algorithm's execution. Also, statistics show that 90% of the mathematical operations executed in the layers of CNNs are convolutions. For these reasons, the key to achieve efficient implementations of CNN-driven algorithms relies on simultaneously reducing data movements and optimizing the convolution operation.

In the literature, two distinct approaches for optimizing the convolution operation are widely adopted. One consists of using dedicated accelerators capable of leveraging convolution's potential parallelism, and data proximity. The other exploits the adoption of lower precision operands in CNNs aiming at speeding up their execution while not degrading severely the quality of the results.

The use of dedicated accelerators aims at leveraging both the convolution's potential parallelism and the high bandwidth to the memory, which is a characteristic of accelerators. As an example, ISAAC [4] re-purposes the hardware resources of *Resistive Random-Access Memory* (RRAM) devices to enable massive parallel computation that can be used to accelerate certain layers of CNNs. ISAAC is not only capable of performing thousands of operations simultaneously but also does so in-situ, i.e., it does not require to move the operands out of the memory device. An important shortcoming of ISAAC, however, is that it hardly fits the power constraints of embedded systems since RRAM devices require a significant amount of energy to operate. Plus, in general, dedicated accelerators that do not operate at memory level like ISAAC present an overhead associated with transferring the operands from the memory hierarchy that is only surpassed by the benefits of processing large datasets. Thus, when the dataset is not big enough, the benefits of using the accelerator might not cover the cost of transferring the data to and from the accelerator. Since CNN-driven algorithms executing on embedded devices usually work with small datasets, suitable for the device's capacity, most accelerators are not suited for such systems.

In parallel, the use of lower precision operands in CNNs is also widely adopted, aiming at simplifying the operations executed by the several layers and, consequently, increasing performance. Intel's bfloat16 is a floating-point format using only 16 bits that was created with the purpose of being used by CNNs. Ultimately, the precision of the operands can be reduced to the limit of 1 bit per operand. *Binary Neural Networks* (BNNs), CNNs that use only 1 bit per operand, show significant performance boosts over CNNs and drastically reduce the memory requirements as they require only 1 bit to store each operand. Although reducing the precision of the operands to the limit sacrifices the quality of the results to some level, studies show that XNOR-Nets, a class of BNNs, still achieve admissible quality for many applications. Due to the drastic reduction of requirements, some BNNs can be efficiently implemented in embedded systems.

An additional advantage brought by BNNs is the increase in data redundancy. Part of the operands involved in the mathematical operations in the CNN layers are intrinsic to those layers. These operands, called weights, are grouped in the form of kernels, which are often small in size (typical values are 3×3, 5×5, and 7×7). When using 32-bit integers or floating-points to represent the weights, it is unlikely to find two kernels whose weights are exactly the same. However, when using only 1 bit, chances are that some kernels will have exactly the same weights by the same order. Thus, such kernels are redundant and there is no need to have them both stored in memory.

The system proposed in this work [5] leverages all the three aspects discussed in the last paragraphs (dedicated hardware structures, lower-precision operands, and data redundancy brought by the adoption of lower-precision operands) to accelerate the execution of BNNs in embedded systems. To achieve this, we propose a novel *Functional Unit* (FU) based on the work presented on [6], the *Binary Dot Product Engine* (BDPE), to be integrated into the execution path of a general-purpose *Central Processing Unit* (CPU). The purpose of the BDPE is both to store the most used kernels, hence avoiding transferring them from the memory, and accelerate the binary convolution operation, by leveraging the low-level properties of the RRAM technology. Results show that the proposed system provides significant benefits both in terms of performance improvements and energy efficiency over the high-efficiency processor ARM Cortex-A53 at a cost of a negligible area overhead.

All in all, the main contributions of this work are:

1. We revisit the work proposed in [6] and modify their artifact to create a novel FU [5];
2. We propose the architecture of a BDPE capable of storing redundant binary kernels and executing the binary convolution operation efficiently;
3. We integrate the novel BDPE with the execution path of the ARM Cortex-A53;
4. We propose an ARMv8 *Intruction Set Architecture* (ISA) extension for supporting the functionality of the novel BDPE;
5. We present a simulation methodology using accurate models and complete frameworks to assess the benefits of the proposed system.

Throughout the following sections, we will discuss the proposed system, namely how the different components were implemented and the methods and

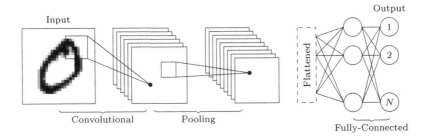

Fig. 1. CNN overview highlighting the three most common types of layers: Convolutional, Pooling, and Fully-Connected.

tools that were used. The rest of this Chapter is organized as follows: Sect. 2 introduces the most important concepts about CNNs and BNNs as well as the process of leveraging RRAM-enabled computing to perform convolutions; Sect. 3 summarizes the working principles of the binary convolution block used as base for the novel BDPE. Section 4 details the architecture of the proposed system. The evaluation methodology and the main results of this work are presented in Sect. 5. Section 6 presents some related work. Finally, Sect. 7 closes this Chapter.

2 Background

This section introduces the reader to important concepts that are used in this work. First, the basic structure and working principles of CNNs are explained, focusing on the particular kind of CNNs used in this work, BNNs. Then, the working principle of RRAM computation applied to CNNs is detailed.

2.1 Convolutional Neural Networks

CNNs constitute a class of Deep Learning algorithms that are particularly useful for Computer Vision applications. Applied to that field, a CNN assigns importance (learnable weights) to the features of images that allows differentiating different objects depicted in those frames. First, several images are presented to the CNN together with known information about them (e.g., a picture of a cat and the information that the picture contains a cat). The image is processed by the CNN and the weights are updated depending on the deviation of the obtained result from the expected result. This process goes on until certain convergence conditions are met. This phase is called training. After training a CNN, it can be used for inferring information from images that were not shown to it during the training phase. For instance, given a picture of a cat different from those shown during training, the CNN will be able to detect that there is a cat in the picture based on all the cat pictures it has seen during training. This phase is called inference.

A CNN is composed of different phases called layers. The type, quantity, and order of those layers are responsible for the properties, namely the accuracy, of

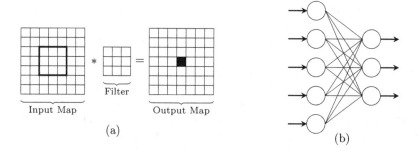

Fig. 2. (a) Convolutional layer; (b) Fully-Connected layer.

the *Convolutional Neural Network* (CNN). Each layer of a CNN takes inputs (in the case of the first layer, the inputs are the pixels of an image), performs a group of mathematical operations over those inputs and export outputs. The inputs of a layer are organized in the form of an input feature map, whereas the set of outputs is called output feature map. Except for the last layer, the outputs of the layers serve as inputs for the next layer. Depending on the mathematical operations realized over the input data, the layers are grouped under different categories. The three most common layer categories are convolutional, fully-connected and pooling, as shown in Fig. 1. Convolutional layers perform the convolution operation between the input and a given kernel (a kernel is an organized array of weights), as shown in Fig. 2a. In fully-connected layers, each element of the input has a weighted influence over each element of the output, as shown in Fig. 2b. Polling layers are transformation layers that perform a mathematical, possibly non-linear, operation over the elements of the input. Such layers can be used for transforming the input such as resizing or rectifying. Examples of possible transformations are max-pooling and *Rectified Linear Unit* (ReLU), respectively, which are depicted in Fig. 3. Note that two of the three most common types of layers, convolutional and fully-connected, implement mathematical operations that can be unrolled in a set of convolutions.

Both the convolutional and the fully-connected layers of CNNs use operands that are intrinsic to those layers (the kernels of the convolutional layers and the weights of the fully-connected layers). Those values are responsible for the quality

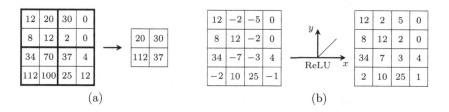

Fig. 3. Two widely used Pooling layers in CNNs: (a) Max-Pool; (b) ReLU.

of the results exported by the CNN, and are calculated during the training phase. At the beginning of the operation, all the weights are initialized to random values. Then, a set of images and corresponding information are fed to the CNN. The CNN processes those inputs, and based on the deviation between the calculated results and the expected, updates the weights using feedback processes.

Depending on several factors such as the quality of the training set, the training configuration and duration and the architecture of the CNN itself, the trained CNN is able to detect more or less accurately objects in new frames that were not shown during the training phase. A popular metric to assess the quality of the inference is the *mean Average Precision* (mAP). The *mean Average Precision* (mAP) is defined as the average value of another metric called *Average Precision* (AP), which is a composed metric that takes into account several factors, such as precision, recall, and *Intersection over Union* (IoU). Precision measures the accuracy of the CNN's predictions, i.e., the percentage of correct predictions; recall is the percentage of positives that the CNN is able to detect, regardless of the assigned class; and *Intersection over Union* (IoU) measures the overlap between the real area where an object is located in a frame and the area where it is detected by the CNN. mAP values are included in the interval $[0, 1]$, being 1 optimal. The mAP can also be used to compare CNNs, which is particularly useful when assessing the loss of quality due to applying heuristics for increasing execution performance (e.g., when reducing the precision of the operands).

2.2   XNOR-Based Binary Convolution

BNNs are a particular class of CNNs where both the inputs of the layers and the weights are specified by only one bit and their values are limited to -1 and 1. Duo to this representation, the atomic operations of the regular convolution can be replaced by simpler operations. The element-wise multiplication is replaced by the XNOR operation whereas the accumulation is replaced by bit-count [7]. Binarizing the operands and replacing the costly operators in the convolution by simpler ones significantly increases the performance of the convolution operation. Since convolutions constitute approximately 90% of the total operations implemented by CNNs [8], optimizing this operation significantly impacts the overall performance and energy efficiency associated with executing the CNN.

Furthermore, binarizing a CNN also reduces significantly the memory requirements duo to each operand being represented by a single bit. For instance, when comparing with a 32-bit representation of the operands and the weights, the memory requirements are reduced 32×. However, reducing the precision of the operands to the limit of 1 bit comes at the cost of sacrificing accuracy. While CNNs such AlexNet suffer from accuracy losses lower than 10% when binarized, some other networks may be rendered totally useless. Therefore, not all CNNs are viable for binarization.

2.3 YOLO: You Look only Once

Similarly to AlexNet, YOLO [3] is another example of a CNN that can be binarized without sacrificing severely its accuracy. YOLO is a state-of-art CNN for real-time object detection targeting low-end devices. It divides the image into regions and predicts bounding boxes and associated probabilities for each region. Unlike expensive object-detection-oriented CNNs such as R-CNN [9] and Fast R-CNN [10], which require thousands of network evaluations to detect multiple objects, YOLO looks at the whole image at testing time, so its predictions are informed by global context. As a result, the YOLO performs 1000× faster than R-CNN and 100× faster than Fast R-CNN [3]. By sizing the network, YOLO also allows trading accuracy for performance by reducing the number of network layers. This represents an advantage for embedded devices characterized by low computing power. When binarized using the definitions in [7], the XNOR-Net version of a given configuration of YOLO, YOLOV3-tiny XNOR-Net, shows approximately the same mAP as the full-precision network, while reducing the size of the weights approximately 32× and thus executing up to 58× faster. For the *Street View House Numbers* (SVHN) dataset [11], the YOLOV3-tiny XNOR-Net shows a mAP decrease of only 0.43%, while increasing the number of detections by 75%.

Duo to the binary nature of both the inputs and the operands in binary convolutions, which allows replacing the expensive multiply and accumulate operations by simpler XNOR and bit-counts, BNNs have great potential to be further accelerated using dedicated structures in hardware. One of the most popular approaches to do so is to re-purpose the hardware resources of RRAMs to enable computation.

2.4 RRAM-Powered Convolution Acceleration

Resistive Random-Access Memory (RRAM) bit-cells, also called memristors, are devices with two terminals composed by metal electrodes and a switching oxide stack [12]. The application of a certain programming voltage between the two electrodes changes the conductivity of the metal oxide, which leads to a switch between two stable resistance states: *Low-Resistance State* (LRS) and *High-Resistance State* (HRS). Thus, allowing to encode the binary values 1 and 0, respectively. The switching from *High-Resistance State* (HRS) to *Low-Resistance State* (LRS) is called a set process and can be achieved through the application of a positive programming voltage. The complementary process is denominated a reset process and involves the use of a negative programming voltage.

Although the classic applications of memristors only use two possible states to encode binary data, the physical characteristics of memristors allow the LRS to assume a wide range of values. This particular feature allows to use RRAM cells to store non-binary values (encoded as physical impedance), which can be used to implement hardware analog dot-products. To do that, the RRAM cells are organized into a crossbar of passive arrays, removing all the access transistors. The output current becomes the sum of the currents flowing through

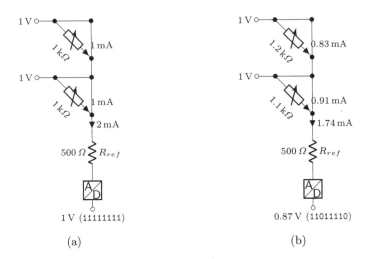

Fig. 4. Operation principle of the RRAM-powered analog dot product: (a under perfect conditions; (b) in the presence of variations. When subjected to variations, the final sum of the currents flowing to the memristors has an associated error which is reflected in the output of the 8-bit ADC.

each memristor, which has encoded a certain non-binary value in the form of impedance, and thus, it becomes the sum of the input voltages weighted by the values encoded in the memristors, as shown in Fig. 4a. Duo to the high density of RRAMs, in theory, using RRAM-based analog computation enables massive parallelism leading to remarkable performance and energy efficiency benefits. However, RRAM-based analog computation suffers from two limitations that largely reduce its applicability. First, it requires a massive quantity of *Digital-Analog Converters* (DACs) and *Analog-Digital Converters* (ADCs) that are area- and power-hungry. This limits the scalability of RRAM-based analog compute devices. Second, memristors are subjected to variability, which has its source in process variations during fabrication as well as temperature oscillations during the device operation. This severely decreases the usability of the analog capabilities of RRAMs, as the results are severely tampered by the lack of precision of the resistance values. The effect of varying the resistance values of the memristors is depicted in Fig. 4b.

The work presented in [6], which also uses RRAM arrays to perform computation, mitigates this effect by allowing only two levels of resistance and performing the dot product in a purely digital way, without relying on an analog sum of currents. Unlike analog-based RRAM computation, the approach used in that work allows obtaining reliable results that minimize the possibility of errors. Thus, the convolutional block presented in [6] served as inspiration for this work and was further developed to become a fully-functional *Functional Unit* (FU) and integrated within the pipeline of a general-purpose *Central Processing Unit* (CPU).

3   RRAM-Based Binary Convolution Block

The use of dedicated accelerators to increase performance when executing CNN-based applications is one of the most well-succeeded approaches. Dedicated accelerators take the most advantage of the hardware resources for a very specific task, enabling massive performance boosts. Furthermore, they usually have their own high-bandwidth channels to memory. However, such accelerators are expensive in terms of hardware and power demand, rendering them unsuitable for embedded devices, which are highly hardware- and power-constrained. Therefore, our system uses a custom *Binary Dot Product Engine* (BDPE) that is integrated within the processor execution path. Our unit is based in the binary convolution engine presented [6] that efficiently implements the binary convolution operation.

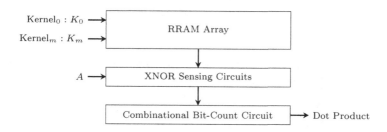

Fig. 5. Structure of the RRAM-based binary convolution block proposed in [6].

Due to the nature of the operands in a binary convolution (each element of the operands has only 1 bit), the costly operations of multiplication and accumulation required by the regular convolution can be replaced by XNOR and bit-count, respectively [7], which can be implemented efficiently in hardware using the low-level properties of memristors and some additional circuitry. Note that in the context of CNNs, convolutions are implemented as a sequence of several dot products. Therefore, the block that implements the binary convolution executes a sequence of dot products, one per cycle, until producing the final result of the convolution.

Figure 5 shows the top-level structure of the convolutional block proposed in [6]. The sequences of binary weights are stored in the RRAM array, one per row. To perform one dot product with an input vector, the line of the RRAM containing the binary weights is selected and the input data is applied to the RRAM array. The bit-wise XNOR of the input and the binary weights stored in the selected line is performed as a readout of the RRAM array. Then, the result of the XNOR operation is applied to the input of the bit-count circuit, which counts the number of bits set to '1'. Finally, the bit-count circuit exports the result of the dot product.

Structure-wise, the part of the convolution block responsible for implementing the XNOR operation is composed of three parts: the precharge circuit; the programming circuit; and the XNOR circuit, as shown in Fig. 6. The precharge circuit loads the outputs (*out* and $\overline{out}$) to V_{DD} before the reading. The programming circuit serves to store the kernels in the RRAM array prior to computation. The XNOR circuit is responsible for performing the XNOR operation between the input and the kernel stored in the selected row of the RRAM.

Overall, the operation of the convolutional block is divided into two phases: (1) the kernel storage phase; and (2) the computing phase.

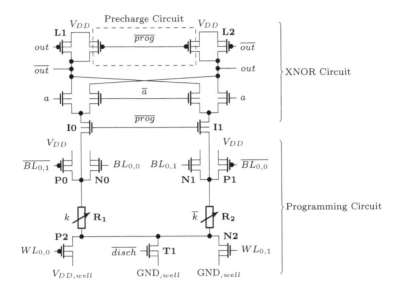

Fig. 6. 1-bit RRAM-based XNOR cell that serves as unit of the RRAM array used in the convolution block. All terminals illustrated as disconnected are connected to GND.

During the programming phase (*prog* = 1), both the outputs, *out* and $\overline{out}$, are precharged to V_{DD} and the RRAM array is isolated from the XNOR circuit through transistors $I0$ and $I1$. Additionally, $\overline{disch}$ is set to GND, turning $T1$ off. The value of k is stored in the RRAM in a complementary way. For example, when $k = 0$, R_1 is set to HRS and R_2 to LRS. R_1 is set to HRS by turning on transistors $N0$ and $P2$ and turning off transistors $P0$, $P1$, $N1$ and $N2$. During the reset process of R_1, $V_{DD,well}$ and $GND_{,well}$ are switched to $2 \times V_{DD}$ and V_{DD}, respectively. As such, the voltage difference across R_1 becomes $-V_{prog} = -2 \times V_{DD}$, which triggers a reset process. Similarly, R_2 is set to LRS by turning on transistors $P1$ and $N2$ and turning off transistors $P0$, $P2$, $N0$ and $N1$. Considering $k = 1$, R_1 is set to LRS and R_2 to HRS in a similar way.

The computing phase consists of calculating the XNOR between an input a and a weight k stored in the memory, which is performed as a single memory readout thanks to the XNOR sense amplifiers. The read sequence goes as follows: first, $V_{DD,well}$ and $GND_{,well}$ are switched to V_{DD} and GND respectively. Signals *prog* and $\overline{disch}$ are set to '0' and '1', respectively. Hence, nodes *out* and $\overline{out}$

are grounded through the RRAMs and transistor $T1$. During this phase, the complementary resistances of the Resistive Random-Access Memories control the discharge currents, so that the memristor in LRS is discharged faster than the one in HRS. Using a deep N-well also eliminates any breakdown risk or reliability degradation on the transistors [13]. When out or $\overline{out}$ reach the voltage $V_{DD} - V_{T,pmos}$ ($V_{T,pmos}$ denotes the threshold voltage of transistors $L1$ and $L2$), the associated $pmos$ transistor is turned on, pulling up the other node (out or $\overline{out}$) to V_{DD}. The resulting output is the XNOR of a and k.

Considering the operation principles above described, it is possible to organize several XNOR cells into a matrix. Figure 7 shows a $m \times l$ RRAM matrix array, where m is the number of kernels to be stored and l is the number of weights of each kernel. For example, storing ten 3×3 kernels requires a 10×9 RRAM array. From the proposed bit-cell structure of Fig. 6, all the XNOR part is shared between all the structures in each pair of columns and is put at the bottom acting as a digital sense amplifier. Similarly, the programming circuits are shared at each column and row to be able to individually address all the RRAM lines. Sharing the programming transistors also allows parallel programming.

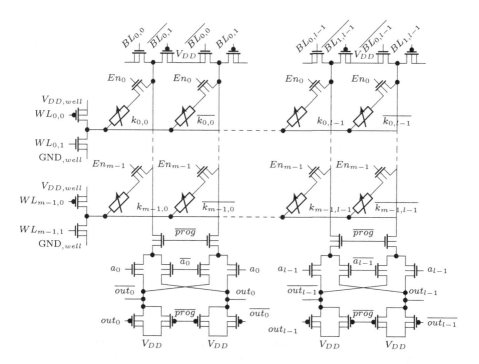

Fig. 7. RRAM-based XNOR $m \times l$ array organization. All terminals illustrated as disconnected are connected to GND.

As shown in Fig. 8, a convolution between an input feature map of size $n \times n$ and a kernel (also $n \times n$, for simplicity) leads to an output feature map with n^2

elements. The kernel is unrolled into a vector so the n^2 weights are encoded in the n^2 pairs of RRAM cells. In this example, n^2 is the number of columns of the RRAM array illustrated in Fig. 7 ($N^2 = l$). Element $o_{i,i}$, the central element of the output feature map, is calculated by performing the dot product of the unrolled input feature map ($A = \{a_{0,0}, \ldots, a_{n-1,n-1}\}$) with the unrolled kernel ($K = \{k_{0,0}, \ldots, k_{n-1,n-1}\}$) by selecting the row of the RRAM where the kernel is stored through signal En_x and summing the partial results, $out_h (h \in [0, n^2])$, through an external circuit to perform the bit-count operation.

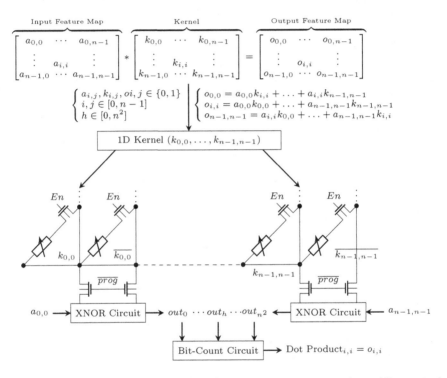

Fig. 8. Example of binary dot product between two $n \times n$ matrices. All terminals illustrated as disconnected are connected to GND.

Results reported by [6] show that the binary convolutional block surpasses previous analog RRAM-based accelerators in terms of reliability against RRAM and CMOS process variations. Furthermore, it shows significant energy efficiency increase when compared both with conventional *Multiply-Accumulate* (MAC) solutions and state-of-the-art accelerators such as ISAAC [4].

4   CPU Integration

To be able to take advantage of the convolutional block presented on [6] and fully integrate it within the execution path of a general-purpose CPU as a regular

FU, some adaptations to the original architecture of the convolution block were required, as explained in [5].

The advantages of using the convolutional block are two: (1) performing the XNOR operation efficiently using the RRAM array; (2) calculating the bit-count atomically. To use the RRAM array to calculate the XNOR between an input and a vector of binary weights it is required the vector of binary weights to be stored in the RRAM array. However, having all the weights stored in the RRAM array is not feasible as it would result in a tremendous chip area overhead. Therefore, only a small number of weights can actually be stored inside the BDPE. Nevertheless, the bit-count circuit does not depend on the weights being stored in the RRAM array. Therefore, to avoid rendering useless the entire convolutional block whenever the weights are not stored in the RRAM array, additional logic was added that allows performing the XNOR operation between two binary input vectors using classic CMOS logic gates. This way, the benefit of performing the bit-count using the circuit of the original block can still be leveraged. Figure 9 illustrates the architecture of the novel BDPE highlighting the modifications to the original convolution block.

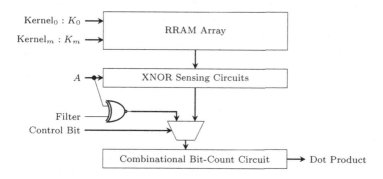

Fig. 9. Block diagram of the proposed BDPE.

The integration of the BDPE with a general-purpose CPU is divided into three phases: (1) the integration with the processor's pipeline; (2) the creation of new instructions in the CPU *Intruction Set Architecture* (ISA) to use the unit; and (3) provide compiler support to use the added ISA instructions in the software side. The CPU choice for integrating the BDPE was the ARMv8-A ARM Cortex-A53 due to both being a high-efficiency low-end processor that provides a competitive baseline and also the available simulations models for this particular CPU.

As shown in Fig. 10, the BDPE is integrated with the processor's pipeline in the *Execute* stage, similarly to the *Arithmetic and Logic Unit* (ALU), and stores the results of the computation in the *Execute/Memory Access* pipeline register. According to the ARM Architecture Reference Manual for the ARMv8-A architecture profile [14], the ARMv8 ISA has unused *opcodes* that can be re-purposed to expand the functionality of the CPU. Using two of the unused *opcodes*, two instructions were created and assigned to the novel BDPE.

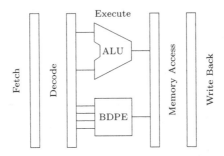

Fig. 10. Simplified block diagram of a generic processor pipeline integrating the proposed BDPE.

Figure 11 illustrates the format of the new instructions and denotes the purpose of each distinct set of bits. Each of the new instructions is decoded in the *Decode* stage such that the content of the register specified by rm serves as input data of the BDPE; the content of the register represented by rn is the input kernel; imm6 specifies the address of the kernel stored in the RRAM array; and the second *Most Significant Bit (MSB)* of the *opcode* designates the control bit.

opcode	rm	imm6	rn	rd
31	21 20 16	15 10	9 5	4 0

Fig. 11. Format of the new instructions added to the ARMv8 ISA to allow the processor to issue instructions to the BDPE. The *opcodes* 10000011000 and 11000011000 were re-purposed to specify the custom instructions. rm and rn specify addresses of 64-bit registers; imm6 represents a 6-bit immediate; and rd specifies the address of the destination 64-bit register.

As shown in Fig. 12, the workflow for running a *Binary Neural Network* (BNN) using the novel BDPE is divided into profiling and execution. During the profiling, the BNN is used to perform a single inference while the kernel space is profiled, selecting the most frequently used kernels. The selected kernels are stored in the RRAM, and a configuration file is generated containing the information about the content of the RRAM. Then, the CNN is recompiled, and the code responsible for implementing the binary convolution is replaced by custom code that utilizes the BDPE. If the kernel being used is stored in the RRAM, the compiler inserts a special instruction to perform the binary convolution using the RRAM array. Otherwise, the compiler inserts a load instruction to fetch the kernel from memory, followed by a special instruction that performs the binary convolution using the two data inputs of the BDPE.

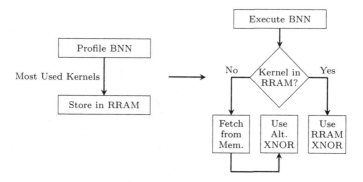

Fig. 12. Simple example that illustrates the process of storing the most used kernels inside the RRAM and running a BNN using the novel BDPE.

5   Results and Discussion

To assess the performance and energy efficiency improvements enabled by the BDPE, a light configuration of the YOLOV3 XNOR-Net was used, the YOLOV3-tiny. First, the network was trained using Darknet [15], a C-based CNN framework on a general-purpose computer for the dataset *Street View House Numbers* (SVHN) [11]. Then, the network was profiled to obtain statistics about the usage of the kernels during the inference phase. Due to the number of kernels used by the CNN, storing all of them inside the RRAM array would lead to a prohibitively large circuit. Thus, only the kernels that are used the most are stored inside the RRAM array while the remaining kernels have to be transferred from memory during inference. As result of profiling YOLOV3-tiny XNOR-Net, it was concluded that a small portion of the kernels is used in a significant percentage of the convolution operations, as suggested by Fig. 13. More specifically, 0.07% of the kernels are used in 9.74% of the convolutions. Therefore, those kernels are stored in the RRAM array.

To further evaluate the impact of storing different amounts of kernels inside the BDPE, five scenarios were considered where the RRAM usage rate (percentage of convolutions that use kernels locally stored in the RRAM) varies between 10% and 50% when executing YOLOV3 XNOR-Net.

5.1   Performance Analysis

A modified version of the gem5 architectural simulator [16] was used to assess the proposed system performance benefits. Due to gem5's known inaccuracies [17], the default ARM model was improved with the gem5-X framework [18], allowing to reduce the ARM model's error margin from 10% to 4% for the ARM Cortex-A53. The system was simulated in *System Emulation* (SE) mode by compiling all the inputs of the network into a single executable binary file. Additionally, the Darknet framework was modified at assembly level to use the custom BDPE

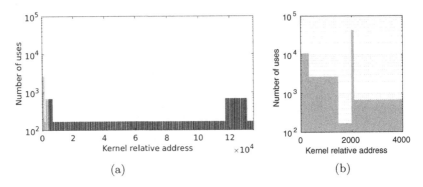

Fig. 13. Number of times each kernel is used during YOLOV3-tiny XNOR-Net inference: (a) entire kernel space; (b) zoom in showing a spike on the usage of a very limited set of kernels.

instead of the processor's *Arithmetic and Logic Unit* (ALU) when performing binary convolutions.

To determine the most used kernels and populate the RRAM array, the following two-step procedure was used: (1) Darknet was ran using gem5 and the kernel space was profiled; (2) The most used kernels were selected and stored in the RRAM. After populating the RRAM, the gem5 module responsible for emulating the BDPE was rebuilt. Because the framework was not recompiled, gem5 in *System Emulation* (SE) mode mapped the data structures to the same addresses used in (1), and the application flow was kept the same except for the binary convolutions involving the most frequently used kernels stored in the RRAMs. In those cases, the RRAM array was used instead of the alternative XNOR mechanism to perform the XNOR operation. The complete system featuring the modified ARM Cortex-A53 and four DRAM ranks of 1 GB each operating at 2400 MHz was emulated and the entire workflow of Darknet was executed.

As result of offloading the execution of binary convolutions to the BDPE, the kernels that are stored in the RRAM array are not requested from memory during inference. Thus, a reduction in memory accesses equal to the RRAM usage rate is observed, as shown in Fig. 14a. Additionally, it can be observed that over 99% of the memory accesses reduction happens at the L1 cache, suggesting that the system has the maximum benefits of caching effects.

However, avoiding the transfer of sequential kernels to the processor whenever the RRAM array is used produces irregularities in the memory access patterns. This situation leads to more evictions and cache collisions, thus causing additional cache misses, as shown in Fig. 14b. Nevertheless, the increase of the cache misses is lower than 0.01% relative to the total number of memory accesses. Hence, this side-effect is negligible and does not affect the overall performance.

All in all, as illustrated in Fig. 14c, for a usage rate of 10% the performance improvement is 11.3%. Also, the performance gains show no significant variation with the RRAM usage rate. This effect has two main causes: (1) both the data

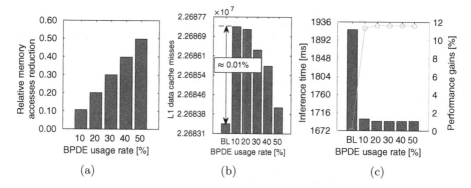

Fig. 14. (a) Number of memory accesses spared depending on the RRAM usage rate when compared with the baseline system; (b) Number of L1 data cache misses caused by BDPE-driven memory access irregularities; (c) Inference time and performance gains of the baseline system and the proposed system considering five RRAM usage rates.

paths in the BDPE take exactly one cycle to perform a binary convolution; (2) due to caching effects, the kernels are stored in the L1 cache 94% of the time, substantially reducing the time required to fetch them. Consequently, using the alternative method for performing the XNOR of the kernel and the input data takes approximately the same time as using the RRAM array and does not impact negatively the overall performance.

5.2   Hardware Resources

Circuit-level metrics were obtained through electrical simulations using a commercial 28 nm *Fully Depleted Silicon On Insulator* (FD-SOI) design kit to assess the hardware requirements and the power demand of the devised BDPE. Delay and power results were extracted from Eldo simulations, to be used in models for the architectural evaluation. These metrics were extracted for the two possible cases to consider when the XNOR is performed using a kernel locally stored in the RRAM or a kernel coming from the processor's registers, respectively. In order to consider an average case, it was assumed that half of the data inputs, as well as the kernels, are zeros and the other half is ones. For the area estimation, the full-custom layout of the RRAM array and its associated control path were modeled using Cadence Virtuoso. The bit-count circuit was synthesized with Synopsys Design Compiler from *Register Transfer Level* (RTL) netlists and integrated into a Place & Route flow using Cadence Innovus to obtain the complete layout of a 256×64 RRAM-based BDPE.

Table 1 shows the hardware requirements, power demand and delay for the BDPE. In practice, since a 10% RRAM usage rate allows achieving the best trade-off between hardware requirements, performance improvements and energy savings, that scenario was used to obtain the results in this section.

The die area required to implement the novel mechanism is only $3,845\,\mu\text{m}^2$ per CPU core, using a *Fully Depleted Silicon On Insulator* (FD-SOI) 28 nm

Table 1. Hardware resources and average power demand of the BDPE considering the two possible paths data paths considering a RRAM usage rate of 10%. When *control bit=0*, the RRAM array is used to implement the XNOR operation. Otherwise, the alternative XNOR mechanism is used.

	Area/Hardware resources [μm²]	Power [mW]	Delay [ps]
control bit=0	3,845	1.24	408
control bit=1		3.23	214

process, while a dual-core ARM Cortex-A53 in an equivalent process requires $2.8\,\mathrm{mm^2}$ [19]. Therefore, the BDPE represents less than 0.3% of the total CPU area. The energy spent for a single operation when using the RRAM array (*control bit=0*) is reduced by 37% comparing to using the alternative mechanism (*control bit=1*). This is allowed by the intrinsic energy efficiency of the RRAM array [6]. Although this advantage comes at a cost of a delay overhead at circuit level, the maximum operating frequency allowed is still 2.5 GHz. Thus, as the target platform is the ARM Cortex-A53 with an operating frequency of 2 GHz, the BDPE can be integrated with the system without constraining its overall frequency.

5.3 Energy Efficiency

As a secondary result of running the modified version of Darknet, gem5 produced timing results, statistics on memory accesses and usage of the CPU's several modules. Such results were applied to 28 nm FD-SOI power models for ARMv8 in-order cores, proposed by [18] and [20], allowing to estimate energy consumption.

The total energy spent by the baseline system (ARM Cortex-A53) and the five scenarios using the BDPE is illustrated in Fig. 15a. Then, Fig. 15b shows the energy consumption for the same circumstances subtracted by the energy spent by the DRAM. As shown in Table 2, the total energy spent by the BDPE is negligible when compared with the rest of the system, and so the energy savings are mostly due to the reduction in the execution time. As the execution time is approximately constant regardless of the RRAM usage rate, so are the energy savings. When considering only the processing system (excluding the DRAM main memory), the use of the BDPE allows for average energy savings of 7.4%.

Table 2. Total energy spent by the BDPE and the CPU during the inference phase of YoloV3 XNOR-Net.

RRAM usage rate [%]	Baseline	10	20	30	40	50
BDPE [μJ]	0	0.870	0.279	0.271	0.263	0.255
CPU [μJ × 10_6]	0.542	0.502	0.501	0.501	0.501	0.502

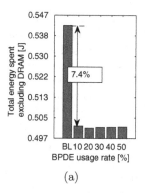 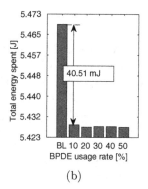

(a)   (b)

Fig. 15. Energy spent by the baseline and the proposed system during the inference phase of YOLOV3-tiny XNOR-Net: (a) excluding the energy spent by the DRAM; (b) including the energy spent by the DRAM.

6   Related Work

As the need for executing compute- and power-hungry CNNs in hardware- and power-constrained devices arises, novel approaches to execute these algorithms efficiently are proposed. Accelerators such those presented in [21–24] aim at reducing data movements by taking advantage of data redundancy, which results in significantly increasing the energy efficiency. Other approaches such as that presented in [25] consist of a method to tolerate errors resulting from aggressive memory voltage scale down, which also allows increasing the energy efficiency significantly.

The use of the compute capabilities of RRAM devices is also an approach to further improve the energy efficiency of CNNs that has shown great interest in the past few years. Shafiee *et al.* [4] proposed using the memristors of the RRAM arrays to store the weights in the form of impedance and perform dot products in an analog fashion. However, the impedance precision of memristors is limited by the ADCs and DACs used to interface the analog RRAM array as well as variations that affect the resistive devices both during its fabrication, operation, and lifetime. Furthermore, ADCs and DAC consume a lot of energy and occupy a lot of chip area, which limits the circuit scalability.

Recent works such as [26,27] proposed using RRAMs to implement dot products in a binary using *Current Sense Amplifiers* (CSAs) or reduced precision ADCs. These approaches use only two logical levels per memristor, which not only improves energy efficiency but also increases the robustness of the devices when compared with RRAM-based analog computation. However, these solutions failed to study important design issues such as the offset voltage of the *Sense Amplifiers* (SAs), which may lead to operational failures [28].

Xiaoyu *et al.* [29] proposed a parallel XNOR-RRAM array using CSAs. Their work shows that by carefully partitioning the RRAM-array, the *Sense Amplifier* (SA) offset issue was alleviated and the proposed architecture is robust against

CMOS and RRAM process variations. However, the assumed RRAM resistance variation was very optimistic (4.5% whereas some work reported around 20% of resistance variation [30]), and the operation of the proposed architecture still may fail under realistic assumptions. Moreover, most of the recent works either did not investigate the impact of RRAM process variations at the circuit level [4,27,31–33] or mainly focused on the architectural level, lacking of proper circuit level evaluations [4,26,27].

Furthermore, previous work still fails to provide embedded-systems-oriented devices that are capable of operating under tight hardware and power constraints. Our work aims at filling these gaps. It has its base on a fully digital RRAM convolutional block that mitigates the limitations of previous RRAM-based solutions, such as errors due to RRAM process variations. Plus, our engine is tiny compared to previous solutions, presenting a chip overhead of merely 0.3% over the CPU used for assessment. Nevertheless, it allows performance improvements up to 11.3% and energy savings as high as 7.4%. Another important contrast between previous solutions and our proposal is the methodology for using the device. While previous approaches rely on non-standard interfaces and protocols for programming and sending data (when such methodology is addressed at all), our system provides a full-stack implementation of a FU that can be easily addressed using assembly language.

7   Conclusions

Our work consists of a novel RRAM-based BDPE suited for accelerating the inference phase of BNNs and meant to be integrated within the pipeline of a general-purpose CPU. To our knowledge, this is the first attempt at exploring the acceleration of CNNs through custom RRAM-based CPU-integrated FUs, which makes it an important contribution. The power demand, hardware resources and propagation delay of the devised mechanism were modeled, and its impact on the considered base system was comprehensively evaluated using the Darknet framework and gem5. Results showed that the novel BDPE achieved performance improvements of 11.3% and 7.4% energy savings. Furthermore, the integration of the novel mechanism requires only few modifications to the baseline CPU, while representing less than 0.3% of the total die area, and does not lower the operation frequency of the system.

The reported advantages allowed by the devised system are tightly coupled with the considered baseline CPU and the used CNN model. Since this work uses an ARM Cortex-A53, which is a high-efficiency CPU, the compute power and energy efficiency enabled by the baseline puts it among the most efficient embedded systems. Nevertheless, the use of the devised BDPE still allows achieving significant performance improvements and energy savings at the cost of a minor area overhead. It is also worth saying that should the baseline be a more rudimentary processing system (e.g., an ultra-low-power embedded system), and the novel BDPE would allow for bigger improvements. Furthermore, the RRAM usage rate is highly affected by the CNN choice. While YoloV3-tiny XNOR-Net allowed for a RRAM usage rate of 10%, other CNNs might allow for higher usage rates. While this may not be relevant performance-wise, as explored in Sect. 5, higher RRAM usage rates lead to fewer data movements and also to performing the XNOR operation using the RRAM array instead of the alternative CMOS mechanism, which impacts positively the energy efficiency.

Acknowledgements. This work was primarily supported by the grant 2016016 from the United States-Israel Binational Science Foundation.

Other supporting grants are SFRH/BD/144047/2019 from Fundação para a Ciência e a Tecnologia (FCT), Portugal; ERC Consolidator Grant COMPUSAPIEN (GA No. 725657); ERC starting grant Real-PIM-System (GA No. 757259); and EC H2020 EUROLAB4HPC2 project (GA No. 800962).

References

1. Collobert, R., Weston, J.: A unified architecture for natural language processing: deep neural networks with multitask learning. In: ICML. ACM International Conference Proceeding Series, vol. 307, pp. 160–167. ACM (2008)
2. Silver, D., et al.: A general reinforcement learning algorithm that masters chess, shogi, and go through self-play. Science **362**(6419), 1140–1144 (2018)
3. Redmon, J., Divvala, S.K., Girshick, R.B., Farhadi, A.: You only look once: unified, real-time object detection. In: CVPR, pp. 779–788. IEEE Computer Society (2016)
4. Shafiee, A., et al.: ISAAC: a convolutional neural network accelerator with in-situ analog arithmetic in crossbars. In: ISCA, pp. 14–26. IEEE Computer Society (2016)
5. Vieira, J., et al.: A product engine for energy-efficient execution of binary neural networks using resistive memories. In: VLSI-SoC, pp. 160–165. IEEE (2019)
6. Giacomin, E., Greenberg-Toledo, T., Kvatinsky, S., Gaillardon, P.: A robust digital RRAM-based convolutional block for low-power image processing and learning applications. IEEE Trans. Circ. Syst. **66-I**(2), 643–654 (2019)
7. Rastegari, M., Ordonez, V., Redmon, J., Farhadi, A.: XNOR-Net: imagenet classification using binary convolutional neural networks. In: Leibe, B., Matas, J., Sebe, N., Welling, M. (eds.) ECCV 2016. LNCS, vol. 9908, pp. 525–542. Springer, Cham (2016). https://doi.org/10.1007/978-3-319-46493-0_32
8. Cong, J., Xiao, B.: Minimizing computation in convolutional neural networks. In: Wermter, S., et al. (eds.) ICANN 2014. LNCS, vol. 8681, pp. 281–290. Springer, Cham (2014). https://doi.org/10.1007/978-3-319-11179-7_36
9. Girshick, R.B., Donahue, J., Darrell, T., Malik, J.: Rich feature hierarchies for accurate object detection and semantic segmentation. In: CVPR, pp. 580–587. IEEE Computer Society (2014)
10. Girshick, R.B.: Fast R-CNN. In: ICCV, pp. 1440–1448. IEEE Computer Society (2015)
11. Netzer, Y., Wang, T., Coates, A., Bissacco, A., Wu, B., Ng, A.Y.: Reading digits in natural images with unsupervised feature learning. In: NIPS Workshop on Deep Learning and Unsupervised Feature Learning 2011 (2011)
12. Wong, H.P., et al.: Metal-oxide RRAM. Proc. IEEE **100**(6), 1951–1970 (2012)
13. Tang, X., Giacomin, E., Micheli, G.D., Gaillardon, P.: Circuit designs of high-performance and low-power RRAM-based multiplexers based on 4t(ransistor)1r(ram) programming structure. IEEE Trans. Circ. Syst. **64-I**(5), 1173–1186 (2017)

14. ARM: Arm architecture reference manual (2018)
15. Redmon, J.: Darknet: Open source neural networks in c (2013–2016). http://pjreddie.com/darknet/
16. Binkert, N.L., et al.: The gem5 simulator. SIGARCH Comput. Archit. News **39**(2), 1–7 (2011)
17. Butko, A., Garibotti, R., Ost, L., Sassatelli, G.: Accuracy evaluation of GEM5 simulator system. In: ReCoSoC, pp. 1–7. IEEE (2012)
18. Qureshi, Y.M., Simon, W.A., Zapater, M., Atienza, D., Olcoz, K.: Gem5-x: A gem5-based system level simulation framework to optimize many-core platforms. In: SpringSim, pp. 1–12. IEEE (2019)
19. Abouzeid, F., et al.: 30% static power improvement on ARM cortex -a53 using static biasing-anticipation. In: ESSCIRC, pp. 37–40. IEEE (2016)
20. Pahlevan, A., et al.: Energy proportionality in near-threshold computing servers and cloud data centers: Consolidating or not? In: DATE, pp. 147–152. IEEE (2018)
21. Du, L., et al.: A reconfigurable streaming deep convolutional neural network accelerator for internet of things. IEEE Trans. Circ. Syst. **65-I**(1), 198–208 (2018)
22. Chen, Y., Krishna, T., Emer, J.S., Sze, V.: Eyeriss: an energy-efficient reconfigurable accelerator for deep convolutional neural networks. J. Solid-State Circuits **52**(1), 127–138 (2017)
23. Jo, J., Kim, S., Park, I.: Energy-efficient convolution architecture based on rescheduled dataflow. IEEE Trans. Circ. Syst. **65-I**(12), 4196–4207 (2018)
24. Sim, J., Park, J., Kim, M., Bae, D., Choi, Y., Kim, L.: 14.6 A 1.42tops/w deep convolutional neural network recognition processor for intelligent IOE systems. In: ISSCC, pp. 264–265. IEEE (2016)
25. Kim, S., Howe, P., Moreau, T., Alaghi, A., Ceze, L., Sathe, V.S.: Energy-efficient neural network acceleration in the presence of bit-level memory errors. IEEE Trans. Circ. Syst. **65-I**(12), 4285–4298 (2018)
26. Ni, L., Liu, Z., Yu, H., Joshi, R.V.: An energy-efficient digital reram-crossbar-based CNN with bitwise parallelism. IEEE J. Explor. Solid-State Comput. Dev. Circ. **3**, 37–46 (2017)
27. Tang, T., Xia, L., Li, B., Wang, Y., Yang, H.: Binary convolutional neural network on RRAM. In: ASP-DAC, pp. 782–787. IEEE (2017)
28. Agbo, I., et al.: Quantification of sense amplifier offset voltage degradation due to zero-and run-time variability. In: ISVLSI, pp. 725–730. IEEE Computer Society (2016)
29. Sun, X., Yin, S., Peng, X., Liu, R., Seo, J., Yu, S.: XNOR-RRAM: a scalable and parallel resistive synaptic architecture for binary neural networks. In: DATE, pp. 1423–1428. IEEE (2018)
30. Chen, A., Lin, M.R.: Variability of resistive switching memories and its impact on crossbar array performance. In: 2011 International Reliability Physics Symposium, p. MY-7. IEEE (2011)
31. Xia, L., et al.: Switched by input: power efficient structure for RRAM-based convolutional neural network. In: DAC, ACM, pp. 125:1–125:6 (2016)
32. Chen, X., Jiang, J., Zhu, J., Tsui, C.: A high-throughput and energy-efficient RRAM-based convolutional neural network using data encoding and dynamic quantization. In: ASP-DAC, pp. 123–128. IEEE (2018)
33. Chi, P., et al.: PRIME: a novel processing-in-memory architecture for neural network computation in ReRAM-based main memory. In: ISCA, pp. 27–39. IEEE Computer Society (2016)

Semi- and Fully-Random Access LUTs for Smooth Functions

Y. Serhan Gener[1], Furkan Aydin[2], Sezer Gören[3(✉)], and H. Fatih Ugurdag[4]

[1] Department of Computer Science, University of California Riverside,
Riverside, CA, USA
ygene001@ucr.edu

[2] Department of Electrical and Computer Engineering,
North Carolina State University, Raleigh, NC, USA
faydn@ncsu.edu

[3] Department of Computer Engineering, Yeditepe University, Istanbul, Turkey
sgoren@cse.yeditepe.edu.tr

[4] Department of Electrical and Electronics Engineering, Ozyegin University,
Istanbul, Turkey
fatih.ugurdag@ozyegin.edu.tr

Abstract. Look-Up Table (LUT) implementation of complicated functions often offers lower latency compared to algebraic implementations at the expense of significant area penalty. If the function is smooth, MultiPartite table method (MP) can circumvent the area problem by breaking up the implementation into multiple smaller LUTs. However, even some of these smaller LUTs may be big in high accuracy MP implementations. Lossless LUT compression can be applied to these LUTs to further improve area and even timing in some cases. The state-of-the-art in the literature decomposes the Table of Initial Values (TIV) of MP into a table of pivots and tables of differences from the pivots. Our technique instead places differences of consecutive elements in the difference tables and result in a smaller range of differences that fit in fewer bits. Constraining the difference of consecutive input values, hence semi-random access, allows us to further optimize designs. We also propose variants of our techniques with variable length coding. We implemented Verilog generators of MP for sine and exponential using conventional LUT as well as different versions of the state-of-the-art and our technique. We synthesized the generated designs on FPGA and found that our techniques produce up to 29% improvement in area, 11% improvement in timing, and 26% improvement in area-time product over the state-of-the-art.

1 Introduction

Computationally complex functions often need to be efficiently implemented in hardware so that they can be part of real-time systems. Look-Up Table (LUT) based methods (see [1] for a comprehensive survey) offer a good balance between latency and area in comparison to algebraic methods by a priori computing of the

© IFIP International Federation for Information Processing 2020
Published by Springer Nature Switzerland AG 2020
C. Metzler et al. (Eds.): VLSI-SoC 2019, IFIP AICT 586, pp. 279–306, 2020.
https://doi.org/10.1007/978-3-030-53273-4_13

function values. LUT-based methods usually have shorter latency as compared to algebraic methods. A straight-forward LUT method, where function value f(x) is stored in (read-only) memory's location x, and the input x is tied to the address port of the memory and the output f(x) is tied to the dataOut port of the memory (without any additional logic) is what we call the Conventional LUT (ConvLUT) method shown in Fig. 1. However, for large bit widths of x, the area of a ConvLUT blows up.

What we are proposing in this work is a "lossless LUT compression method" that can shrink the hardware area of complex functions (sometimes even with improvements in latency) when applied to:

- ConvLUTs or
- the below smarter methods with multiple LUTs

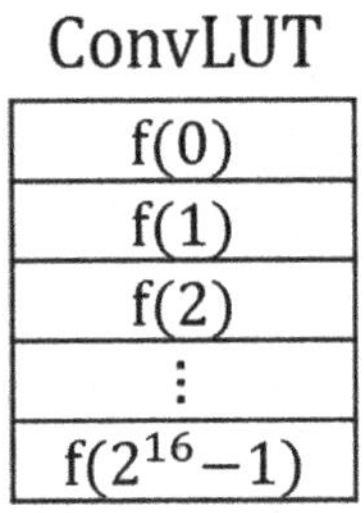

ConvLUT

f(0)
f(1)
f(2)
⋮
f($2^{16}-1$)

Fig. 1. LUT contents of a ConvLUT.

When a ConvLUT blows up due to large input bit width, "multi-LUT methods" (including ours) come to rescue. Although our lossless compression method can be directly applied to ConvLUT, better results are obtained if a lossy multi-LUT method is used first, and our method is applied to the LUTs within. Multi-LUT methods use some arithmetic logic to combine the values in multiple tables. These methods do not produce the exact same output as the ConvLUT method but can stay within a prescribed error range. Some such popular methods are BiPartite method (BP) [2,3], Symmetric Bipartite Method (SBTM) [4], Symmetric Table Addition Method (STAM) [5], MultiPartite method (MP) [6,7], and Hierarchical MultiPartite method (HMP) [8].

BP [2,3] uses approximation by the first two terms of the Taylor expansion of a function using two LUTs: i. Table of Initial Values (TIV) and ii. Table of Offsets (TOs). The microarchitecture in Fig. 2 becomes BP, when the three TOs are combined into a single TO. BP uses an adder to add TIV and TO outputs. TIV downsamples the function values and hence stores a subset of them (at $x0$ values), whereas TO stores the derivative times $\Delta x(= x - x0)$.

For further reduction in TO size, TO can be partitioned into multiple smaller LUTs, which thus leads to the MP method. MP combines STAM [5] and the approach in [9]. In MP, there are multiple TOs and a single TIV. Figure 2 depicts an MP

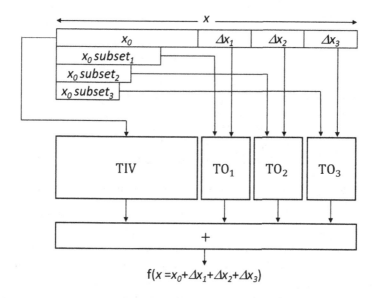

Fig. 2. MP microarchitecture.

microarchitecture with 3 TOs. A smaller Δx can work with a derivative with fewer bits, hence the smaller the Δx the narrower the $x0$ bits (subset) it uses. Each additional table reduces the total number of bits in all of the tables but then increases the combinational logic complexity - all in all reduces the total area.

In the recently proposed HMP method [8], the TIV is further decomposed into the sum of another TIV and TOs. HMP also performs global bit width optimization over all LUTs.

Figure 3 sketches the LUT compression approach within the context of MP. For any given function f, with any given input bit resolution (w_i), i.e., bit width, output resolution (w_o), and m value (which represents the number of TOs to be generated), MP can be implemented as shown in Fig. 3, where TIV_{new} is a new TIV with fewer entries than TIV, while TIV_{diff}'s store differences of missing entries from the entries TIV_{new}. Our lossless LUT compression and the one in [11] can actually be applied to any LUT, hence TIV or TOs or both. However, we applied it on TIV, as there is more compression opportunity in TIV because it is bigger. Also, [11] is applied on TIV, and we wanted to compare our work to theirs.

The concept of general-purpose lossless LUT compression for hardware design was first introduced in [10]. The work in [10] proposes what we here classify as Semi-Random Access differential LUT (SR-dLUT), where differential LUT (dLUT) is a sort of TIV_{diff}. Note that [10] calls the dLUT in this chapter as cLUT, short for "compressed LUT". SR-dLUT can output any LUT location within the range $[i - k, i + k]$ in a given cycle if location i is output in the previous cycle and k is the number of difference tables (dLUT). Note that there is no TIV_{new} in SR-dLUT, there are only difference tables (cLUT in the case of [10]).

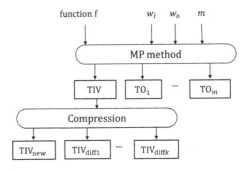

Fig. 3. MP method combined with LUT compression for TIV.

In [11], a lossless LUT compression approach was proposed and was used to compress the TIV of MP method. Two schemes were proposed in [11], namely, 2-table decomposition and 3-table decomposition. We abbreviate them as 2T-TIV and 3T-TIV, respectively. Details of both methods are discussed in Sects. 2.1 and 2.2. Furthermore, in [8] an improvement over the 2T-TIV method was introduced, which we call 2T-TIV-IMP and discuss in detail in Sect. 2.3.

In this chapter, we propose four lossless LUT compression methods, namely, Fully-Random Access differential LUT (FR-dLUT) and Semi-Random Access differential LUT (SR-dLUT), "Variable Length" encoded FR-dLUT (FR-dLUT-VL), and "Variable Length" encoded SR-dLUT (SR-dLUT-VL). Note that FR-dLUT and FR-dLUT-VL microarchitectures were first proposed in our earlier paper [16] and an earlier version of SR-dLUT (cLUT) was introduced in [10]. SR-dLUT-VL is unique to this chapter. Also, SR-dLUT is here used as a building block of MP. Note that although this chapter targets hardware implementation, software implementation of our proposed methods are also possible.

Section 2 below covers the details of the state-of-the-art, namely, 2T-TIV [11], 3T-TIV [11], and 2T-TIV-IMP [8] (which we call T-TIV methods), while Sect. 3 presents our proposed methods. Section 4 gives synthesis results (area, time, and area-time product) of all of the above methods and compares them, and Sect. 5 concludes the chapter.

2 State-of-the-Art

In this section, previous state-of-the-art of fully-random access lossless LUT compression are outlined, namely, T-TIV methods.

2.1 2T-TIV Microarchitecture

2T-TIV [11] decomposes TIV of the MP method into 2 LUTs, TIV_{new} and TIV_{diff} (i.e., a form of dLUT) as shown in Fig. 4, where the original TIV can be recovered from TIV_{new} and TIV_{diff} without introducing any errors.

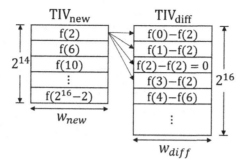

Fig. 4. LUT contents of 2T-TIV for s = 2.

In Fig. 4, we have $w_i = 16$ and $s = 2$ such that for every 2^s consecutive entries, TIV_{new} stores one TIV value (i.e., the one in the middle of 2^s). That is why TIV_{new} has 2^{wi-s} entries. TIV_{diff} is used to store differences between the original TIV values and their corresponding entries in TIV_{new}. Equation (1) shows how TIV is reconstructed back from TIV_{new} and TIV_{diff}.

$$\text{TIV}(i) = \text{TIV}_{new}(i') + \text{TIV}_{diff}(i)$$
$$\text{where } i' = integer\left(\frac{i}{2^s}\right) \tag{1}$$
$$\text{and } \text{TIV}_{new}(i') = \text{TIV}\left(i' * 2^s + 2^{s-1}\right)$$

Note that every 2^s entries of TIV_{diff} contains one zero entry (i.e., entries 2, 6, 10, etc. in Fig. 4).

2.2 3T-TIV Microarchitecture

3T-TIV [11] exploits the "almost symmetry" of function values around the entries of TIV_{new}. 3T-TIV has 3 LUTs as shown in Fig. 5 for a given function with $w_i = 16$ and $s = 3$. In 3T-TIV, TIV_{new} serves the same purpose as in 2T-TIV. Figure 5 shows an example, where $w_i = 16$ and $s = 3$. Hence, there is one entry in TIV_{new} for every $8(= 2^{s=3})$ entries of the original TIV. The entries in TIV_{new} correspond to f(4), f(12), f(20), and so on. The values of f(0), f(1), and up to f(7) need to be computed from f(4) in TIV_{new}. Half of those values, i.e., f(0), f(1), up to f(3) are calculated using the differences stored TIV_{diff1} as in 2T-TIV, hence (2) where i' is the same as in (1).

$$\text{TIV}(i) = \text{TIV}_{new}(i') + \text{TIV}_{diff1}\left(2^{s-1} * i' + j\right)$$
$$\text{for } j < 2^{s-1} \text{ where } j = mod\left(i, 2^s\right) \tag{2}$$

However, for f(4) through f(7), the second-order differences in TIV_{diff2} are also added on top of TIV_{new} and TIV_{diff1}. The value of f(7) is computed from f(1), while f(6) is derived from f(2), and so on. That can be expressed as in (3).

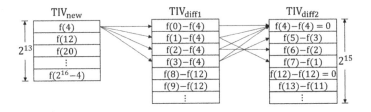

Fig. 5. LUT contents of 3T-TIV for s = 3.

$$
\begin{aligned}
\mathrm{TIV}\,(i) = {}& \mathrm{TIV}_{new}\,(i') + \mathrm{TIV}_{diff1}\left(2^{s-1} * i' + j\right) \\
& + \mathrm{TIV}_{diff2}\left(2^{s-1} * i' + j - 2^{s-1}\right) \text{ for } j \geq 2^{s-1} \\
& \text{where } \mathrm{TIV}_{diff2}\,(k) = \mathrm{TIV}\left(k' + 2^{s-1}\right) \\
& \qquad\qquad\qquad - \mathrm{TIV}\left(k' - 2^{s-1}\right) \\
& \text{and } k' = 2 * integer\left(\tfrac{k}{s^{s-1}}\right) + mod\left(k, 2^{s-1}\right)
\end{aligned}
\tag{3}
$$

In summary, when we group values of function f in groups of 2^s, the first 2^{s-1} values in every group of 2^s use TIV_{new} and TIV_{diff1}, while the second 2^{s-1} values use all three tables. Note that every 2^{s-1} entries of TIV_{diff2} contains one zero entry (i.e., entry 0, 4, 8, etc. in Fig. 5).

2.3   2T-TIV-IMP Microarchitecture

2T-TIV-IMP [8] improves 2T-TIV [11] by reducing the bit width of TIV_{new}. This is possible when every TIV_{diff} entry is summed offline with least significant w_{diff} bits of the corresponding TIV_{new} entry. As a result of this, the least significant w_{diff} bits of all TIV_{new} entries can be zeroed out, hence do not need to be stored, which leads to a bit width of $w_{new} - w_{diff}$ bits as shown in Fig. 6. On the other hand, TIV_{diff} entries become 1-bit larger (the $w_{diff} + 1$ in Fig. 6) if any TIV_{diff} entry overflows when summed with w_{diff} bits of TIV_{new}. If there is no overflow, then the bit width of TIV_{new} stays the same (w_{diff}).

This optimization not only reduces the bit width of TIV_{new} but also makes the subcircuit that sums TIV_{new} and TIV_{diff} smaller, when there is overflow resulting in 1 overlap bit, hence TIV_{diff} with $w_{diff} + 1$ bits. The optimization can even completely eliminate summing when there is no overflow during offline addition performed to compute the new TIV_{diff} values. In that case, summing TIV_{new} and TIV_{diff} can simply be realized by concatenating them.

One thing that is not addressed in [11] is that if TIV_{new} entries are truncated, TIV_{diff} entries may have to be 2-bit larger. For a guarantee on at most 1-bit larger TIV_{diff}, TIV_{new} entries have to be rounded down to $w_{new} - w_{diff}$ bits from w_{new} bits.

Note that the described improvement on 2T-TIV cannot be applied to 3T-TIV because this optimization breaks the symmetry property 3T-TIV uses.

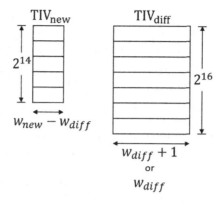

Fig. 6. 2T-TIV-IMP version of Fig. 4.

3 Proposed Methods

In this section, our proposed microarchitectures, FR-dLUT and SR-dLUT as well as their variable length coded variants, namely, FR-dLUT-VL and SR-dLUT-VL, are presented. The critical difference between our approach and the previous state-of-the-art (2T-TIV and variants) is that TIV_{diff} (which we call dLUT) entries store the difference from the neighboring function value instead of the difference from the corresponding value in TIV_{new} as shown in (4) and (5). This allows elimination of TIV_{new} if what is desired is only semi-random access [10]. If fully-random access is desired, we still need a TIV_{new} table but our dLUTs store smaller differences compared to the above explained state-of-the-art. Below, we will describe FR-dLUT, SR-dLUT, FR-dLUT-VL, and SR-dLUT-VL.

3.1 FR-dLUT Microarchitecture

FR-dLUT can be implemented with any number of dLUTs. Figure 7 shows an FR-dLUT with 4 dLUTs, which implements a function f with $w_i = 16$ and $s = 3$ (hence $2^3 = 8$ difference values per each TIV_{new} entry). If TIV_{diff} in 2T-TIV and variants contain differences, dLUTs in FR-dLUT, in a way, contain difference of differences. More specifically, the entries in the dLUTs that correspond to points that neighbor TIV_{new} entries (shown as shaded in Fig. 7) contain the same values as in 2T-TIV, while the other differences are equal to the differences of neighboring TIV_{diff} entries in 2T-TIV (see (4) and (5)).

This allows us to store smaller values (i.e., fewer bits) in our difference tables. However, there is a tradeoff since the summation circuit gets bigger because we have to sum multiple difference values in our case. Note that, in the actual implementation, the last dLUT (i.e., dLUT3 in Fig. 7) has half the number of entries of the other dLUTs. (If logic synthesis is used, logic minimization would do area reduction when unused entries are specified as don't cares.)

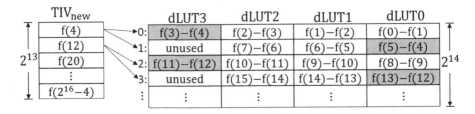

Fig. 7. LUTs of FR-dLUT for $w_i = 16$, $s = 3$ (i.e., $\Delta = 2^{3-1} = 4$).

Equations (4) and (5) are two specific examples of how original TIV values are constructed from TIV_{new} and dLUTs in FR-dLUT. They are based on the tables in Fig. 7.

$$\underbrace{f(10)}_{\text{TIV}} = \underbrace{f(12)}_{\text{TIV}_{new}} + \underbrace{f(11) - f(12)}_{\text{dLUT3}} + \underbrace{f(10) - f(11)}_{\text{dLUT2}} \tag{4}$$

$$\underbrace{f(13)}_{\text{TIV}} = \underbrace{f(12)}_{\text{TIV}_{new}} + \underbrace{f(13) - f(12)}_{\text{dLUT0}} \tag{5}$$

The generalized construction of TIV from TIV_{new} and dLUTs for FR-dLUT method is given in (6) and (7). There are separate construction formulae for odd (7) and even (6) rows of dLUTs. Note that i' and $\text{TIV}_{new}(i')$ below use the definitions given earlier in (1). Also, in the summations of (6) and (7), if the upper index (finish index) is smaller than the lower index (start index), then the summation returns zero.

$$\text{TIV}(i) = \text{TIV}_{new}(i') + \sum_{k=j}^{\Delta-1} \text{dLUT}k(2i') \text{ for } j \leq 2^{s-1}$$
$$\text{where } j = mod(i, 2^s), \text{ and} \tag{6}$$
$$\text{dLUT}k(2i') = \text{TIV}(i' * 2^s + k) - \text{TIV}(i' * 2^s + k + 1)$$

$$\text{TIV}(i) = \text{TIV}_{new}(i') + \sum_{k=0}^{q} \text{dLUT}k(2i' + 1) \text{ for } j > \Delta = 2^{s-1}$$
$$\text{where } j = mod(i, 2^s), q = j - 2^{s-1}, \text{ and} \tag{7}$$
$$\text{dLUT}k(2i' + 1) = \text{TIV}(i' * 2^s + 2^{s-1} + k + 1) - \text{TIV}(i' * 2^s + 2^{s-1} + k)$$

The top-level of FR-dLUT microarchitecture is shown in Fig. 8 for a function f with n-bit input ($w_i = n$), hence 2^n possible output values, k-bit output resolution ($w_o = k$), Δ dLUTs ($\Delta = 2^s$), and d-bit differences. The top-level of FR-dLUT consists of 5 submodules, namely, AddressGenerator, TIV_{new}, a set of dLUTs, DataSelection, and SignedSummation.

If there are Δ dLUTs, where Δ is a power of 2 (to make address generation is simple), TIV_{new} stores k-bit $\text{TIV}(\alpha)$, where $\alpha = \Delta, 3\Delta, 5\Delta, 7\Delta, \ldots,$ $2^n - \Delta$. The number of locations in TIV_{new} is $2^{(n-1)}/\Delta$. We denote the output of TIV_{new} with $mval$ (short for main value). The address line of TIV_{new}, named as $directAddress$, has a bit width of $n - 1 - lg\Delta$ (lg denotes $\log_2$). dLUTs store

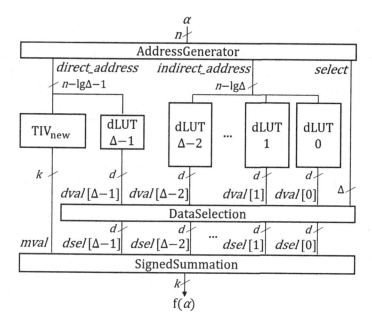

Fig. 8. Top module of FR-dLUT microarchitecture.

d-bit 2's complement differences. The number of locations in "dLUT $\Delta - 1$" is half the number of locations in the other dLUTs and is the same as in TIV_{new}. "dLUT of index $\Delta - 1$" shares the same address bus as TIV_{new}. The bit width of the address lines of other dLUTs, named as *indirectAddress*, is $n - lg\Delta$. The output of a dLUT is named *dval* (stands for "difference value").

AddressGenerator, detailed in Fig. 9, generates three signals: *directAddress*, *indirectAddress*, and *select*. For every 2Δ value in TIV, there is only one entry in TIV_{new} (as well as in "dLUT $\Delta-1$"), thus *directAddress* signal is the $n-1-lg\Delta$ most significant bits of the n-bit input α part-selected as $\alpha[n-1:lg\Delta+1]$. Moreover, for each value in TIV_{new} there are two entries in each dLUT (except "dLUT $\Delta - 1$"), that is why *indirectAddress* signal is the higher $n - lg\Delta$ bits of n-bit input $\alpha(\alpha[n-1:lg\Delta])$.

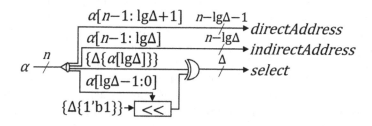

Fig. 9. AddressGenerator module.

Signal named *select* is a thermometer vector, which consists of Δ consecutive ones, each bit representing whether the corresponding *dval* will be summed (by SignedSummation module). Consider (4), which shows how we compute f(10) using the differences in the dLUTs. In the case of f(10), signal *select* is 1100, i.e., *select*[3] = 1 (the MSB) and *select*[2] = 1. Therefore, the outputs of dLUT3 and dLUT2 (find the terms in (4) in Fig. 7) are summed. Positions of signal *select*'s bits match the dLUT locations in Figs. 7 and 8, and the related figures to follow.

Now, consider f(13), which is given by (5). Its *select* vector is 0001 because only dLUT0's output is summed with TIV_{new}. If we were computing f(15), *select* would be 0111. Note that unused dLUT entries always have a *select* bit of 0. On the other hand, f(9) and f(8) would have *select* of 1110 and 1111, respectively. If the α of f(α) we are computing corresponds to an even row of dLUTs (i.e., row 0, 2, 4, etc.), then *select* is a contiguous block of 1's starting with the LSB. On the other hand, If the α corresponds to an odd row (i.e., row 1, 3, 5, etc.), then *select* is a contiguous block of 1's starting with the MSB.

Let us now look at how we generate *select* from α. Figure 9 shows how. Let us apply Fig. 9 to f(10), where Δ is 4, and hence $lg\Delta$ is 2. 10 in base 10 is 1010 in binary and $\alpha[lg\Delta - 1 : 0]$, lower $lg\Delta$ bits of α is binary 10(= 2). We start with $\Delta 1'b1$, i.e., Δ 1's in Verilog notation. That is, binary 1111. Left-shift it by 2 positions to get $\Delta = 4$ bits, and we get 1100. Bitwise XOR that with $\alpha[lg\Delta]$ (bit 2 of α), which is 0, and we get 1100. That is indeed the *select* signal.

Let us do the same for f(13). 13 (α) in base 10 is 1101 in binary. Left-shift 1111 by binary 01 ($\alpha[lg\Delta - 1 : 0]$) positions, and we get 1110. Bitwise XOR that $\alpha[lg\Delta] = 1$, and all bits flip, resulting in 0001, which is the correct value.

DataSelection module shown in Fig. 10 is quite straight forward. It is practically a vector-multiplication unit or some sort of multiplexer as expressed in (8). It multiplies every *dval* (i.e., dLUT output) with the corresponding *select* bit, resulting in signal *dsel*. This can be done with an AND gate provided that each *select* bit duplicated d times (i.e., *dselect*[i]), which happens to be the bit width of *dval* as well as *dsel*.

$$dsel[i] = \begin{cases} dval[i], & \text{if } select[i] = 1 \\ 0, & otherwise \end{cases} \text{ where } i < \Delta = 2^{s-1} \qquad (8)$$

After masking out some *dval*'s and obtaining *dsel*'s, we need to sum *dsel*'s and the corresponding entry from TIV_{new}. That is best done with a Column Compression Tree (CCT). In our work, the summation is done by SignedSummation shown in Fig. 11, which is based on the CCT generator proposed in [13] (called RoCoCo). RoCoCo handles only the summation of unsigned numbers, which is why the following conversion had to be done.

Consider the summation when *mval* is 16 bits, hence $\underline{a}$ and 15 x's in (9). The *dsel*'s are 4 bits each, and there are 4 dLUTs. That is why we have four 4-bit numbers in (9). These numbers are 2's complement, which is why their MSBs are negative. The underbar a, b, c, d, e show that these numbers are negative. In other words, a, b, c, d, e can be 0 or 1, and $\underline{a}$, $\underline{b}$, $\underline{c}$, $\underline{d}$, $\underline{e}$ are either $-0 = 0$ or -1. In summary, we need to perform the summation in (9), where

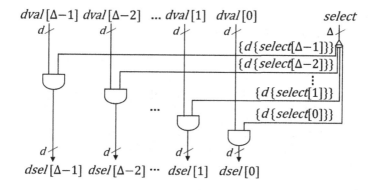

Fig. 10. DataSelection module.

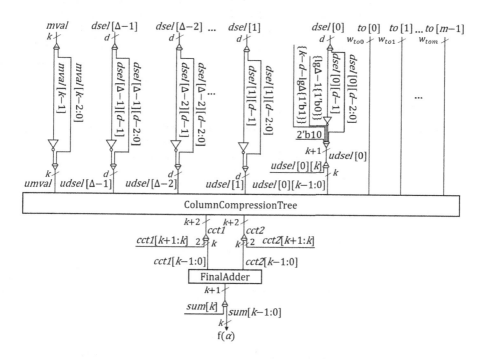

Fig. 11. SignedSummation module.

most bit positions have 0 and 1, while two bit positions have 0, 1, and −1. We can apply unsigned summation techniques only when −1 can be present in the highest bit position, that is, bit position 15 (the bit position a̲). For this, we may sign-extend the 4-bit 2's complement numbers in (9) to 16 bits. Then, the result will also be 16-bit 2's complement, that is, a binary number with negative bit 15. We also have to make sure that the summation does not overflow. If it may, we need to sign-extend all numbers to 17 bits. However, in our case, the sum is also guaranteed to be 16-bit 2's complement.

$$\underline{a}xxxxxxxxxxxxxxxx + \underline{b}xxx + \underline{c}xxx + \underline{d}xxx + \underline{e}xxx \tag{9}$$

$$\begin{aligned}= \ &\bar{a}xxxxxxxxxxxxxxxx + \underline{1}000000000000000 + \bar{b}xxx \\ &+ \underline{1}000 + \bar{c}xxx + \underline{1}000 + \bar{d}xxx + \underline{1}000 + \bar{e}xxx + \underline{1}000\end{aligned} \tag{10}$$

$$\begin{aligned}= \ &\bar{a}xxxxxxxxxxxxxxxx + \bar{b}xxx + \bar{c}xxx + \bar{d}xxx + \bar{e}xxx \\ &+ \underline{1}0111111111100000\end{aligned} \tag{11}$$

$$= \bar{a}xxxxxxxxxxxxxxxx + \bar{b}xxx + \bar{c}xxx + \bar{d}xxx + \underline{1}011111111110\bar{e}xxx \tag{12}$$

$$= \bar{a}xxxxxxxxxxxxxxxx + \bar{b}xxx + \bar{c}xxx + \bar{d}xxx + 011111111110\bar{e}xxx \tag{13}$$

Having said all that, a smarter (more area and speed efficient) approach, is to use the identity in Table 1, and hence, to replace the $\underline{a}$ in (9) with $\bar{a} + \underline{1}$, where $\bar{a}$ is an unsigned 0 or 1 and is the NOT of a. Through this we get (10), which is a summation of variable unsigned numbers and some 2's complement constant numbers with still varying positions for the negative bits. However, these 2's complement constants can be summed offline to obtain a single 16-bit 2's complement number, hence (11). Then, we happen to have negative bits only in bit position 15. Equation (12) does a little optimization by adding the rightmost two numbers in (10) offline and hence combining them into a single number ($\underline{1}011111111110\bar{e}xxx$). Equation (13), on the other hand, eliminates bit position 16 of that combined number as the sum is guaranteed to be 16 bits (bit positions 0 through 15).

Table 1. Proof of $\underline{a} = \bar{a} + \underline{1}$.

$\underline{a}$	$\bar{a} + \underline{1}$
$\underline{0}$	$\bar{0} + \underline{1} = 1 + (-1) = 0$
$\underline{1}$	$\bar{1} + \underline{1} = 0 + (-1) = -1$

The SignedSummation module in Fig. 8 is detailed in Fig. 11. It is composed of CCT and a Final Adder. The little cones in Fig. 11 expose bits of signals and recombine them. The bit-level manipulation before the CCT is a pictorial representation of equations (9) through (13). Note that the number of zeros to the left of $\bar{e}$ does not have to be one as in (13) in the general case. It is $lg\Delta - 1$ zeros (assuming Δ is a power of 2) as in Fig. 11 (look under $dsel[0]$). Also, note that the CCT in Fig. 11 not only sums TIV_{new} and dLUT outputs but also the outputs of TOs (shown in Fig. 2). There is no reason why we should do two separate summations.

3.2   FR-dLUT-VL Microarchitecture

FR-dLUT-VL has a similar microarchitecture to FR-dLUT. They both have Δ dLUTs and a TIV_{new}. The contents of TIV_{new} are the same for both architectures. The difference between FR-dLUT-VL and FR-dLUT is the dLUT contents (compare Fig. 12 with Fig. 7). FR-dLUT-VL's dLUTs store the compressed versions of the differences stored in the FR-dLUT's dLUT. Due to the nature variable length coding, dLUTs of FR-dLUT-VL are wider than those of FR-dLUT. However, unused bits of those dLUTs' entries are don't care, and logic synthesis can optimize them out.

Figure 12 shows the entries of the FR-dLUT-VL with 4 dLUTs for a function with $w_i = 16$ and $w_o = 16$.

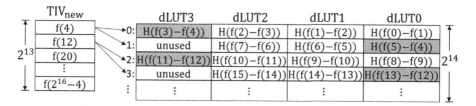

Fig. 12. LUT contents of FR-dLUT-VL implementation for $\Delta = 4$.

It is obvious that one can apply any compression method on dLUT contents. In this work, Huffman coding [12] is chosen for this purpose. For each dLUT, the frequency of the values is calculated. According to the frequency, each value is assigned a Huffman code. Frequency for each value in a dLUT is calculated separately from the other dLUTs. Additionally, due to the encoded values stored in the dLUTs, after each value is read from its respective dLUT, it needs to go through a Decoder module before it can be used in SignedSummation module.

In FR-dLUT-VL microarchitecture, instead of encoding the whole value, a portion of the entry is taken and then the encoding method is applied. For example, if three MSBs are selected, each entry's three MSBs are encoded. To determine the separation point in a dLUT, starting from the two MSBs of an entry to all bits of entry, each possible combination is tested. For each combination, dLUT sizes and the decoder sizes are calculated. Calculation of dLUT sizes are done by adding encoded values' bit width and the bit width of the remaining bits that are not used in the encoding. Among these combinations, the one with the lower bit count is selected for implementation. Pseudocode of separation point selection is shown in Algorithm 1.

Algorithm 1. MSB calculation of FR-dLUT-VL design.

Input: w_i : *input bit width*, w_o : *output bit width*
 1: $LUTsizeMin \leftarrow 2^{w_i} * w_o$
 2: $MSBcountMin \leftarrow 0$
 3: **for** $MSBcountMin \leftarrow 2 \ to \ w_o$ **do**
 4:     compute encoded representation of every entry
 5:     $LUTsize \leftarrow 0$
 6:     $DecoderSize \leftarrow 0$
 7:     **for all** unique encoded value **do**
 8:         $LUTsize \leftarrow LUTsize + (\text{encoded value bit length}) * (\text{frequency of the value})$
 9:         $DecoderSize \leftarrow DecoderSize + (\text{encoded value bit length})$
10:     **end for**
11:     $LUTsize \leftarrow LUTsize + 2^{w_i} * (w_o - MSBcount) + DecoderSize$
12:     **if** $LUTsize < LUTsizeMin$ **then**
13:         $LUTsizeMin \leftarrow LUTsize$
14:         $MSBcountMin \leftarrow MSBcount$
15:     **end if**
16: **end for**

Encoded part of the accessed dLUT entry is sent to the Decoder module. After the encoded value is decoded, output bits and the non-encoded segment of the stored value in dLUT is concatenated and sent to the DataSelection module. Top module of FR-dLUT-VL method is shown in Fig. 13. As shown in Fig. 13, after the values are read from the dLUT (*dvals*), part of *dval* goes through the Decoder, then the decoded value merges with the rest of the *dval* and becomes the decoded difference value (*ddval*) which is the input for the DataSelection module.

3.3   SR-dLUT Microarchitecture

The main idea in SR-dLUT is to eliminate the TIV_{new} in FR-dLUT and instead add dLUT entries on top of the previous function value. This can be done when not only the function f is smooth but also the input (x in f(x)) is smooth. Smoothness of x means the consecutive values of x are close to each other. This is, for example, the case when x comes from a sensor for example in a closed-loop control application, or when x is a timer tick or a smooth function of time. Elimination of TIV_{new} makes SR-dLUT quite competitive in terms of area.

Figure 15 shows the top level of the proposed SR-dLUT microarchitecture, which consists of AddressGenerator (Fig. 16), dLUTs, DataSelection (Fig. 19), and SignedSummation (Fig. 20).

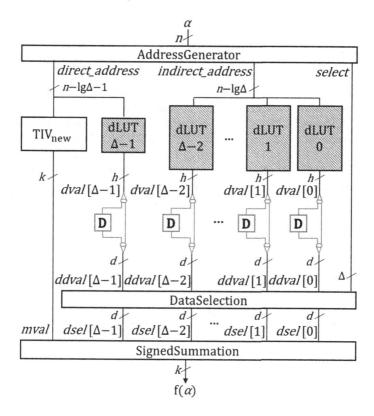

Fig. 13. Top module of FR-dLUT-VL microarchitecture.

Note that Δ of SR-dLUT is not the same as Δ of FR-dLUT. For FR-dLUT, Δ is a purely internal parameter stating the number of dLUTs, and hence, it has nothing to do with how it functions. For SR-dLUT, Δ is not only an internal parameter but also shows how smooth x is, that is the maximum amount of change between consecutive x values.

AddressGenerator module calculates the required addresses of dLUTs for input α. One register stores the previous input value. The previous input is subtracted from the current input to find *magnitude* and *diff_sign* that determines whether the shift direction may be forward or backward. The `thermo` vector is shifted in direction of *diff_sign* as the amount of the magnitude. (Fig. 18) shows the ThermoRegulator block that resolves the overflow issue due to the shift operation. The `thermo` vector is XOR'ed with the shifted `thermo` vector. Then, the output of the first XOR is shifted by 1 in a backward direction, and the resulting signal is named *tmp0*. The specific bit portion of *tmpO* is XOR'ed to determine *select* signals. Similarly, the specific bit portion of thermo is ORed to determine *dLut_Out_En* which is used in control mechanisms of both ThermoRegulator and DataSelection modules. (Fig. 17) shows the AddressSelection module that uses a conditional control mechanism by using *tmp_α* signals as input *tmpO* signals as select to determine addresses of dLUTs.

Note that SR-dLUT has access to much more than $\pm\Delta$ values, since each TIV value is coupled with multiple TO tables in MP. In Fig. 2, we can see that the same TIV value is used for $2^{(\Delta x_1 + \Delta x_2 + \Delta x_3)}$ in the case of $m = 3$. While we can access $2 * \Delta$ different entries in dLUTs, we can compute the function for $2 * \Delta * 2^{(\Delta x_1 + \Delta x_2 + \Delta x_3)}$ different x values. For the reasons explained above, $\Delta = 1$ is a meaningful case for SR-dLUT unlike FR-dLUT.

There are Δ parallel dLUTs that store difference values in SR-dLUT microarchitecture. Figure 14 shows an example of SR-dLUT with 4 dLUTs, which implements a function f with $w_i = 16$. SR-dLUTs store subsequent differences values in-order and each dLUT stores same amount of data with a length of $2^{(n-lg\Delta)}$. Since the SR-dLUT method does not require a TIV_{new} table, we can no longer have half entries for one of the dLUTs like in Fig. 7. In other words, there is no unused memory location in dLUTs.

	dLUT0	dLUT1	dLUT2	dLUT3	
0:	f(1)−f(0)	f(2)−f(1)	f(3)−f(2)	f(4)−f(3)	
1:	f(5)−f(4)	f(6)−f(5)	f(7)−f(6)	f(8)−f(7)	
2:	f(9)−f(8)	f(10)−f(9)	f(11)−f(10)	f(12)−f(11)	2^{14}
3:	f(13)−f(12)	f(14)−f(13)	f(15)−f(14)	f(16)−f(15)	
⋮	⋮	⋮	⋮	⋮	

Fig. 14. LUT contents of SR-dLUT implementation for $w_i = 16$ and $\Delta = 4$.

DataSelection module of SR-dLUT is similar to DataSelection module of FR-dLUT. The difference from FR-dLUT is that there is an extra control mechanism that determines which signal is multiplied by the select signal. The multiplication is implemented using an AND gate. The results of multiplication are *dsel* signals that are connected to the SignedSummation module.

SignedSummation module of SR-dLUT is different from the FR-dLUT's SignedSummation. Since it needs to hold the previous value of the TIV output in a register, and it could not use a single CCT to add dLUT outputs and the TOs output from MP method. Therefore, there is an additional CCT. The first CCT uses the current values of *dsel* and the previous outputs of the CCT. It outputs two values, which are the values generated just before going through the second CCT. The outputs of the first CCT are saved in registers for the next iteration, at the same time used in the second CCT as inputs together with the TOs outputs. As a conclusion, a final adder sums outputs of the second CCT.

One of the differences between SR-dLUT and the earlier version of this work [10] is the form of thermo vector. While the size of thermo vector is 3Δ-bit SR-dLUT, the size of the thermo vector is Δ-bit in [10]. The advantage of using this new form of thermo vector is to find the dLUT addresses easier. In other words, the AdressSelection module in our proposed SR-dLUT is simpler than in [10]. Additionally, we used CCTs for the summation of *dsels* in our proposed SR-dLUT. On the other hand, conventional addition units are used in [10].

Our proposed summation module has an advantage in terms of area when Δ increases because the addition unit in [10] is proportional to Δ.

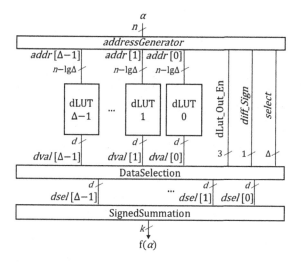

Fig. 15. Top module of SR-dLUT microarchitecture.

3.4 SR-dLUT-VL Microarchitecture

Difference between SR-dLUT-VL and SR-dLUT is similar to the difference between FR-dLUT and FR-dLUT-VL, where values inside dLUTs are partially compressed according the algorithm shown in Algorithm 1. As in FR-dLUT-VL, partial output of dLUTs' (*dval*) in SR-dLUT-VL first go through a decoder, then output of the decoder is concatenated with the remaining part of the *dval*. The concatenated value represents the actual *dval* from the SR-dLUT microarchitecture, which can now be used in the SignedSummation module.

4   Results

In this section, we compare our proposed microarchitectures with the state-of-the-art (T-TIV methods) as well as ConvLUT (i.e., RegularTIV). For each of the 8 TIV construction methods listed above, we wrote a code generator in Perl that generates Verilog RTL for a complete MP design. The code generators take in w_i, w_o, and m (number of MP's TOs) as well as parameters related to the specific TIV construction method such as Δ for our methods.

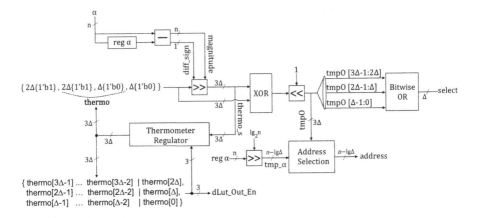

Fig. 16. SR-dLUT AddressGenerator module.

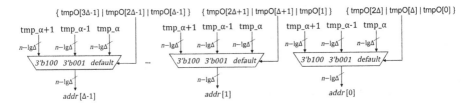

Fig. 17. SR-dLUT AddressSelection module.

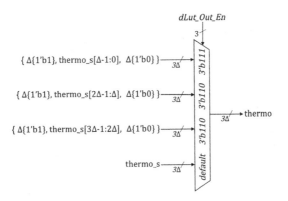

Fig. 18. SR-dLUT ThermometerRegulator module.

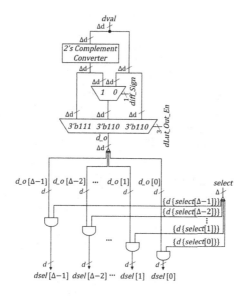

Fig. 19. SR-dLUT DataSelection module.

Generation of the original TIV (RegularTIV) and TOs, i.e., the MP method [6], is done using a tool [14], which is also part of FloPoCo [15]. This tool (written in Java) generates RTL code in VHDL targeting various mathematical functions and parameters W_i, W_o, and m. Our Perl script runs the Java MP generator with W_i, W_o, and m, where W_o shows the precision of the output rather than the bit width of any of the embedded tables. MP generator decides what sizes RegularTIV and TOs have to be for the given set of w_i, w_o, and m. This information is embedded into Table 2 of [6] which, for example, shows that $w_i = 10$ and $w_o = 17$ for the RegularTIV part, when the function is sine and $w_i = 16$, $w_o = 16$, and $m = 1$. Our Perl takes in w_i, w_o, and m, runs the Java MP generator with the input parameters. Then, it parses the VHDL produced by the MP generator, extracts w_i and w_o, and runs the TIV generator. Then, our script produces Verilog, in which we have an MP design equivalent to the input VHDL but the RegularTIV is replaced with our TIV of choice (one of FR-dLUT, FR-dLUT-VL, SR-dLUT, SR-dLUT-VL, 2T-TIV, 2T-TIV-IMP, 3T-TIV). Our script automates verification as well as design. We exhaustively test all function values by comparing the output of the VHDL and Verilog designs.

We generated the above listed 8 designs for $\sin(x)$ ($x = [0, \pi/2[$) and 2^x ($x = [0, 1[$) functions with $w_i = 16$, $w_o = 16$ and $w_i = 24$, $w_o = 24$, both with various m for each resolution. We then synthesized them on to a Xilinx Artix-7 FPGA (more specifically XC7A100T-3CSG324). FR-dLUT and FR-dLUT-VL were synthesized for four Δ values (2, 4, 8, and 16) where SR-dLUT and SR-dLUT-VL synthesized for an additional Δ value, where $\Delta = 1$. For 24-bit resolution, m values of 1, 2, 3, and 4 were implemented. For 16-bit resolution, m values (number of TOs) of 1, 2, and 3 were implemented, since the Java tool at

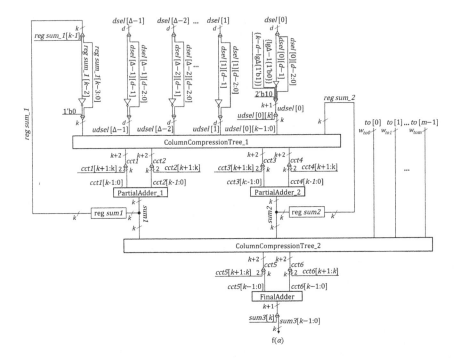

Fig. 20. SR-dLUT SignedSummation module.

[14] gave an error and did not produce any VHDL. Note that all LUTs (Regular-TIV, dLUTs, TIV_{new}, TIV_{diff}, TIV_{diff1}, and TIV_{diff2}) are logic-synthesized instead of instantiating memory blocks. This yields designs with smaller area for all methods including the original TIVs. The synthesis option of Area with High effort is selected for better area minimization in Xilinx ISE.

Tables 2, 3, and 4 show the Area, Time, and Area-Time Product (ATP) results we obtained for sine and exponent function (2^x) for 16-bit resolutions, respectively. Similarly, Tables 5, 6, and 7 show the Area, Time, and ATP results we obtained for 24-bit versions of sine and exponent function. Area results are in terms of FPGA LUTs. Time (also called timing) is the latency (i.e., critical path) of the circuit measured in terms of nanoseconds (ns). ATP simply shows the product of Area (#LUTs) and Time (ns) columns divided by 10^3. ATP of a design shows the tradeoff between area and timing, also ATP is usually correlated with power consumption. The best Area, Time, and ATP results are shaded for each m value in the tables.

In Table 2 through 7, all designs (60 for 16-bit and 80 for 24-bit) are equivalent at MP level. That is, they all produce the same function with the same resolution. However, the TIV microarchitectures are equivalent within the

Table 2. Area results for 16-bit resolution

Function	m	RegularTIV	2T-TIV	2T-TIV-IMP	3T-TIV	Full Random			Semi Random		
						Δ	FR-dLUT	FR-dLUT-VL	Δ	SR-dLUT	SR-dLUT-VL
Sine 16-bit	1	346	343	346	357	2	249	277	1	245	268
						4	249	271	2	285	306
						8	313	349	4	368	380
						16	435	454	8	521	547
	2	188	192	187	212	2	208	215	1	253	257
						4	245	245	2	287	293
						8	320	320	4	362	364
						16	451	448	8	606	610
	3	147	157	159	185	2	181	187	1	205	210
						4	220	222	2	242	244
						8	277	277	4	317	325
						16	402	406	8	550	555
2ˣ 16-bit	1	341	334	N/A	365	2	255	262	1	251	258
						4	265	283	2	293	306
						8	323	320	4	375	382
						16	438	438	8	521	551
	2	196	199	196	230	2	215	214	1	259	262
						4	247	242	2	290	295
						8	321	320	4	368	372
						16	443	442	8	591	588
	3	156	165	156	200	2	191	188	1	217	221
						4	232	231	2	252	257
						8	292	288	4	331	330
						16	420	416	8	553	552

Table 3. Timing results for 16-bit resolution

Function	m	RegularTIV	2T-TIV	2T-TIV-IMP	3T-TIV	Full Random			Semi Random		
						Δ	FR-dLUT	FR-dLUT-VL	Δ	SR-dLUT	SR-dLUT-VL
Sine 16-bit	1	6.69	8.22	6.67	9.66	2	8.46	8.16	1	9.94	11.30
						4	9.09	8.85	2	10.62	15.90
						8	10.58	10.02	4	12.77	12.69
						16	10.97	11.25	8	14.28	14.75
	2	7.34	9.02	7.68	9.47	2	7.82	8.09	1	10.32	10.04
						4	8.35	7.94	2	11.75	11.27
						8	9.16	9.16	4	12.38	12.71
						16	10.98	12.83	8	14.70	15.07
	3	7.39	8.62	7.73	9.15	2	7.73	8.09	1	10.95	10.40
						4	7.77	7.60	2	11.76	12.07
						8	9.70	10.50	4	12.69	12.35
						16	10.40	13.49	8	15.02	14.73
2ˣ 16-bit	1	6.69	8.31	N/A	9.81	2	8.32	7.88	1	10.19	11.11
						4	9.08	9.08	2	10.94	11.42
						8	9.38	9.45	4	12.57	11.42
						16	10.78	11.38	8	14.97	15.20
	2	7.77	9.14	7.65	9.27	2	8.14	8.14	1	9.45	10.07
						4	8.70	8.66	2	12.34	11.81
						8	10.16	12.92	4	12.96	13.08
						16	10.97	16.13	8	15.72	15.38
	3	8.16	8.69	7.81	8.44	2	7.60	7.50	1	10.45	10.50
						4	7.57	7.95	2	12.55	12.70
						8	9.90	12.36	4	13.61	12.43
						16	11.14	13.61	8	15.62	15.90

Table 4. ATP results for 16-bit resolution

Function	m	RegularTIV	2T-TIV	2T-TIV-IMP	3T-TIV	Full Random			Semi Random		
						Δ	FR-dLUT	FR-dLUT-VL	Δ	SR-dLUT	SR-dLUT-VL
Sine 16-bit	1	2.31	2.82	2.31	3.45	2	2.11	2.26	1	2.44	3.03
						4	2.26	2.40	2	3.03	4.86
						8	3.31	3.50	4	4.70	4.82
						16	4.77	5.11	8	7.44	8.07
	2	1.38	1.73	1.44	2.01	2	1.63	1.74	1	2.61	2.58
						4	2.05	1.95	2	3.37	3.30
						8	2.93	2.93	4	4.48	4.63
						16	4.95	5.75	8	8.91	9.19
	3	1.09	1.35	1.23	1.69	2	1.40	1.51	1	2.24	2.18
						4	1.71	1.69	2	2.85	2.95
						8	2.69	2.91	4	4.02	4.01
						16	4.18	5.48	8	8.26	8.18
2^x 16-bit	1	2.28	2.78	N/A	3.58	2	2.12	2.06	1	2.56	2.87
						4	2.41	2.57	2	3.21	3.50
						8	3.03	3.02	4	4.71	4.36
						16	4.72	4.98	8	7.80	8.38
	2	1.52	1.82	1.50	2.13	2	1.75	1.74	1	2.45	2.64
						4	2.15	2.10	2	3.58	3.48
						8	3.26	4.13	4	4.77	4.87
						16	4.86	7.13	8	9.29	9.04
	3	1.27	1.43	1.22	1.69	2	1.45	1.41	1	2.27	2.32
						4	1.76	1.84	2	3.16	3.26
						8	2.89	3.56	4	4.51	4.10
						16	4.68	5.66	8	8.64	8.78

same m. Therefore, it is best to compare the 8 microarchitectures separately for every m. However, out of curiosity we compare all solutions for each of the 4 cases (16-bit sine, 16-bit 2^x, 24-bit sine, 24-bit 2^x).

Tables 2, 3, and 4 implement 16-bit sine and 2^x 60 different ways each, where 57 comes from (RegularTIV + 2T-TIV + 2T-TIV-IMP + 3T-TIV + 4×FR-dLUT + 4×FR-dLUT-VL + 4×SR-dLUT + 4×SR-dLUT-VL) × (3 m values). In the above tables, one result is missing for 2T-TIV-IMP because TIV_{new} and TIV_{diff} in the corresponding 2T-TIV have equal bit width, hence no optimization is possible.

Tables 5, 6, and 7 implement 24-bit sine and 2^x for an additional 20 different ways due to the $m = 4$ case. The Time and ATP of RegularTIV for $m = 1$ are missing for both functions and for 2T-TIV-IMP for 2^x function in Table 6 and 7 because the synthesis tool was not able to complete routing. The tool reported the Area but did not report the timing (Time).

Looking at Tables 2, 3, and 4, we can see that, except for 5 cases (2 in Area, 1 in Timing, and 2 in ATP), the proposed method is surpassed by the RegularTIV and the T-TIV variants for 16-bit implementations. Though in a few cases, our proposed methods offer up to 29%, 4%, 9% improvement in area, timing, ATP, respectively over the state-of-the-art and RegularTIV. The area improvements come from SR-dLUT. Time and ATP improvements come from FR-dLUT and FR-dLUT-VL.

Looking at Tables 5, 6, and 7 show the results for 24-bit implementations of sine and 2^x. In area, SR-dLUT (and a few times SR-dLUT-VL) gives the best results. In timing, FR-dLUT gives the best result in 3 out of the 8 cases

Table 5. Area results for 24-bit resolution

Function	m	RegularTIV	2T-TIV	2T-TIV-IMP	3T-TIV	Full Random			Semi Random		
						Δ	FR-dLUT	FR-dLUT-VL	Δ	SR-dLUT	SR-dLUT-VL
Sine 24-bit	1	54045	36068	51145	30472	2	30907	30801	1	28175	29776
						4	29402	29643	2	28132	29131
						8	28755	29525	4	28088	28240
						16	28461	28942	8	28502	28702
	2	4922	4064	4687	3817	2	3468	3579	1	2923	2956
						4	3291	3378	2	2968	3024
						8	3172	3208	4	3235	3317
						16	3575	3628	8	3589	3652
	3	3015	2673	2890	2572	2	2468	2490	1	2248	2293
						4	2379	2405	2	2376	2424
						8	2525	2545	4	2528	2570
						16	2797	2821	8	2901	2977
	4	2583	2225	2500	2156	2	2083	2103	1	1849	1871
						4	1934	1965	2	1939	1993
						8	2073	2097	4	2099	2135
						16	2345	2993	8	2466	2538
2^x 24-bit	1	57511	57400	55059	48156	2	45849	45721	1	46925	46888
						4	44484	44649	2	43715	45061
						8	43910	43989	4	43371	43271
						16	43765	44004	8	43655	43694
	2	5845	4703	5658	4970	2	4594	4626	1	4126	4126
						4	4283	4331	2	4157	4179
						8	4234	4415	4	4427	4480
						16	4545	4626	8	4798	4880
	3	3512	3341	3434	3235	2	3071	3090	1	2862	2883
						4	3004	3037	2	2989	3022
						8	3117	3120	4	3154	3198
						16	3267	3265	8	3526	3591
	4	2844	2614	2804	2515	2	2390	2413	1	2206	2217
						4	2325	2363	2	2281	2312
						8	2441	2453	4	2452	2492
						16	2345	2572	8	2822	2886

(2 different designs and 4 different ms for each design). FR-dLUT-VL, on the other hand, is the best in 3 cases. 2T-TIV and RegularTIV each are the best in 1 case. In ATP, FR-dLUT, FR-dLUT-VL, and SR-dLUT are best in 4, 3, and 1 case, respectively. Our proposed methods offer up to 23%, 11%, 26% improvement in area, timing, ATP, respectively over the state-of-the-art and RegularTIV.

In summary, proposed methods offer, in greater bit widths, significant improvement in all of Area, Time, and ATP even beyond the state-of-the-art T-TIV methods.

The bar graphs (Fig. 21) summarize the results by comparing RegularTIV, the best of T-TIV methods, the best of FR-dLUT methods, and the best of SR-dLUT methods. RegularTIV and T-TIV methods combined are, on the average, superior to proposed FR-dLUT and SR-dLUT methods in 16-bit results.

Table 6. Timing results for 24-bit resolution

Function	m	RegularTIV	2T-TIV	2T-TIV-IMP	3T-TIV	Full Random Δ	FR-dLUT	FR-dLUT-VL	Semi Random Δ	SR-dLUT	SR-dLUT-VL
Sine 24-bit	1	Can't Route	14.72	24.48	16.49	2	14.77	14.78	1	17.49	17.94
						4	15.62	16.02	2	16.46	17.37
						8	16.39	17.27	4	16.26	17.47
						16	17.51	17.45	8	17.39	18.45
	2	12.44	11.46	11.63	12.18	2	10.70	10.79	1	13.50	12.41
						4	10.45	11.16	2	13.75	13.78
						8	11.01	11.73	4	14.98	15.49
						16	12.27	11.96	8	16.08	16.73
	3	11.71	10.99	11.21	11.59	2	10.01	10.16	1	11.79	13.15
						4	9.80	10.13	2	13.60	14.48
						8	11.16	10.98	4	14.40	14.44
						16	11.21	11.29	8	16.55	16.69
	4	12.49	10.52	11.53	10.87	2	10.11	10.57	1	12.58	12.73
						4	11.29	9.99	2	14.72	14.36
						8	10.89	11.02	4	15.17	15.78
						16	11.51	12.98	8	18.00	17.93
2^x 24-bit	1	Can't Route	16.11	Can't Route	17.92	2	16.14	15.99	1	17.85	18.66
						4	16.95	16.80	2	16.38	17.27
						8	17.43	16.63	4	17.10	17.41
						16	18.45	18.66	8	17.65	17.82
	2	10.86	11.76	12.07	12.15	2	11.13	11.68	1	13.35	12.58
						4	10.98	11.21	2	12.95	12.82
						8	12.42	12.19	4	15.53	15.13
						16	12.37	12.21	8	15.48	15.20
	3	11.06	11.98	11.54	12.21	2	10.38	10.25	1	12.17	12.19
						4	10.71	10.49	2	13.08	13.05
						8	11.35	11.32	4	14.20	14.38
						16	11.59	11.88	8	16.00	15.79
	4	12.15	10.94	11.24	11.42	2	9.72	10.08	1	12.42	12.57
						4	10.27	10.34	2	14.02	14.77
						8	11.58	10.77	4	14.57	15.09
						16	11.51	11.84	8	17.06	16.77

However, in 24-bit results either FR-dLUT or SR-dLUT method ore their variants (-VL) are superior. Only with one m value, we lose to our competition for each function (sine and 2^x), and that is in time metric. In each of the two 24-bit functions, there are 4 cases (i.e., 4 different m's), and 3 metrics (Time, Area, ATP). Therefore, we are speaking of 12 ways to compare the TIV microarchitectures. Ours are better in 11 out of 12.

Figure 21(a) and (b) shows the 16-bit results. For 16 bits, RegularTIV has the best outcome in 8 out of 18 cases, 2T-TIV-IMP is the best in 7 cases, and our proposed metods are the best in 5 cases. Te total is 20, not 18, because there are 2 cases with a tie.

Table 7. ATP results for 24-bit resolution

Function	m	RegularTIV	2T-TIV	2T-TIV-IMP	3T-TIV	Full Random			Semi Random		
						Δ	FR-dLUT	FR-dLUT-VL	Δ	SR-dLUT	SR-dLUT-VL
Sine 24-bit	1	N/A	530.85	1252.13	502.36	2	456.56	455.18	1	492.75	534.15
						4	459.20	474.73	2	462.91	505.86
						8	471.15	509.84	4	456.68	493.38
						16	498.27	505.12	8	495.65	529.49
	2	61.24	46.57	54.53	46.51	2	37.12	38.60	1	39.46	36.70
						4	34.38	37.69	2	40.80	41.66
						8	34.93	37.63	4	48.47	51.38
						16	43.87	43.37	8	57.69	61.08
	3	35.29	29.38	32.40	29.81	2	24.70	25.30	1	26.50	30.16
						4	23.31	24.36	2	32.31	35.10
						8	28.17	27.95	4	36.40	37.11
						16	31.35	31.83	8	48.00	49.70
	4	32.26	23.41	28.81	23.43	2	21.07	22.23	1	23.25	23.81
						4	21.83	19.63	2	28.53	28.62
						8	22.58	23.10	4	31.84	33.68
						16	26.98	38.84	8	44.40	45.51
2^x 24-bit	1	N/A	924.66	N/A	862.91	2	740.09	731.08	1	837.38	875.02
						4	753.91	750.06	2	716.14	778.11
						8	765.44	731.63	4	741.64	753.18
						16	807.55	820.94	8	770.69	778.80
	2	63.47	55.32	68.27	60.37	2	51.14	54.01	1	55.07	51.88
						4	47.04	48.55	2	53.84	53.59
						8	52.58	53.82	4	68.76	67.76
						16	56.24	56.48	8	74.25	74.19
	3	38.84	40.04	39.63	39.50	2	31.89	31.66	1	34.83	35.15
						4	32.17	31.85	2	39.09	39.43
						8	35.37	35.33	4	44.77	45.99
						16	37.87	38.78	8	56.42	56.69
	4	34.55	28.60	31.52	28.72	2	23.24	24.33	1	27.39	27.86
						4	23.88	24.44	2	31.98	34.15
						8	28.28	26.42	4	35.72	37.59
						16	26.98	30.44	8	48.13	48.40

In Fig. 21(c) and (d), due to the routing errors we removed the results of $m = 1$ from the bar graphs. From the remaining m values (2, 3, and 4) we can see that proposed method is the best in terms of area, time, and ATP except for one case where $m = 2$, in which RegularTIV shows better timing results. When comparing FR-dLUT and SR-dLUT, we can see that SR-dLUT has the best performance in terms of area, and FR-dLUT has the best timing. In the current implementation of SR-dLUT, FR-dLUT shows much better timing performance but only falls behind a little in terms of area, that is why for almost all cases, FR-dLUT outperforms SR-dLUT in terms of ATP.

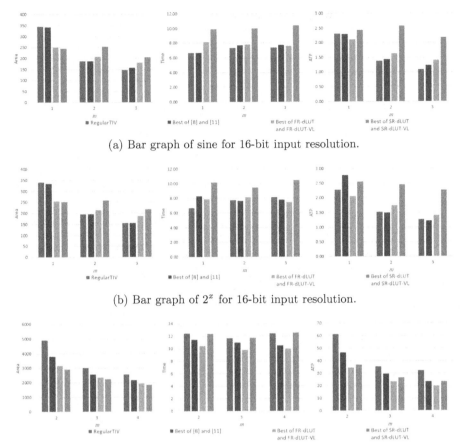

(a) Bar graph of sine for 16-bit input resolution.

(b) Bar graph of 2^x for 16-bit input resolution.

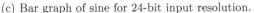

(c) Bar graph of sine for 24-bit input resolution.

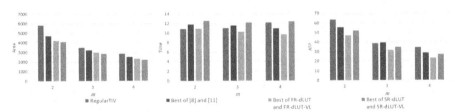

(d) Bar graph of 2^x for 24-bit input resolution.

Fig. 21. Bar graphs of Area, Time, and ATP for sine and 2^x.

5   Conclusion

In this chapter, we have presented lossless LUT compression methods, called
FR-dLUT and SR-dLUT as well as their variants FR-dLUT-VL and SR-
dLUT-VL, which can be used to replace TIVs of Multi-Partite (MP) function

evaluation method among other applications. It is possible to use our methods and the previous state-of-the-art within the context of any LUT-based method for evaluation of smooth functions. Although it is possible to implement these techniques in software, we implemented our proposed methods in hardware (i.e., low-level Verilog RTL) and benchmarked at 16-bit and 24-bit resolutions within MP implementations of sine and exponential.

It was observed that our four methods yield significant and consistent improvements at high resolution (i.e., 24 bits) over the previous state-of-the-art, which we also implemented through design generators for fair comparison. We synthesized the generated designs on FPGA and found that our methods result in up to 29% improvement in area, 11% improvement in latency, and 26% improvement in ATP over the previous state-of-the-art.

This chapter introduces SR-dLUT-VL for the first time. SR-dLUT is, on the other hand, is based on [10]. Yet, it is optimized and plugged into MP here, besides getting compared with the other methods in many cases. Moreover, FR-dLUT and FR-dLUT-VL are presented in greater detail compared to [16].

In future work, SR-dLUT can be modified to utilize pre-fetching. That may make SR-dLUT better than all other techniques in latency at the expense of some additional area. Since SR-dLUT is already efficient in area, it can afford some additional area. However, pre-fetching can also allow memory packing, which can lower area at the expense of some additional latency.

References

1. Lih, L.J.Y., Jong, C.C.: A memory-efficient tables-and-additions method for accurate computation of elementary functions. IEEE Trans. Comput. **62**, 858–872 (2013)
2. Hassler, H., Takagi, N.: Function evaluation by table look-up and addition. In: Proceedings of Symposium on Computer Arithmetic (ARITH), pp. 10–16 (1995)
3. Sarma, D.D., Matula, D.W.: Faithful bipartite ROM reciprocal tables. In: Proceedings of Symposium on Computer Arithmetic (ARITH), pp. 17–28 (1995)
4. Schulte, M.J., Stine, J.E.: Approximating elementary functions with symmetric bipartite tables. IEEE Trans. Comput. **48**, 842–847 (1999)
5. Stine, J.E., Schulte, M.J.: The symmetric table addition method for accurate function approximation. J. VLSI Sig. Proc. **21**, 167–177 (1999)
6. Dinechin, F.D., Tisserand, A.: Multipartite table methods. IEEE Trans. Comput. **54**, 319–330 (2005)
7. Detrey, J., Dinechin, F.D.: Multipartite tables in JBits for the evaluation of functions on FPGA. Diss. INRIA (2001)
8. Hsiao, S.F., Wen, C.S., Chen, Y.H., Huang, K.C.: Hierarchical multipartite function evaluation. IEEE Trans. Comput. **66**, 89–99 (2017)
9. Muller, J.-M.: A few results on table-based methods. Reliable Comput. **5**, 279–288 (1999)
10. Unlu, H., Ozkan, M.A., Ugurdag, H.F., Adali, E.: Area-efficient look-up tables for semi-randomly accessible functions. In: Proceedings of WSEAS Recent Advances in Electrical Engineering, pp. 171–174 (2014)

11. Hsiao, S.F., Wu, P.H., Wen, C.S., Meher, P.K.: Table size reduction methods for faithfully rounded lookup-table-based multiplierless function evaluation. IEEE Trans. Circ. Syst. II Express Briefs **62**, 466–470 (2015)

12. Huffman, D.A.: A method for the construction of minimum-redundancy codes. Proc. IRE **40**, 1098–1101 (1952)

13. Ugurdag, H.F., Keskin, O., Tunc, C., Temizkan, F., Fici, G., Dedeoglu, S.: RoCoCo: row and column compression for high-performance multiplication on FPGAs. In: Proceedings of East-West Design and Test Symposium (EWDTS), pp. 98–101 (2011)

14. Dinechin, F.D.: The multipartite method for function evaluation. http://www.ens-lyon.fr/LIP/Arenaire/Ware/Multipartite/. Accessed 8 Mar 2020

15. Dinechin, F.D., Pasca, B.: Designing custom arithmetic data paths with FloPoCo. IEEE Des. Test Comput. **28**, 18–27 (2011)

16. Gener, Y.S., Gören, S., Ugurdag, H.F.: Lossless look-up table compression for hardware implementation of transcendental functions. In: Proceedings of IFIP/IEEE International Conference on Very Large Scale Integration (VLSI-SoC), pp. 52–57 (2019)

A Predictive Process Design Kit
for Three-Independent-Gate
Field-Effect Transistors

Patsy Cadareanu$^{(\boxtimes)}$, Ganesh Gore, Edouard Giacomin,
and Pierre-Emmanuel Gaillardon

Electrical and Computer Engineering Department, University of Utah,
Salt Lake City, UT, USA
{patsy.cadareanu,ganesh.gore,edouard.giacomin,
pierre-emmanuel.gaillardon}@utah.edu

Abstract. The *Three-Independent-Gate Field-Effect Transistor* (TIGFET) is a promising beyond-CMOS technology which offers multiple modes of operation enabling unique capabilities such as the dynamic control of the device polarity and dual-threshold voltage characteristics. These operations can be used to reduce the number of transistors required for logic implementation resulting in compact logic designs and reductions in chip area and leakage current.

However, the evaluation of TIGFET-based design currently relies on a close approximation for the *Power, Performance, and Area (*PPA) rather than traditional layout-based methods. To allow for a systematic evaluation of the design area, we present here a publicly available Predictive *Process Design Kit* (PDK) for a 10 nm-diameter silicon-nanowire TIGFET device. This work consists of a SPICE model and full custom physical design files including a *Design Rule Manual*, a *Design Rule Check*, and *Layout Versus Schematic* decks for Calibre®. We validate the design rules through the implementation of basic logic gates and a full-adder and compare extracted metrics with the FreePDK15nm^{TM} PDK. We show 26% and 41% area reduction in the case of an XOR gate and a 1-bit full-adder design respectively. Applications for this PDK with respect to hardware security benefits are supported through a differential power analysis study.

1 Introduction

In the past decade, the semiconductor industry has seen exponential growth in computationally intensive applications such as artificial intelligence, augmented reality, and machine learning. Scaling down the standard semiconductor technologies based on standard *Metal-Oxide-Semiconductor Field-Effect Transistors* (MOSFET) devices has been the primary solution for achieving these performance requirements. However, with a reduction in transistor size, undesired short-channel effects such as increased leakage current start dominating the device operation. Several 3D semiconductor structures such as *Fin Field-Effect Transistor* (FinFET) or *Gate-All-Around* (GAA) configurations have been proposed to enhance channel electrostatic control and reduce leakage current [1]. However, their fabrication in the sub-10 nm regime is increasingly difficult and

© IFIP International Federation for Information Processing 2020
Published by Springer Nature Switzerland AG 2020
C. Metzler et al. (Eds.): VLSI-SoC 2019, IFIP AICT 586, pp. 307–322, 2020.
https://doi.org/10.1007/978-3-030-53273-4_14

expensive [2] and so there is a need to investigate devices which can be scaled functionally rather than physically.

To continue supporting ever-increasing performance demand substantial research has been devoted to novel semiconductor structures with enhanced functionality [3–5]. Device level innovations such as novel geometries and materials are used in improved logic devices including Spintronics-based FETs, Tunnel FETs, and Ferroelectric FETs [6, 7].

Of particular interest are *Multiple Independent Gate FETs* (MIGFETs), which are Schottky-based devices using additional gate terminals to configure the device to different modes of operation [8–11]. Due to their compatibility with the standard CMOS manufacturing process and their increased logic benefits, these devices are considered promising both as superlatives and alternatives to conventional MOSFETs. A wide range of studies showing the benefits of these devices have been carried out in different domains including digital, analog, and RF design [12, 13].

One promising MIGFET device is the *Three-Independent-Gate FET* (TIGFET) [14], which introduces two gate terminals called *Polarity Gates* (PG) to a traditional FET structure. The PG terminals are used to modulate Schottky-barriers at the source and drain of the FET and effectively allow for a dynamic configuration of the device to *n*- or *p*-type. A massive benefit to these devices is their extremely low leakage current when compared to standard MOSFETs, which is due to the current cutoff provided by the Schottky-barriers. Meanwhile, the ability to dynamically control device polarity gives TIGFETs a higher expressive logic capability than conventional devices, resulting in a compact logic gate implementation and lower leakage current per cell. As a result, the circuit-level benefits of TIGFETs have been largely investigated in literature in the past few years and have shown promising implementations for a wide range of logic circuits such as multiplexers [15], adders [16], flip-flops [17] or for use in differential power attack mitigation techniques with reduced power line variation [18].

However, performance evaluation of TIGFET-based design currently relies on an area approximation rather than traditional layout-based methods since no TIGFET-based *Process Design Kit* is publicly available.

In this work, we introduce an open-source TIGFET PDK available online [19], created for simple integration with Cadence® Virtuoso.

The *Design Rule Manual* for the proposed PDK is derived from previously fabricated MIGFET devices [4] and the publicly available FreePDK15nm™ [20]. Our PDK consists of a SPICE Verilog-A model for a 10 nm diameter *Silicon Nanowire* (SiNW) TIGFET and includes full custom design files, *Design Rule Check* (DRC), and *Layout Versus Schematic* (LVS) decks. The availability of this PDK will allow universities and researchers to explore the benefits of TIGFETs in various domains. The benefits of the proposed PDK are as follows:

- It provides design rules and a layout consistency check for a more reliable and reproducible system design,
- It allows accurate metric evaluations, such as area or delay, of TIGFET-based designs,
- It enables the system designer to explore higher-level designs using state-of-the-art TIGFET circuit techniques,
- It showcases the area benefits of compact TIGFET gates for an XOR and a 1-bit full adder.

- It provides a detailed regular cell placement method which helps mitigate additional routing overhead.

The rest of this chapter is organized as follows: Sect. 2 provides an overview of TIGFET technology including its circuit-level opportunities. Section 3 introduces the TCAD work and resulting electrical SPICE model of the proposed TIGFET device. Section 4 describes the physical TIGFET design and briefly describes the DRC and LVS decks. Section 5 evaluates the regular layout technique for TIGFETs, and Sect. 6 includes a differential power analysis which further showcases the benefits of TIGFET-based applications. Finally, Sect. 7 concludes the chapter.

2   Technical Background

In this section, we establish the necessary background to understand TIGFET technology. We then briefly review circuit-level opportunities brought by TIGFET devices and discuss publicly available design kits.

2.1   TIGFET Operation

The TIGFET is composed of drain and source contacts as well as three independent gate contacts, as shown in Fig. 1 (a). The *Control Gate* (CG) controls the potential barrier in the channel in the same manner the gate contact works in a conventional MOSFET device and turns the device *on* or *off*.

The *Polarity Gates* (PG) at the source and drain modulate their respective Schottky-barriers, selecting the type of carriers (electrons or holes) which will enter the channel and dominate the current flow; the ability to make this selection is called device reconfigurability and is unique to Schottky-barrier-based devices. TIGFET devices have been successfully fabricated with several channel technologies such as FinFET [21], 2D materials [22], and SiNW [23]. In this paper, we will consider a SiNW TIGFET which is fabricated using a fully CMOS-compatible process. A scanning electron microscopy picture of a previously fabricated TIGFET device with labeled terminals is seen in Fig. 1 (b) [23].

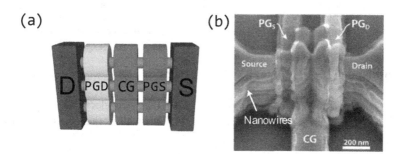

Fig. 1. (a) TIGFET general structure; (b) scanning electron microscopy image of a fabricated TIGFET device comprising of four vertically stacked silicon nanowires [23].

2.2   Circuit-Level Opportunities

Due to their reconfigurability, TIGFETs show richer switching capabilities per given transistor and this ability is used to implement compact logic gates. For instance, as shown in Fig. 2 (a), a TIGFET NAND requires 1 fewer transistor than its CMOS counterpart. Similarly, as illustrated in Fig. 2 (b) and (c), while a CMOS two-input XOR and three-input majority gate require 8 and 10 transistors respectively, using TIGFETs reduces this amount to only 4 transistors in both cases. This leads to an area reduction, as is demonstrated in Sect. 5. Note also that a two-input XOR, three-input XOR, and three-input majority gate can all be made from the same four TIGFET transistors by adjusting the terminal voltages [10]. This essentially means that a TIGFET circuit does not need to be programmed until after it has been fabricated and can also be reprogrammed for multiple differing functions, a feat not possible with standard CMOS technology.

2.3   Publicly Available Physical Design Kits

Previous PDKs based on predictive technologies include the FreePDK45nm[TM] [24] and FreePDK15nm[TM] [20] which present the design rules and standard cell library [25] for planar and FinFET CMOS technologies respectively. In addition, the ASAP7 PDK [26] was created to describe the aggressive 7 nm FinFET technology node. The set of realistic assumptions included in the ASAP7 PDK simplifies its use in an academic setting. Most recently, an add-on for the FreePDk15nm[TM] was proposed for CMOS-compatible Resistive RAM technology [27].

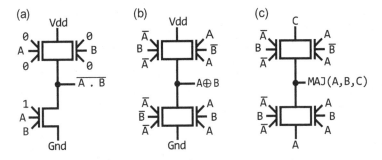

Fig. 2. TIGFET compact gates: (a) 2-input NAND; (b) 2-input XOR; (b) 3-input majority gate.

3   Proposed TIGFET Device Properties

In this section, we evaluate the proposed TIGFET device electrical properties and present the TIGFET SPICE model used in the PDK as well as the TCAD model upon which it is based.

3.1 Device TCAD Work

TCAD simulations of a 10 nm SiNW TIGFET device with gates of 10 nm and separations of 10 nm were performed in Synopsys Sentaurus. Nickel silicide-silicon is the assumed Schottky barrier contact and the dielectric layer is HfO_2 with a thickness of 8 nm. Electrical properties, such as the ON-current (I_{ON}), the OFF-current (I_{OFF}) and the nominal voltage V_{DD} were extracted from these simulations. The maximum current drive for n-type operation is 90.20 $\mu A/\mu m$ and for p-type is 89.25 $\mu A/\mu m$, as seen in Fig. 3. Thanks to the Schottky barrier cutoff, I_{OFF} is extremely low at 3.3 nA/μm and 0.1 nA/μm for n- and p-type operation respectively. Further work and discussion of this simulation is available in [28].

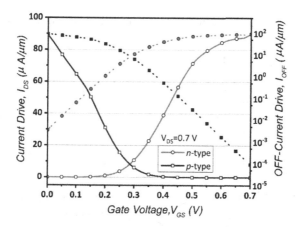

Fig. 3. I_{DS}-V_{GS} characteristics of the simulated device at $V_{DD} = 0.7$ V. The switching is centered around $V_{GS} = 0.3$ V. The linear scale results show the maximum ON-current and the log scale results show the minimum OFF-current.

These current drives are approximately 10 X lower than the previous 22 nm TIGFET device simulations [7] which used a supply voltage of 1.2 V. This loss is primarily due to the 0.7 V supply voltage used in the 10 nm devices as is standard for technology at this node. This lowered supply voltage is necessary for fair comparisons with the corresponding CMOS technology.

The real benefit to these devices is their reconfigurability, as used in Sect. 5 and this is enhanced with this new model: the 10 nm TIGFET device was designed in TCAD to be extremely symmetric in its ON-current drives for p-type and n-type switching. This is seen in Fig. 4 which compares the 10 nm TIGFET TCAD device to the previously used 22 nm TIGFET TCAD device using normalized drain current and gate voltage characteristics; from this plot we can see a decrease in asymmetry from approximately 9% with the 22 nm simulations to less than 1% with this new model.

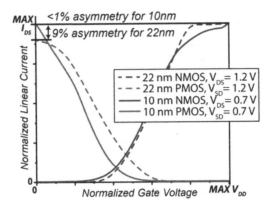

Fig. 4. Normalized I_{DS}-V_{GS} characteristics of the simulated 10 nm and 22 nm TIGFET devices.

3.2 SPICE Verilog-A Model

The TCAD simulation results have been used to develop a TIGFET macro model in Verilog-A, as shown in Fig. 5.

The nonlinear current source $I(D, S)$ is modeled using TIGFET macro model

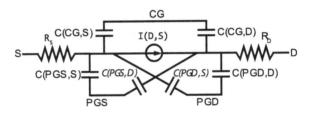

Fig. 5. Macro model of a SiNW TIGFET.

approach and a function of the drain, source and all three gate voltages. The table stores the current $I(D, S)$ for each bias point combination applied on the device terminals. We chose a bias point granularity of 0.1 V on the PG gates at the source and drain and the CG terminal, and a 0.05 V bias on the drain terminal, totaling to 67,536 bias points. For other bias points, the model uses linear interpolation and extrapolation techniques. Linear interpolation provides relatively better convergence in transient simulation and avoids any spurious false peaks. To model transient behavior, the capacitance between each terminal pair is extracted by AC simulations from TCAD and the average value obtained under all the bias conditions is considered in the proposed model. The terminal access resistances are also extracted using TCAD simulations. The coupling capacitance between gate terminals is very small and omitted from the model. Since TIGFETs are built using vertically stacked SiNWs, as explained in Sect. 2, the proposed SPICE model assumes a single SiNW by default. To change the number of wires in the stack, a *nw* design parameter can be changed. A comparison of SPICE model and TCAD simulation result indicates less than 0.1% mean square error for both DC and transient simulations.

4 TIGFET Physical Design

In this section, we briefly present the TIGFET fabrication process requirements and corresponding constraints. Then, we summarize the sets of DRC and LVS rules. Finally, we discuss the implications of a TIGFET-based physical design.

4.1 Process Assumptions

The fabrication of a SiNW-based TIGFET is completely CMOS-compatible and straightforward, the most challenging step for fabricating these devices at the 10 nm node being patterning. Each TIGFET has three independent gates, which are patterned with a spacing of 15 nm and reliable fabrication of these features is required for correct functionality of the device. The traditional 193 nm (ArF) lithography process is inadequate for realizing features this small, and the most advanced lithography process of *Extreme Ultraviolet Lithography* (EUVL) is as yet prohibitively expensive for high volume production [29]. An alternative option to the latter is *Dual Patterning Lithography* (DPL) at 193 nm. DPL allows patterning at half the pitch size of the corresponding single patterning technique [29]. Hence, in the proposed PDK, we consider DPL for patterning of the gate layer and the first four metal layers. Every DPL layer requires decomposition before the fabrication process. In commercial PDKs this decomposition is achieved by providing different colors for each DPL layer. When two patterns have to be drawn in the same layer with spacing smaller than the pitch, double patterning is realized by using two separate colors which correspond to different masks. These two separate masks are then connected together by inserting a stitch to form an electrical connection between them [30]. A minimum number of stitches must be introduced into each layer to stall printability degradation [31]. Process modeling is also recommended to ensure correct decomposition of layers. In an academic setting, placement and design using all the constraints of the DPL technique can get increasingly difficult. The layer decomposition task is better automated using many proposed layout decomposition EDA tools [32]. To simplify the use of the proposed PDK, we represent each DPL layer with a single color. This results in the gate layer and the first four metal layers being represented using a single color. To simplify further, this PDK does not provide any additional layers for threshold adjustment or a gate cut mask. The proposed PDK's *Back-End-Of-Line* (BEOL) process supports ten layers of metal. The list of key layers is given in Table 1.

Table 1. List of key layers in the proposed PDK.

Layer name	Drawn width (nm)	Pitch (nm)
Active	166	32
GATE	20	64*
PG-CG	20	35
SDC	28	40
GC	56	40
IL	24	40
V0	28	36
Metal 1-4	28	36
VM0 5-10	28	36
Metal 5-10	56	72
VM5 5-10	56	72

*Pitch between the gate of two different devices.

4.2   Single Device Layout and Dimensions

The layout of a single TIGFET is shown in Fig. 6. As discussed earlier, all three gates of the TIGFET are drawn using the same color to represent the gate layer; these are separated later using EDA tools for fabrication of separate PG and CG masks. Vertical strips of polysilicon are patterned uniformly across the chip with a *Contacted Poly Pitch* (CPP) of

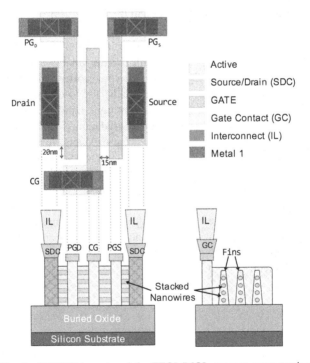

Fig. 6. TIGFET layout and the FEOL/MOL process cross-section.

44 nm. The gate cut mask generated using the automated EDA tools is used to cut the excess polysilicon from around the active region with a 20 nm extension. Figure 6 shows the cross-section view of the *Front-End-Of-Line* (FEOL) and *Middle-Of-Line* (MOL) of the proposed predictive process model. Contact to all the gate terminals is made using the *Gate Contact* (GC) layer. Source and drain terminals of the device are connected using *Source Drain Connect* (SDC) layer. Both GC and SDC layers are connected to the first layer of the metal using *Interconnect Layer* (IL).

The drain and source terminals of the device have a height and width of 100 nm and 30 nm respectively. The side view in Fig. 6 shows the channel as formed with a maximum stack of four SiNW. Based on the height of the active region, multiple such stacks can be formed with a pitch of 40 nm. Figure 6 depicts a device with a total of 5 stacks of 4 nanowires. Some of the other key layers are summarized in Table 1, along with the drawn width and minimum pitch.

4.3 Cell Layout and DTCO Consideration

Meeting fabrication yield and cost targets are particularly challenging tasks when fabricating new semiconductor structures. *Design for Manufacturability* (DFM) and *Design Technology Co-optimization* (DTCO) are widely used techniques to ensure successful device fabrication using novel processes. Using the DTCO approach, manufacturing yield and device density can be improved by customizing the layouts of some widely used structures [26, 33]. In the traditional fabrication processes, the DTCO approach is used for optimizing the highly regular pattern such as an SRAM cell. The SRAM pattern can be carefully tuned using actual manufacturing data allowing tighter tolerance, higher device density, but very few variations in the layout.

In the case of TIGFET-based designs, transistors connected in series (i.e., with shared source and drain contacts) and tied polarity gates are very common, and these are called grouped devices. We use the DTCO approach to optimize the layout of the grouped devices. Figure 7 shows the schematic and the layout of two grouped TIGFETs. The polarity gates of both devices are shorted together by allowing horizontal routing of the gate layer to the top of the device. The DRC rule for vertical spacing of gates with different potentials is compromised to achieve higher device density. This structure is also very helpful in designing a regular layout using TIGFET devices, as will be shown in Sect. 5.

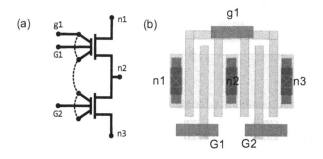

Fig. 7. TIGFET grouped transistors: (a) schematic; (b) layout view.

4.4   Sea-of-Tile Implementation

The enhanced functionality of TIGFETs comes at the cost of two additional gate terminals per device. Using traditional layout and routing methods, the TIGFET-based physical design may not give the best possible results due to the addition of these extra gates. Here, we explore some techniques to mitigate the additional routing complexity. In particular we look at the dual metal power grid routing and then explore the novel layout approach for increasing regularity of the TIGFET-based design, which was first proposed in [34, 35].

At advanced technology nodes, one of the prerequisites for robustness is a layout regularity. This makes the design less sensitive to process variation and improves the yield of fabrication. *Sea-of-Tiles* (SoT) is a fully configurable architecture in which an array of logic tiles is uniformly spread across the chip. A tile is an array of TIGFET devices in which the devices are placed horizontally and adjacent to each other with shorted polarity gates in case they share the same logic on polarity gates. If the devices share the same logic on the control gate, they are aligned vertically with shorted control gates. Based on the number of devices grouped together, many different sizes of tiles are possible. In this work, we will consider $Tile_{G1}$ and $Tile_{G2}$ [35], whose corresponding schematics are shown in Fig. 8 (a) and (b) respectively.

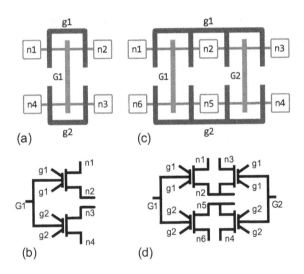

Fig. 8. Logic tiles: (a) $Tile_{G1}$ stick diagram; (b) $Tile_{G1}$ schematic; (c) $Tile_{G2}$ stick diagram; (d) $Tile_{G2}$ schematic.

Each tile can be configured for different logical operation based on the input provided to its nodes (n1–n6) and gates (g1, g2, G1, and G2).

Many other configurations are possible using $Tile_{G2}$, and these are listed in Table 2.

Table 2. Area comparison of tile-based logic gates implementation.

Logic gate	Tile	Area TIGFET (μm^2)	Area CMOS (μm^2)
1-bit HA	$2 \times Tile_{G2}$	0.34	0.59
XNOR2	$Tile_{G2}$	0.37	0.49
NAND2	$Tile_{G2}$	0.17	0.15
NOR2	$Tile_{G2}$	0.17	0.15
INV	$Tile_{G1}$	0.10	0.10
BUF	$Tile_{G1}$	0.10	0.10

We implement $Tile_{G1}$ and $Tile_{G2}$ using the proposed design rules in Cadence® Virtuoso, as shown in Fig. 9.

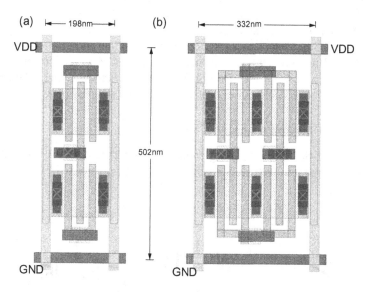

Fig. 9. SoT layout using the proposed PDK: (a) $Tile_{G1}$ (Area = 0.10 μm^2); (b) $Tile_{G2}$ (Area = 0.17 μm^2).

4.5   Grid Based Power Routing

A TIGFET device can be configured as a pull-up (p-type) network by applying logic 0 to its polarity gates or a pull-down (n-type) by applying logic 1. This additional requirement creates a sparse connection of V_{DD}/GND connectivity in the cell. Consequently, traditional power distribution schemes with alternate V_{DD} and GND lines are not efficient. As proposed in [35], we used two metal approach to route power around the cell. Figure 8 shows the horizontal V_{DD} and vertical GND lines. Comparison of this approach with tradition single metal based power routing has been demonstrated in [34] and shows delay reduction by approximately 28% with minimum routing complexity.

5   PDK Showcases

In this section, we showcase the area benefits of TIGFET technology by presenting two TIGFET compact logic cells designed using the proposed PDK.

5.1   Compact XOR Cell

Using the higher expressive logic capabilities of the TIGFET device, it is possible to build a compact XOR gate. As illustrated in Fig. 2 (b), a TIGFET-based XOR gate only requires 4 transistors, whereas its CMOS counterpart requires 8 transistors. This compact implementation of a TIGFET-based XOR gate results in an area benefit and leakage power reduction. It is interesting to note that the TIGFET design requires a single device for a pull-up or a pull-down operation, unlike CMOS which requires a series of two transistors. As a result, it reduces the total resistance in the charging and discharging load paths. A TIGFET-based XOR is implemented using 2 X $Tile_{G2}$. One is configured as two individual inverters, and another as an XOR gate, as shown in Fig. 2. The complete layout of the CMOS-based XOR gate. The resulting area of the TIGFET-based XOR cell is 0.37 μm^2, which is $\sim 26\%$ smaller than the CMOS implementation which resulted in an area of 0.49 μm^2. Due to its symmetric structure, the TIGFET-based XNOR has the same area and power benefits. This work was previously shown in [36].

5.2   Compact 1-Bit Full Adder

We also built a 1-bit full adder using compact TIGFET-based XOR and MAJ logic gates, and compared it to its CMOS counterpart [25], the schematic of which is seen in Fig. 10.

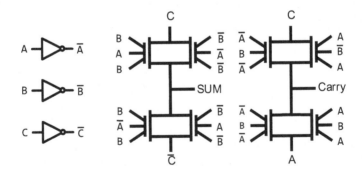

Fig. 10. TIGFET-based compact implementation of a 1-bit full adder.

The layout of the TIGFET (Area = 0.66 μm^2) and CMOS-based (Area = 1.13 μm^2) full adder are shown in Fig. 11 (a) and (b) respectively. As explained, the richer switching capabilities of TIGFET devices allow them to realize the same CMOS logic function while reducing the number of devices. In the case of the 1-bit full adder, this results in a 41% area reduction. [36]

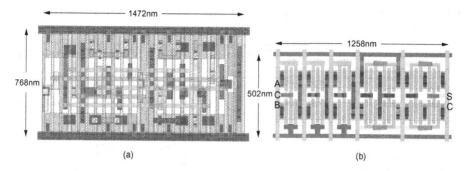

Fig. 11. Layout view of a full adder: (a) CMOS; (b) TIGFET.

Similar to the XOR and MAJ gates, various logic functions can be realized by configuring $Tile_{G1}$ and $Tile_{G2}$.

6 Differential Power Analysis Resilience Study

Simulations for power line variation and integral charge were performed using the TIGFET 10 nm PDK for various TIGFET-based logic gate designs including XOR-only, XOR-XNOR, DCVSL-XOR, NAND HP, NAND LL, DCVSL-NAND, NOR HP, NOR LL, and DCVSL-NOR. These results were then compared to simulations performed using a PTM 10 nm LSTP CMOS design. Table 3 shows these simulation results.

Power line variation was lower for almost all TIGFET-based gate configurations (the only exception being for the XOR-XNOR gate). One of the most impressive of these was for a TIGFET-based NAND design which showed 2 X the power line variation when compared to its CMOS-based counterpart. The integral charge was similarly consistently and significantly lower for the TIGFET-based design, with benefits of over 7 X being seen for the DCVSL-XOR simulations. These two metrics are extremely important in designing circuits that are resilient to hardware attacks.

Table 3. Power line variation and integral charge studies for TIGFET-based designs compared to CMOS-based designs.

		TIGET 10 nm			PTM 10 nm LSTP CMOS-CMG		
XOR		*TIGFET XOR*	*TIGFET XOR-XNOR*	*TIGFET DCVSL XOR*	*CMOS XOR*	*CMOS XOR-XNOR*	*CMOS DCVSL NOR*
		I_{SUPPLY} (μA)					
	Power Line Variation (%)	21.16	5.81	0.58	57.46	4.51	38.52
	Integral Charge (10^{-16} C) (|Max-Min|)	0.65	0.01	1.05	0.76	0.17	7.34
NAND		*TIGFET NAND HP*	*TIGFET NAND LP*	*TIGFET DCVSL NAND*	*CMOS 4T NAND*	*CMOS DCVSL NAND*	
		I_{SUPPLY} (μA)					
	Power Line Variation (%)	34.55	32.38	18.64	51.77	24.64	
	Integral Charge (10^{-16} C) (|Max-Min|)	0.23	0.11	0.96	0.94	1.65	
NOR		*TIGFET NOR HP*	*TIGFET NOR LP*	*TIGFET DCVSL NOR*	*CMOS NOR*	*CMOS DCVSL NOR*	
		I_{SUPPLY} (μA)					
	Power Line Variation (%)	34.55	32.38	18.64	51.77	24.64	
	Integral Charge (10^{-16} C) (|Max-Min|)	0.05	0.17	0.95	1.61	1.89	

7 Conclusion

This work has exhibited a predictive PDK for a 10 nm-diameter SiNW TIGFET. The design kit is derived using TCAD simulations and realistic assumptions made for large-scale production of TIGFET-based systems. We detailed key assumptions made while designing the PDK and derived the set of design rules for physical design in Cadence® Virtuoso. Using the TIGFET PDK, we evaluated previously proposed grouped transistor and grid-based power-line distribution overhead introduced because of the TIGFET's additional terminals. We validated the design rules by implementing an XOR and a 1-bit full adder, and compared those with the FreePDK15nm™ CMOS process, which shows 26% and 41% area reduction respectively. The TIGFET PDK was also used to compare against CMOS-based logic cell designs for power variation analysis, and it was showed to be optimal when compared to the CMOS designs for almost all logic cells.

Acknowledgements. This work was supported by the NSF Career Award number 1751064, and the SRC Contract 2018-IN-2834.

References

1. Cui, Y., et al.: High performance silicon nanowire field effect transistors. Nano Lett. **3**(2), 149–152 (2003)
2. Colinge, J.P.: FinFET and Other Multigate Transistors, 1st edn. Springer, Cham (2007). https://doi.org/10.1007/978-0-387-71752-4
3. Sutar, S., et al.: Graphene p-n junctions for electron-optics devices. In: IEEE DRC (2013)
4. De Marchi, M., et al.: Polarity control in double-gate, gate-all-around vertically stacked silicon nanowire FETs. In: IEDM Tech. Dig., vol. 8, no. 4, pp. 1–4 (2012)
5. Heinzig, A., et al.: Reconfigurable silicon nanowire transistors. Nano Lett. **12**(1), 119–124 (2011)
6. Rai, S., et al.: Emerging reconfigurable nanotechnologies: can they support future electronics?. In: Proceedings of ICCAD, p. 13 (2018)
7. Romero-González, J., et al.: BCB evaluation of high-performance and low-leakage three-independent-gate field-effect transistors. IEEE JXCDC **4**(1), 35–43 (2018)
8. Trommer, J., et al.: Reconfigurable nanowire transistors with multiple independent gates for efficient and programmable combinational circuits. In: DATE, pp. 169–174 (2016)
9. Mathew, L., et al.: Multiple independent gate field effect transistor (MIGFET) – multi-fin RF mixer architecture, three independent gates (MIGFET-T) operation and temperature characteristics. VLSI Technology (2005)
10. Rai, S., et al.: Designing efficient circuits based on runtime-reconfigurable field-effect transistors. IEEE TVLSI **27**(3), 560–572 (2019)
11. Ben-Jamaa, M.H., et al.: An efficient gate library for ambipolar CNTFET logic. IEEE TCAS **30**(2), 242–255 (2011)
12. Gaillardon, P.-E., et al.: Three-independent-gate transistors: opportunities in digital, analog and RF applications. In: LATS (2016)
13. Rostami, M., et al.: Novel dual-Vth independent-gate FinFET circuits. In: ASPDAC (2010)
14. Zhang, J., et al.: Configurable circuits featuring dual-threshold-voltage design with three-independent-gate silicon nanowire FETs. IEEE TCAS I **61**(10), 2851–2861 (2014)

15. Giacomin, E., et al.: Low-power multiplexer designs using three-independent-gate field effect transistors. In: NanoArch (2017)
16. Romero-Gonzalez, J., et al.: An efficient adder architecture with three-independent-gate field-effect transistors. In: IEEE ICRC (2018)
17. Tang, X., et al.: TSPC flip-flop circuit design with three-independent-gate silicon nanowire FETs. IEEE ISCAS (2014)
18. Giacomin, E., et al.: Differential power analysis mitigation technique using three-independent-gate field effect transistors. VLSI-SoC (2018)
19. A 10-nm TIGFET PDK (2019). https://github.com/LNIS-Projects/TIGFET-10nm-PDK
20. Bhanushali, K., et al.: FreePDK15: an open-source predictive process design kit for 15nm FinFET technology. IEEE ISPD (2015)
21. Zhang, J., et al.: A schottky-barrier silicon FinFET with 6.0 mV/dec subthreshold slope over 5 decades of current. IEDM Tech. Dig., pp. 339–342 (2014)
22. Resta, G.V., et al.: Doping-free complementary logic gates enabled by two-dimensional polarity-controllable transistors. ACS Nano **12**, 7039–7047 (2018)
23. Zhang, J., et al.: Polarity-controllable silicon nanowire transistors with dual threshold voltages. IEEE TED **61**(11), 3654–3660 (2014)
24. Stine, J.E., et al.: FreePDK: an open-source variation- aware design kit. In: IMSE (2007)
25. Martins, M., et al.: Open cell library in 15nm FreePDK technology. IEEE ISPD (2015)
26. Clark, L.T., et al.: ASAP7: a 7-nm FinFET predictive process design kit. Microelectron. J. **53**, 105–115 (2016)
27. Giacomin, E., et al.: A resistive random access memory addon for the NCSU FreePDK 45nm. IEEE TNANO **18**(1), 68–72 (2018)
28. Cadareanu, P., et al.: Nanoscale three-independent-gate transistors: geometric TCAD Simulations at the 10nm-Node. In: IEEE NMDC (2019)
29. Finders, J., et al.: Double patterning lithography: the bridge between low k1 ArF and EUV. Microlithogr. World **17**(1), 2 (2008)
30. Yuan, K., et al.: Double patterning layout decomposition for simultaneous conflict and stitch minimization. IEEE TCAD **29**(2), 185–196 (2010)
31. Pan, D.Z., et al.: Layout optimizations for double patterning lithography. In: ASICON (2009)
32. Kahng, A.B. et al.: Layout decomposition for double patterning lithography. In: ICCAD (2008)
33. Ryckaert, J., et al.: DTCO at N7 and beyond: patterning and electrical compromises and opportunities. In: Proceedings of SPIE, vol. 9427 (2015)
34. Zografos, O., et al.: Novel grid-based power routing scheme for regular controllable-polarity FET arrangements. In: IEEE ISCAS (2014)
35. Bobba, S., et al.: Process/design co-optimization of regular logic tiles for double-gate silicon nanowire transistors. In: NanoArch (2012)
36. Gore, G., et al.: A predictive process design kit for three-independent-gate field-effect transistors. In: VLSI-SoC (2019)

Exploiting Heterogeneous Mobile Architectures Through a Unified Runtime Framework

Chenying Hsieh$^{(\boxtimes)}$, Ardalan Amiri Sani, and Nikil Dutt

Department of Computer Science,
University of California, Irvine, CA 92697, USA
{chenyinh,ardalan,dutt}@uci.edu

Abstract. Modern mobile SoCs are typically integrated with multiple heterogeneous hardware accelerators such as GPU and DSP. Resource heavy applications such as object detection and image recognition based on convolutional neural networks are accelerated by offloading these computation-intensive algorithms to the accelerators to meet their stringent performance constraints. Conventionally there are device-specific runtime and programming languages supported for programming each accelerator, and these offloading tasks are typically pre-mapped to a specific compute unit at compile time, missing the opportunity to exploit other underutilized compute resources to gain better performance. To address this shortcoming, we present SURF: a Self-aware Unified Runtime Framework for Parallel Programs on Heterogeneous Mobile Architectures. SURF supports several heterogeneous parallel programming languages (including OpenMP and OpenCL), and enables dynamic task-mapping to heterogeneous resources based on runtime measurement and prediction. The measurement and monitoring loop enables self-aware adaptation of run-time mapping to exploit the best available resource dynamically. Our SURF framework has been implemented on a Qualcomm Snapdragon 835 development board and evaluated on a mix of image recognition (CNN), image filtering applications and synthetic benchmarks to demonstrate the versatility and efficacy of our unified runtime framework.

1 Introduction

Mobile computing has benefited from a virtuous cycle of powerful computational platforms enabling new mobile applications, which in turn create the demand for ever more powerful computational platforms. In particular contemporary mobile platforms are increasingly integrating a diverse set of heterogeneous computing units[1] that can be used to accelerate newer mobile applications (e.g., augmented reality, image recognition, inferencing, 3-D gaming, etc.) that are computationally demanding. The privacy and security needs of these mobile applications

---

[1] In this article we use the terms "compute unit" and "device" interchangeably.

© IFIP International Federation for Information Processing 2020
Published by Springer Nature Switzerland AG 2020
C. Metzler et al. (Eds.): VLSI-SoC 2019, IFIP AICT 586, pp. 323–344, 2020.
https://doi.org/10.1007/978-3-030-53273-4_15

(i.e., safely compute on the mobile platform, rather than suffer the vulnerability of sending to the cloud for processing) place further computational stress on emerging mobile platforms. Consequently, as shown in Table 1, contemporary mobile platforms typically include a diverse set of compute units such as multiple heterogeneous multi-processors (HMPs), and programmable accelerators such as GPUs, DSPs, NPUs, as well as other custom application-specific hardware accelerators.

Table 1. Contemporary mobile SoCs [10]

Vendor	SoC	CPU	GPU	Other IPs
Qualcomm	Snapdragon	HMP	Adreno	Hexagon DSP
TI	OMAP	HMP	PowerVR	Tesla DSP
NVIDIA	Tegra	HMP	NVIDIA	-
Samsung	Exynos	HMP	Mali	Neural processor
Apple	A series	HMP	Apple	Neural processor

However, current mobile platforms and their supporting software infrastructures are unable to fully exploit these heterogeneous compute units for two reasons: 1) existing runtime systems are typically designed for one or a few compute units, thus unable to exploit other heterogeneous compute units that are left idle, and 2) conventional wisdom dictates that certain application codes are best accelerated by specific compute units (e.g., embarassingly parallel codes by GPUs, and filtering/signal processing by DSPs). Consequently, some compute units (e.g., GPUs) can get heavily overloaded with high resource contention resulting in overall poor performance. Indeed, in our recent study [10], we made the case for exploiting underutilized resources in heterogeneous mobile architectures to gain better performance and power; and even counterintuitively using a slower/less efficient but underused compute unit to gain overall performance and power benefits when the platform is saturated. To fully exploit such situations, we believe there is a need for a unified runtime framework for parallel programs that can accept applications and dynamically map them to fully utilize the available heterogeneous architectures.

Towards that end, this article motivates the need for, and presents the software architecture and preliminary evaluation of **SURF**, our Self-aware Unified Runtime Framework for parallel programs, that exploits the range of mobile heterogeneous compute units. SURF is a unified framework built on top of existing parallel programming interfaces to provide resource management and task schedulability for heterogeneous mobile platforms. Using SURF application interfaces, application designers can accelerate application blocks by creating schedulable SURF tasks. The SURF runtime system includes a self-aware task mapping module that considers resource contention, the platform's native scheduling scheme, and hardware architecture to perform performance-centric task mapping. We have implemented SURF in Android on a Qualcomm Snapdragon 835 development board, supporting OpenMP, OpenCL and Hexagon SDK as the programming interfaces to program CPU, GPU and DSP respectively. Our initial experimental results – using a naive, but self-aware scheduling scheme – shows that SURF achieves average performance improvements of 24% over contemporary runtime systems, when the system is saturated with mutliple applications. We believe this demonstrates the potential upside of even larger performance improvements when more sophisticated scheduling algorithms are deployed within SURF.

The rest of this article is organized as follows. Section 2 presents background on existing mobile programming frameworks. Section 3 outlines opportunities to exploit heterogeneous compute units for mobile parallel workloads, and motivates the need for the SURF framework through a case study. Section 4 presents SURF's software architecture. Section 5 presents early experimental results using SURF to execute sample mobile workloads. Section 6 discusses related work, and Sect. 7 concludes the article.

2   Background

Modern mobile heterogeneous system-on-Chip (SoC) platforms are typically shipped with supporting software packages to program the integrated heterogeneous hardware accelerators. However, there is no unified programming framework. Open Computing Language (OpenCL) was designed to serve this purpose but it ends up being mostly limited to GPU only among mobile platforms. Other compute units such as DSP or FPGA need their own software supporting packages instead of relying on OpenCL. As a consequence, existing infrastructures require a static mapping of the workload to compute units at compile time. severe resource contention for one unit (e.g., the GPU) while underutilizing other units (e.g., DSP). Besides, there is no information sharing between individual device runtimes, which makes it difficult to make intelligent task-mapping decisions even if the schedulability is provided. Hence, existing software infrastructures are unable to exploit the full heterogeneity of compute units. In our previous case study [10], we showed how underutilized heterogeneous resources can be exploited to boost performance and gain power saving when the platform is saturated with workloads – an increasingly common scenario for mobile platforms where users are multi-tasking between mobile games, image/photo manipulation, video streaming, AR, etc. Our study highlighted the need for a new runtime that can dynamically manage and map applications to heterogeneous resources at runtime. To address these challenges, we have built SURF, a unified framework that sits on top of existing parallel programming interfaces to provide resource management and task schedulability for mobile heterogeneous platforms. Using SURF application interfaces, application designers can accelerate application blocks by creating schedulable SURF tasks. Next we analyze the performance of several popular mobile data parallel workloads on heterogeneous compute units to illustrate the potential for SURF to map these computations across these units.

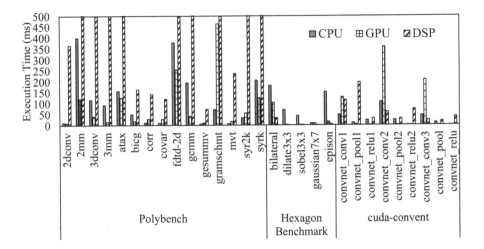

Fig. 1. Execution time of benchmarks on different compute units

Data-Parallel Workload Characterization. Data-parallel computations are common in several mobile application domains such as image recognition (using CNNs) and image/video processing/manipulation where the same function is applied to a huge amount of data. Due to the simplicity of this programming pattern, they can be easily offloaded to hardware accelerators such as GPUs without substantial programming effort. In order to highlight the opportunity for gaining performance improvement through task mapping/schedulability across heterogeneous compute units, we measured the execution time of two benchmark suites (Polybench benchmark suite [7] and Hexagon SDK benchmark suite [16]), as well as for the critical layers in a CNN (cuda-convnet) that contain several common data-parallel kernels across different domains. In addition to their original implementations, we added OpenMP/CPU, OpenCL/GPU or C/DSP implementations to execute them on different compute units (CPU, GPU, DSP).

Figure 1 shows the measurement results of running each benchmark on the CPU, GPU and DSP respectively. As expected, we typically see one "dominant" version for best performance on a specific compute unit, e.g., syrk and convnet_pool1 have the lowest execution time on GPU, whereas bilateral and convnet_conv2 runs best on the DSP. However, note that the non-dominant (slower) versions (e.g., syrk and convnet_pool1 on CPU or DSP; and bilateral and convnet_conv2 on CPU or GPU) – while seemingly inferior in performance – can be opportunistically exploited by our SURF runtime to improve overall system performance, especially as the mobile platform suffers from high contention when popular apps (e.g., image recognition, photo manipulation/filtering) compete for a specific compute unit (e.g., the GPU for data parallel computations).

3   Motivational Case Study

With abundant compute resources on a mobile chip, a developer typically partitions an application into task kernels to be executed on compute units and accelerators (e.g., CPU, GPU, DSP) that correspondingly promise a boost in performance. For instance, a convolutional neural network (CNN) application with multiple layers can be partitioned into data-parallel tasks for each layer and mapped onto GPUs for boosting performance. Intuitively, this strict partitioning of tasks to execute them on the highest-performing compute units should result in overall better performance. Mobile platforms often face resource contention when executing multiple applications, saturating these high-performing compute units. In such scenarios – contrary to intuition – offloading of computational pressure to other underutilized and seemingly under-performing compute units (e.g., DSPs) can actually result in overall improvements in performance and energy. Indeed, in an earlier experimental case study [10], we observed an average improvement of 15–46% in performance and 18–80% in energy when executing multiple CNNs, computer vision and graphics applications on a mobile Snapdragon 835 platform by utilizing idle resources such as DSPs and considering all available resources holistically.

In this section, we present this motivational study executing a mix of popular data-parallel workloads and show that both performance and energy consumption of mobile platforms can be improved by synergistically deploying these underutilized compute resources. We select and run three classes of applications: image recognition, image processing and graphics rendering workload, to emulate when the system is heavily-exercised by high computation-demanding applications such as augmented reality and virtual reality applications.

3.1   Experimental Setup

Table 2. Keywords used in experiments [10]

Experiment	Description
CPU-float, CPU-8bit	Run the original or quantized version on the CPU
GPU-float, GPU-8bit	Run the original or quantized version on the GPU
DSP-float	Run the original version on the DSP
DSP-8bit	Run the quantized version on the DSP w/ batch processing
DSP-8bit-nob	DSP-8bit w/o batch processing
Hetero	Layers or stages are statically configured to run on highest-performing compute unit
Hetero-noGPU	Like Hetero but avoid using GPU

Platform: We use a Snapdragon 835 development board with the Android 6 operating system (which uses the Linux 4.4.63 kernel). The board's SoC integrates custom CPUs with big-LITTLE configurations that conform to ARM's ISA. It also integrates a GPU with unified shaders, all capable of running compute and graphics workloads. The 835 board has two Hexagon DSPs: a cellular modem DSP dedicated to signal processing, and a compute DSP for audio, sensor, and general purpose processing. We target exploiting the compute DSP since it is typically idle.

Applications: For the CNN applications, we select two Caffe CNNs: *lenet-5* and *cuda-convnet* using datasets MNIST and CIFAR10, respectively. MNIST represents a lightweight network with a few layers and low memory footprint whereas CIFAR10 has more layers and high memory footprint. We also implemented a quantized version of Caffe, which supports quantized matrix multiplication using 8-bit fixed-point for convolutional and fully-connected layers. The other layers still perform floating-point computation. The experiments include floating-point and fixed-point versions of CNN models running on CPU, GPU and DSP. For the CED application, we modified Chai CED [9] to support all heterogeneous compute resources for each stage.

Table 2 summarizes the different experiments by executing the above applications on various compute units (CPU, GPU, DSP, and heterogeneous – including all compute units). In addition to the original floating-point version of CNNs, we also deploy 8-bit quantized versions to exploit the DSP effectively. The row *DSP-8-bit* represents a single function call for batch processing of 100 images to amortize the communication overhead, whereas the row *DSP-8bit-nob* represents no batch processing, i.e., separate function calls for each image.

3.2   Opportunities for Exploiting Underutilized Resources

Figure 2 presents the performance of the convolutional layers of MNIST and CIFAR10. Since the Hexagon DSP is fixed-point optimized, the quantized version (*DSP-8bit*) of the conventional layers are able to outperform some of the other versions. Therefore – following intuition – the performance of a single application can be boosted by allocating the workload to the corresponding highest-performing compute unit. *However – counterintuitively – we may be able to exploit seemingly slower compute units to gain overall performance and energy improvements.* Figure 3 illustrates this scenario, showing the execution time of running one to three instances of CIFAR10 in parallel. When executing only one CIFAR10 instance, the *GPU-only* version yields the best result compared to *GPU-CPU* and *GPU-DSP* versions (as expected). However, when we execute multiple instances of CIFAR10 (i.e., panels showing *CIFAR10*2* and *CIFAR10*3*), we observe that offloading to the other seemingly inferior compute units (e.g., CPU & DSP) yields overall better performance. Indeed, when executing 3 instances of CIFAR10 (*CIFAR10*3*), we see that the performance of *GPU-CPU* and *GPU-DSP* significantly outperform the *GPU-only* version, since the GPU is saturated. This simple example motivates the opportunity to exploit underutilized resources such as DSPs as outlined in Sects. 3.3 and 3.4.

3.3 Optimization for Single Application Class

Intuitively, the performance and energy consumption of an application (e.g., CNN) can be improved by partitioning and executing on specific accelerators (e.g., GPUs). But frameworks such as Tensorflow and Caffe run the CNN model on the same GPU, saturating that compute unit while missing the opportunity to improve performance and energy consumption by exploiting other underutilized compute units (e.g., CPU and DSP). Therefore, we partition the neural network at the layer level so each layer can be executed as a task running on a different compute unit to exploit heterogeneity. Figure 4a, 4b shows the execution time, average power and energy consumption of running different versions of MNIST and CIFAR10. For MNIST, *conv2* runs on DSP and the others run on CPU.

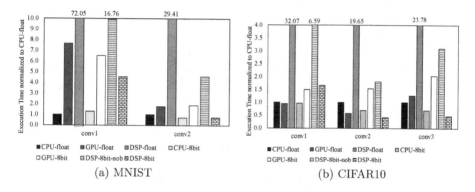

(a) MNIST   (b) CIFAR10

Fig. 2. Performance of convolutional layers [10]

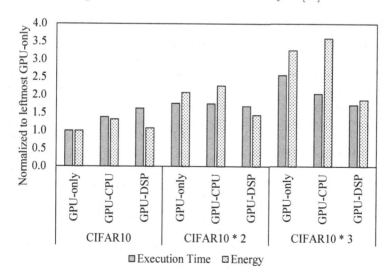

Fig. 3. Performance of executing multiple CIFAR10 instances on different compute units [10]

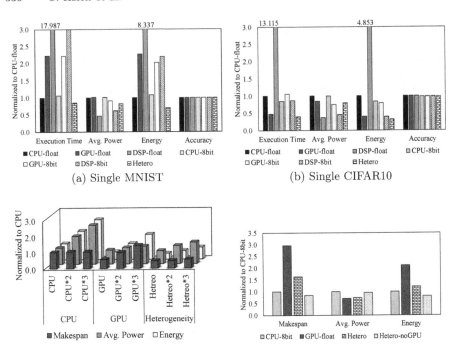

(a) Single MNIST   (b) Single CIFAR10

(c) Running multiple CIFAR10 instances   (d) Running CIFAR10 with graphics applications

Fig. 4. Performance, power, and energy consumption for single or multiple CNNs/CED with different task mapping [10]

For CIFAR10, *conv2*, and *conv3* run on DSP, and the others run on GPU. Although *DSP-8bit* has better performance over convolution layers in general as shown in Fig. 2, it performs worse due to the floating-point computation in other layers such as the Pooling and ReLu layers. For all quantized models, the accuracy drops 1.4% on average. *Hetero* represents the results of utilizing diverse compute units to gain performance and energy improvements. Indeed, the *Hetero* results show a 15.6% performance boost and a 25.4% energy saving on average compared to *CPU-float* and *GPU-float* (which respectively perform best for MNIST and CIFAR10).

Figure 4c shows the results of running multiple CIFAR10 instances. The results are grouped by CPU, GPU and heterogeneous resources and the values are normalized to *CPU-8bit*. For *CPU-8bit*, the performance is scalable but the power and energy consumption increases drastically with more instances because more cores are exercised. The performance of *GPU-8bit* downgrades along with the increase of instances because they contend for the GPU. *Hetero* shows more stability than the others due to the distribution of the workload over all compute resources. We also simulate the scenario when the GPU is saturated by rendering high-quality graphics. We use the GPU Performance Analyzer benchmark to produce a high quality graphics workload. As Fig. 4d shows, the performance of GPU-float and *Hetero* decreased significantly because the GPU is fully-saturated by the above-mentioned graphics workload. *Hetero-noGPU* is statically configured to offload the *conv2*, *conv3* and *relu* layers to DSP while the other layers run on CPU. As *Hetero-noGPU* specifically avoided using the GPU, its performance and energy consumption outperforms the others.

3.4 Optimization for Multiple Application Classes

When executing multiple application classes on a system, both the task partitioning and the exploitation of heterogeneous resources help for better distribution of workload, which in turn leads to better performance and energy consumption. Figure 5a presents the results of running different combinations of CED and CIFAR10. *CPU/CPU* represents the static task mapping policy that CED runs only on the CPU and CIFAR10 also runs on the CPU. The other terms in the figure follow the same convention. Makespan is from when we execute all the applications in parallel to when the last application terminates. By exploiting all heterogeneous (including underutilized) resources efficiently, we can achieve better results: the fully heterogeneous with *Hetero* mapping outperforms CPU-only and GPU-only up to 51% for performance and 55% for energy consumption.

Figure 5b presents the results of running all three workload including CED, CIFAR10 and the graphics benchmark. The mapping policy Hetero/Hetero/Grahpics contends for GPU and therefore fail to achieve better outcome. However, the Hetero-noGPU/Hetero-noGPU/Grahpics policy where we adjust the CED and CIFAR10 to map only on CPU and DSP outshadows the previously policy since GPU becomes the bottleneck due to severe contention.

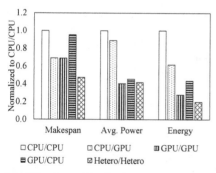 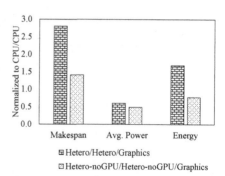

(a) Mixed workload of image processing and recognition

(b) Mixed workload of image processing, recognition and graphics rendering

Fig. 5. Performance of mixed workload

This scenario highlights the need for runtime decision making for pairing workload from different applications with compute unit according to the system status – something not possible in existing runtimes. Hence, we proposed our runtime model, SURF, to deal with the problem which will be detailed in the next section.

4   SURF: Self-aware Unified Runtime Framework

SURF [11] is a unified runtime framework built on top of existing programming interfaces and device runtime to provide adaptive, opportunistic resource management and task schedulability that exploits underutilized compute resources. Figure 6 shows the architectural overview of SURF. In a nutshell, mobile applications create SURF tasks through SURF APIs. When a SURF task is submitted, a self-aware task mapping algorithm is invoked referencing runtime information of compute units provided by SURF service. After the task mapping decision is made, the corresponding parallel runtime stub executes that task.

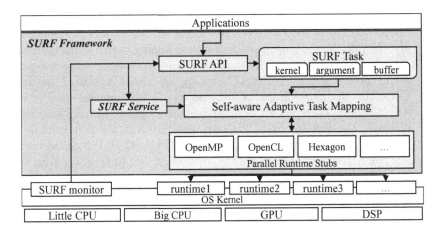

Fig. 6. SURF Architecture

4.1   Application and Task Model

Figure 7 shows the hierarchy of SURF's application model. At the highest level, the mobile platform admits new applications at any time. A newly entering application (e.g., CNN in Fig. 7) can create and submit tasks to SURF dynamically. A task (e.g., conv1, pool and relu1 in Fig. 7's CNN application) represents a computational chunk (parallel algorithm or application block) that could be a candidate for acceleration. A kernel residing in a task represents the programming-interface-specific implementation artifact to program one compute unit (e.g., OpenMP, OpenCL and Hexagon DSP kernels as shown on the right side of Fig. 7). SURF opportunistically maps each task (encapsulating multiple

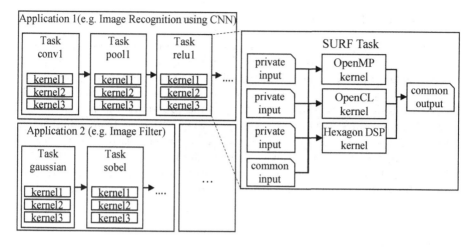

Fig. 7. Application and task model

kernels) for scheduling execution on a specific compute unit. All kernels in a task share a set of common inputs and outputs,

The code block in Fig. 8 demonstrates an example of how to use the application interfaces to create and execute a 2-dimensional convolution task with three kernels including an OpenMP, a OpenCL and a Hexagon DSP kernel. Lines 1–2 create the input and output SURF buffer; Line 4 creates a task; Lines 5–8 add common arguments for all kernels; Lines 9–11 create three kernels to run on CPU, GPU and DSP with user-provided OpenMP binary, OpenCL source code, Hexagon DSP binary respectively, and associate the kernels with the task; and Lines 11–12 execute and destroy the task.

```
1   surf_buffer_t in = surf_buffer_create(size_in);
2   surf_buffer_t out = surf_buffer_create(size_out);
3   /* fill in input buffer */
4   surf_task_t task = surf_task_create(3);
5   surf_task_add_args(task, 0, in, size_in, SURF_MEM_READ | SURF_MEM_BUFFER);
6   surf_task_add_args(task, 1, out, size_out, SURF_MEM_WRITE | SURF_MEM_BUFFER);
7   surf_task_add_args(task, 2, &ni, sizeof(int), 0);
8   surf_task_add_args(task, 3, &nj, sizeof(int), 0);
9   surf_task_create_kernel(task, "conv2D_cpu", SURF_DEV_CPU, SURF_KERNEL_OPENMP |
        SURF_KERNEL_USE_BINARY, "res/libpb.so", 0);
10  surf_task_create_kernel(task, "conv2D_gpu", SURF_DEV_GPU, SURF_KERNEL_OPENCL |
        SURF_KERNEL_USE_SOURCE, "res/2dconv.cl", 0);
11  surf_task_create_kernel(task, "conv2D_dsp", SURF_DEV_DSP, SURF_KERNEL_HEXAGON |
        SURF_KERNEL_USE_BINARY, "res/libconv.so", 0);
12  surf_task_enqueue(task);
13  surf_task_destroy(task);
```

Fig. 8. Sample code of SURF application interfaces including SURF buffer, task and kernel creation as well as SURF task execution and termination.

4.2   Memory Management and Synchronization

SURF assumes compute units are sharing the system memory which is also the dominant architecture in mobile SoCs. Hence, the expensive data movement between device memory can be ignored if the memory is mapped to all the devices correctly. The SURF buffer object is a memory region mapped to all the device address space through device-specific programming interfaces e.g., OpenCL Qualcomm extension and Hexagon SDK APIs for Qualcomm SoCs. Memory synchronization is still necessary when the buffer is used among different devices to ensure the running device can see the most recent update of data. SURF automatically synchronizes memory objects when the memory object is going to be used by a different device; this memory overhead is included in SURF's task mapping decision.

4.3   Self-aware Adaptive Task Mapping

SURF employs a self-aware adaptive task mapping strategy. SURF exhibits self-awareness [5] by creating a model of the underlying heterogeneous resources, assessing current system state via the SURF monitor, and using predictive models to guide mapping decisions. This enables SURF to act in a self-aware manner, combining both *reactive* (e.g., as new applications arrive or when active applications exit), as well as *proactive* (e.g., through the use of predictive models to enable evaluation of opportunistic mapping to underutilized compute units) strategies to enable efficient, adaptive runtime mapping.

SURF's current implementation deploys a variant of the heterogeneous earliest finish time (HEFT) [17] task mapping algorithm, enhanced to incorporate the cost of runtime resource contention. We consider two types of contention:

Intra-compute-Unit. the contention happens when multiple tasks are submitted to a compute unit. The cost of the contention depends on the device runtime and the hardware architecture. For compute unit accelerators such as GPU and DSP, the task execution is usually exclusive due to costly context switch overheads. A FIFO task queue is implemented for each compute unit, so we include the wait time in the queue when calculating the finish time for a task. We also consider device concurrency (i.e., how many tasks can run concurrently on a device) in the analysis. Contemporary mobile GPUs can only accommodate one task execution at a time. Other devices such as DSPs may have more than one concurrent task execution (e.g. Qualcomm Hexagon DSP supports up to 2 when setting to 128-byte vector context mode [16]). And of course for the CPU cluster we can have multiple, concurrent tasks executing across the big.LITTLE cores, that typically employs an existing sophisticated scheduler such as the Linux Completely Fair Scheduler (CFS) [14].

Inter-compute-Unit. Typically memory contention is the major bottleneck when there are concurrent memory-intensive task executions in different compute units, resulting in the execution makespan of a task increasing significantly.

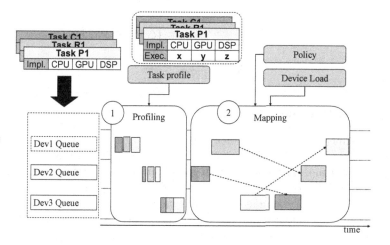

Fig. 9. SURF task mapping scheme

Figure 9 shows SURF's dynamic task mapping scheme. SURF proposes a heuristic-based scheme to estimate the finish time for a task running on different compute units considering both intra- and inter-compute-unit contention. First, to determine which compute unit has the fastest execution time, a new task starts within a profile phase to measure the execution time for all kernels in the task. Mapping phase comes after the profile phase is finished where it begins to find the earliest finish time based on the runtime information. Policy determines how to perform the task mapping according to the task profile and device load. Equation 1 shows how we estimate the finish time. T_{task}^{cu} is the finish time when executing task t on compute unit cu. T_{inter} is the execution time considering inter-compute-unit contention. The influence of memory contention to execution time is difficult to estimate at runtime because the micro-architecture metrics for hardware accelerators are usually not feasible; hence we use a history-based method to model that effect. A history buffer is introduced to track execution time of the latest n runs. T_{inter} is the average of the history buffer. T_{intra} is the execution time considering intra-compute-unit contention. For GPU/DSP, T_{intra} is the sum of execution time of earlier submitted tasks. For CPU, T_{intra} is complicated to estimate if left unbounded. So we estimate the worst execution time based on OpenMP programming model and assume the active CPU threads have the same priority under CFS policy (each thread is allocated with the same time slice). SURF configures an OpenMP kernel to execute on a CPU cluster with a thread on each core. Hence, we approximate the worst execution time by Eq. 2. *TPC* is the number of concurrent OpenMP tasks in the CPU cluster. T_o represent the overhead of deploying the task to the compute units and the memory synchronization if it is necessary (e.g., memory buffer is written by GPU and CPU is going to use the results). SURF finds the kernel with the minimum T_{task}^{cu} and submits it to the SURF device queue for execution.

$$T_t^{cu} = T_{inter}^{cu} + T_{intra}^{cu} + T_o, cu \in \{CPU, GPU, DSP\} \tag{1}$$

$$T_{intra}^{cpu} = TPC * T_{inter}^{cpu} \tag{2}$$

4.4   Parallel Runtime Stub

Parallel runtime stub is an abstract layer on top of the existing programming interfaces. This layer utilizes their interfaces to communication with the corresponding runtime. The corresponding stub provides the following features: a) Initialization of programming resources for different programming interfaces accordingly; b) Memory management and synchronization: while the shared system memory model between heterogeneous compute units is dominant in mobile SoCs, and saves expensive data movement, it still needs to perform memory synchronization between cache and system memory before another compute unit accesses the memory; and c) Computation kernel execution. SURF currently supports three programming interfaces: OpenMP, OpenCL and Hexagon SDK to program CPU, GPU and DSP respectively.

4.5   SURF Service and Monitor

The SURF service is a background process that synchronizes the system information with application processes. The SURF Monitor collects system status and profile results. For example, we collect execution time of OpenMP threads from the entity *sum_exec_runtime* through sysfs so to estimate how long an OpenMP kernel runs.

5   Experimental Results

5.1   Experimental Setup

Figure 10 shows our experimental setup. We have implemented the SURF framework using C/C++ in Android 7 running on Qualcomm Snapdragon 835 development board, which has two CPU clusters (big.LITTLE configuration), and integrated GPU and DSP. SURF considers the little CPU cluster, big CPU cluster, GPU and DSP as four compute units when making task mapping decisions where GPU and DSP are exclusive for 1 and 2 tasks respectively. SURF kernels can be created by the programming interfaces of OpenMP, OpenCL and Hexagon SDK to program CPU, GPU and DSP respectively. We deploy the Caffe convolutional neural network framework [12], Canny Edge Detector (CED), Polybench benchmark suite and Hexagon SDK benchmarks to run on SURF. We also use the Snapdragon Profiler [15] to measure the utilization for each compute unit. Power consumption is measured by averaging the product of voltage and current read from the power supply module through Linux *sysfs* interface (e.g. */sys/class/power_supply*). Energy consumption is the product of makespan and average power consumption. We also access Android Debug Bridge (adb) through WiFi instead of USB connection so the USB charging will not compromise the results. The big.LITTLE processor governors are set to performance mode so as to not interfere with our performance-centric task mapping.

In our experimental sets, we run two applications: image recognition (cuda-convnet within Caffe and with Cifar10 dataset) and image filter (CED) representing foreground processes that have 9 and 4 SURF tasks respectively. We also run two GPU-dominant benchmarks (*syrk* and *gemm* from Polybench) and two DSP-dominant benchmarks (*bilateral* and *epsilon*) representing background processes and each of the benchmarks runs one SURF task. We characterize application workloads as heavy and light workloads by changing batch processing size (how many images are processed each iteration) and benchmark workloads as heavy, medium and light workload by changing their input size. Light workload is characterized as real-time workload which can be done within 20 ms. Medium and heavy workload are the ones can be done within 20–100 ms and above 100 ms respectively. Tables 3 and 4 summarizes the configurations of applications and benchmarks used in our experimental sets.

Table 3. Details of applications and benchmarks used in our experimental sets

Name	Source	Category	#tasks	Dominant device
CUDA-convnet	Caffe	Image recognition	9	Mixed
Canny Edge Detector	Synthetic	Image filter	4	Mixed
syrk	Polybench	Linear algebra	1	GPU
gemm	Polybench	Linear algebra	1	GPU
bilateral	Hexagon SDK	Image filter	1	DSP
epsilon	Hexagon SDK	Image filter	1	DSP

Table 4. Details of applications and benchmarks used in our experimental sets (continuation)

Name	#Iteration	Workload		
		Heavy(H)	Medium(M)	Light(L)
CUDA-convnet	150	Batch = 100, 32×32	n/a	Batch = 10
Canny Edge Detector	150	Batch = 100, 640×354	n/a	Batch = 1
syrk	200	512×512	384×384	256×256
gemm	200	768×768	512×512	256×256
bilateral	200	3840×2160	1920×1080	1280×960
epsilon	200	7680×4320	3840×2160	1920×1080

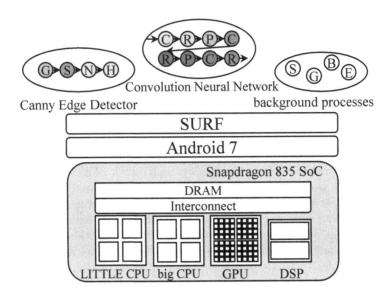

Fig. 10. Experimental setup

5.2   Experimental Results

As Table 5 shows, we run six test sets composed of combinations of heavy/light applications and heavy/medium/light benchmarks. Figure 11 shows the execution makespan of running our six test sets with static best-performing task mapping and SURF dynamic task mapping. The static best-performing mapping configures each task to run on their best-performing compute unit according to the profiling results without SURF. SURF's dynamic task mapping outperforms static mapping by 24% on average. Table 5 also shows that the speedup increases with the level of the background benchmark workload because for heavy background benchmarks, a single run of them will occupy the compute resources for long time in GPU and DSP, which creates opportunities to map alternative kernels to exploit other underutilized compute units. The light applications have better speedup than heavy applications because the light application setup

Table 5. Speedup for different test sets

	Foreground-background workload	Speedup	Makespan difference (s)
Set1	H-H	1.33	19.07
Set2	H-M	1.17	7.15
Set3	H-L	1.04	1.43
Set4	L-H	1.34	12.60
Set5	L-M	1.34	5.07
Set6	L-L	1.22	1.72

experiences more contention with background processes during the entire makespan and it's easy to find alternative kernels because the kernels in one task tend to have similar performance in light workload configuration. Figure 12 shows the sum of all device utilization of the makespan including little/big CPUs, GPU and DSP utilization when running each test set (max 400% across the 4 classes of units). GPU and DSP utilization are similar (increased by 4.51% and 3.38% respectively) across all in general, since the GPU and DSP are heavily exercised. Here the Big CPU is better utilized (increased by 30.6%) by our dynamic scheme, and is the major contributor to the speedup.

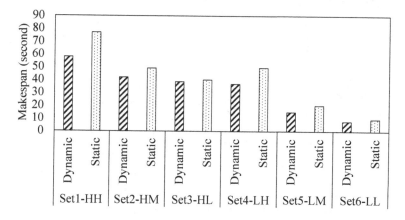

Fig. 11. Makespan of static and SURF dynamic task mapping

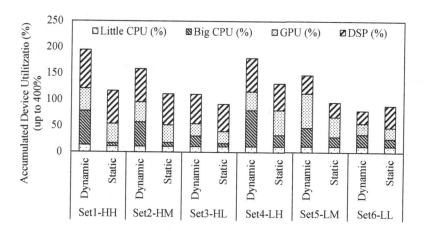

Fig. 12. Device utilization of makespan for each test set

Further experiments were conducted where DSP-dominant background processes (bilateral and epsilon) are not executed, but only foreground applications and GPU-dominant background processes. Figure 13 and 14 show the results of makespan and utilization respectively. SURF's dynamic scheme outperforms static mapping by 27% in performance which is slightly better than the previous experiments because there are more available resources while GPU is saturated. The utilization for big CPU and DSP increased by 43.15% and 8.13% respectively which shows part of the computation are offloaded to them.

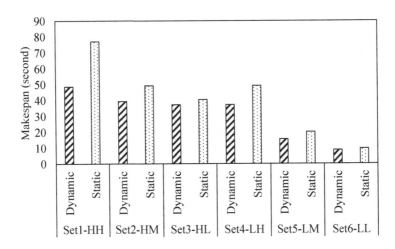

Fig. 13. Makespan of static and SURF dynamic task mapping w/o DSP-dominant background processes

While these preliminary experimental results demonstrate SURF's efficacy in exploiting underutilized compute units for improving performance, the current policy which applies the HEFT algorithm introduced in Sect. 4.3 is not power- and energy-aware. As a result, the power and energy consumption increase by 62.8% and 31.6% on average shown in Fig. 15. We speculate that the current implementation for the computational kernels make SURF infeasible to deploy energy-aware policy because they are not optimized according to the hardware architecture. Hence, the trade-off between performance and energy becomes trivial - either high performance and energy consumption or low performance and low energy consumption. We expect to see reductions in energy consumption once the kernels are optimized with an energy-aware policy. This development is currently ongoing.

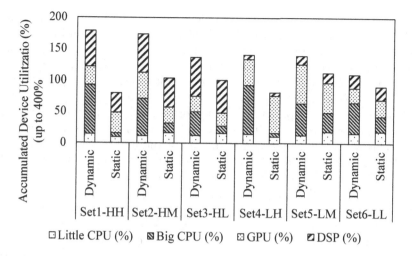

Fig. 14. Device utilization of makespan for each test set w/o DSP-dominant background processes

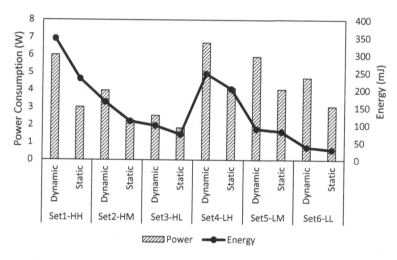

Fig. 15. Power and energy consumption for adaptive HEFT policy in SURF

6 Related Work

Heterogeneous resource management has been widely studied, with a large body of existing work on task scheduling/mapping algorithms [4, 8, 13, 17]. For instance, Topcuoglu et al. [17] proposes the heterogeneous earliest finish time (HEFT) algorithm that schedules tasks in a directed acyclic graph (DAG) onto a device to minimize execution time. Choi et al. [4] estimates the remaining execution time for tasks on CPU and GPU by using a history buffer and selects the most suitable device. The StarPU [2] framework targets high performance computing and enables dynamic scheduling between CPU and GPU based on static knowledge of the tasks. Zhou et al. [19] perform task mapping onto heterogeneous platforms for fast completion time. Some recent efforts also address domain-specific platforms: Wen et al. [18] and Bolchini et al. [3] propose dynamic task mapping schemes specific for OpenCL; Georgiev et al. [6] proposes a memetic algorithm based task scheduler for mobile sensor workload; and Aldegheri et al. [1] presents a framework allowing multiple programming languages and exploit their different level of parallelism for computer vision applications which achieves better performance and energy consumption.

SURF distinguishes from these works in two directions. First, the SURF framework is composed of a runtime system for task mapping and APIs for mobile systems. SURF is built on top of existing programming interfaces and dynamically profiles task execution and perform task mapping without user-provided static knowledge. Second, SURF is *self-aware*: aware of the heterogeneous hardware architecture, existing scheduling scheme and the runtime system status. It takes care of resource contention of single compute units while other works make assumptions that all the compute unit are exclusive to a single task (e.g., CPU should not be exclusive). The device concurrency of hardware accelerators is also ignored in these previous works.

7   Conclusion

In this article, we presented the architecture of SURF, a self-aware unified runtime framework built on top of existing programming interfaces including OpenMP, OpenCL and Hexagon DSP SDK for mapping tasks onto CPU, GPU, and DSP respectively in mobile SoCs. We illustrated how to use SURF's application interfaces to create and execute a SURF task. SURF performs task mapping while being aware of existing scheduling schemes, intra- and inter-compute-unit contention and heterogeneous hardware architectures to select the compute unit with the earliest finish time for the given tasks without user-provided static information about the tasks. Our early experimental results show an average of 24% speedup by running mixed mobile workloads including two applications, image recognition by using convolution neural networks and an image filter with couple of background processes sharing workload on the compute units. Our ongoing work is incorporating more sophisticated mapping and prediction algorithms, and analyzing the performance as well as energy benefits of deploying SURF on emerging heterogeneous mobile platforms.

References

1. Aldegheri, S., Manzato, S., Bombieri, N.: Enhancing performance of computer vision applications on low-power embedded systems through heterogeneous parallel programming. In: IFIP/IEEE International Conference on Very Large Scale Integration, VLSI-SoC 2018, Verona, Italy, October 8–10, 2018, pp. 119–124 (2018). https://doi.org/10.1109/VLSI-SoC.2018.8644937

2. Augonnet, C., Thibault, S., Namyst, R., Wacrenier, P.A.: StarPU: a unified plat-form for task scheduling on heterogeneous multicore architectures. Concurr. Comput.: Pract. Exp. **23**(2), 187–198 (2011). https://doi.org/10.1002/cpe.1631

3. Bolchini, C., Cherubin, S., Durelli, G.C., Libutti, S., Miele, A., Santambro-gio, M.D.: A runtime controller for OpenCL applications on heterogeneous system architectures. SIGBED Rev. **15**(1), 29–35 (2018). https://doi.org/10.1145/3199610.3199614

4. Choi, H.J., Son, D.O., Kang, S.G., Kim, J.M., Lee, H.H., Kim, C.H.: An efficient scheduling scheme using estimated execution time for heterogeneous computing systems. J. Supercomput. **65**(2), 886–902 (2013). https://doi.org/10.1007/s11227-013-0870-6

5. Dutt, N.D., Jantsch, A., Sarma, S.: Toward smart embedded systems: a self-aware system-on-chip (SoC) perspective. ACM Trans. Embed. Comput. Syst. **15**(2), 22:1–22:27 (2016). https://doi.org/10.1145/2872936

6. Georgiev, P., Lane, N.D., Rachuri, K.K., Mascolo, C.: Leo: scheduling sensor infer-ence algorithms across heterogeneous mobile processors and network resources. In: Proceedings of the 22nd Annual International Conference on Mobile Computing and Networking, MobiCom 2016, pp. 320–333. ACM, New York (2016). https://doi.org/10.1145/2973750.2973777

7. Grauer-Gray, S., Xu, L., Searles, R., Ayalasomayajula, S., Cavazos, J.: Auto-tuning a high-level language targeted to GPU codes. In: 2012 Innovative Parallel Com-puting (InPar), pp. 1–10 (May 2012)

8. Gregg, C., Boyer, M., Hazelwood, K., Skadron, K.: Dynamic heterogeneous schedul-ing decisions using historical runtime data. In: Workshop on Applications for Multi-and Many-Core Processors (A4MMC) (2011)

9. Gómez-Luna, J., et al.: Chai: collaborative heterogeneous applications for integrated-architectures. In: 2017 IEEE International Symposium on Performance Analysis of Systems and Software (ISPASS) (2017)

10. Hsieh, C., Sani, A.A., Dutt, N.: The case for exploiting underutilized resources in heterogeneous mobile architectures. In: 2019 Design, Automation Test in Europe Conference Exhibition (DATE) (March 2019)

11. Hsieh, C., Sani, A.A., Dutt, N.: SURF: self-aware unified runtime framework for parallel programs on heterogeneous mobile architectures. In: 2019 IFIP/IEEE 27th International Conference on Very Large Scale Integration (VLSI-SoC), pp. 136–141 (October 2019)

12. Jia, Y., et al.: Caffe: Convolutional architecture for fast feature embedding. In: Proceedings of the 22nd ACM International Conference on Multimedia, MM 2014, pp. 675–678. ACM, New York (2014). https://doi.org/10.1145/2647868.2654889

13. Kadjo, D., Ayoub, R., Kishinevsky, M., Gratz, P.V.: A control-theoretic app-roach for energy efficient CPU-GPU subsystem in mobile platforms. In: 2015 52nd ACM/EDAC/IEEE Design Automation Conference (DAC), pp. 1–6 (June 2015)

14. Kumar, A.: Multiprocessing with the completely fair scheduler (2008)

15. Qualcomm: Snapdrgon profiler (2013). https://developer.qualcomm.com/software/hexagon-dsp-sdk

16. Qualcomm: Hexagon DSP SDK (2017). https://developer.qualcomm.com/software/snapdragon-profiler

17. Topcuoglu, H., Hariri, S., Wu, M.-Y.: Performance-effective and low-complexity task scheduling for heterogeneous computing. IEEE Trans. Parallel Distrib. Syst. **13**(3), 260–274 (2002)

18. Wen, Y., Wang, Z., O'Boyle, M.F.P.: Smart multi-task scheduling for OpenCL programs on CPU/GPU heterogeneous platforms. In: 2014 21st International Conference on High Performance Computing (HiPC), pp. 1–10 (December 2014)
19. Zhou, H., Liu, C.: Task mapping in heterogeneous embedded systems for fast completion time. In: 2014 International Conference on Embedded Software (EMSOFT), pp. 1–10 (October 2014)

Author Index

Atienza, David 257
Atishay 139
Aydin, Furkan 279

Bandeira, Vitor 115
Brendler, Leonardo H. 89
Butzen, Paulo F. 69

Cadareanu, Patsy 307

da Rosa Jr., Leomar S. 69
Dutt, Nikil 323

Falas, Solon 165
Forlin, Bruno 209
Franco, Denis T. 69

Gaillardon, Pierre-Emmanuel 257, 307
Gener, Y. Serhan 279
Giacomin, Edouard 257, 307
Gore, Ganesh 307
Gören, Sezer 279
Grosso, Michelangelo 1
Gupta, Ankit 139

Henker, Ronny 235
Hsieh, Chenying 323

Jenihhin, Maksim 21

Konstantinou, Charalambos 165
Köse, Selçuk 187
Kvatinsky, Shahar 257

Meinhardt, Cristina 45, 89
Michael, Maria K. 165
Moraes, Leonardo B. 45

Ost, Luciano 115
Oyeniran, Adeboye Stephen 21

Pliva, Jan 235
Prasanth, B. 139

Qureshi, Yasir 257

Raik, Jaan 21
Reinbrecht, Cezar 209
Reis, Ricardo 45, 89, 115
Rinaudo, Salvatore 1
Rosa, Felipe 115

Sani, Ardalan Amiri 323
Schvittz, Rafael B. 69
Seçkiner, Soner 187
Sepúlveda, Johanna 209
Sonawat, Rashmi 139
Sonza Reorda, Matteo 1
Szilágyi, László 235

Tang, Xifan 257
Thacker, Helik Kanti 139

Ubar, Raimund 21
Ugurdag, H. Fatih 279

Vieira, João 257

Wang, Longfei 187

Zapater, Marina 257
Zimpeck, Alexandra Lackmann 45, 89

Printed in the United States
by Baker & Taylor Publisher Services